D1709135

Prodigy Houses of Virginia

Prodigy Houses

OF VIRGINIA

ARCHITECTURE AND THE NATIVE ELITE

Barbara Burlison Mooney

University of Virginia Press | *Charlottesville & London*

University of Virginia Press
© 2008 by the Rector and Visitors of the University of Virginia
Printed in the United States of America on acid-free paper
First published 2008

9 8 7 6 5 4 3 2 1

Library of Congress Cataloging-in-Publication Data
Mooney, Barbara Burlison, 1952–
    Prodigy houses of Virginia : architecture and the native elite /
Barbara Burlison Mooney.
        p.   cm.
    Includes bibliographical references and index.
    ISBN 978-0-8139-2673-5 (cloth : alk. paper)
    1. Mansions—Virginia. 2. Architecture, Domestic—Virginia
—18th century. 3. Architecture and society—Virginia. 4. Social
status in art—Virginia. I. Title.
NA7613.V8M66 2008
728.809755—dc22   2007021534

To Bob and Will

Contents

Acknowledgments

I am greatly indebted to the institutions and individuals who made the completion of this book possible. Through an Arts and Humanities Grant, the University of Iowa generously funded my research, travel, and photography during 2004 and 2005. The University of Iowa's commitment to the humanities was also demonstrated by the Office of the Vice President for Research in a generous subvention toward procuring images and reproduction rights for this book. The fellowship of scholars from across many disciplines at the Obermann Center for Advanced Studies greatly facilitated and encouraged my work that semester.

For more than fifteen years, the architectural historians at the Colonial Williamsburg Foundation have shared their expertise and patiently discussed ideas about Virginia's colonial buildings with me. Mark R. Wenger, Edward A. Chappell, William J. Graham, and especially Carl R. Lounsbury have been magnanimous in offering the most recent information on the buildings that form the core of this study. Cary Carson, former Vice President of Research at the Colonial Williamsburg Foundation, graciously allowed me to exploit the files of the Foundation and the accumulated knowledge of its historians. Many of the insights of this book come from these scholars; all of the errors are mine.

Thanks to the art historian Sally Mills, many errors were prevented. Her careful reading and gentle inquiries have made the text more readable and clearly argued. The illustration of this book has been greatly enhanced by the work of Megan D. Roy, my research assistant from the University of Iowa's Undergraduate Scholar Assistant Program. Ms. Roy applied her enthusiasm for architecture and her expertise in AutoCad and Photoshop to create plans and to improve a number of photographs.

Finally and most importantly, I want to thank my husband, Robert T. Mooney, and son, William A. Mooney. Throughout the long process from dissertation to completed book, my husband has continuously and faithfully offered his support in innumerable ways. My son, now an adult, has endured my preoccupation with the subject of Virginia's colonial mansions literally all his life. Both have sustained me emotionally and intellectually. To them, I wish to express my profound gratitude.

Prodigy Houses of Virginia

Introduction

"An Art Which Shews So Much"

Thomas Jefferson firmly grasped the alliance between architecture and the construction of self, whether that self was a person or a country. In recommending the study of buildings as a worthy intellectual pursuit, Jefferson justified architecture on the basis of its practical utility, aesthetic potential, and ability to reveal its owner's character. He explained the value of studying buildings in a list of objectives and inquiries meant to guide and make profitable the European travel of two young Americans in 1788. After encouraging them to evaluate the agricultural, mechanical, and horticultural practices of other countries, Jefferson instructed them to look critically at the built environment: "Architecture [is] worth great attention. As we double our numbers every 20 years we must double our houses. Besides we build of such perishable materials that one half our houses must be rebuilt in every space of 20 years. So that in that term, houses are to be built for three fourths of our inhabitants. It is then among the most important arts: and it is desireable to introduce taste into an art which shews so much."[1] Note that, at first, Jefferson argues for the practical benefits of adequate shelter, accompanied by convincing statistics. He continues by touching only briefly on the issue of taste, cognizant perhaps that the importance of good design would be self-evident to his well-heeled correspondents. Jefferson's last clause, however, is particularly intriguing. At first, his words "an art which shews so much" might be taken to suggest that architecture has a large physical presence—that it is noticeable. His phrase can also be construed to mean that architecture reveals the character and judgment of its maker and owner.

In this book, I reverse Jefferson's claim to demonstrate how analyzing members of Virginia's eighteenth-century elite shows much about the mansions they created. Virginia's colonial mansions stand as icons of American architecture, well known to many outside of the architectural history profession. Over the years, these buildings have come to represent far more than examples of attractive architectural design. Instead, they have become flash points onto which conflicting interpretations of America's past adhere. Some view Tidewater mansions as patriotic emblems of a glorious past infused with a beauty and grace that is worthy of emulation. Some see the very same buildings as redolent of the stink of the exploitation of poor white farmers and the barbarous treatment of black slaves. Many others hold conflicting opinions about Virginia's mansions: attracted to their design and repelled by their social and economic foundation. This book does not ask readers to reject the elegant and aesthetically appealing mansions of Virginia. It does, however, require that readers acknowledge the precondition that made these exquisitely handsome dwellings in Virginia and similar ones throughout all of British North America possible, namely slavery. Make no mistake, the seductive attraction of a house such as Stratford Hall was purchased with stripes on the backs of Africans aboard "a Negro Ship consign'd to the Hon. Thomas Lee, Esq., lately arriv'd at Hampton, and is gone up to Potomack," as the *Virginia Gazette* reported in 1738, the same year Stratford Hall was built.[2] With this fundamental and unresolved tension in mind, my investigation presents a more detailed and nuanced interrogation of the dynamics of ownership and wealth. Whether a reader esteems or reviles Virginia's mansions, I argue that our understanding of them is amplified by examining the lives of the men and women who caused them to be built and first inhabited them.

Clarifying the title of my book defines its scope and approach more narrowly. The phrase "prodigy house" was first used by the British architectural historian John Summerson to denote the excessively large and luxurious country houses that were built at enormous, even ruinous, expense during the reigns of Elizabeth I and James I.[3] According to Summerson, these mansions were also built with the expectation of personal and political advancement in an era of social and economic change. With wealth and prestige recently acquired by supporting Henry VIII's rejection of papal authority and his dissolution of the monasteries, high-ranking ministers and court officials embarked on a frenzy of building. Hoping to garner favor with Elizabeth I (a sovereign whose religion and legitimacy to rule were none too secure), some landowners whose titles were only three or four generations old lavished huge capital assets on the construction of residences that might be used to lodge and entertain the queen and her large retinue during her summer travels, or progresses, through England. According to Summerson, these relatively new earls and barons and their families "sought outlets of a more fantastic and brilliant kind than the collection of land or the attainment of office." They did so through architecture and the performance of novel and prestigious ornamental rhetoric. Prodigy houses self-consciously displayed decorative features and planning practices whose origins can be traced to the Italian Renaissance, and that stood in contradistinction to more indigenous English notions of proper architecture.[4] The adaptation and transliteration of those continental characteristics constitutes one of the critical narratives in the history of England's elite houses and, as we shall see, represents an equally critical theme in the story of Virginia's elite houses.

The main title of this book seeks to draw a social, though not stylistic, parallel between England's prodigy houses and those constructed later in Virginia. Summerson's term, first applied to Virginia's colonial mansions by the historian Cary Carson, cogently summarizes the way that Virginia mansions functioned in an eighteenth-century colonial rather than a sixteenth- and seventeenth-century English context.[5] In the context of Virginia, the term "prodigy houses" refers to a small group of dwellings that, like those in England, seem to have had a disproportionate influence on the imagination of later designers and historians. Unlike the British aristocracy, Virginia's elite planters were less directly dependent on the government for their emoluments. And in terms of absolute wealth, Virginia's richest men never approached the standards of the British aristocracy. Yet, like the country houses of Elizabethan and Jacobean England, the mansions of eighteenth-century Virginia were built at enormous expense by those whose wealth and rank were not entirely beyond question. And like England's prodigy houses, Virginia's prodigy houses were built with the expectation of securing their owners' relatively new status at the pinnacle of society.

The second part of the title refers to the Virginia families who, like their earlier British counterparts, embarked on building campaigns that were extravagant in both cost and style. Historians have variously named these politically powerful and often related families the "governing elite," the "ruling elite," or the "native elite."[6] The historian Allan Kulikoff concisely defined the native elite as a "ruling class that not only increasingly monopolized power and wealth but formed its own culture as well."[7] Around 1720, these families sought to perpetuate their relatively new and by no means secure status with architecture, as well as by other displays of material distinction.

In order to scrutinize the relationship between Virginia's native elite and their mansions, I employ a methodological approach known in art history as "patronage." For those who think that architectural historians study only buildings while historians study only documents, the term may require explanation. Patronage methodology claims that those who commission, purchase, and use buildings, paintings, sculpture, or any other kind of material culture are not passive consumers held hostage to the whims of the artisan or craftsperson who fashioned those objects. Instead, a patronage approach acknowledges the fact that the style and meaning of artistic production results from the collaboration between those who pay for the product and those who produce it. In the case of Virginia's prodigy houses, a patronage approach focuses on the ways that the owners took an active role in determining, either directly or indirectly, the appearance and use of the building they owned and first occupied. Once the role of the patron is recognized, documentary evidence yielding insight into their lives becomes as vital as studying the building itself. In this book, the buildings serve as background, while the men and women who first inhabited them stand in the foreground. Of course, the patronage methodology is only one of several ways that the built environment can be approached. My study is intended to complement, not supplant, in-depth monographs on individual buildings and investigations into construction practices.

In referring to the first owners of Virginia's colonial mansions as "patrons," I am deliberately eschewing the word "client." In modern usage, the term "client" suggests a dependent role in which deference is shown to the architectural expertise of a trained design professional. The term "patron" lays claim to a more collaborative relationship between the owner and the skilled workmen that he or she hired. Similarly, I avoid the term "architect" in this book. Its current meaning connotes a specially educated and artistically inspired individual in charge of the design and occasionally the building process and is inappropriate in the context of colonial Virginia. There is little evidence of men making their living strictly as design professionals. Instead, skilled builders such as carpenters, joiners, and masons routinely made design decisions in collaboration with whose who owned the property. Shared responsibility would be the norm in America until the professionalization of architecture in the second half of the nineteenth century eroded the notion of diverse design competence.

The perspective taken in this book—namely, that an intensely personal relationship exists between inhabitants and their houses—has a long and sometimes troubled history. For a number of post–Civil War historians, mansions such as Mount Airy exuded the glow of a past golden age of Virginia political and cultural prestige (fig. 1). To writers such as Thomas Allen Glenn, Edith D. T. Sale, and Robert A. Lancaster, Virginia's eighteenth-century mansions enhanced their builders' historical luster and that of the state because, as Sale would write in 1930, "they bear witness that their owners were not only persons of wealth but of culture." Virginia's mansions served as testaments to the superior culture of the Old South and the ancient relics of what she considered a "more pleasing era of plantation life, founded by men whose names are high enrolled in the book of history, and whose homes were little kingdoms worthy of the sincere study of our less picturesque generation."[8] Agnes Rothery, in her popular 1929 *New Roads in Old Virginia,* claimed that "every man's house is the extension of his personality." She also rooted the colony's famous architecture in an economic system. Bemoaning the "sadly shabby" appearance of Virginia's mansions in the late 1920s, Rothery laid the blame squarely on the end of slavery. For Rothery, the faded and bedraggled condition of Virginia's mansions in the twentieth century was only logical insomuch as their owners "no longer draw incomes from tobacco and cotton and slave labour."[9]

Fig. 1. Mount Airy, Richmond County, 1760. View of central projecting pavilion on the garden façade. (Photograph by author)

Not all early commentators looked upon Virginia's great houses with unalloyed admiration. Writing in the 1850s, William Meade, Episcopal bishop of Virginia, saw the construction of Rosewell's "richly carved mahogany wainscotings and capitals and stairways" as a "great folly," costing so much that the enterprise verged uncomfortably close in his mind to the sin of pride. Meade believed that "no one of the name of him who built it has owned it or could afford to own it for generations."[10] Now a romantic ruin after being destroyed by fire in 1916, Mann Page I's Rosewell stands as the most infamous example of the enormous expenses incurred by patrons when building their prodigy houses (fig. 2). The burden of debt that Rosewell settled on the Page family was not, however, unusual. Thomas Jefferson, George Washington, and other Virginia planters left enormous debts as well as enormous houses to their heirs. Architectural extravagance, however, was only one part of a larger pattern of spending beyond their means. The unrestrained acquisition of the finest consumer goods, the inability to reign in hemorrhaging debt, as well as gambling led some prominent planters such as William Byrd III to choose suicide as a way of avoiding the embarrassment that accompanied financial collapse.

As compelling as is the dynamics of wealthy Virginians' obsession with the prestige of material objects, it does not represent the only important story that can be told about the colony's built environment.[11] In fact, for more than a quarter century, the dwellings of the poor rather than the mansions of the rich have constituted the most exciting research direction in the architectural history of the region. That research has unveiled a new picture of a scruffy, untidy landscape comprised of a few planted tracts adjacent to many spent, infertile fields and punctuated by small, rough-and-tumble dwellings that often became uninhabitable within two decades. The vernacular landscape not only provides the setting for Virginia's mansions, it serves as the foil that makes them intelligible. Against a background of mostly crude and rudimentary habitations, Virginia's mansions presented an extraordinarily overt display of permanence, comfort, and visual sophistication. Not many Virginians were either capable of or inclined to undertake the difficult, expensive, and lengthy building campaign that was required to create an aesthetically superior dwelling. Many wealthy planters in the Tidewater region decided to forego lavish homes in favor of modest habitation. In short, Virginia's mansions were not only remarkable, they stood out in high relief.

While many colonists were content with more sensible shelter, a number of wealthy and politically powerful Virginians embarked on monumental, and in some cases foolhardy building campaigns, and this study investigates those patterns of behavior that affected the decision to build these more extravagant architectural gestures. Among the questions posed are:

Fig. 2. Rosewell, Gloucester County, 1726, destroyed by fire in 1916. View of ruins in 2005. (Photograph by Robert T. Mooney)

what demographic characteristics did patrons share, how were they able to build such costly buildings, what were the patrons' aesthetic values, and to what purposes were they put? I address these questions in a series of somewhat independent chapters exploring various aspects of patronage and social use. The first chapter, which analyzes the visual rhetoric of Virginia mansions, will be useful to those with only a limited familiarity with the colony's buildings and draws upon the research of the past generation of scholars in the field. The second chapter analyzes the demographic characteristics of the people who built these extraordinary dwellings. The middle three chapters delve into specific aspects of patronage: how marriage impacted architecture, how owners participated in design and construction, and what patrons knew about building fashions. The last two chapters take a more speculative gamble by examining a female epistemology of space within the mansion and by interrogating the political efficacy of architectural patronage.

To address these questions, I have drawn upon literary evidence not only from such well-known eighteenth-century writers as William Byrd II and Philip Vickers Fithian but also from a study group of twenty-five Virginians who built mansions between the early 1720s and the American Revolution. Buildings in the study group were chosen because they were the products of a single building campaign and hence reflect the values of one person or one married couple. While George Washington's Mount Vernon and the Randolph mansion, Tuckahoe, have fascinating stories to tell, they were excluded from the study group because of their multiple building campaigns. Mansions were additionally selected if the building could be dated with some measure of accuracy and if some biographical information for the owners could be found. Initially created for my dissertation in the early 1990s, the study group sample relied almost entirely on documentary evidence for building dates.[12] In the intervening period, the science of dating buildings by tree rings, known as dendrochronology, has refined and amended some of the original dates assigned to individual mansions. In many instances, I have made subjective choices, and the book should not be construed as representing a scientific sample. The study group can, however, serve as a model to be compared and tested against other examples of high-style colonial architecture.

Readers should note that the architectural plans in chapter 1 have been drawn to a consistent scale, but they have been simplified and should not be construed as measured drawings. Sources for the statistical tables are given in the appendix. The issue of Old Style/New Style dating also requires clarification. Although under the Julian calendar in use before 1752 the new year began on 25 March, in this book the year dates have silently been changed to begin on 1 January, so that, for example, 12 February 1742 becomes 12 February 1743.

Readers attuned to methodological nuances will notice that I have taken a few cues from New Historicism. For me, incidental anecdotes reveal small and vital epiphanies of truth. I am also reluctant to reduce the meaning of Virginia's colonial architecture to one master narrative. Throughout the book I propose that the most privileged members of the elite class created imposing houses in order to inscribe inherited privilege more permanently on the cultural landscape of the colony. That, however, stands as only one of several critical interpretations of Virginia mansions. My book explores several perspectives; many more remain.

Defining the Prodigy House

Architectural Aesthetics and the Colonial Dialect

The Role of Design

Whether he was a sincere, objective critic or merely a fawning political lackey, the eighteenth-century historian Robert Beverley II (1673–1722) knew how to flatter his readers as well as Virginia governor Alexander Spotswood: he appealed to their sense of aesthetic superiority. In the 1722 edition of *The History of Virginia in Four Parts,* Beverley emphasized Spotswood's improvements to the architectural environment of Williamsburg, noting his work in rebuilding the fire-ravaged College of William and Mary; erecting a new brick church, a new brick powder magazine, and a new debtor's prison; and regularizing the town's street pattern from its previously "fanciful" layout. Spotswood made several significant architectural contributions to the town, yet Beverley drew his readers' attention to the Governor's Palace. Although an earlier administration had begun construction, the Governor's Palace, according to Beverley, had "received its Beauty and Conveniency, for the many Alterations and Decorations, of the present Governor Colonel Spotswood."[1]

Beverley used a self-consciously literate vocabulary more familiar to avid readers of architectural treatises than to everyday Virginians. His encomium assumed that the buyers and readers of his book would possess the linguistic competency necessary to appreciate the architectural meaning of the words "beauty" and "conveniency." By evoking an elite, international vocabulary of architectural aesthetes, Beverley also invited his readers to believe they were participating in a gentlemanly conversation within the larger British cultural sphere. The number of eighteenth-century Virginians recognizing the author's articulate speech or attuned to architectural aesthetics and theory must have been exceedingly small. Yet, Beverley perceptively foresaw that his audience was literate in both print and architectural culture. To Beverley and the architectural patrons of Virginia's prodigy houses, aesthetics mattered.

Beverley's knowledgeable audience was comprised of extremely wealthy colonial Virginians who are referred to by historians today as the "native elite." Beginning in the last decade of the seventeenth century, a small segment of Virginia planters accumulated great wealth based on slave labor. Most were native-born Virginians, and their increasingly powerful position in the colonial hierarchy was the product of a symbiotic relationship between their wealth and the political offices they held. Their money was new, their ascent was rapid, and their authority extraordinary. Compared to the sickly, malarial, economically unstable, and often anarchic decades of the seventeenth century, the new order of the eighteenth appears, at least at first glance, stable, orderly, and appealing. Members of Virginia's eighteenth-century native elite knew how lucky they were. Richard Ambler saw the hand of God in this new and, for him, happy state of affairs when he advised his sons, "You cannot therefore, sufficiently Adore the Divine Providence who has placed your Parents above the lower Class."[2] Not surprisingly, men like Ambler did not rely on Providence to sustain their position, but devised legal and economic strategies to perpetuate their exalted status and extend it to their descendents. Material culture served a vital role in this strategy.

Beginning around 1720, a number of the most privileged members of the native elite began to construct dramatically large, classically inflected houses at enormous expense. They spent prodigious amounts of money in creating dwellings with design features that were carefully calculated, they hoped, to mirror their personal honor and the social worth of their family. Like the other prestigious objects with which they surrounded themselves, such as carriages, matched ceramic assemblages, and clothing made of smooth and elaborately patterned fabric, architecture functioned as a prop in their self-invention and their presumptuous claim to social and political authority.[3] Virginia's prodigy houses declared their owners' worthiness to rule. Via the superior aesthetic character of their architecture, the native elite attempted to naturalize and make permanent their superior social and economic position. The formal values they considered efficacious were not just attractive reflections of the prestige of the native elite. Rather, architecture was meant to serve as an active agent in legitimizing the social order the wealthiest planters envisioned.

Understanding how Virginia's native elite exploited the built environment in the expectation of perpetuating their authority requires understanding, as Beverley did, the architectural language they spoke. Eighteenth-century Virginia architecture was not completely autochthonous but was inflected by ideals from within and without the colony. Taking the measure of Virginia mansions by comparing them to broader colonial and European architectural contexts not only situates their design more precisely, but it more accurately identifies the cultural sphere in which Virginia's gentry operated. For the colony's native elite, the cultural sway of British culture was particularly strong and frequently renewed. The laws and religion they imposed on less wealthy settlers and native peoples were British, and they were able to maintain cultural contacts in ways that other, poorer Virginia inhabitants were not. Unlike yeoman farmers, tenants, indentured servants, and slaves, some wealthy Virginia planters were personally entangled in the wider world of British Atlantic politics. The emigrant Richard Lee is one example. Lee moved to Virginia from England in the middle of the seventeenth century, traveled to Holland in support of the exiled King Charles II during the Commonwealth, and thought of himself as British.[4] The magnetic pull of British cultural and material production appears undiminished in the next century, especially among those rich and powerful enough to take a role in colonial politics.[5] William Byrd II and later William Beverley, for instance, both played their hand in English politics as they sought to maintain their power in the Virginia Council, the most prestigious governmental body in the colony. Unlike poor or even middling inhabitants, the native elite possessed wealth that allowed them to purchase consumer goods that daily reinforced the aesthetic and social values of Britain. Acquiring and displaying the kind of design that reflected contemporary English taste functioned as an essential component of the self-image of the colonial elite. Even the English place-names attached to Virginia plantations, such as Stratford, Battersea, and Wilton, illustrate that some members of the Virginia gentry set their compass by England. Not every prosperous Virginian, however, was held in the thrall of British cultural imperatives. As the architectural historian Clifton Ellis has shown, wealthy planters who dissented from the theology and liturgy of the Anglican Church in Halifax County seemed happy to live in less pretentious dwellings.[6]

Because emulating British culture was a conscious choice on the part of certain segments of the Virginia gentry, it is important to determine how prodigy houses related to architecture in Britain and more generally to the architectural values of early modern Europe. Rather than providing specific prototypes for Virginia mansions, British architecture provided aesthetic and social ideals, such as the increasing specialization of rooms and the privileging of interior life and privacy. The cultural influence of the wider Atlantic world upon Virginia's mansions also extended to decorative schemes, particularly the selective use of design principles and ornamental features whose origins lie in the Italian Renaissance but that were modified in different European regions.

There is, however, another and equally important context: the vernacular building traditions of colonial Virginia. The visual impact of the prodigy house and its social claim to authority was, in fact, only meaningful when it stood within a larger built environment.[7] At its most rudimentary, Virginia's seventeenth-century vernacular houses were cheap, flimsy, short-lived, and supported not on masonry foundations but on posts placed in holes, which were then backfilled. Wooden posts rot in soil. Consequently, buildings constructed in this manner survive only a short time. Historians in the field have estimated that if the rotted post ends were not replaced, post-in-hole buildings lasted no longer than about fifteen years. Not all builders using hole-set technology were compelled to use small-dimensioned studs and simplified joints of tenuous strength. Carpenters occasionally constructed sturdy timber frames underpinned with earthfast posts. One such example with more substantial carpentry survives at Cedar Park, Maryland, but it endures because it was later encased in brick. The Matthew Jones house was also initially framed with earthfast posts in 1720, and it too remains because nine years later the walls were bricked.[8]

A more representative image of the kind of impermanent houses experienced by average Tidewater settlers has been erected in the re-created seventeenth-century village at Historic St. Mary's City, Maryland (fig. 3). Walls made of small-dimensioned studs were covered with crudely riven clapboards that minimally sheltered inhabitants from the weather and gave the building only a small measure of lateral bracing. Dirt floors and stick-and-mud-daub chimneys were common. Amenities were rare, although a noticeable number of polychrome Dutch tiles found at some St. Mary's houses as well as Spanish, Italian, and Chinese ceramics unearthed at Jamestown, Virginia, imply a more complex international trade network.[9]

Because hole-set construction technology was so common in Virginia, it became synonymous with the colony's architecture. By common linguistic consent, it was termed the "Virginia House." In 1684, an act was passed by the General Assembly codifying the construction of county prisons. To assure uniformity, the act specified that "a good strong and substantiall prison, after the forme of Virginia housing be built."[10] Three years later the ambitious planter William Fitzhugh claimed that tenants could build an "ordinary Virginia House" on their own without construction specialists.[11] Almost eighty years later this widespread construction method was still generally understood without the benefit of additional description. In providing for the future welfare of his son, Charles Carter instructed his executors to build "at the expense of my estate, an overseer's house, a quarter, a cow house and two 40 foot Tobo. [tobacco] Houses, according to the common method of building in Virginia."[12]

Impermanent architecture was no regional Tidewater aberration. Archaeologists have discovered similar building technology used in England, New Netherlands, and New England.[13] By the middle of the eighteenth

Fig. 3. Reconstruction of typical seventeenth-century hole-set dwelling, Historic St. Mary's City, Maryland. (Photograph by author)

century, post-in-ground buildings began to be supplanted by another cheap but more substantial building technology, namely unhewn or roughly hewn notched and horizontally positioned logs. Thomas Jefferson's slaves lived and worked in buildings along Mulberry Row made of logs, and it was this kind of simple construction that would become identified with the American frontier experience. In 1793, Francisco Hector Carondelet, the Spanish governor of what would become known as the Louisiana Territory, condemned American settlers for their guns, corn bread, and easy-to-build and easy-to-abandon log cabins. The Baron de Carondelet saw log houses as proof of a dangerous, restless, and "wandering spirit" accompanied by a rapacious appetite for ever more land.[14]

Between the extremes of post-set dwellings and grand mansions lay the houses of various striation belonging to the middling sort. Many houses for the middle class were small and of frame construction. More prosperous landowners occasionally marked their transition from rudimentary to polite architecture by paying for the hallmarks of domestic gentility: plastered walls, a separate chamber to hold a prized feather bed, or the dishes necessary to serve tea. Further along the scale of polite architecture, wealthier Virginia planters lived in substantial one-and-a-half-story brick houses embellished with fashionable interior wall paneling. In this category belongs the Jacob Faulcon House, also known as Smith's Fort Plantation, built about 1765 in Surry County (fig. 4) or the Thoroughgood House in Princess Anne County, now known, through the science of tree-ring analysis, or dendrochronology, to have been under construction around 1719.[15]

Virginia's prodigy houses, on the other hand, were far more than polite. Their owners went to extraordinary lengths to acquire aesthetic features that distinguished them not only from humble hole-set houses but also from the dwellings of competing prosperous planters. The process of social distinction through architectural refinement becomes clearer by examining twenty-five mansions and their owners (table 1).[16] Analyzing the physical characteristics of this sample—specifically their scale, materials, fenestration, and ornamental details—shows the way that Virginia's native elite put aesthetic distance between themselves and other colonial inhabitants. I begin by analyzing the most obviously distinct quality, the sheer size of the houses built by the newly rich and powerful, buildings that I am calling the prodigy houses of Virginia.

Fig. 4. Jacob Faulcon House (Smith's Fort Plantation), Surry County, ca. 1765. (Photograph by author)

Table 1
Prodigy house study group

Date	House	Location	Patron
1720	Corotoman	Lancaster County	Robert Carter I
1721	Germanna	Spotsylvania County	Alexander Spotswood
1725	Kingsmill	James City County	Lewis Burwell III
1726	Berkeley	Charles City County	Benjamin Harrison IV
1726	Rosewell	Gloucester County	Mann Page I
1738	Sabine Hall	Richmond County	Landon Carter
1738	Stratford Hall	Westmoreland County	Thomas Lee
1741	Belvoir	Fairfax County	William Fairfax
1746	Marlborough	Stafford County	John Mercer
1746	Cleve	King George County	Charles Carter
1750	Carter's Grove	James City County	Carter Burwell
1751	Brooke's Bank	Essex County	Sarah Taliaferro Brooke
1751	Carlyle House	Alexandria	John Carlyle
1751	Wilton	Henrico County	William Randolph III
1752	Gunston Hall	Fairfax County	George Mason IV
1758	Laneville	King and Queen County	Richard Corbin
1758	Tazewell Hall	Williamsburg	John Randolph II
1760	Mount Airy	Richmond County	John Tayloe II
1761	Chantilly	Westmoreland County	Richard Henry Lee
1763	Salubria	Culpeper County	John Thompson
1767	Battersea	Dinwiddie County	John Banister III
1767	Mannsfield	Spotsylvania County	Mann Page II
1769	Blandfield	Essex County	Robert Beverley
1769	Chatham	Stafford County	William Fitzhugh
1770	Monticello I	Albemarle County	Thomas Jefferson

Scale and Relative Size

Compared to the hole-set slave houses at seventeenth-century Littletown Plantation outside Williamsburg, or the log slave dwellings along late eighteenth-century Mulberry Row at Monticello, Virginia's prodigy houses were immense.[17] They were also huge compared to habitations of free white, well-off Virginians (fig. 5). Because virtually all of the smaller dwellings have disappeared, it is easy to lose sight of the dramatic difference in scale between mansions and the way most people lived in colonial Virginia. Take for example, William Randolph III's mansion, called Wilton, which was built in 1751 (fig. 6). The two-story house measures 64 feet, 3 inches x

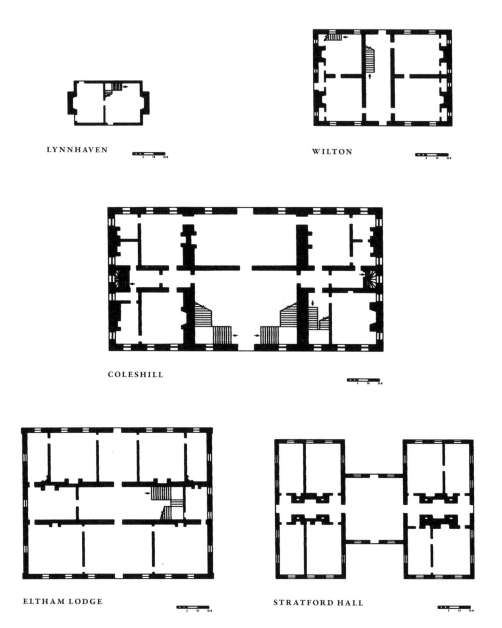

Fig. 5. Relative size of Virginia prodigy houses; scale bar equals 15 feet. (Megan D. Roy after Willie Graham, Thomas T. Waterman, and John Summerson)

43 feet, 5 inches and contains four rooms plus a generously wide central passage on each floor.[18] By comparison, Lynnhaven House (also known as the Francis Thelaball II House), a more modest though far from typical one-and-a-half-story house started in 1724, measures approximately 30 x 20 and enclosed only two rooms plus a now-missing one-story wing measuring perhaps 10 x 13 feet (fig. 7).[19] To put Wilton in perspective, its two

Fig. 6. Wilton, Richmond, originally in Henrico County, 1751. River façade. (Photograph by Robert T. Mooney)

Fig. 7. Lynnhaven House (Francis Thelaball II House), Virginia Beach, originally in Princess Anne County, 1724–25. (Photograph by Robert T. Mooney)

full stories allowed William Randolph III's family about 5,632 square feet of living space. Francis Thelaball II's family at Lynnhaven House, on the other hand, inhabited about 1,330 feet. Wilton was more than four times the size of Lynnhaven House.

The size of Wilton and Lynnhaven House becomes more impressive by contextualizing it among more typical colonial dwellings. Pear Valley, a yeoman farmer's house, is located in Northampton County on the Eastern Shore of Virginia and has been dated to 1740 by dendrochronology (fig. 8).[20] The one-and-a-half-story house is a miraculous extant example of the kind of modestly proportioned houses that dominated the Tidewater. Its brick foundation, brick chimney, brick chimney-end wall, and plastered interior walls, however, made it much more comfortable than the dwellings of other yeoman farmers. More typically, the carpenters at Pear Valley used simplified false plates to connect rafters to the two wood-framed walls with a minimum of complex and expensive carpentry. Pear Valley's original inhabitants conducted life in a startlingly minimal living space: the house

Fig. 8. Pear Valley, Northampton County, 1740. (Photograph by Robert T. Mooney)

measures 20 feet, 10 inches x 16 feet, 3 inches.[21] The square footage, roughly 336, is significant. It satisfies, barely, the legal minimal dimensions of a so-called Virginia House. In order to secure title to frontier property, prospective landowners needed to make certain "improvements" to the land, among which was the erection of a habitation of minimal dimension. An act of November 1713, for example, specified that even on less fertile land "such patentee shall be obliged, within three years after the passing such grant, to erect and build on some part of the said tract, one good dwelling house, after the manner of Virginia building, to contain at least twenty foot in length, and sixteen foot in breadth."[22] Pear Valley's dimensions can be compared with Tidewater habitations in both Virginia and Maryland. Tenants leasing property on Kent Manor, Maryland, in 1767 lived in houses averaging 484 square feet.[23] At the end of the century, the average dwelling in Baltimore County, Maryland, was slightly smaller, measuring about 20 x 18 feet with a median area of only 360 square feet.[24] Advertisements in the *Virginia Gazette* between 1736 and 1780 indicate that most property owners were sheltered in homes of less than 576 square feet.[25] In Berkeley Parish in Spotsylvania County, Virginia, at the end of the century, almost two-thirds of the dwelling houses were less than 600 square feet.[26]

The diminutive form of most colonial Virginia habitation compared to Wilton dramatically illustrates how the size of prodigy houses fairly shouted a declaration of aesthetic and social superiority in the colonial landscape. Placed in the English landscape, however, Wilton would have conveyed a more modest, though nonetheless genteel, aspect. Coleshill, designed by Roger Pratt and constructed in Berkshire in the 1650s, has exterior features that have often been compared to Virginia's early eighteenth-century buildings, particularly its rectangular massing, regularized fenestration, and hipped roof (fig. 9). It measures an impressive 127 x 65 feet.[27] Eltham Lodge, designed by Hugh May and built in Kent in 1664, is somewhat smaller (fig. 10). Eltham Lodge measures about 90 x 70 feet. Considered a prime example of the impact of Dutch Palladianism on England, Eltham Lodge has also been associated with Virginia elite architecture by virtue of the colorful contrast between its brick walls and its stone trim, hipped roof, and compact massing. Builders in Virginia eliminated the colossal pilasters but adopted similar rectangular massing and regularized fenestration at a smaller scale, seen at the 1723 Brafferton building at the College of William and Mary (fig. 11).[28] The similarity, however, lies in exterior design, not plan. The elaborate arrangement of rooms at Coleshill and Eltham Lodge finds little parallel in early eighteenth-century Virginia. While Wilton was decidedly smaller, Thomas Lee's Stratford Hall, built in 1738, measured 92 feet, 6 inches x 62 feet, 8½ inches, and fit more comfortably within the standards of England's gentry houses.

Fig. 9. Coleshill, Berkshire, England, 1650s, designed by Roger Pratt, destroyed by fire in 1952. (Country Life Picture Library)

Fig. 10. Eltham Lodge, Kent, England, 1664, designed by Hugh May. (Country Life Picture Library)

Fig. 11. The Brafferton, College of William and Mary, Williamsburg, 1723. (Photograph by author)

Building Materials

After scale and size, the second necessary, but not sufficient, characteristic defining Virginia prodigy houses was the use of load-bearing brick walls. Aside from practical considerations such as permanence and fire retardancy, brick was desirable because it so obviously declared the wealth of the owner within the Virginia context. The laborious complexity of brick construction prior to the modern building industry can be easily underestimated, but brick making and bricklaying were not ordinary or everyday endeavors. Moreover, every aspect of brick construction proclaimed that the owner had surplus wealth that could be diverted from productive use to aestheticized display. The smooth, finely wrought textiles depicted in John Wollaston's portrait of William Randolph III (fig. 12) that elites throughout the colonies prized for clothing had their parallel in the uniform coursework, regular surfaces, and coloristic effects of the brickwork at Randolph's mansion, Wilton. By announcing aesthetic distance from the rough, irregular, and unpainted riven clapboards that covered most Virginia habitations, Randolph's bricks announced social distance as well.

Fig. 12. John Wollaston, *Portrait of William Randolph III,* oil on canvas, mid-eighteenth century. (Virginia Historical Society, Richmond, Virginia)

Whereas the production of brick for local sale to builders may have occurred in England as early as the late medieval period, in colonial Virginia bricks were usually made on site and for a particular building campaign as they were for Carter's Grove. Finding suitable clay deposits represented an important step in the building process. William Byrd II noted in his diary on 5 April 1709 that "the brickmaker came this evening" and two days later that "the men began to work this day to dig for brick."[29] Brick-making toil signaled to viewers that the architectural patron was able to locate clay deposits and could arrange for the digging and hauling of clay and sand, often by taking slave labor out of the field and away from crop production. Brick making also demonstrated that the patron could hire a specialist who knew the correct proportions of clay, sand, and moisture to produce the proper consistency for molding. Although much of the physical labor could be carried out by apprentices, indentured servants, or unpaid slaves, a skilled professional directed the project. That specialist had to know how to mold bricks and, more importantly, to determine how long to let them dry out of direct sunlight. He had to be someone experienced in building a kiln, in efficiently stacking raw bricks in the kiln, and in estimating the amount of fuel necessary to reach an ideal firing temperature between 1,850°F and 1,950°F. Without the aid of a thermometer, a brick maker judged the color of the heat and raised the temperature gradually lest the water in the bricks turn to steam and explode. He made the critical decision whether the heat had permeated all parts of the kiln and if the bricks were sufficiently fired or well burnt. Once the bricks were fired, they were sorted according to quality and color. The hardest and most uniform bricks, often referred to as stock bricks, were reserved for the exterior face of load-bearing walls. Lesser-quality bricks, many times called common bricks, were used within the interior core of the wall. In the firing process, the surfaces of some bricks vitrified. These vitrified, or glazed, bricks displayed a darker, glassy, somewhat reflective surface and might be sorted and stacked separately for ornamental purposes.[30]

Architectural patrons also needed to find, hire, and pay a bricklayer, often the same person as the brick maker. Joseph Moxon's *Mechanick Exercises, or the Doctrine of Handyworks,* published in London in 1678, may have offered building patrons valuable advice about how to judge the quality of workmanship, but it did not provide the depth of expertise necessary to learn the trade. Consequently, a professional bricklayer was needed to oversee wall construction. He ensured sound bonding between stock and common brick in the depth of the wall mass, and strove for uniform mortar beds and straight vertical wall surfaces. In laying up his masonry wall, a bricklayer gave careful forethought to the level placement of the voids on the interior face of the walls in which joists rested. Creating multiflue or funnel chimneys with a hearth on each floor required more skills and had to be planned when the chimney foundation was laid.[31]

Before this point, however, patrons and their bricklayers determined the brick bond. The older, and perhaps more structurally firm, English bond was composed of alternating courses of all headers and all stretchers (fig. 13). English bond was employed for the foundations and upper walls at Bacon's Castle (1665), the James City Parish church tower (1680), and the foundations of the row houses built in Jamestown (after 1662). Interestingly, recent research suggests that the patterning of English bond may not have been noticeable to viewers. After closely examining the building fabric at Bacon's Castle, the painting expert Susan Buck found that the bricks as well as the mortar were covered with red pigment that disguised flaws in the brick bonding and created a wall surface in striking contrast with the lighter plastered window surrounds. There is some evidence, moreover, that pigmentation was also applied to the exquisitely wrought brickwork around the entrances of Christ Church, Lancaster County (fig. 14).[32] The visual impact of colonial elite architecture, therefore, presented a startlingly more brilliant impression than these buildings do today.

Fig. 13. Bacon's Castle (Arthur Allen House), Surry County, 1665. English bond brickwork. (Photograph by author)

Fig. 14. Christ Church, Lancaster County, ca. 1732–35. Brick segmental arch, entablature, and pilasters at entrance. (Photograph by author)

English bond was also employed in the foundation and upper walls of John Custis II's three-story house in Northampton County called Arlington, built about 1670. Arlington represented the apogee of refinement in seventeenth-century Virginia, but certain parts of its building fabric were marked by a feature that would disappear from the vocabulary of Virginia's eighteenth-century prodigy houses, pebblecast. Made by throwing small stone against unhardened plaster, the technique is related to roughcast, wherein quartz, gravel, or glass are added to lime mortar before it is applied to the wall. In crowded urban areas like Boston, house owners such as Thomas Stanbury, who added roughcast to the exterior of his new 1680 frame house, might have imagined that it served to retard fire (fig. 15). The real advantage to both processes was in allowing a greater variety in textural surface effects. Custis heightened the visually complicated elevation design by adding heart-shaped blocks of masonry to his exterior walls.[33]

By contrast, eighteenth-century mansion owners and their builders came to prefer Flemish bond, in which each course was composed of al-

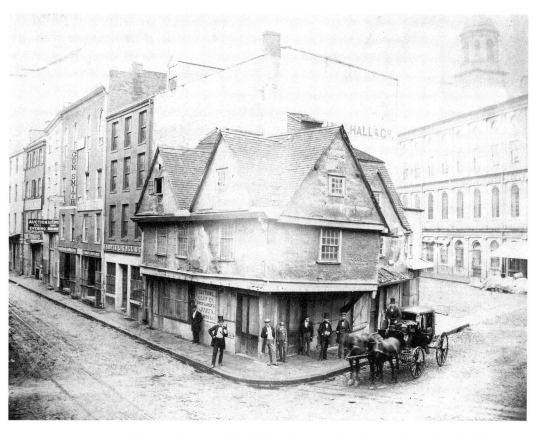

Fig. 15. Thomas Stanbury House, Boston, 1680, photograph ca. 1870–80. (Courtesy of the Bostonian Society/Old State House)

ternating headers and stretchers, like that found at Brooke's Bank (fig. 16). Architectural historians believe that Flemish bond was introduced into English practice when Samuel Fortrey, a wealthy London merchant with commercial and family ties to Flanders and the Netherlands, remodeled a mid-sixteenth-century house in Richmond, England, in 1631, now known as Kew Palace or the Dutch House (fig. 17).[34] Flemish bond did not dominate English building until the eighteenth century, and in Virginia, too, the transition was gradual.[35] English bond was still employed for both the foundation and upper walls of the genteel but modestly sized Lynnhaven House.[36] At the nearby Thoroughgood House (1719), bricklayers built only one wall with the fashionable new Flemish bond and more cautiously or conservatively retained English bond for the other façades. In a number of prodigy houses, masons utilized English bond for the foundation and Flemish bond for the upper exterior wall face.

Some architectural patrons demanded more complex and time-consuming decorative brick patterning. At Stratford Hall, for instance, every header in the Flemish bond of the lower level is glazed, creating a checkered pattern (fig. 18). At Brooke's Bank, a vertical diamond pattern of glazed bricks enlivens each long face of the chimney stacks. The pattern showed off not only the taste of the owner, Sarah Taliaferro Brooke, for flamboyant decoration but also her ability to pay for an expert bricklayer who could use variations in brick color to advantage (fig. 19). Such expertise in masonry was not plentiful in colonial Virginia, nor did it come cheaply. Yet, surprisingly refined brickwork appears on more vernacular dwellings, too. The chimney-end wall of the small frame yeoman's cottage called Pear Valley was not only constructed of brick but was also embellished with bands of darker, glazed bricks paralleling the steep slope of the roof (fig. 20). After 1750, fewer buildings used glazed bricks for geometric designs.

Wealthy seventeenth-century colonial Virginians utilized brick construction more often than the handful of surviving examples would indicate.[37] In addition to Bacon's Castle and Arlington, several other important dwellings are known to have had a brick superstructure as well as a brick foundation: a row of townhouses at Jamestown, the mansion complex at Green Spring, and the Page House on the fringes of Williamsburg (1662) were all built of brick. The Page House is dated from the decorative carved brick panel with the date 1662 found in its archaeological remains, and Benjamin Harrison IV inserted a similar stone commemorative device into the upper wall of Berkeley in 1726.[38] Like the prodigy houses of the eighteenth century, the Arlington and the Page Houses made architectural claims for social superiority. The features they used to declare these claims, however, would be eclipsed by a different vocabulary.

Fig. 16. Brooke's Bank, Essex County, 1751. Flemish bond brickwork. (Photograph by author)

Fig. 17. Kew Palace, also known as the Dutch House or the Samuel Fortrey House, Surrey, England, 1631. (© Historic Royal Palaces)

Fig. 18. Stratford Hall, Westmoreland County, begun in 1738. Glazed headers in Flemish bond brickwork on lower level. (Photograph by author)

Fig. 19. Brooke's Bank, Essex County, 1751. Diamond pattern created with glazed bricks on chimney stacks. (Photograph by author)

Fig. 20. Pear Valley, Northampton, 1740. Glazed headers on gable end. (Photograph by author)

Whether English bond or Flemish bond, most colonial Virginians found the lengthy and arduous process of creating brick buildings beyond their means. They survived, even flourished, in houses built of wood, which were either knitted to hole-set posts or, if they were more fortunate, rested on masonry foundations. Set against a prevailing context of timber houses, a large brick prodigy house presented a prominent and remarkable profile. The contrast seemed particularly noticeable to travelers to the colony. In 1724, Hugh Jones, an associate of the embattled Governor Alexander Spotswood, painted a promising picture of Virginia under his political patron's administration. His comments provide a snapshot, albeit a biased one, of domestic construction and the plantation landscape. Jones claimed that "the gentlemen's seats are of late built for the most part of good brick, and many of timber very handsom, commodious, and capacious; and likewise the common planters live in pretty timber houses, neater than the farm houses are generally in England."[39] In 1732, the traveler William Hugh Grove painted a less flattering image of Virginia architecture. After casting a critical eye over Yorktown, he judged only ten out of the thirty dwelling houses to be "good." Out of those thirty houses, only four were made of brick. The others seem to have been significantly less substantial. Grove described them as constructed of "Pine Planks Covered with shingles of Cypress."[40] Forty-five years later, Ebenezer Hazard, a surveyor for the postal service, continued to take the measure of a town by judging its architecture. Raised in Philadelphia and trained at Princeton, Hazard recorded his impressions while on a trip through the South and noted that Alexandria, Virginia, was a "small town." He said that the town's Church of England and Presbyterian churches were built of brick and were "large neat Buildings," but the houses were "mostly wooden, & small." Likewise, he found that the "Houses in Fredericksburgh are built some of Wood & some of Brick, the former are the most numerous." He characterized Port Royal as a "small wooden town," and also summarized Williamsburg as "chiefly framed."[41]

Anecdotal evidence finds support in statistical analysis of the documentary record. From a close and nuanced reading of the advertisements in the *Virginia Gazette* between 1736 and 1780, the architectural historian Camille Wells discovered that fully 90 percent of houses in Virginia were made of wood.[42] Ashli White reached the same conclusion from her study of the built environment of Berkeley Parish in Spotsylvania County. Out of 190 dwellings in the parish noted in the 1798 Federal Direct Tax Lists, 82 percent were listed as either log, frame, or simply "wood."[43] From the same tax records, Liz Gallow determined that 70.9 percent of all the dwellings in Baltimore County, Maryland, were built with logs while only 15.2 percent utilized frame construction.[44]

Not all wooden buildings, however, were flimsy, impermanent, and devoid of aesthetic grace. The size of the wood-frame Randolph mansion at Tuckahoe (started in 1733 and substantially enlarged in 1740 or 1754) or the wood frame plus brick-end walls of the Hill mansion at Hillsborough (perhaps mid-eighteenth century) could also convey the visual prestige, especially through interior woodwork or expensive material contents (figs. 21 and 22).[45] But they could never communicate the same level of expense as entire brick buildings, nor signal the owner's ability and willingness to divert prodigious amounts of money to secure materials and pay for the required levels of expertise.

The traditional hierarchy of building materials privileged stone over brick. A greater number of ambitious patrons might have used stone more extensively if better quality stone had been available. Aquia Creek freestone from the Northern Neck region was notoriously coarse. John Carlyle built his house in Alexandria with a rubble core faced with Aquia Creek freestone that at some point received a protective coat of plaster. The smooth finish one sees today is deceptively refined because the mansion was refaced with finer-grained Indiana limestone during restoration in the 1970s (fig. 23). Charles Carter was probably referring to Aquia Creek freestone when he wrote sarcastically to his brother about his "Nasty Sorry Soft Stone."[46]

Carter nevertheless employed stone to draw attention to decorative elements set against the brick walls of Cleve. John Tayloe, however, elected to build his entire dwelling house and two large dependencies with local stone. However it was used, stone, even more so than brick, would have embodied the owner's social and economic superiority, as evidenced by his or her ability to absorb the astronomical costs of quarrying stone, carting it, and finding someone trained to carve it into decorative shapes that imitated fashionable metropolitan ideals.

Because of its ability to heighten the rhetoric of architectural aesthetics, stone remained the most prestigious of building materials. Consequently, some wealthy colonials attempted to imitate stone in wood. At the end of the century, George Washington curtained the wooden frame of the main block and dependencies at Mount Vernon not with beaded weatherboard but with beveled wood blocks painted with a sand admixture that imitated ashlar stone masonry (fig. 24).[47] Washington's fake stone walls were not novel. In fact, his siding was remarkably similar to that on the west façade of the Isaac Royall House in Medford, Massachusetts, remodeled in 1739 (fig. 25).[48] Even more elaborate imitation stone embellishments covered

Fig. 23. Carlyle House, Alexandria, Virginia, 1751. Main façade. (Photograph by author)

Fig. 24. Mount Vernon, Fairfax County. Beveled wood sheathing on principal façade of the north dependency known as the "servants' hall," mid-1770s. (Photograph by author)

Fig. 25. Isaac Royall House, Medford, Massachusetts, ca. 1739. West façade with beveled faux masonry. (Photograph by author)

Governor William Shirley's midcentury house in Roxbury, Massachusetts.[49] At the end of the century, Thomas Jefferson enhanced the prestige of his remodeled Monticello by covering the brick exterior walls of the new north entrance with plaster incised to look like stone (fig. 26). Sometime probably in the late eighteenth century, the descendants of the first owners, John Thompson and his wife, Anne Butler Brayne Spotswood Thompson, chose to coat the exterior walls of Salubria with plaster and to score the surface to look like stone blocks (fig. 27). Whether they knew the published source or not, Washington, Jefferson, and the Thompson descendents were following the advice of the Renaissance architect Andrea Palladio, who advised his readers that brick buildings could be made more impressive by covering them with stucco.[50] The dogma of truth to materials still awaited Ruskin and the nineteenth century.

Fig. 26. Monticello II, Albemarle County, after 1796. East portico. Faux-ashlar masonry on right. (Photograph by author)

Fig. 27. Salubria, Culpeper County, 1763. Stucco scored to look like stone masonry. (Photograph by author)

Symmetry

The third essential characteristic of Virginia's prodigy houses was symmetry, made manifest in an equal and regularized pattern of fenestration on either side of a central door. Following Renaissance ideals, all openings should align vertically, creating a pattern of void over void and solid over solid. In other words, load-bearing walls must be positioned over load-bearing walls, while windows must be located directly above either windows or doors. It sounds simple, but the principle is not a natural but a learned value essential to classicizing architectural design. Symmetry, however, was not invented by prodigy house owners of the eighteenth century. The fenestration pattern at the Arthur Allen House, known better as Bacon's Castle (1665), also reflects a Renaissance understanding of the vertical and symmetrical alignment of windows (fig. 28). More than a hundred years later, Robert Beverley, like Arthur Allen, made a conscious decision to insist on regularized vertical and horizontal alignment of fenestration at Blandfield (fig. 29).

Fig. 28. Bacon's Castle (Arthur Allen House), Surry County, 1665. (Photograph by author)

Fig. 29. Blandfield, Essex County, 1769. Land façade. (Photograph by author)

Windows and Window Glass

Glazing within this symmetrical arrangement of fenestration did, however, change from the seventeenth to the eighteenth century, and it too dramatically signaled the superior aesthetic and financial status of the native elite from more humble Virginians. The visual sensation and practical effects of good window glass are greatly underappreciated, and it is difficult to imagine the startling consequences and delightful aesthetic effects of clearer and larger pieces of glass. In England, glazing was routine only after about 1590, and the kind of glass that was inserted into the previously open windows, known as broad sheet glass, was replete with imperfections and had a dull, murky surface. Glassmakers cut broad sheet glass into small rectangular pieces called quarrels, or quarries, because the H-shaped strips of soft lead, called cames, that held them in place could not support much weight. Lead cames, in turn, were supported within iron casement frames that turned on hinges like doors.

While not without flaws, pieces of crown glass were, comparatively speaking, amazingly transparent. Produced in quantity in London starting in 1678, this new kind of window glass first appeared in the urban centers of British North America a few decades later. At least one Boston government official found its effect revelatory when he visited the new Boston

City Hall in 1713. Recognizing the metaphorical connotations of its increased transparency, Samuel Sewall jotted a rather cynical prayer to the Almighty in his diary: "Let this large, transparent, costly Glass serve to oblige the Attorneys always to set things in a True Light."[51]

The novel effect of crown glass went hand in hand with other innovations, namely the shift from iron casement windows to wooden sash windows. The English builder William Samwell first used the new device at Inigo Jones's Prince's Lodging at Newcastle in 1669, and installed them in 1674 on the newly remodeled south façade of Ham House in Surrey, England (fig. 30).[52] His original sash windows there still employed lead cames and quarrels, but soon it was discovered that wooden glazing bars, or muntins, could hold larger pieces of glass. The size of crown glass, about 6 x 9 inches, when placed in wooden muntins offered the considerable luxury of increased illumination and the possibility of increased interior social activity.[53]

The shift from casement windows with lead cames and quarrels to wooden sash windows with crown glass did not take place in Virginia overnight. Sash windows are first mentioned in the documentary records at the turn of the eighteenth century in the context of the new public buildings

Fig. 30. Ham House, Surrey, England, south façade, 1672–74, attributed to William Samwell. (Country Life Picture Library)

at Williamsburg, specifically the Capitol and the College of William and Mary. But more traditional casements and quarrels continued to be used for some time, even in one of the grandest of Virginia mansions. Robert Carter I decided to use iron casement frames, presumably for quarrel glass, for at least a few of the windows at Corotoman. Archaeological evidence from Lynnhaven House, built in 1724-25, for instance, indicates that its interior was illuminated with casement windows containing lead, which in turn held quarrels rather than prized crown glass. Small openings in the Capitol at Williamsburg did not receive sash window treatment until 1730.[54] Building owners continued to use quarrels of glass held in lead cames into the middle of the century, but sash windows were considered more fashionable. As scientific paint analysis at Colonial Williamsburg has proved, their prestige value was emphasized by a brilliant white paint finish applied to the wooden sashes that sharply contrasted with the surrounding brickwork.[55]

The novelty of clear illumination did not fade in the second half of the eighteenth century. Sewall's prayer notwithstanding, it connoted prestige and wealth, not honesty. The luxury of light proved so desirable that it caused men of supposedly high ideals to compromise their principles. When Jefferson was building his first house, Monticello I, he found construction hindered by his own fastidious standards, by his inability to find a construction supervisor (whom he referred to as an architect), and by official colonial resolutions limiting trade with England. Restrictions placed on the procurement of building materials from England after passage of the Non-Importation Resolutions of June 1770 proved particularly vexing and ultimately embarrassing. Construction went on throughout the early 1770s, and by 9 December 1774 at least part of the house was ready to be enclosed.[56] On that date, Jefferson wrote an apologetic letter to Archibald Cary and Benjamin Harrison V in which he explained the circumstances behind his apparent disregard for a new set of nonimportation regulations. He explained that in May 1774 the general feeling was that only tea would be prohibited. Accordingly, so he claimed, "two or three days therefore after this I wrote to Cary and co. of London for 14. pair of sash windows to be sent to me ready made and glazed with a small parcel of spare glass to mend with." Shortly after ordering, however, the nonimportation restrictions were expanded to include glass. He wrote to Cary and Company to stop shipment, but the message was delivered too late. The windows were expected to arrive soon.[57] Jefferson's eagerness to do business with British merchants for a luxury item on the eve of a high-profile boycott of British imports offers some measure of the contemporary desirability of sash glass windows. Large and expensive expanses of glass-filled windows portended more than simple openings in the wall fabric. They offered a luxurious, perhaps even miraculous, portal of light into the interior and extended productive and leisurely close work such as reading and needlecraft, activities that would have been difficult for those who inhabited houses with less refined interior illumination.

The Use of the Orders

After size and a regularized elevation characterized by broad expanses of glazed openings, the feature that most distinguished the prodigy houses of Virginia from the dwellings of the poor or middling sort was the use of the Orders, the ornamental vocabulary of classical architecture. Virginia patrons and their builders, however, were inclined to use the Orders, or parts of the Orders, in a relatively restrained manner. The earliest influx of classical motifs into colonial America may have taken place in the largest urban center in the seventeenth century, Boston. One of the first known examples of this new ornamental system might have been displayed across the façade of the brick house that the merchant John Foster built about 1690-92 (fig. 31). Foster's house is gone, but at least one of the Ionic pilaster caps survives (fig. 32). If the pilasters were part of the original building campaign, instead of later additions, then a surprisingly sophisticated classical vocabulary was exhibited by Foster's urban contemporaries engaged in the building industry. The architectural historian Abbott Lowell Cummings suggested that classical ornament like that at the Foster House could be in part attributed to Foster's commercial ties to England. Cummings put more store in the impact of immigrant English artisans who had rebuilt London following the Great Fire of 1666 and brought new metropolitan architectural ideas with them.[58] Twenty years later, some of Boston's prosperous urban artisans continued to erect brick houses that also exhibited postfire design principles (fig. 33). With its windows of diminishing height, simple stringcourse dividing floor levels, and two-room plan separated by a central stair passage, the glazier Moses Pierce's 1711 dwelling reflected the direction of London's new housing standard.[59]

Impressive examples of classical ornament can be found in early eighteenth-century America. The entrance of St. Philip's in Charleston, South Carolina (1722–23), was marked by three porticoes composed of freestanding monumental Tuscan columns. Considered a remarkable example of colonial sophistication, St. Philip's was illustrated in a 1753 issue of the *Gentleman's Magazine,* an English periodical to which a few of the most wealthy Virginia planters subscribed (fig. 34). The Venetian window on the eastern façade of Christ Church in Philadelphia (fig. 35), which was added during the building campaign of 1735, likewise appropriated high-fashion motifs from the British capital. Its east end echoed that found at James Gibbs's St. Martin-in-the-Fields, London (1722–26) and illustrated in his

Fig. 31. John Foster House, Boston, 1690–92. Elevation published in the *American Magazine of Useful and Entertaining Knowledge* 3 (February 1836). (Special Collections, University of Iowa)

Fig. 32. John Foster House, Boston, 1690–92. Imported stone pilaster cap. (Courtesy of Historic New England)

1728 *Book of Architecture* (fig. 36).[60] Drayton Hall, located just outside of Charleston, stands as another example of cutting-edge British architecture. Begun in 1738, the building was remarkable for its correspondence to published British prototypes, including its Palladian two-story portico and interior chimneypiece. Throughout urban British America, colonial elites strove to compensate for their provincial status by imitating high-style and English building forms.

The Upper South was the richest region in the British North American colonies and maintained vigorous economic ties to England throughout the colonial period. Yet Virginia architectural patrons and their craftsmen chose to use the Orders in a noticeably more reserved manner. By eschewing the overt use of columns or pilasters, Virginia patrons and their builders expressed their taste for a more astylar interpretation of classical architecture. Take, for example, the exterior ornament of Rosewell, known in

Fig. 33. Moses Pierce House, Boston, 1711. (Photograph by author)

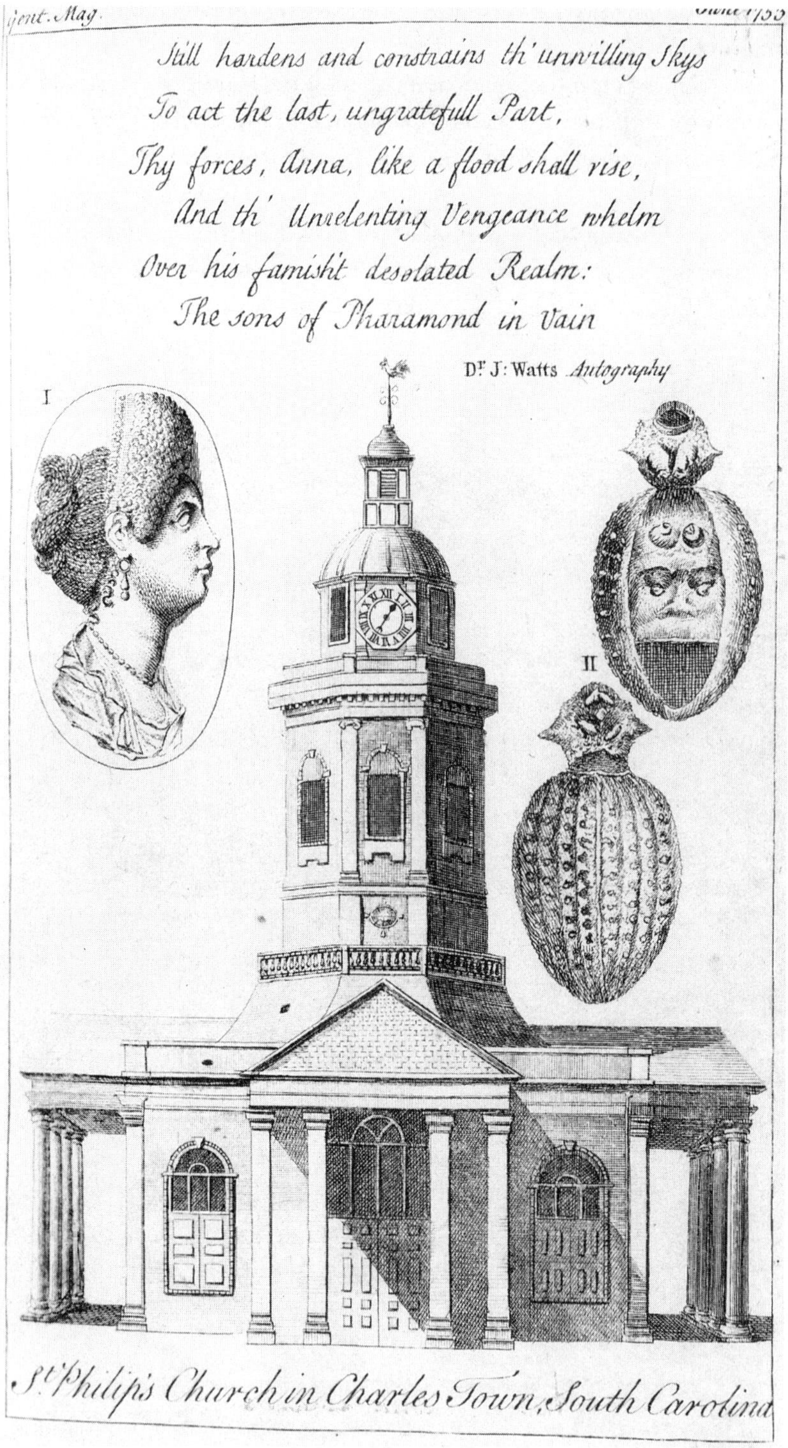
Gent. Mag.
Still hardens and constrains th' unwilling Skys
To act the last, ungratefull Part,
Thy forces, Anna, like a flood shall rise,
And th' Unrelenting Vengeance whelm
Over his famish't desolated Realm:
The sons of Pharamond in Vain
Dr J: Watts Autography
I
II
St. Philip's Church in Charles Town, South Carolina

Fig. 34. St. Philip's Church, Charleston, South Carolina, ca. 1722–23. Illustration from the *Gentleman's Magazine* (London, 1753). (Butler Library, Columbia University)

Fig. 35. Christ Church, Philadelphia. Eastern façade, begun 1735. (Historic American Building Survey, Prints and Photographs Division, Library of Congress)

the colonial period as the best house in Virginia. Mann Page I paid dearly for complex molded brick embellishment around his doors. An old image of one entrance shows that Rosewell's patron desired lavish brick doorways comprised of a pediment, dentiled cornice, scrolled brackets, and molded pilaster shafts (fig. 37). Yet Rosewell had no complete pilasters with capitals reaching the full height of the building like those of the John Foster House in Boston. The double portico on the façade of the second Capitol in Williamsburg, built in the early 1750s, might have been the first use of a pedimented double portico with freestanding columns in the colony (fig. 38). It was built roughly at the same time that the merchant and Rhode

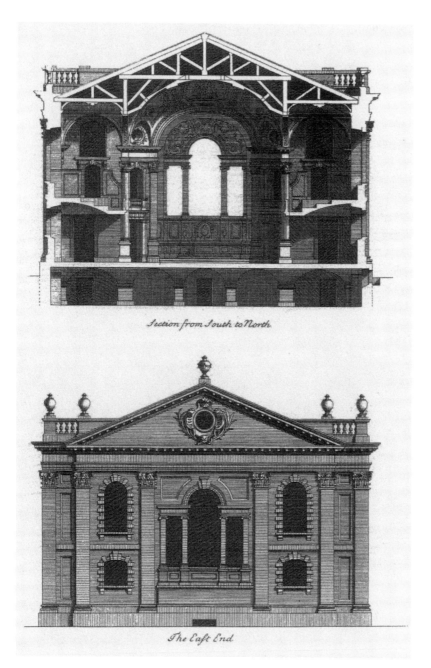

Section from South to North.

The East End

Fig. 36. St. Martin-in-the-Fields, London, 1722–26, designed by James Gibbs. The illustration is plate 4 from Gibbs's *A Book of Architecture* (London, 1728). (From the collections of The Rare Book & Special Collections Library, The University of Illinois, Urbana-Champaign)

Island architect Peter Harrison was designing sophisticated paired Corinthian columns for King's Church, Boston, along with monumental Ionic columns for its porch (though these were not actually added to the building until 1787). Harrison had already established his reputation in 1749 by exploiting his knowledge of Anglo-Palladian architectural publications for the stylized temple façade of the Redwood Library in Newport, Rhode Island.

None of the above should imply that members of the native elite of Virginia or their craftsmen were ignorant about the Orders, or unaware of the intellectual prestige they conveyed. A full complement of base, pilaster, and entablature appears in formal reception rooms of Stratford Hall (fig. 39), Gunston Hall, Wilton, and Carter's Grove. There is also the pos-

Fig. 37. Rosewell, Gloucester County, 1726. Poor-quality photograph of the brickwork around the court-side doorway. (Virginia Historical Society, Richmond, Virginia)

Fig. 38. Howard Pyle, *Old State House, Williamsburg,* oil painting, late nineteenth or early twentieth century. (Colonial Williamsburg Foundation)

sibility that a more fully elaborated classical vocabulary existed in colonial Virginia buildings that have subsequently disappeared. The evidence at hand, however, indicates that Virginians waited until the mid-eighteenth century before incorporating freestanding exterior columns supporting an entablature into the design of their prestige buildings.

One possible explanation for the conservative quality of Virginia's high-style architecture has been suggested by the architectural historian Carl Lounsbury. Examining the design development of Anglican churches, Lounsbury surmised that Virginia's early founding firmly planted conservative basilican church plans in the minds of its settlers. Maryland's later seventeenth-century Anglicans, by comparison, made the colony more amenable to new building concepts, particularly church plans influenced by Christopher Wren's post-1666 auditory plans. Another plausible explanation lies in Virginia's nonurban character. The Boston building industry was established early in the seventeenth century yet was receptive to an influx of new architectural fashions. English metropolitan fashions were even selectively adopted by Non-Conformists for their places of worship. The 1729 Old South Meeting House in Boston, for example, was built by Puritans whose earlier coreligionists had dominated the region in the seventeenth century and had eschewed Anglican liturgy and liturgical fittings. Trading ports such as Boston, Philadelphia, and Charleston may have functioned as more effective *entrepôts* for the importation of cultural capital and craftsmen conversant with *au courant* fashion in the early eighteenth century than Norfolk, Virginia's largest port town.[61]

Whatever the reason, Virginia's prodigy house patrons and craftsmen employed a reticent classical dialect, restricting exterior ornament to cornices, doorways, water tables, stringcourses, and quoins. The overall effect of classical decoration served as pointing devices that seemed intended to draw a viewer's attention to specific parts of a building, particularly those that indicated wealth. Virginia patrons purchased costly ornament that in effect divided the elevation design into parts rather than united those parts into a whole. Their restrained classical vocabulary, however, still spoke unambiguously: the owner of this house possesses great wealth and special knowledge that other planters do not.

Fig. 39. Stratford Hall, Westmoreland County, begun in 1738. Great Hall. (Historic American Buildings Survey, Prints and Photographs Division, Library of Congress)

Cornices—only the upper third of a full entablature—represented one of the principal means by which Virginia's architectural patrons advertised their knowledge of classicizing architectural fashion to viewers outside of the house. Men like Charles Carter and his brother Landon were not only personally interested in the elegant embellishment of their mansions, but they also possessed the linguistic competency to use the word "cornice." Another important opportunity to display erudition was to ornament a doorway with a triangular or segmental pediment supported by flanking pilasters. The molded, gauged brick and carved stonework still found at the entrance to Christ Church, Lancaster County, or only glimpsed in old and poor-quality photographs of Rosewell's once-magnificent doorways, were exceptionally elaborate. Other doorways, like the molded brick pediment and pilaster strips at Stratford Hall, seem almost archaically plain (fig. 40). Most wooden cornices and frontispieces have rotted and been replaced, but the south frontispiece of Wilton was believed to be original when the house was moved from Henrico County to Richmond in the early 1930s (fig. 41). If true, then its Ionic pilasters supporting a cushionlike pulvinated frieze and pediment match the refined use of the Orders in the parlor, which were executed in part by the joiner Samson Darrel in 1753. His pride in workmanship and hidden signature allows us to date the building to 1751.[62]

Ornamental water tables on the exterior also called attention to the owner's superior aesthetic knowledge. Positioned on the exterior where the thicker brick foundation walls yield to the thinner walls above, water tables were composed of specially molded bricks intended to dispense water away from the wall. At Blandfield, built by Robert Beverley, the grandson of the historian, expensive molded bricks in the classical form of a concave cavetto and a convex torus accomplished the transition (fig. 42). John Thompson paid for a plain water table composed of only a course of simple, sloping bricks added to the top of the foundation (see fig. 27 on p. 34).

Horizontal rows of bricks that visually articulated one floor from another on the elevation—a feature architectural historians call a string-course, or belt course—drew the viewer's attention to the owner's ability to build a multistoried dwelling. In keeping with his preference for a "plain neat" style, Robert Beverley's masons created a rather severe stringcourse at Blandfield, composed of four projecting unmolded courses of brick (fig.

Fig. 40. (*Opposite, top*) Stratford Hall, Westmoreland County, begun in 1738. Brick pedimented doorway and clustered chimney stack. Stairway added in the 1930s. (Photograph by Robert T. Mooney)

Fig. 41. (*Opposite, bottom*) Wilton, Richmond, originally in Henrico County, 1751. Doorway on river façade. (Photograph by Robert T. Mooney)

Fig. 42. Blandfield, Essex County, 1769. Detail of water table and gauged brick jack arches over basement windows. (Photograph by author)

43). About eighteen years earlier, Sarah Taliaferro Brooke's masons laid a more decoratively complex stringcourse composed of forms derived from the base of a column: ovolo, torus, astragal, fascia, and cyma reversa (see fig. 19 on p. 28). Unlike Blandfield's, the stringcourse at Brooke's Bank stops short of the rubbed brick corner, only to be taken up again on the other exterior wall.

In lieu of stone architraves, architectural patrons surrounded the windows of their mansions with specialized brickwork that emphasized glazing. At Blandfield, the flat arches over windows, also known as jack arches, were created by Robert Beverley's craftsmen, who abraded, or rubbed, the surface of each brick with a file, perhaps even sawing them into precise, angled, or gauged shapes, and then positioned them with a minimum of mortar (fig. 42). At Wilton, William Randolph III's windows were surrounded by rubbed and closely gauged bricks, creating light pink rectangular halos around the apertures and, of course, signaling to viewers the patron's ability to pay for these special effects. Thomas Jefferson's window architraves, on the other hand, adhered to more bookish classical precedents.

Architectural patrons and their builders also emphasized the corners of their dwellings. While William Randolph III's water table was composed of two elegantly curved brick courses, his corners were stressed by abraded or rubbed bricks that created splendid coloristic effects (fig. 44). At Gunston Hall, George Mason IV's builders visually underscored the structural importance of corners more emphatically by emphasizing them with stone quoins (fig. 45).

Some owners paid for a far more dramatic use of stone ornament. At Cleve, for instance, Charles Carter directed his stonecutters and masons to place stone blocks of alternating size not only at the corners but around doors and the windows (fig. 46). Because the structural walls were made of brick, the contrasting stone—probably the same as his "Nasty Sorry Soft Stone"—resulted in a showy and textural façade. Architectural historians now refer to these alternating fenestration blocks as "Gibbs surrounds" because of their prominent use by the architect James Gibbs at his well-known buildings such as St. Martin-in-the-Fields (fig. 47).[63] The coloristic and textural manipulation of stone dressings against brick walls pre-dates Gibbs by many decades. Strongly articulated stone dressings were part of the ornamental vocabulary of late sixteenth- and early seventeenth-century English prodigy houses, including Blickling Hall, begun in 1619, but they enjoyed a revival in the second half of the eighteenth century (fig. 48).[64] At

Fig. 43. Blandfield, Essex County, 1769. Detail of stringcourse and gauged brick jack arches over first-floor windows. (Photograph by author)

Fig. 44. (*Opposite, top left*) Wilton, Richmond, originally in Henrico County, 1751. Detail of rubbed brick corner and molded brick water table. (Photograph by author)

Fig. 45. (*Opposite, top right*) Gunston Hall, Fairfax County, 1752. Detail of stone quoins against brick wall. (Photograph by author)

Fig. 46. (*Opposite, bottom*) Cleve, King George County, 1746, destroyed by fire in 1917. Photograph from early twentieth century. (Virginia Historical Society, Richmond, Virginia)

Fig. 47. St. Martin-in-the-Fields, London, 1722–26, designed by James Gibbs. Side elevation showing the so-called "Gibbs surrounds." (Photograph by author)

Fig. 48. (*Opposite, top*) Blickling Hall, Norfolk, England, 1619. West range to right remodeled 1765–71 by Thomas Ivory. (Photograph by author)

Fig. 49. (*Opposite, bottom*) Sabine Hall, Richmond County, 1738. Porch not original. (Valentine Richmond History Center)

Landon Carter's Sabine Hall, ornamental stonework linked the doorway and upper window and conferred greater prominence to the vertical axis and entrance (fig. 49). Compared to Wilton's 1751 relatively sedate exterior, the earlier façades of Landon Carter's 1738 Sabine Hall and Charles Carter's 1746 Cleve exhibit a greater visual exuberance.

Toward a "Plain Neat Manner"

Between the seventeenth and eighteenth century, wealthy Virginians shifted from preferring more extroverted rhetorical gestures associated with what Summerson coined "artisan mannerism" to a style that Robert Beverley, the patron of Blandfield, referred to in 1771 as a "plain neat Manner."[65] But this generalization requires qualification. First, a plain, neat manner does not mean that the elite eliminated ornamental details. Rather it refers to a preference for more restrained classic features in lieu of a highly embellished rococo dialect. Second, we should be cautious not to impose a strict linear pattern of development or an organic model of growth, achievement, and decline upon Virginia's eighteenth-century mansions. A conceptual model that describes a period of experimentation followed by a period of standardization would also be inappropriate. The rectangular massing, hipped roof, and fenestration pattern found at the Brafferton (1723) were features still attractive to William Byrd II when he built Westover more than a quarter century later (fig. 50). The same decade that witnessed the construction of the Brafferton and Berkeley also saw Mann Page I's extravagantly embellished Rosewell.

Nevertheless, one does witness definite changes in the aesthetic decisions made by Virginia's eighteenth-century native elite. Changes in chimney-stack design exemplify this shift in taste. Multiple ornamental shafts are present at Bacon's Castle (fig. 51) and also appear in old photographs of the now-lost late seventeenth-century mansion known as Fairfield in Gloucester County (fig. 52). Historians consider Fairfield a key transitional house foreshadowing eighteenth-century classicism. The complex chimney shafts there demonstrate how wealthy planters continued to find them an attractive symbol of prestige in the last decade of the seventeenth century.

Multiple chimney stacks like those at Bacon's Castle and Fairfield advertised the presence of multiple fireplaces, the expending of more fuel, and the inhabitants' greater physical comfort. Similarly aestheticized places of

Fig. 50. Westover, Charles City County, 1750. South façade. (Photograph by Robert T. Mooney)

Fig. 51. (*Opposite, top*) Bacon's Castle (Arthur Allen House), Surry County, 1665. Side elevation with multiple chimney stacks and stepped and scrolled gable ends. (Photograph by author)

Fig. 52. (*Opposite, bottom*) Fairfield, Gloucester County, 1690s, destroyed by fire ca. 1899. Photograph ca. 1880s. (Virginia Historical Society, Richmond, Virginia)

smoke disgorgement were also found in English architecture, and some of the cultural fascination with the design potential of chimney stacks might arise from their relative novelty, even in the seventeenth century. It had not been too many decades before when many English gentry houses were warmed only by open hearths. Smoke hoods and later fireplaces became widespread only by the late 1500s, and architectural historians see them as an important innovation of the so-called Great Rebuilding of England.[66] At the grandest sixteenth-century country houses, chimney stacks also displayed the owner's acquisition of northern Renaissance decorative features.

Eighteenth-century Virginia prodigy house patrons rejected highly sculptural multishaft chimneys in favor of tall, plain chimney stacks, sheathing multiple funnels behind a simple rectangular form. Their aesthetic evolution was gradual. John Custis's now-lost house in Williamsburg, built after 1715, was conventionally called "Six Chimneys" well into

the nineteenth century, when it, as well as Bacon's Castle, served as a model for the deliberately archaizing design of Bremo Recess in Fluvanna County.[67] The enormous visual impact of the chimneys at Stratford was created by building two groups of four individual flues that were linked by arches. Set within the body of the house, each unit was nonetheless far enough apart to allow a corridor to pass between them along the longitudinal axis. The uppermost portions of many colonial chimney stacks have been rebuilt, making it difficult to know how they were originally topped. Most likely they were capped with several courses of projecting, molded brick, which, while more aesthetically quiet than Fairfield's angled flues, still bespoke the owner's wealth and more up-to-date taste.

The Plan: Art and Social Patterns

Virginia's native elite shaped the plan as well as the elevation according to their social and aesthetic values. Any analysis of prodigy house plans must keep both of these imperatives in mind. Interior spaces responded not only to the permutations of art but to evolving social relations. The exterior of the mansion spoke to social cohorts as they approached the house for entertainment, to poorer landowning neighbors and tenants who came to conduct business, and to field slaves trudging from one field to another to hoe weeds or pick insects off tobacco leaves. Inside the mansion, the master entertained his peers, consigned his tobacco, hired overseers, wrote contracts with tenants, and extended mercy or punishment to emboldened or begging slaves. His wife conducted household business by ordering staff and slaves and presided over more polite, convivial exchanges at the tea table. Toddlers got underfoot when a planter cleaned his gun, and ardent teenagers evaluated prospective marriage partners. Domestic slaves, forced to keep the white household clean and comfortable, slipped in and out of rooms, ideally with minimal visibility. Cherished relatives and friends but also unknown travelers of varied social status appeared fairly regularly and required, by ancient rules of social obligation, some measure of accommodation. The plan of Virginia prodigy houses, therefore, addressed various functions and potential audiences. Certain parts functioned as public space, while an increasing number of rooms were screened from casual view. The concept of the house as a domestic refuge completely separated from public life would not occur until the nineteenth century.

In the plan of Virginia's prodigy houses, fashionable new metropolitan architectural ideals were amended by local social conventions. Because social relations evolve more slowly than aesthetic fashion, the planning principles of Virginia's mansions reveal more conservative tendencies than does the exterior design. For that reason, many scholars of Virginia colonial architecture consider the plan a more meaningful barometer of the owner's architectural intent. Mark R. Wenger, for example, expanding on Dell Upton's ideas, examined probate inventories and argued for social motivation and class distinction as the underlying cause of changes in eighteenth-century plans. Inflected by the theoretical approaches of structural anthropology and linguistics, Upton and Wenger sought to discover an underlying pattern of grammatical rules for the plans of Virginia colonial dwellings.[68] According to Wenger, the appearance of new spatial forms, such as the central passageway through the middle of a house, was not the result of borrowing from published English or Continental sources, but developed as a barrier to protect the planter from the "promiscuous mix of persons and activities." The traditional multipurpose room known in both England and colonial America as the hall—and not to be confused with a passage or corridor—became less accessible and more formal, coming to symbolize "the social authority of the planter." For Wenger, planning decisions reflected "a growing desire on the part of planters to distance themselves, in a ceremonial way, from persons outside their closely knit circle of family and peers."[69] The central passage continued to evolve and widen throughout the eighteenth century from a social barrier into a major living space. Similarities to high-style, particularly Anglo-Palladian, features appear, but to Wenger, "the adaptation of English prototypes in this and other instances represented a momentary correspondence of academic form with local priorities."[70]

The Politics of Access

What scholars like Wenger read into the genteel architecture of eighteenth-century Virginia is the politics of access.[71] In other words, your status as a visitor was demonstrated by your physical location within the mansion. The politics of access unfolded through movement, not stasis. The closer a visitor processed toward the planter, the more socially privileged he or she was. The politics of access offers an attractive explanation integrating social behavior and architectural design. It is, however, not exclusive to Virginia.

Like the vocabulary of classical ornament, the politics of access as expressed in Virginia's most grandiose houses reflects not only local conditions but also wider European developments. The withdrawal of elite families from the public sphere had been evolving for several centuries when Virginia's native elite exerted its power. The increased number of rooms in fifteenth-century Florentine palaces, for example, has been interpreted as reflecting the increased tendency of newly wealthy and competitive, elite families to remove themselves from public scrutiny and communal life. The declining use of urban loggias for the decorous public display of genteel leisure in Renaissance Italy indicates a privatization of social life.[72]

The valorization of private space and private activities began as early as the fourteenth century in England when the withdrawal of the lord and his immediate family from the communal hall to the relatively more private great chamber became noticeable to commentators at the time.[73] Dining ceremonies moved to the more private great chamber and were witnessed by only the most privileged members of the lord's entourage.[74] By the late sixteenth and early seventeenth centuries, commentators decried the separation of the lord from his vassals and laborers and lamented a decline in the ritualized hospitality that had presumably cemented reciprocal obligations between ranks of men in an earlier time.[75] The politics of access can also be seen in the extremely elaborate social protocols associated with seventeenth-century Roman palaces of the Catholic hierarchy. As the architectural historian Patricia Waddy has proposed, Roman palace architecture as well the houses of the prosperous middle class accommodated and enhanced ceremonies that marked visitors' social status via their physical position.[76]

Basic elements of the politics of access also occurred in the far more humble dwellings of seventeenth-century Protestant New England. According to Robert Blair St. George, the most basic division of the chamber/parlor from the hall in New England's seventeenth-century houses embodied the owners' decision to restrict access to the best furniture in the most genteel interior environment. An invitation to the parlor/chamber, where a visitor enjoyed a more exclusive, refined interior, conferred a flattering special status. By withdrawing from the hall, the guest received respite from the noise, offensive odors, and visual clutter of the hall. He or she not only would have been entertained more genteelly but would have been privileged enough to see the owners' most expensive object of household furniture, the conjugal bed.[77] This fundamental difference between two rooms operated at Virginia's Lynnhaven House (see fig. 7 on p. 17). The more public hall is entered through the main door, while the more private parlor opens off this hall and can be closed to visitors.[78] Clearly, it did not require a large number of individual spaces to perform the politics of access effectively.

The politics of access concept of architectural planning, however, poses a problem. While the concept may generate a plan, it does not generate the same plan in all circumstances. Public and hidden transcripts of power can be performed on any number of architectural set designs.[79] In late medieval England, wealthy landowners spun off socially restricted spaces at either end of the communal hall and often placed them on an upper floor. By contrast, visitors to seventeenth-century Roman cardinals negotiated a more linear sequence of rooms. Early eighteenth-century French aristocrats built houses that accommodated the politics of access within elaborate suites of rooms that were further differentiated by gender.[80] In seventeenth-century

Netherlands, reception rooms began to be distinguished from sleeping rooms by removing the best bed from the principal entertainment space. In the next century, Netherlandish patrons adopted a modest version of the French suite plan in their townhouses when they connected two formal rooms with a *porte-brisée,* a set of double doors.[81] Like their European counterparts, elites in colonial Virginia engaged in the politics of access. That fact alone, however, does not fully explain the arrangement of interior rooms.

The interiors of Virginia's mansions mirrored another general trend exhibited in early modern European elite architecture, namely, the increased specialization of room functions. Over the course of the eighteenth-century, the design of Virginia houses—both those of the gentry and those of the middling sort—reflected this greater differentiation by including distinct rooms for dining, for sleeping, and for refined entertainment.[82] Functional differentiation was not merely a function of wealth. The separate dining room that John Custis built at Arlington (ca. 1670) was exceptional. Most wealthy planters in the seventeenth century lived contentedly in comfortable, even fashionable houses comprising relatively fewer rooms. Documentary records show that Thomas Hansford, for example, enjoyed a very high level of material prosperity. In 1677, he was possessed of silver plate, silk-trimmed fabrics, and 1,500 acres of land. The probate record states that he and his family lived in a "very good dwelling house," but it also indicates that his house had only two rooms on the first level, a hall and a parlor, with a bedchamber located above each. Two feather beds, probably the finest Hansford owned, were found in the parlor. Hansford was a very rich man by Tidewater standards, but his ideas concerning architectural refinement were different from those of most wealthy planters of the following century.[83]

Architectural patrons were forced to accommodate sometimes conflicting cultural values when they determined the plan of their mansions. Isolating the circulation routes taken by domestic slaves stood as an important imperative in determining plans. Patrons and builders in Virginia, as in Europe, invented means of moving domestic laborers through and around the house with a minimum number of face-to-face encounters. Such ancillary means of circulation could be inserted in a number of different ways from uncomfortably cramped stair closets to small serving rooms adjacent to entertainment spaces. Patrons additionally wanted to provide for both privacy and the display of valuable consumer items, which lose social value if they are either invisible or too obvious. Patrons also desired to display not only prestige consumer goods but prestige aesthetic knowledge. With both material objects and privileged knowledge of fashionable building forms, they appropriated British cultural production even though no copies of

English buildings exist in colonial Virginia. There are, however, several re-curring themes appearing in the plans of Virginian mansions that make it impossible to discuss them without reference to English architectural con-ventions and innovations. With these multiple social and aesthetic consid-erations in mind, one can discern five basic planning schemes employed by the twenty-five patrons in the study group.[84]

Plan Type One: Vestigial Hall

The first plan type employed in eighteenth-century Virginian prodigy houses relates to the venerable English hall, the central social core of En-glish domestic planning (fig. 53).[85] Briefly described, the traditional English hall was a rectangular space, usually located on the ground floor, and was entered from one end of its long façade. Often, but not always, a partition wall, known as a screens wall, created a transverse corridor starting at the entrance and running to a door at the opposite wall. The screens wall would have separated the entrance from the hall proper. Ancillary rooms called the pantry and the buttery—intended to facilitate the storage and serving of food and drink—were usually positioned near, but separated from, the hall. Important visitors or members of the household would have entered the hall at what was known as the lower, and less prestigious, end. Such a visitor would not have been an impoverished peasant; the poor were fed at the courtyard gate. But assume for the moment that you were a productive and valuable member of the landowner's entourage. Upon accessing the house, you would customarily make a right-angle turn and find yourself at the lower end of the hall. Your gaze would have been drawn to the opposite, more important end of the hall, called the upper end. In the Middle Ages, you would have expected to see the master of the house seated at a raised dais table at the upper end, enjoying a meal with his entourage of various ranks and classes.

As Renaissance architectural ideals of symmetry insinuated themselves into seventeenth-century English architecture, the asymmetrical position-ing of the hall to the side of the main entrance became less attractive, all the more so because the master had likely removed himself and took his meals elsewhere. Designers began to position the main entrance in the cen-ter of the façade but often retained a vestige of the traditional asymmetri-cal positioning of the hall. At Peter Mills's Thorpe Hall, Cambridgeshire (1653), and Roger Morris's Combe Bank, Kent (1725), a symmetrical door-way opens onto an asymmetrical hall.[86] Although no specific English house served as a model for any specific Virginia prodigy house, a vestige of a similar compromise between symmetrical elevation and asymmetrical hall appears in Plan Type One and can be seen at Mann Page I's Rosewell. A vis-

ARLINGTON

BACON'S
CASTLE

ROSEWELL

SHIRLEY

Fig. 53. Plan Type One: Vestigial Hall; scale bar equals 15 feet. (Megan D. Roy after Thomas T. Waterman and Cary Carson)

itor moved through a strictly symmetrical façade and entered at one end of an asymmetrically positioned hall. At the other end, Mann Page I had his builders place an extraordinary display of his largesse, a broad stairway lavishly carved with deep-relief ornament conforming to a style made famous in England by Grinling Gibbons (fig. 54). John Carter's mansion, Shirley in Charles City County (1738), has a similar orientation upon entering and a similarly extravagant display of stairway bravura. Both buildings may be related to the original plan of the Governor's Palace in Williamsburg, although the Palace entry did not include a stairway, or they may recall other prestige dwellings of the seventeenth century. Based on archaeological remains, historians have also proposed an asymmetrical hall, also without a staircase, for Arlington, John Custis's impressive three-story house on Virginia's Eastern Shore, built about 1670.[87] By the second half of the seventeenth century, the hall no longer served to renew the reciprocal bonds of duty between social classes. The imprint of its traditional and potent spatial experience, however, was more long-lived.

Fig. 54. Rosewell, Gloucester County, 1726. Photograph of the stair hall before the fire of 1916. (Cook Collection, Valentine Richmond History Center)

Plan Type Two: Center Transverse Passage

The second plan type used by the architectural patrons of Virginia's prodigy houses became the one most strongly identified with genteel colonial housing (fig. 55). The British traveler William Hugh Grove identified the plan with the mansions he visited along the banks of the Mattaponi River in 1732: "They have a broad Stayrcase with a passage thro the house in the middle which is the Summer hall and Draws the air, and 2 rooms on Each Hand." The cross ventilation afforded by the center passage with doors or windows at each end was also noted in a 1781 diary entry of Sara Nourse of Berkeley County, who wrote that in the heat and humidity of a Virginia summer she dressed only in her shift and remained in the upstairs passage.[88] As Grove also noted, center transverse passage plans were not necessarily double-pile, but also single-pile houses, that is, only one room deep. According to Grove, "some indeed have only one room on a Side and Windows opposite each other."[89]

Marked by the presence of a transverse passage containing the principal stairway in the middle of the ground floor, Plan Type Two must also be positioned within the context of developments inside and outside of the Tidewater.[90] In some sense, the cross passage reveals spatial and functional affinities with the screens passage of a traditional English hall plan. But unlike the traditional hall, cross passages in eighteenth-century Virginia appear in the approximate center of the dwelling, rather than at the lower end of the hall, so that important social rooms (not merely service rooms) could be placed on each side in what must have appeared a newfangled but fashionably symmetrical manner.

And unlike the decorative screens wall, the center passage could block rather than frame visual as well as physical access into the privileged social spaces beyond. As privacy and interior life became a more important modern value, patrons increasingly had walls built to separate strangers from intimates. Functioning as the principal circulation space, the passage allowed for the sorting of public business associates from valued guests. Changes made to the plan of Bacon's Castle underscore the evolution toward separating semipublic space and private space. A center transverse passage was inserted into the asymmetrical hall plan in the early eighteenth century in order to block immediate access to the hall.

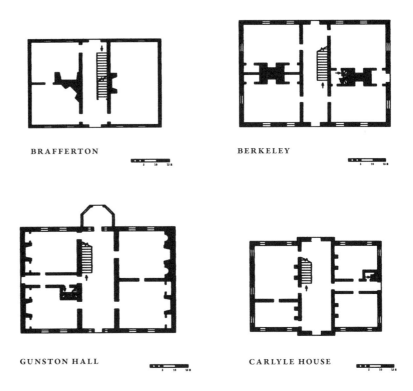

BRAFFERTON

BERKELEY

GUNSTON HALL

CARLYLE HOUSE

Fig. 55. Plan Type Two: Center Transverse Passage; scale bar equals 15 feet. (Megan D. Roy after Thomas T. Waterman and Mark R. Wenger)

As the primary circulation space, the transverse center passage plan in the eighteenth century also served as the site of the principal stairway. As with Plan Type One, the presence of a stairway in the center passage continued to offer wealthy property owners an opportunity to advertise their wealth and ability to pay for skilled joinery and specialized woodcarving. Elaborate newel posts and balusters could impress even those less privileged guests who entered the house and proceeded no farther than the passage.

The cultural origin of the colonial center passage plan remains an intriguing historical mystery. Unlike the asymmetrical hall plan, the central passage plan is not found in the most ambitious English mansions. The historical geographer Daniel Reiff has argued that the cross passage plan developed from the application of Renaissance planning ideals to more modest but stylish houses. Based on visual similarity, the cross passage plan might have evolved from the screens passage or might have grown from the side passages used in urban houses.[91] Reiff's theory of the middle-class origins of the cross passage might find support in Williamsburg.

The John Brush House in Williamsburg, dated through dendrochronology to 1718, stands as one of the earliest documented dwellings with an original rather than added central passage. Built by a gunsmith and keeper of the powder magazine built by Governor Spotswood, the Brush House's novel plan was complemented by plaster walls, but only the most important social rooms were finished at Brush's death.[92] Plan Type Two was also employed in the design of the more ambitious brick Brafferton, constructed for the College of William and Mary in 1723. The plan, however, was not unique to Virginia. Archibald McPheadris and his designer/builder, John Drew, selected the center transverse passage plan for McPheadris's house in Portsmouth, New Hampshire (1716–18). It was also selected by Thomas Hancock—in consultation with his builder, Joshua Blanchard, and perhaps the English architect John James—for Hancock's 1737 mansion in Boston.[93]

Plan Type Three: Divided Passage

The third plan type, the divided passage, represents an elaboration and refinement of the center transverse passage plan (fig. 56). While still maintaining a clear aesthetic preference for symmetry of rooms, this plan divided the center transverse passage into two spaces, suggesting a desire to isolate the circulation function of the stairs. One part, broader than a center transverse passage, served as the entrance hall. The second part, slightly narrower than the entrance hall, contained the stairway. At Gunston Hall, such a separation was suggested by a column that was later replaced in the eighteenth century with the pendant pine cone. The stair halls at Belvoir and Brooke's Bank are also distinct but are positioned vis-à-vis the entrance hall in a less rigidly symmetrical manner. Wenger sees the divided passage plan as an indication that the social sorting function of the center passage was no longer necessary, thus freeing up the central passage from a circulation space into a more important social space. This new scheme, however, was used contemporaneously with the center passage plans. Moreover, it is difficult to identify a definite change in the social behavior of Virginia's elite that might account directly for a deliberate modification in plan. An alternative explanation for elite planters directing their builders to widen the interior entrance may lie in their knowledge of metropolitan architectural ideals, especially the Anglo-Palladian fashion for broad, open rooms at the center of the house.

The center open space stands as a key element of Renaissance architecture that underwent alteration as it traversed different geographical and cultural contexts. Derived from planning schemes of the sixteenth-century Italian architect Andrea Palladio, the centralized open space signified his attempt, under the guidance of humanistic scholars, to interpret, re-create, and adapt the ancient Roman atrium to sixteenth-century elite palaces and villas. The device entered the vocabulary of English elite architecture when Bess of Hardwick constructed her new Hardwick Hall in the 1590s.[94]

BELVOIR

CLEVE

CARTER'S GROVE

BROOKE'S BANK

Fig. 56. Plan Type Three: Divided Passage; scale bar equals 15 feet. (Megan D. Roy after Thomas T. Waterman and Mark R. Wenger)

But it was the English architect Inigo Jones who effectively adapted Palladio's open space to the purposes of English court-style architecture under the Stuarts, seen most famously at the Queen's House in Greenwich, designed in 1616 but not substantially constructed until the late 1630s.[95] While Jones's court-style classicism never dominated seventeenth-century elite architecture in England, the prestige of the central space was manifest in later versions of English classicism. The social attractiveness of the central open space can be seen later in Roger Pratt's plan for Coleshill. Well before Lord Burlington's version of Palladianism appeared in the second quarter of the eighteenth century, some of Palladio's planning principles had already been incorporated into notions of what constituted prestige English domestic architecture. Whether or not Virginia patrons knew this complex architectural lineage is immaterial; they did know that open center spaces were found in some fashionable houses of the English gentry, the class to which elite Virginians aspired.

Plan Type Four: Double-Pile Saloon

The evolution toward an open central space becomes more obvious in the fourth plan type in Virginia mansions (fig. 57). John Tayloe's Mount Airy, Robert Beverley's Blandfield, and probably Landon Carter's Sabine Hall all stressed the social versus circulatory purpose of this centralized room, often called a saloon (anglicized from "salon"), by removing the stairway entirely.[96] At Blandfield, the original plan did not allow for communication between the two center spaces and the two-room deep, or double-pile lateral rooms. Inhabitants were forced to use corridors to access these more private rooms.[97] This was no Virginia invention meant to respond to specific Virginia social tensions. Elites in other colonies also demanded similarly fashionable metropolitan planning conventions. We find wide spaces in the middle of the Stephen Van Rensselaer II mansion in Albany, New York (1765, demolished 1973), and in Governor William Shirley's mansion, Shirley Place, in Roxbury, Massachusetts (ca. 1747).

Plan Type Five: Single-Pile Saloon

The fifth plan type identified among the prodigy houses in the study group maintained the primacy of the Palladian center open space, but abandoned the full double-pile plan (fig. 58). It, too, was characterized by a prominent open space in the middle of the mansion that was flanked by single-pile rooms or smaller wings only one room deep. Patrons and their builders either placed the stairway in front of the open center space, as at Battersea, or moved it to a side room, as at Chatham. Like Plan Types Three and Four, many of these mansions share features associated with eighteenth-century Anglo-Palladianism. Parallels can be drawn to plans published by

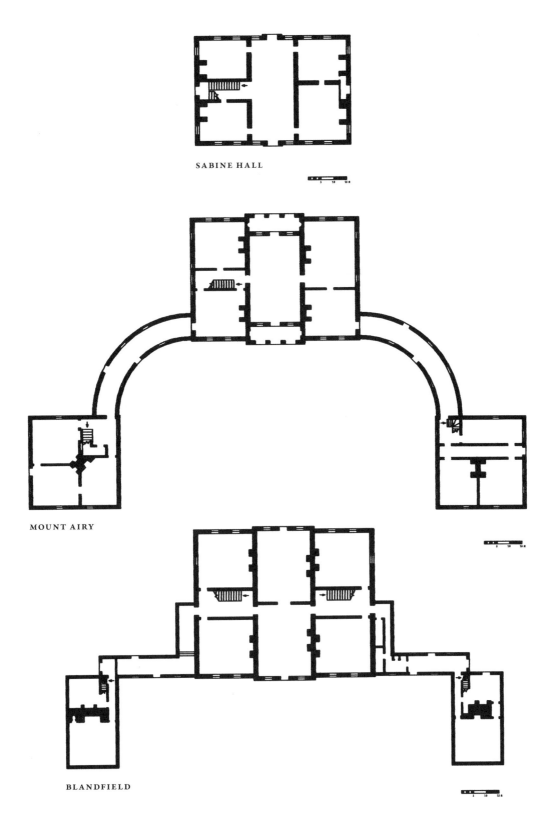

SABINE HALL

MOUNT AIRY

BLANDFIELD

Fig. 57. Plan Type Four: Double-Pile Saloon; scale bar equals 15 feet. (Megan D. Roy after Thomas T. Waterman and Mark R. Wenger)

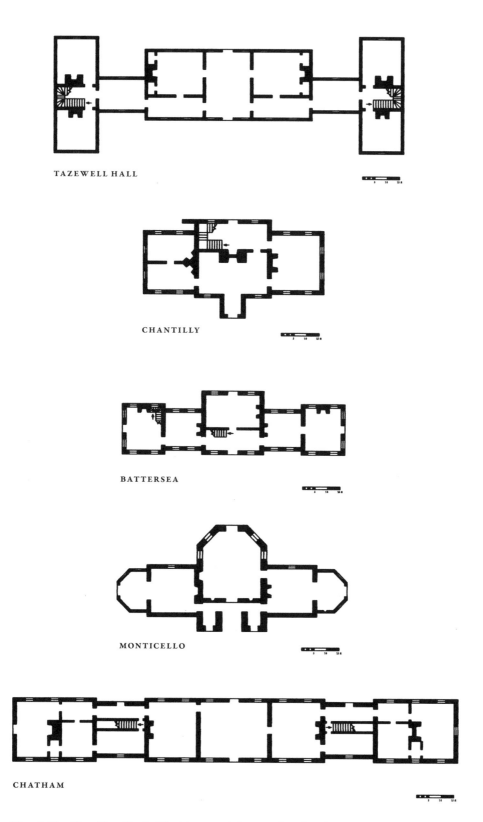

TAZEWELL HALL

CHANTILLY

BATTERSEA

MONTICELLO

CHATHAM

Fig. 58. Plan Type Five: Single-Pile Saloon; scale bar equals 15 feet. (Megan D. Roy after Thomas T. Waterman, S. P. Moorhead, Jeffrey M. O'Dell, and Mark R. Wenger)

James Gibbs and especially Robert Morris. None of the Virginia examples, however, are direct copies. All were adapted and amended to Virginia conditions. While William Fitzhugh built an extraordinarily elongated and large example at Chatham (fig. 59), others like Battersea are more modestly scaled. Once erroneously attributed to Thomas Jefferson, these smaller Anglo-Palladian villas such as Tazewell Hall, Chantilly, and Battersea (fig. 60) had already been constructed when he began leveling the earth at the top of the Monticello site and started to build Monticello I. The basic arrangement of spaces, with variation in stair placement, accommodated genteel functions in an elegant manner without the need for additional rooms. Wenger has proposed that this arrangement was popular with the wealthy planters not only because it was fashionably Anglo-Palladian, but because it efficiently satisfied the minimum number of spatial requirements needed for polite architecture: a hall, dining room, and chamber.[98]

Fig. 59. Chatham, Stafford County, 1769. West façade. (Photograph by Robert T. Mooney)

Fig. 60. Battersea, Petersburg, originally in Dinwiddie County, 1767. South façade. (Photograph by Robert T. Mooney)

Offices and Outbuildings

Some prodigy house owners extended the imposition of formal aesthetic qualities from their mansions to the service buildings that surrounded them. For most Virginia planters of means, a higgledy-piggledy assortment of detached utilitarian structures supported functions that sustained an elite lifestyle. Wealthy landowners recognized certain standards of genteel respectability in plantation landscapes. We can read a codification of these standards in a 1748 law describing the buildings necessary for the support of an Anglican minister. In addition to the dwelling house, the law required each vestry to provide a kitchen, barn, stable, dairy, meat house, corn house, and enclosed garden.[99] Such assemblages of ancillary buildings characterized the plantation landscapes of the elite at least as early as the second half of the seventeenth century. The practice continued in the eighteenth century and struck outsiders as one of the most distinguishing feature of Virginia's built environment. In his 1724 description of the planter domicile, Hugh Jones wrote that there "also are built houses for the overseers and out-houses; among which is the kitchen apart from the dwelling house because of the smell of hot victuals, offensive in hot weather."[100] In 1732, William Hugh Grove was tricked into thinking Yorktown was larger than it really was because of the presence of so many outbuildings: "A Stranger [would] conclude there were at Least 100 houses whereas there are really not 30—for Their Kitchins, Warehouses, etc., are here and generally Elsewhere Seperate from their Dwelling houses and make them appear different habitations." The service structures at Williamsburg also deceived Grove initially, leading him to believe that the town had "about 100 houses, tho by the manner of building their offices separately it shows to be 300."[101] Grove found the conglomeration of ancillary buildings at rural plantations picturesque and remarkable. They "Shew Like little villages, for having kitchins, dayry houses, Barns, Stables, Store houses, and some of them 2 or 3 Negro Quarters all Seperate from Each other but near the mansion houses make a shew to the river of 7 or 8 distinct Tenements, tho all belong to one family."[102] Not all plantations started operations with such a large complement of service buildings. The Matthew Jones House in Newport News, built around 1720, originally was constructed with earthfast walls and two brick chimneys, one of which was used for cooking. Seven years later, Jones built a separate brick kitchen.[103] In her analysis of Berkeley Parish tax records, Ashli White discovered that while most dwellings in 1798 were small and made of wood, they were accompanied by a complement of outbuildings, most often a kitchen, smokehouse, and corn crib.[104] So it appears that it was not the presence of outbuildings that would have set prodigy house plantations apart from other Virginia properties, but rather their formal planning and high-quality construction.

Like the wealthiest mansion owners in Europe, Virginia's native elite subjected secondary structures and service space to the same aesthetic rhetoric exhibited in their main houses. The most elaborate configurations of service space can be found in the eighteenth-century *hôtels particulier* in Paris. Flanked on one side by formal gardens, on the other by a courtyard with service quarters to the right and left, and entered through a formalized gated entrance, the main residential block, or *corps de logis,* as it was known, was framed and enhanced by ordered, aestheticized structures. The balance of beauty and convenience was not accidental and over the course of the eighteenth century became an important programmatic consideration, as evidenced by its treatment in the architectural publications of Jacques-François Blondel.[105] Increasing control of ancillary space also characterized English gentry house developments. According to the British architectural historian Nicholas Cooper, the general trend in England since the late Middle Ages was toward incorporating separate functional buildings into one coherent whole, eventually placing the kitchen in a partially subterranean basement.[106] In colonial Virginia, wealthy planters preferred to separate and isolate service functions, especially those where the chief occupants were black slaves, such as the kitchen and the laundry. This constitutes a significant departure from published European ideals. In *The Four Books of Architecture,* Palladio specifically recommends the basement as a proper place for storage rooms, kitchens, and servants' quarters. He also advised covered ways to link the main house to service buildings.[107] If Virginians took cues directly from architectural publications, those ideas were weighed, and either accepted or rejected according to local building and social practice.

A small number of the native elite elected to arrange their dependencies, which they called offices, in an aestheticized, orderly fashion and to imbue them with design features that complemented the high-style design of the main dwelling house. The result was an ensemble approach to buildings. At Germanna, for example, Alexander Spotswood directed his builders to locate his service buildings parallel and somewhat forward of the axis of the main body of his mansion (fig. 61). Because Spotswood supervised the construction of the Governor's Palace in Williamsburg and lived there for a short time, his plan for Germanna can be read as a way of surpassing his former residence by constructing covered ways between his main dwelling house and offices, covered ways absent from the Governor's Palace (fig. 62). Spotswood's linked buildings at Germanna were unprecedented, but the idea would soon appear elsewhere in the colonies. Short, straight hyphens originally linked dependencies to the main block at the Pennsylvania State-house and are illustrated in a 1732 elevation drawing attributed to Andrew Hamilton (fig. 63).[108] Straight hyphens were selected by Robert Beverley at Blandfield, while John Tayloe added curved, so-called "quadrant hyphens" at Mount Airy that rather awkwardly abut the main block (fig. 64).[109] The feature reappears in Mann Page II's Mannsfield, begun in 1767. Although

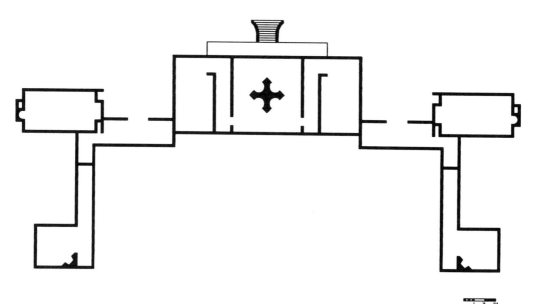

Fig. 61. Germanna, Spotsylvania County, 1721. Conjectural plan; scale bar equals 15 feet. (Megan D. Roy after Germanna Excavation Project plan)

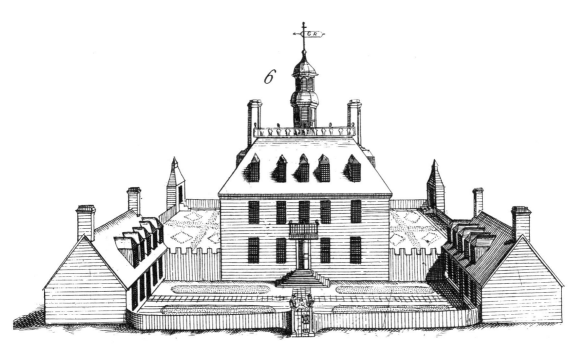

Fig. 62. Governor's Palace from Bodleian Collection, copper-plate engraving, ca. 1740. (Colonial Williamsburg Foundation)

Fig. 63. Attributed to Andrew Hamilton, plans and elevation of the Pennsylvania Statehouse, Philadelphia, 1732. (The Historical Society of Pennsylvania)

the house was destroyed in the Civil War, photographs of the ruins still suggest the impressive amplitude of its main block and dependencies (fig. 65). In the 1720s, however, Spotswood's covered ways would have been a novel feature within the larger British architectural context, and they remained unusual within a colonial context.

Fig. 64. Mount Airy, Richmond County, 1760. East façade. (Photograph by author)

Fig. 65. Mannsfield, Spotsylvania County, 1767. View of the ruins of the main house and dependencies. (Valentine Richmond History Center)

Wealthy planters also formalized their service buildings without the convenience and expense of covered ways. Thomas Lee created an expansive composition by locating ancillary buildings at diagonal angles to the four corners of the main block at Stratford Hall (fig. 66). At Carter's Grove, laundry and kitchen buildings were arranged on either side of, and parallel to, the main block. The configuration of offices in an anonymous water-color painting of about the last decade of the eighteenth century depicting what might be a South Carolina plantation offers another layout (fig. 67). The watercolor is not entirely clear, but the pattern of shadows on the buildings in the background suggests a rectangular forecourt in front of

Fig. 66. Stratford Hall, Westmoreland County, 1738. Main house with two southernmost dependencies. (Photograph by Robert T. Mooney)

Fig. 67. Unidentified artist, *The Old Plantation,* probably in South Carolina, watercolor, ca. 1790–1800. (Abby Aldrich Rockefeller Folk Art Museum, Colonial Williamsburg Foundation, Williamsburg, Virginia)

the mansion. In the distance to the right, a row of small buildings, perhaps slave dwellings, runs at right angles to the mansion and, although not part of the formal composition, amplified a sense of an ordered landscape. In all cases, the intended effect was the same. Formally designed dependencies constructed of permanent materials extended the visual presence and impact of the main dwelling and underscored the owner's ability to control and shape the built environment.

Conclusion

In surveying the domestic aestheticscapes that wealthy planters constructed on their property, it is clear that architectural taste was an essential factor in the decisions they made about building. By manipulating design features, architectural patrons created an environment that conveyed to viewers not only their wealth but, more importantly, a refined design sensibility meant to surpass that of other Virginia inhabitants. Members of the native elite were not aiming to build houses that reflected regional conditions, nor simply genteel homes, but rather, monuments to both English cultural ideas and the social values they hoped to re-create. For the historian Robert Beverley and his knowledgeable English and colonial readers, "Beauty and Conveniency" were essential for the cultivation of prestige. Design details were not superficial, coincidental, or cosmetic. They were manifestations of the native elite's faith in the power of art to create and confer personal worth and power. These were not values shared by all Virginians, not even all wealthy Virginians. We must then consider what kind of circumstances would allow or compel a person to expend prodigious amounts of capital on a house that harkened more to England than to its Virginia neighbors in order to create a monument to ambition.

Chapter 2

"Blind Stupid Fortune"

Profiling the Architectural Patron

Architectural Patrons as a Distinct Social Group

Like any well-educated, outside observer, Philip Vickers Fithian held conflicting opinions about Virginia's colonial elite. His impressions resulted in part from his experience as a tutor at the magnificent plantation complex owned by Robert Carter III, whose portrait by Thomas Hudson shows the Virginian costumed as a seventeenth-century English aristocrat (fig. 68). In the course of working at Nomini Hall in 1773 and 1774, Fithian came to admire the comfortable and genteel style of living enjoyed by his employer and his wife, Frances Anne Tasker Carter, their well-bred manners, and their display, on occasion, of generosity that verged on noblesse oblige. Fithian was more dubious, though, about what he saw as their lax and mechanical religious practices, their treatment of slaves, their extravagant spending, and most of all, their presumption of an entitled superiority. Searching for just the right words to describe the social and moral character of Virginia planters to his successor, Fithian said that, contrary to stereotype, they were fully capable of exerting themselves in hard work. He reassured his correspondent, also a northerner, that planters would deign to converse civilly with white laborers. The bigger problem, as Fithian saw it, was the deleterious effects of enormous wealth on Virginia plantation owners. "Such amazing property," he proffered, "no matter how deep it is involved, blows up the owners to an imagination, which is visible in all, but in various degrees according to their respective virtue, that they are exalted as much above other Men in worth & precedency, as blind stupid fortune has made a difference in their property."[1] Fithian's appraisal may have been mixed, but he unambiguously conceived of wealthy Virginia planters as comprising a distinct social class with well-defined cultural habits and mentalities.

Can a similar consistency of character be discovered among the architectural patrons of Virginia's prodigy houses? What sort of person would have had the audacity to embark on such a large, expensive, and often

Fig. 68. Thomas Hudson, *Portrait of Robert Carter III of Nomini Hall,* oil on canvas,
1753. (Virginia Historical Society, Richmond, Virginia)

frustrating effort to create a dwelling that was so very different from surrounding habitations? William Byrd II and Thomas Jefferson have often dominated our image of colonial architectural patrons. Their large body of extant writing offers vivid and informative insights into colonial life from an elite white male point of view. Creating a more representative profile of the kind of person who built Virginia's monumental houses, however, requires a larger sample. We will again turn to the twenty-five examples in the study group for evidence. Comparing factors such as birth, marriage, education, and sources of wealth can, however, reveal patterns that distinguish architectural patrons from the general white population. These patterns may also throw light on the forces that influenced a planter's ability to construct a genteel house and perhaps on the motivation for doing so.

Constructing a profile of the average colonial Virginia patron may at first appear a fool's errand. We know from our own experience that individuals, their circumstances, and their motivations are exactly that, so very individual. To plumb their statistics with the aim of creating a pattern may seem an academic inquiry that approaches a naïve sort of social determinism. And yet, twenty-four men and one woman produced, in collaboration with the talented craftsmen they hired, architectural products so distinct from average Virginia dwellings, that it is almost impossible not to conceive of these individuals, as Fithian did, as constituting a class that shared similar values and characteristics.

Ancestry

In devising a profile of architectural patrons, we confront some well-honed but competing conventional narratives concerning early American class structure. Did, for instance, the builders of Virginia's eighteenth-century mansions adhere more closely to the Horatio Alger myth of ascent to social success through industriousness and pluck, or did they follow the story of old money, in which inherited wealth carries blue-blooded prestige as well as purchasing power? Living before the upheaval of industrialization, rich architectural patrons might be expected to have been the scions of the earliest and most established colonial settlers. It would seem natural that their ability to construct costly houses was made possible by the successive accumulation of wealth through many generations. In addition to the Horatio Alger and old money models, historians have devised a third social model for colonial Virginia.

An alternative model concerns the native elite, the wealthiest and most powerful planters in eighteenth-century Virginia. Born in Virginia in the seventeenth century, they rose to the top of the social and political hierarchy around 1700. Many scholars believe that the culture of eighteenth-century Virginia, including the creation of high-style buildings, was a manifestation of the rise of this native elite.[2] How do the architectural patrons fit this paradigm? Of the twenty-five persons in the study group, five represent the first generation of their family to live in Virginia, one was the second generation, ten were the third generation, and nine were the fourth generation (table 2). The great majority of patrons in the study group, 80 percent, can be classified as members of the native elite whose ancestors immigrated in the seventeenth century. One could reasonably expect that some third- and fourth-generation Virginia families would have had both the opportunity and time to accumulate the wealth necessary to spend on extravagant houses of seemingly no productive value. Further, the more farsighted among recently arrived immigrants might be expected to invest their money wisely in capital expenditures, namely land and slaves. Yet, evidence from the study group reveals that neither the upper reaches of eighteenth-century Virginia society nor the ability to build a genteel house were entirely closed to ambitious newcomers, especially those who acquired wealth through nonagricultural means. Twenty percent of all the patrons in this study immigrated and ascended to social and economic prominence in the eighteenth century, a period often construed as more rigidly stratified than the previous century.

The analysis of ancestry can be parsed more carefully. Scholars have argued that it was not the descendants of the earliest settlers of Virginia, but rather the children of those arriving later in the seventeenth century who captured and consolidated political, economic, and social power in the following century.[3] Bernard Bailyn, in his analysis of the various power groups operating throughout the colonial period in Virginia, claimed that members of the eighteenth-century political elite were not the progeny of the high-born founders of Jamestown in 1607, nor the later members of the Virginia Company, nor the bootstrapping pioneer immigrants of the 1620s and 1630s. According to Bailyn, the native elite consisted instead of the descendants of middle-class immigrants arriving "for the first time within ten years either side of 1655."[4] Information from the study group affirms Bailyn's theory only in its most general outlines. The twenty-five architectural patrons comprise nineteen separate surnames. The exact date of immigration of the Jefferson and Tayloe families has not been discovered, and William Fairfax, John Carlyle, Alexander Spotswood, John Mercer, and John Thompson were all first-generation immigrants arriving in the eighteenth century. Twelve surnames can be traced through seventeenth-century records. Despite some similarity of surnames, none can be reliably classified as "ancient planters," that is, men who gained legal title to their land through the Virginia Company.[5] No single decade stands out as the most fortuitous moment for founding a future ruling family, although clusters coalesce in 1640s, 1650s and 1670s. The last decades of the seventeenth

Table 2

Ancestry

Patron	House	Building date	Generations in America	Decade of family immigration
John Banister III	Battersea	1767	Third	1670s
Robert Beverley	Blandfield	1769	Fourth	1660s
Sarah Taliaferro Brooke	Brooke's Bank	1751	Fourth	1640s
Carter Burwell	Carter's Grove	1750	Fourth	1640s
Lewis Burwell III	Kingsmill	1725	Third	1640s
John Carlyle	Carlyle House	1751	First	1740s
Charles Carter	Cleve	1746	Third	1640s
Landon Carter	Sabine Hall	1738	Third	1640s
Robert Carter I	Corotoman	1720	Second	1640s
Richard Corbin	Laneville	1758	Third	1650s
William Fairfax	Belvoir	1741	First	1730s
William Fitzhugh	Chatham	1769	Fourth	1670s
Benjamin Harrison IV	Berkeley	1726	Fourth	1630s
Thomas Jefferson	Monticello I	1770	Fourth	Unknown
Richard Henry Lee	Chantilly	1761	Fourth	1640s
Thomas Lee	Stratford Hall	1738	Third	1640s
George Mason IV	Gunston Hall	1752	Fourth	1650s
John Mercer	Marlborough	1746	First	1720s
Mann Page I	Rosewell	1726	Third	1650s
Mann Page II	Mannsfield	1767	Fourth	1650s
John Randolph II	Tazewell Hall	1758	Third	1670s
William Randolph III	Wilton	1751	Third	1670s
Alexander Spotswood	Germanna	1721	First	1710s
John Tayloe II	Mount Airy	1760	Third	Unknown
John Thompson	Salubria	1763	First	1730s

century, however, were characterized by low tobacco prices, making those middling or yeoman planters with few or no slaves less competitive and consequently discouraging white immigration.[6] The study confirms the picture of a depressed Virginia economy; not one of the families is known to have immigrated to Virginia in the 1680s or 1690s.

When the ancestors of architectural patrons landed in Virginia around the middle decades of the seventeenth century, most prospered rapidly and rose to social and political prominence. To be sure, degrees of wealth and political stature existed even among the very wealthy. A Lee or a Burwell possessed far more land than a Banister or a Jefferson. With the possible exception of the Jefferson family, none of the patrons' ancestors who immigrated in the seventeenth century remained obscure landless tenants whose descendants suddenly achieved prestige and wealth in the eighteenth century. Virtually all of the immigrants to Virginia brought with them economic or social capital that they quickly parlayed into colonial success.

Descent from an old Virginia family carried considerable social value in the eighteenth century and was enhanced by an English pedigree. Not only did eighteenth-century scions of well-established colonial families benefit from several generations of accumulated wealth, but they also sought and sometimes bought the social patina of a long association with English inherited power and privilege. Their yearning for nobility was in vain for the social origins of the native elite lay mostly within a respectable but not aristocratic class. As John Oldmixon wrote in 1708, Virginia's elite descended from "men of good families, and small fortunes," who "thrived and grew great by their industry and success" in Virginia. Although "many gentlemen of Virginia may boast as good descents as those in England," Oldmixon wryly noted that "there's no need as yet of an Herald Office to be set up at James Town."[7] Nevertheless, Virginia's native elite ardently tried to establish a record of prestigious ancestry through heraldic devices and genealogy. The metallic Burwell family crests discovered near Kingsmill, a silver cup engraved with Lee arms that was presented to Queen's College, Oxford, by Richard Lee I in 1658, or William Beverley's attempt to have the correct arms used by his father engraved upon a seal in 1739 all point to the desire on the part of Virginia's native elite to create social legitimacy.[8] In Robert Carter I's diary entry of 14 July 1727, he noted that among the items he purchased for his daughter, "all the plate [is] to have my Coat of Arms."[9] Decades later, Carter's grandson Robert Carter III requested information about his family's ancestry from his uncle Landon Carter of Sabine Hall. Landon pursued this inquiry by purchasing at least two genealogical works on the English nobility.[10] A book on heraldry also was listed in the inventory of the personal estate of John Carlyle, a merchant by trade.[11] In 1783, George Washington somewhat haughtily rebuffed Mrs. Ruthy Jones's claim of familial relation, as well as her solicitation for money, by recounting his ancestry. Even Thomas Jefferson, who dismissed the merits of pedigree, bowed to the curiosity of his class- and lineage-conscious readers in the opening paragraphs of his 1821 *Autobiography* when he pointed to his mother's Randolph family heritage.[12] Elite Virginians' pursuit of pedigree suggests a measure of insecurity about their place in the early modern British social order when that order was being reshuffled by the commercial revolution and the power of capitalism to upset old hierarchies of power.

Patterns of Inheritance

The old social order of privilege, for example, would have ensured that by law or custom the greatest benefits of "blind stupid fortune" accrued to the eldest surviving son. In England, where the law of primogeniture was applied uniformly, an eldest son possessed economic advantages denied to his younger brothers. In eighteenth-century Virginia, the strict rule of primogeniture was enforced only in cases of intestacy, that is, when a father died without a will.[13] When a father did leave a will, he usually distributed property, both personal and real, so that neither his wife nor any of his progeny were left destitute.[14] By custom, however, the eldest son in Virginia usually inherited the largest and most valuable portion of his father's estate, including the main residence. Birth order then may represent an important factor in the ability to construct an extravagant display of architectural refinement. Among the twenty-four architectural patrons whose birth order is known, thirteen were either the eldest son, or became the principal heir after the death of an older brother (table 3). The economic benefits of birth order were likely to be even greater if the patron's father died intestate, as was the case for Benjamin Harrison IV, William Fitzhugh, and George Mason IV. Similar advantages fell to the six patrons who were either the only son or sole surviving male heir. They did not have to share inherited real property with other male siblings. Yet, the value of being born the eldest or only male heir existed only if there was valuable property to be passed down, and this was probably not the case for two men, Alexander Spotswood and John Mercer, both of whom were immigrants.

While eleven architectural patrons had a substantial advantage in the accumulation of wealth by reason of birth order, an equal number were able to overcome the disadvantages of being born a younger son or daughter. This is particularly true for two immigrant younger sons, William Fairfax and John Carlyle, who were barred from inheriting their father's landed wealth by stricter primogeniture customs in Britain. Charles Carter and Landon Carter, on the other hand, inherited so much property from their father, Robert Carter I, that the order of their birth was inconsequential. Neither Virginia's economy nor testamentary customs were so rigid as to exclude younger siblings of the very rich from accruing the wealth required to create an academically designed house. Although fate conferred definite advantages to eldest male heirs, this hurdle could be overcome if a father held enormous wealth or if "blind stupid fortune" shined brightly on younger children in other ways.

Instead of birth order, early paternal mortality strongly marks the demographic profile of Virginia's prodigy house owners. Callous though it sounds, patrons stood to gain from the early demise of their fathers. Of

Table 3

Patterns of testation

Patron	Birth order	Father dying intestate	Sole surviving heir	Paternal mortality before patron built house	Paternal mortality before patron reached majority
John Banister III	First son	No	Yes	Yes	No
Robert Beverley	First son	No	Yes	Yes	Yes
Sarah Taliaferro Brooke	First daughter	No	No	Yes	Unknown
Carter Burwell	Second son	No	No	Yes	Yes
Lewis Burwell III	Third son	No	No	Yes	Yes
John Carlyle	Second son	No	No	Yes	No
Charles Carter	Third son	No	No	Yes	No
Landon Carter	Fourth son	No	No	Yes	No
Robert Carter I	Second son	No	Yes	Yes	Yes
Richard Corbin	First son	No	No	Yes	No
William Fairfax	Second son	No	No	Unknown	Unknown
William Fitzhugh	First son	Yes	No	Yes	Yes
Benjamin Harrison IV	First son	Yes	No	Yes	Yes
Thomas Jefferson	First son	No	No	Yes	Yes
Richard Henry Lee	Third son	No	No	Yes	Yes
Thomas Lee	Fourth son	No	No	Yes	No
George Mason IV	First son	Yes	No	Yes	Yes
John Mercer	First son	No	No	Yes	Yes
Mann Page I	First son	No	Yes	Yes	No
Mann Page II	First son	No	No	Yes	Yes
John Randolph II	Third son	No	No	Yes	Yes
William Randolph III	Third son	No	No	Yes	Yes
Alexander Spotswood	First son	No	Yes	Yes	Yes
John Tayloe II	First son	No	Yes	Yes	No
John Thompson	Unknown	No	Unknown	Unknown	Unknown

the twenty-three individuals for whom sufficient biographical information exists, all built their mansions after their father had died, that is, after coming into their inheritance. Moreover, a substantial number had full legal control over their inheritance as young adults and could spend it on architecture. Comparing the date of majority, twenty-one years for males, to the date of the father's death, we find that seven architectural patrons came of age while their fathers were living, but that fifteen were yet minors at the time their father died. Far from constituting an unusually tragic event, orphanhood was frequent and widespread throughout all social classes in eighteenth-century Virginia. In their analysis of Middlesex County, Virginia, Darrett and Anita Rutman found that 57 percent of white children between the years 1710 and 1749 lost at least one parent by the age of thirteen.[15] Most Virginia orphans inherited very little and were further impoverished by paternal mortality. By contrast, most architectural patrons in the study stood to gain land and slaves at the death of their fathers.

Vital Statistics

Mindful that wealth accumulates, or potentially accumulates, over a lifetime, one might expect that owners erected their mansions after they had augmented their fortunes.[16] Although the correlation between advanced age and accumulation of total estate wealth may hold true, the patrons of Virginia's prodigy houses appear surprisingly young when they embarked on their expensive building campaign. Benjamin Harrison IV, for instance was only about twenty-six when he started to build Berkeley (fig. 69). Among the twenty-two patrons in this study whose birth date is known

Fig. 69. Berkeley, Charles City County, 1726. (Photograph by Robert T. Mooney)

with some assurance, the average mean age when mansion construction commenced was 36 years, with the average median of 33.5 (table 4). When divided by decades, the overall youth of architectural patrons appears more pronounced. Eight patrons began construction in their twenties, seven in their thirties, five in their forties, and only two in their fifties, when presumably they were near the apex of their economic lives.

Table 4
Vital statistics

Patron	Building date	Year of birth	Approximate age when house construction commenced	Year of death	Approximate age at death
John Banister III	1767	1734	33	1788	54
Robert Beverley	1769	1740	29	1800	60
Sarah Taliaferro Brooke	1751	Unknown	Unknown	1763 or 1764	Unknown
Carter Burwell	1750	1716	34	1756	40
Lewis Burwell III	1725	Unknown	Unknown	1744	Unknown
John Carlyle	1751	1721	30	1780	59
Charles Carter	1746	1707	39	1764	57
Landon Carter	1738	1710	28	1778	68
Robert Carter I	1720	1663	57	1732	69
Richard Corbin	1758	1714	44	1790	76
William Fairfax	1741	1691	50	1757	66
William Fitzhugh	1769	1741	28	1809	68
Benjamin Harrison IV	1726	ca. 1700	26	1745	45
Thomas Jefferson	1770	1743	27	1826	83
Richard Henry Lee	1761	1732	29	1794	62
Thomas Lee	1738	1690	48	1750	60
George Mason IV	1752	1725	27	1792	67
John Mercer	1746	1705	41	1768	63
Mann Page I	1726	1691	35	1730	39
Mann Page II	1767	1719	48	1780	61
John Randolph II	1758	1727	31	1784	57
William Randolph III	1751	1723	28	1761	38
Alexander Spotswood	1721	1676	45	1740	64
John Tayloe II	1760	1721	39	1779	58
John Thompson	1763	Unknown	Unknown	1772	Unknown

Architectural patrons, however, were not motivated by modern actuarial standards but by their own perceptions of life expectancy. At age sixty, Landon Carter considered himself an old man and cited the biblical three score and ten life span.[17] In a 1789 letter to James Madison, Jefferson estimated average life expectancy to be fifty-five years: "Let the ripe age be supposed of 21 years, and their period of life 34 years more, that being the average term given by bills of mortality to persons who have already attained 21 years of age."[18] By their own reckoning, then, architectural patrons thought they were building their mansions when they were in their middle years.

Virginia's architectural patrons also undermine the conventional twentieth-century association between youth and avant-garde design. In 1726, a twenty-six-year-old Benjamin Harrison IV utilized a center transverse passage plan for Berkeley. Twenty-five years later, a twenty-eight-year-old William Randolph III employed the same plan type for Wilton. Conversely, the willingness to depart from conventional planning principles appears at Jefferson's Monticello I when he was only twenty-six, but also at Thomas Lee's Stratford Hall, built when he was forty-seven. Neither youthful exuberance nor sage maturity constituted a salient factor in determining the stylistic qualities of a mansion.

Modern science has also conditioned us to expect a correlation between living conditions and life span. Accordingly, we would anticipate that capacious, well-lighted, ventilated, and generously heated domestic spaces maintained by servants would increase longevity. The study group data corroborated this supposition. Of the twenty-three patrons whose birth dates are known, the average mean age at death was 58 with a median age of 60.5. This means that, on average, the architectural patrons of Virginia's mansions lived five to ten years longer than most white males reaching maturity in the colonial South. In Perquimans County, North Carolina, for example, the average life expectancy in the eighteenth century was 48.9 years, but for Maryland legislators, who represented a wealthier and presumably healthier sector of the population, the average was 55 years.[19] The men in the study group, however, were not quite as long-lived as the English elite they sought to emulate; among eighteenth-century British ducal families, average life span rose to 61.3 years.[20]

Marriage

Among all the demographic data, the most striking and intriguing corollary is between the date of construction and the date of marriage. Of the twenty-five patrons in the study group, only two, Alexander Spotswood and Thomas Jefferson, began to construct their houses before they married (table 5). All the rest waited until marriage, and the same economic prerequisites affecting the decision to marry may have likewise influenced their decision to commence building. Among the twenty men in the study group for whom adequate biographical data exist, the average mean age at the time of first marriage was twenty, with an average median age of twenty-three. Economic demographers often hypothesize that men choose to marry when they feel capable of supporting a family economically. Laws encouraged mature alliances and household formation. A father's legal consent to marry was required if his son was younger than twenty-one or daughter younger than eighteen.[21] If men decide to marry when they were confident of their prospects, then the age at which architectural patrons married indicated that most felt very assured. Governor Francis Fauquier gave voice to at least some of their enthusiasm for marriage when he wrote in 1763 that Virginia's growing population "is owing in part to the laudable Custom prevalent in the Colony of every Persons [*sic*] marrying very early in Life."[22] Samples from the Chesapeake and among the British ruling class confirm Fauquier's more subjective impressions. The economic historian Gloria Main, for instance, found that the average age at marriage for seventeenth-century Maryland men was about thirty, but she also discovered that over 25 percent of men in the colony never married, largely because of a shortage of females.[23] Among British ducal families between the years 1680 to 1779, the average mean age at marriage was 28.6.[24] Marriage among wealthy Virginia men in the study group conforms more closely to data from two other regions in the eighteenth-century South. In Perquimans County, North Carolina, men married at a mean average of 23.8 years. In Charles Parish, York County, Virginia, the mean average was 24.8.[25]

Some factor emboldened eighteenth-century Virginia men, and not only those from extremely wealthy families, to marry while young. For members of the native elite, that factor may have been the relatively early death of their fathers and the subsequent control over their inheritance. Of the twenty men whose age at first marriage is known with some certainty, only three married before their fathers died, two married sometime during the same year that their fathers died, and sixteen married after their father's death. The need to construct a new house would be most urgent among younger sons, who, because they were not the principal heir, would not inherit their father's home. Among the nine patrons starting construction in their twenties, one was a second son, three were third sons, and four others were either first or only sons whose mothers were still alive at the time of construction and probably retained a life interest in the father's dwelling house. House construction, therefore, can be seen as a response to new nuclear family formation, but that fails to explain why the new dwelling was a high-style edifice.

Because almost all patrons married before they built the houses in the study group, these particular mansions could not have been constructed

Table 5
Marriage

Patron	Year of birth	Date of first marriage	Building date	Approximate age at first marriage	Marriage before or after paternal mortality	First wives related to other patrons	Number of spouses	Raised in a substantial house and married first spouse from prominent family
John Banister III	1734	1755	1767	21	Before	Unrelated	Three	Unknown
Robert Beverley	1740	1763	1769	23	After	Related	One	Yes
Sarah Taliaferro Brooke	Unknown	Unknown	1751	Unknown	Unknown	Unrelated	One	Unknown
Carter Burwell	1716	1738	1750	22	After	Unrelated	One	Yes
Lewis Burwell III	Unknown	Unknown	1725	Unknown	After	Unknown	One	Unknown
John Carlyle	1721	1747	1751	26	After	Related	Two	Unknown
Charles Carter	1707	1728	1746	21	Before	Related	Three	Unknown
Landon Carter	1710	1732	1738	22	Same year	Unrelated	Three	Yes
Robert Carter I	1663	1689	1720	26	After	Unrelated	Two	Unknown
Richard Corbin	1714	1737	1758	23	Before	Related	One	Unknown
William Fairfax	1691	Unknown	1741	Unknown	Unknown	Unknown	Three	Unknown
William Fitzhugh	1741	1763	1769	22	After	Related	One	Yes
Benjamin Harrison IV	ca. 1700	1722	1726	22	After	Related	One	Yes
Thomas Jefferson	1743	1772	1770	29	After	Unrelated	One	Unknown
Richard Henry Lee	1732	1757	1761	25	After	Unrelated	Two	Unknown
Thomas Lee	1690	1722	1738	32	After	Related	One	Yes
George Mason IV	1725	1750	1752	25	After	Unrelated	Two	Unknown
John Mercer	1705	1725	1746	20	After	Related	Two	Unknown
Mann Page I	1691	1712	1726	21	After	Unrelated	Two	Yes
Mann Page II	1719	1741	1767	22	After	Unrelated	Two	Yes
John Randolph II	1727	1751	1758	24	After	Unrelated	One	Yes
William Randolph III	1723	Unknown	1751	Unknown	Unknown	Related	One	Yes
Alexander Spotswood	1676	1724	1721	48	After	Unrelated	One	Unknown
John Tayloe II	1721	1747	1760	26	Same year	Unrelated	One	Yes
John Thompson	Unknown	1742	1763	Unknown	Unknown	Related	Two	Unknown

in order to impress a prospective spouse's family. Yet patrons wed very well, and one enticement to matrimony may have included the dwelling in which a potential spouse was raised. Of the twenty-three patrons whose first wife's name is known, nine were able to wed women who were closely related to the families of other patrons in this study. The wives of Benjamin Harrison IV, Robert Beverley, John Carlyle, John Thompson, and William Randolph III had lived previously in one of the other houses considered in this study. Eight other men first married women whose families figured prominently in either Virginia or Maryland politics and were, or came to be, associated with a large residence: Carter Burwell, Robert Carter I, William Fitzhugh, Mann Page I, John Tayloe II, Mann Page II, Landon Carter, and John Randolph II. Although twelve men remarried a second or third time, their social status was evident at the first marriage, that is, before they built their mansions.

A prospective father-in-law might have gladly handed his daughter and her dowry to a man whose family's wealth and social status was visually demonstrated by a fine residence. Little is known about the architectural character of many of these earlier dwellings, but at least twelve of the seventeen architectural patrons who won the hand of a socially prominent woman grew up in residences larger and more comfortable than those of average Virginians. Newcomers John Carlyle, John Mercer, and John Thompson, on the other hand, attracted prestige wives without any prior architectural evidence in the colony of their families' wealth and standing, so property likely counted for more in terms of matrimonial capital. Aside from such notable exceptions, however, living in substantial housing represents a common bond among both patrons and their spouses and created an inter- and intragenerational web of architectural alliances.

Progeny

The point of marriage alliances among Virginia's native elite was to concentrate wealth and privilege in the hands of their progeny. Offspring of advantageous matches were blessed with property and status from both mother and father. Such boys and girls would also, presumably, benefit from better nutrition and too, the warmth, comfort, and cleanliness of high-quality housing. Wealthy mansion owners might be expected to have produced more and longer-lived offspring than poor tenant farmers inhabiting cold, drafty, and dirty earthfast or log dwellings. Among the twenty-four persons in the study group for whom evidence exists, an average mean of 9.1 offspring were born per patron, with family size ranging from 2 to 19 children (table 6). Twelve men married more than once, so not all of the children were born of one woman. The progeny of John Banister III and Lewis Burwell III cannot be attributed to specific partners, but

Table 6

Progeny

Patron	Total number of children	Birth of first child compared to date of construction	Majority of children born before or after construction	Marriage alliances to other patrons' children
John Banister III	6	Before	Unknown	No
Robert Beverley	16	Before	After	One
Sarah Taliaferro Brooke	2	Before	Before	No
Carter Burwell	9	Before	Before	One
Lewis Burwell III	Unknown	Unknown	Unknown	No
John Carlyle	10	About same time	After	No
Charles Carter	13	Before	After	One
Landon Carter	9	Before	After	Daughter to other patron
Robert Carter I	15	Before	Before	Two daughters to other patrons
Richard Corbin	8	Before	Before	One
William Fairfax	7	Before	Before	Daughter to other patron
William Fitzhugh	6	After	After	No
Benjamin Harrison IV	11	Before	After	Daughter to other patron
Thomas Jefferson	6	After	After	No
Richard Henry Lee	9	About same time	After	No
Thomas Lee	11	Before	Before	One
George Mason IV	12	About same time	After	No
John Mercer	19	Before	Before	No
Mann Page I	9	Before	Unknown	No
Mann Page II	10	Before	Before	Two
John Randolph II	3	Before	Unknown	No
William Randolph III	8	Unknown	Unknown	No
Alexander Spotswood	4	After	After	No
John Tayloe II	11	Before	After	Four
John Thompson	5	Before	After	One

other patrons produced an average mean of 5.6 recorded births per marriage. These averages represent only the known children born; determining survival rates and completed family size is more difficult. Often the only evidence of children comes from a will, and offspring who died before the will was written have been lost to recorded history. In sum, there were likely more children born whose existence is unknown. Genealogical records are incomplete for the children of Carter Burwell, Lewis Burwell III, Mann Page I, and William Randolph III. For the other twenty-one architectural patrons, an average mean of 6.7 children per architectural patron survived childhood, that is, lived to thirteen years. Surprisingly, the most luxuriously sheltered children survived about as long as the more miserably housed poor white children of the Chesapeake region. According to Allan Kulikoff's research, "the average number of children in all families rose by a third, from 5.5 to 7.4" between the years 1650 to 1750 and declined to 5.5 in the next fifty years.[26] Sadly, the comforts found within a genteel house offered little protection from colonial childhood disease.

Virginia's prodigy houses were not logical responses to the practical requirements of family size. Of the twenty-three patrons whose first child's birth date is known with some certainty, seventeen had at least one child born before construction, three had their first child born at about the same time, and three became parents after the dwelling was started. Nor did an expanding household population serve as a major impetus behind the erection of a pretentious dwelling. Among those twenty patrons for whom sufficient data exist concerning the birth dates of all progeny, eight had most of their offspring born before the mansion was commenced, and twelve had most of their children born afterwards. Like other wealthy planters, the architectural patrons in the study group carried on family life in genteel though less imposing structures.

Architecture as Legacy

While the motivation behind construction of a high-style house does not seem directly linked to the functional accommodation of family life, it may have been associated with a patron's perceived need to provide his children with social status. In addition to leaving a substantial landed inheritance, fathers occasionally played a more direct role in their sons' future homes by providing them with building materials; money specifically for construction; designs; and designated building sites. Robert Carter I was not alive when Sabine Hall or Cleve were erected, but in 1725 he engaged a glazier and obtained the glass for Nomini Hall, the mansion of his son Robert Carter II.[27] Another of Carter's son, Charles, continued this tradition. Charles Carter specified in his will of 1762 that the tract of land he gave his son was intended "for the seat of my son, Landon, I desire the Mansion House may be built at the place I have laid off and called View Mount, as it commands a beautiful prospect of the great ledge of Mountains."[28] Other fathers also took an interest in ensuring suitable housing for their heirs. Thomas Lee bequeathed each of his younger sons with land but also £200 "toward building and Finishing each a house."[29] In 1758, Richard Corbin wrote to his son, then studying in England, to inform him that "I am now repairing with all expedition the loss of my house and shall provide materials for a house for you [before] you arrive."[30] In 1792, when George Mason IV was sixty-seven years old, he not only procured building materials for his son Thomson's house but directed the workmen.[31] Perpetuating family stature via substantial architecture found expression even in unusual circumstances. John Custis IV specified in his will that his executor build Custis's beloved manumitted mulatto son a "handsome strong convenient dwelling house according to the dimensions I shall direct and a plan thereof drawn by my said friend John Blair Esquire."[32] For wealthy Virginia fathers, bequeathing impressive architecture was almost as important as land and political influence.

Possessing an imposing residence increased the matrimonial assets of a patron's children and expanded the web of architectural alliances. Of the twenty-five patrons in this study, all had at least one child who married into families with politically prominent names. In addition, four of these twenty-five patrons had daughters who married other patrons in this study, and eight had children who married children of other patrons. It would be foolish to place too much emphasis on the role of architecture as a cause of valuable marriage alliances. Undoubtedly, large dowries and inheritances were the primary prizes, but as we have seen, most patrons who first married prominent women grew up in substantial dwellings. If a substantial house facilitated advantageous marriages for architectural patrons, they, in turn, may have been more willing to build extravagantly in order to encourage similarly beneficial alliances for their children. Prodigy houses functioned as an efficacious way of knitting together families of compatible wealth and prestige.

Education

The architectural patrons of Virginia's mansions were also drawn together by a shared emphasis on education. Access to elite cultural knowledge put a wide gulf between the colony's native elite and most Virginians, who were either illiterate or only functionally literate. Through superior education, the truly wealthy in eighteenth-century Virginia regularly reconfigured an intellectual compass that pointed to British social and aesthetic values. Most eighteenth-century Virginians survived remarkably well without access to elite cultural values. Although formal schooling alone did not constitute an absolute prerequisite for the construction of a mansion, the overall high level of education sets these men apart from the general white population of eighteenth-century Virginia.

Literacy can be measured in several ways, the most fundamental being the capacity to sign one's name. The historian Kenneth A. Lockridge estimated that the ability to write one's name on a will extended to about 62 percent of adult white males during the entire eighteenth century.[33] In the older, more settled regions, such as Westmoreland and Middlesex Counties, the rate was higher, 68 to 74 percent, while in the newer frontier areas the rate was only about 50 percent in the mid-eighteenth century, rising to about 60 percent by 1776.[34] The figures for females are more difficult to determine, but Lockridge claimed that no more than 50 percent of women were able to sign their names in the mid-eighteenth century.[35]

Writing one's name, however, is distinct from the ability of an individual to understand a deed of indenture, keep an account book, or read a newspaper.[36] An alternative method of measuring literacy is to evaluate the opportunities for formal schooling beyond that which the parent could provide within the home. Formal elementary-level education was tied to the higher income brackets of parents and did not involve a particularly lengthy period of matriculation. In 1724, there was only one teacher for every hundred white households. While 30 percent of wealthy fathers, namely those with £1,000 or more in personal property, made educational bequests in their wills, only 10 percent of those with personal property of less than £400 provided for their children's education. Among those families who had the financial means to provide formal education, boys usually received two years of training, acquiring skills in reading, writing, and occasionally arithmetic. Girls, if they were taught at all, usually attended school for only one year, gaining perhaps the ability to read. Functional literacy among eighteenth-century Virginians can also be gauged by the possession of books, as recorded in probate inventories. Based on these documents, a little more than half of the white households owned reading material, usually a Bible or other devotional texts.[37]

Just as there is a profound chasm between the ability to sign one's name and the ability to read the *Virginia Gazette* or a passage from the Bible, so too is there a deep gulf between functional literacy and high, or cultural, literacy. The proportion of colonial Virginians falling into this latter category appears to have been exceedingly small and was signaled primarily by the ability to translate Latin.[38] Whereas the rudiments of English and simple computation were taught in primary school, the study of Latin usually occurred within the setting of a grammar school, that is, a Latin grammar school. Whether it occurred within an institutional setting or at the hands of a private tutor, this level of schooling required several more years of study and, of course, a great deal more money. Grammar school–level education introduced the pupil not only to an ancient language but also to a world of literature that gave him the intellectual polish that set him apart from the merely functionally literate, as well as from those whose status within the upper levels of society was based on accumulated wealth alone.[39] The majority of the twenty-five architectural patrons in the study group fall within the privileged ranks of the culturally literate. Their Virginia parents paid dearly for this gift of what is now called cultural capital.

The cost of obtaining education beyond the primary level effectively restricted cultural literacy to a very small number of families. While the cost of employing a primary or grammar school teacher could be shared among the families utilizing his services, a Latin grammar school teacher commanded a higher total salary. Advertisements in the *Virginia Gazette* offered between £20 and £30 per annum for tutors able to teach English, writing, and arithmetic, but from £50 to £80 per annum for instructors of classical languages.[40] Finding capable teachers within the colony who met the high standards set forth by English educational theorists such as John Locke was difficult even for wealthy Virginia planters. William Beverley, the father of the builder of Blandfield, complained to his London agent, "I would willingly have such a person as Mr. Lock [*sic*] describes, but can't expect on such wages as I can afford." Beverley also expressed his reservations about Scottish teachers, telling Micajah Perry that "the usual wages here for a Latin master from Scotland is £20 year, but they commonly teach the children the Scotch dialect which they never can wear off."[41] Eventually Beverley decided to place his son Robert, the builder of Blandfield, in the Wakefield Grammar School in Yorkshire, England.[42] Robert Carter III was more successful and in 1773 contracted with the Princeton-trained Philip Vickers Fithian

> to teach his Children, Five Daughters, & three Sons, who are from five to seventeen years old—The young Ladies are to be taught the English Language. And the Boys are to study the English Language carefully; & to be instructed in the Latin, & Greek—And he proposed to give thirty five Pounds Sterling, which is about Sixty Pounds currency, Provide all Accommodations; allow him the undisturbed Use of a Room; And the Use of his own Library, find Provender for a Horse; & a Servant to Wait.[43]

In order to pursue education beyond the plantation grammar school Fithian conducted, wealthy Virginians faced fewer and more costly choices.

Six architectural patrons pursued this more exclusive level of education entirely in Virginia, either in the grammar school or the collegiate level of the College of William and Mary (table 7).[44] Tuition at the College of William and Mary cost 20s. per year for both the grammar school and college, while board at the college building amounted to £13 per year.[45] Some ambitious parents found the college a less than desirable place for their sons. Robert Carter III warned Fithian about the institution's lax moral environment but surprised the tutor by telling him that the "Necessary Expence for each Scholar yearly is only 15£ Currency."[46] This charge was far beyond the reach of most colonial Virginia families. Among the free heads of households leaving wills in Tidewater Virginia in 1774, the average net worth, not income, equaled about £527 sterling.[47] Sending one son to the grammar school of the College of William and Mary would have decreased an average white father's entire estate by a minimum of 3 percent each year, fluctuations of currency aside. Most of this estate, though, was not easily converted into cash. The amount of wealth comprised of personal property was even smaller among average colonial Virginians. Between 1731 and 1740, the median value of personal estates in Lancaster County was only £54 2s. sterling.[48] Attending the College of William and Mary for one year would have decreased the value of personal property substantially. It would have been difficult for Fithian, who earned £35 sterling a year from Carter, to send his own sons to the college. The exclusivity of the institution is reflected in attendance figures. Exact data have been lost, but conjectural estimates place the total enrollment between the years 1699 and 1776 at only 589 students, or about 7.5 students per year.[49]

Other, more prestigious schools of higher learning existed in Britain, and eleven architectural patrons in the study group received at least part of their schooling there. Five attended grammar school, and six studied at a college or one of London's Inns of Court, which trained lawyers. Enrollment figures illustrated how privileged these men were. Up until 1776, a total of only thirteen Virginians studied at Oxford and twenty-one at Cambridge. During the same period, only forty-nine native Virginians are known to have attended one of the Inns of Court.[50] Colleges in Great Britain were considerably more expensive than grammar schools. Tuition, room, and board at these institutions was about £12 sterling per quarter, not per year, and additional fees and the cost of living made a college education in Britain beyond the reach of even prosperous Virginians. Depending on the standard of living assumed by the student, a year at Oxford or Cambridge required an allowance of between £90 and £191 sterling.[51] Members of the British nobility, however, reportedly gave their sons larger stipends, as much as £400 per annum.[52] At the University of Edinburgh, considered the least expensive collegiate institution, tuition and living expenses in the second half of the eighteenth century ran between £100 and £120 per annum. The combined cost of tuition, room, board, books, and the other details of maintenance at one of the London Inns of Court could total £250 per annum. Expenses for English grammar schools varied according to the location and reputation of the institution. Famous preparatory schools, such as Eton, Westmoreland, and Harrow, ranged from £80 to £100 per year, but less well-known schools still cost from £21 to £50 in the eighteenth century.[53] By comparison, Robert Carter I claimed that his education in London during the 1670s was no more £30 per year.[54]

Table 7

Education

Patron	Attended College of William and Mary or its grammar school	Attended grammar school in England	Attended English college or Inns of Court	Unknown education or illiterate
John Banister III	—	—	Yes	—
Robert Beverley	—	Yes	Yes	—
Sarah Taliaferro Brooke	—	—	—	Illiterate in 1737
Carter Burwell	Yes	—	—	—
Lewis Burwell III	Yes	—	—	—
John Carlyle	—	—	—	Unknown
Charles Carter	—	Yes	—	—
Landon Carter	Yes	Yes	—	—
Robert Carter I	—	Yes	—	—
Richard Corbin	Yes	—	—	—
William Fairfax	—	Yes	—	—
William Fitzhugh	—	—	—	Unknown
Benjamin Harrison IV	—	—	—	Unknown
Thomas Jefferson	Yes	—	—	—
Richard Henry Lee	—	Yes	—	—
Thomas Lee	—	—	—	Unknown
George Mason IV	—	—	—	Unknown
John Mercer	—	—	Yes	—
Mann Page I	—	Yes	Yes	—
Mann Page II	Yes	—	—	—
John Randolph II	—	—	Yes	—
William Randolph III	Yes	—	—	—
Alexander Spotswood	—	—	—	Unknown
John Tayloe II	—	—	—	Unknown
John Thompson	—	—	Yes	—

Virginia fathers wealthy enough to invest in education did so not only to provide their sons with practical skills and Christian values, nor only to give their sons the more abstract intellectual enrichment of the liberal arts, but to imprint the social advantages associated with an advanced education. Some parents made the connection between social rank and education clear to their children. Richard and Elizabeth Ambler emphasized this point exactly when they admonished their sons to make wise use of their time at the Wakefield Grammar School in England. In a passage from a 1748 letter that still resonates among parents, Richard claimed that education was the key determinant of status:

> I shall think the expense I am at (tho' great) well laid out provided you make proper use of it and acquire such an Education as may set you above the common level & drudgery of Life, of which be mindfull. You are now entering into Years which will enable you to reflect, that many Children capable of learning, are condemn'd to the necessity of Labouring hard, for want of ability in their Parents to give them an Education. You cannot therefore, sufficiently Adore the Divine Providence who has placed your Parents above the lower Class and thereby enabled them to be at the expense of giving you such an Education (which if not now neglected by you) will preserve you in the same Class & Rank among mankind.[55]

Richard Ambler reminded his sons again of the social consequences of sloth the following year:

> You have at present an advantage which was never in the power either of my Father or my Self, I have often heard Him lament his want of Learning, and I my self am very sensible of my own defects, and have frequently condemned my self for neglecting the opportunity I once had! for how stinging is the [affliction?] when we fall into the Company of the learned, we cannot bear a part in the conversation for want of Learning.[56]

His remarks reveal his own social insecurities and indicate as well that even the wealthiest members of the native elite were not entirely secure in their own station. Perhaps Ambler's anxiety concerning the future of his sons was no more than the insecurity of the new rich whose wealth was based on commerce. Similar concerns, however, were voiced by members of older families whose wealth was derived from the land. When Nathaniel Burwell became aware of the academic deficiencies of his ward and younger brother, Lewis Burwell III, he was worried not only about his sibling's ability to support himself but also that Lewis's ignorance would embarrass the good name of the family. He warned that Lewis would prove in "noways capable of the management of his own affairs and unfit for any gentleman's conversation, and therefore a scandalous person, and a shame to his relations, not having one single qualification to recommend him."[57] Both Ambler and Burwell allude to intellectual discourse as the essential way of measuring education and therefore social status.

Attaining cultural proficiency came from a curriculum focused primarily but not exclusively on classical languages and literature. In 1751, John Smith wrote to Edward Ambler, who was then still in England, about the various educational options for his son and insisted that "the foundation must be laid in the Classics or he will make a poor figure in anything."[58] Some members of the Virginia gentry were able to compensate for shortcomings in their formal education through personal initiative. According to one relative, Thomas Lee was an exemplary autodidact (fig. 70). Although born to an extremely wealthy family, he was a younger son and received a meager education compared to that of his older brothers. Based on a later, and perhaps biased, memoir, Lee, who had nothing "but a common Virginia Education, yet having strong natural parts, long after he was a man he learned the Languages without any assistance but his own genius, and became a tolerant adept in Greek and Latin."[59]

Figure 70. Attributed to Charles Bridges, *Portrait of Thomas Lee,* oil on canvas, after 1735. Reproduction located at Stratford Hall. (Jessie Ball duPont Memorial Library, Robert E. Lee Memorial Association, Inc., Stratford Hall Plantation)

Because of the expense and rarity of education, students were made cognizant of their privileged rank within Virginia society; a position which, judging from the admonitions of Ambler or Burwell, was not guaranteed by birth, not even among the native elite, but achieved or sustained by external evidence of success. The purpose of expending large sums of money on education was the outward display of erudition, not intellectual stimulation for its own sake. The ability to comport oneself with dignity, speak the King's English correctly, discuss fashionable literature, and drop the occasional Latin phrase were the distinguishing signs of gentility and personal worth.[60]

Education offers a key metaphor to academic architecture. Like the performance of classical learning before a similarly trained audience, a genteel house displayed a visible sign of status before one's peers. To build a prodigy house, they needed a more fundamental resource, money.

Wealth

The characteristic that most sharply defined members of Virginia's elite class, according to Fithian, was their great wealth. It was their "amazing property," he claimed, that blew up their inflated sense of self-importance even though that property was acquired by accident of birth instead of their own hard work and even if that property was mortgaged against debts. Fithian was correct; the disparity between the wealth of Virginia's native elite and that of poor and middling planters was enormous. But to say that Virginia's architectural patrons were able to undertake extravagant building projects because they were rich is to state the obvious. A more pertinent question to ask would be how they became rich and why they believed their pockets were sufficiently deep to finance such huge projects. On this point, Fithian's emphasis on luck needs more careful consideration. The architectural patrons in the study group exhibit behavior that indicates they were not entirely secure in their own economic rank and needed to devise schemes to ameliorate and consolidate their wealth. To be sure, there are no Horatio Alger stories to be told here. Even those architectural patrons who inherited very little through the accidents of birth started adult life with social and educational advantages that set them far above the ranks of other colonials. Nevertheless, there is an element of restless ambition in their economic behavior. To judge by the way they diversified their agricultural production, pursued lucrative professional occupations, attempted to manufacture goods, and engaged in commercial ventures, these are people who do not appear to believe in the inevitability of their own status.

Inheritance

Attempts to solidify a place more firmly in the social and economic hierarchy, however, must be seen against the background of the wealth that most already possessed through chance: their inheritance. Although the size of patrimony varied greatly, it was always enough to create a wide gulf between architectural patrons and other colonial Virginia landowners. Among the twenty-one individuals in the study group whose paternal inheritance is known, two were left cash bequests only (table 8). The remaining nineteen inherited land. Among those inheriting land, no reasonable estimate of real property can be made for either Landon Carter or John Randolph II. Not all land in Virginia was of equal value. Income from land planted in tobacco varied according to type, Sweet Scented or Oronoco. In other words, in any particular year, 100 acres in Lancaster County may not have been as productive and profitable as 100 acres in York County. Human labor was required to make any amount of land productive, and consequently usually only a fraction of land was under cultivation at any one time. Determining landholdings is, moreover, a highly conjectural exercise, but evidence from wills indicates that the average mean inheritance of the other seventeen men equaled 20,390 acres, with the average median at about 13,310 acres.[61] A wide disparity existed among the sizes of landed inheritance, ranging from Thomas Lee's 1,650 acres to Robert Beverley's 136,665 acres. Yet, even the smallest patrimony was substantially larger than most early eighteenth-century colonial Virginia plantations when estimates have been calculated. Keeping temporal distances in mind, the average size of landholding per county in 1704 ranged from 166 acres in Elizabeth City County to 936 acres in Henrico County, with a composite mean average of 496 acres.[62]

Only a slim majority of the patrons in the study group built their mansions upon inherited property. Thirteen patrons constructed their residences on land they inherited, ten on land acquired by purchase or patent, one by lease, and in one case, land acquisition is unclear. The amount of land inherited also does not seem to have affected the size or visual features of mansion design. Robert Beverley inherited the largest landed estate, about 136,665 acres. His main dwelling house at Blandfield can surely be counted as one of the largest, about 7,668 square feet, and the most formal in terms of planning principles of any of the houses in this study. Large size and a high degree of formality in plan also characterize Stratford Hall, about 9,730 square feet, built by Thomas Lee, who inherited a much more modest amount of land, about 1,650 acres. The more moderate scale of John Banister III's Battersea, about 3,705 square feet, and Richard Henry Lee's Chantilly, about 3,660 square feet, may reflect their more modest landed

Table 8

Inheritance

Patron	House	Building date	Cash bequest	Land bequests	Source of land on which mansion built
John Banister III	Battersea	1767	—	ca. 2,970 acres and 4 town lots	Inherited
Robert Beverley	Blandfield	1769	—	ca. 136,665 acres	Inherited
Sarah Taliaferro Brooke	Brooke's Bank	1751	£200 sterling	None	Unknown
Carter Burwell	Carter's Grove	1750	£100	ca. 14,372 acres	Inherited
Lewis Burwell III	Kingsmill	1725	—	ca. 6,200 acres	Inherited
John Carlyle	Carlyle House	1751	£300 sterling	None	Purchase or patent
Charles Carter	Cleve	1746	—	ca. 25,807 acres	Purchase or patent
Landon Carter	Sabine Hall	1738	—	Amount unknown	Purchase or patent
Robert Carter I	Corotoman	1720	—	ca. 13,310 acres	Inherited
Richard Corbin	Laneville	1758	—	ca. 14,000 acres	Inherited
William Fairfax	Belvoir	1741	Unknown	Unknown	Purchase or patent
William Fitzhugh	Chatham	1769	—	ca. 34,146 acres	Inherited
Benjamin Harrison IV	Berkeley	1726	—	ca. 14,600 acres	Inherited
Thomas Jefferson	Monticello I	1770	—	ca. 5,450 acres	Inherited
Richard Henry Lee	Chantilly	1761	£200	ca. 4,200 acres	Lease
Thomas Lee	Stratford Hall	1738	—	ca. 1,650 acres	Purchase or patent
George Mason IV	Gunston Hall	1752	—	ca. 14,032 acres	Inherited
John Mercer	Marlborough	1746	Unknown	Unknown	Purchase or patent
Mann Page I	Rosewell	1726	£2,000 sterling	ca. 7,900 acres	Inherited
Mann Page II	Mannsfield	1767	—	ca. 35,640 acres	Inherited
John Randolph II	Tazewell Hall	1758	—	Amount unknown	Inherited
William Randolph III	Wilton	1751	—	ca. 1,000 acres	Purchase or patent
Alexander Spotswood	Germanna	1721	Unknown	Unknown	Purchase or patent
John Tayloe II	Mount Airy	1760	—	ca. 19,662 acres	Inherited
John Thompson	Salubria	1763	Unknown	Unknown	Purchase or patent

inheritances, about 2,972 acres and 4,200 acres respectively. But Benjamin Harrison IV's mansion at Berkeley, about 4,920 square feet, and Lewis Burwell III's Kingsmill, about 4,880 square feet, are similar in size, material, and style, even though Harrison inherited more than twice as much land as Burwell: 14,600 acres as compared to 6,200 acres. The patrimony of George Mason IV, 14,032 acres, was substantially larger than the 7,900 acres inherited by Mann Page I, or the 5,450 acres left to Thomas Jefferson, yet the external form and interior plan of Mason's Gunston Hall was generally more traditional than Page's Rosewell or Jefferson's Monticello I, both of which demonstrated a stronger departure from conventional architectural norms. Clearly, degrees of wealth did not necessarily translate into distinct degrees of architectural refinement.

Sources of Income

While "blind stupid fortune" placed most architectural patrons in a category of wealth that was far removed from poor and middling Virginians, they needed to exploit that capital to produce the sort of money that both ensured their rank and allowed them to build monumental houses. All of them had to earn a living, and the source of that living was usually based on tobacco planting. The prodigy houses of eighteenth-century Virginia are, in fact, often referred to as the houses of the great planters. Yet even a cursory glance at the biographical record reveals the difficulty of assigning architectural patrons to a single occupational category (table 9).[63] Although the lack of complete data makes a precise account of the finances of an individual impossible, sufficient documentary data survive to show that many of these dwellings were built by persons for whom tobacco planting was not the sole source of income. Indeed, for a few of them, it did not even constitute the primary source of income. That the ability to build on a large scale, and the motivation for doing so, were not always confined to successful tobacco planting is most clearly demonstrated by the first-generation architectural patrons climbing to the ranks of wealth and prestige. Alexander Spotswood, William Fairfax, John Mercer, John Carlyle and John Thompson eventually accumulated large landed estates and engaged in agricultural pursuits, but none initially became rich as tobacco growers.

This is not to say that tobacco planting did not dominate the economy and the economic decisions made by mansion owners. Throughout the colonial period, tobacco represented the colony's single-largest cash crop, its chief source of government revenue, and the largest and most valuable export commodity from the North American mainland to Britain. Not only did fluctuations in the production and price of the staple affect the economy and political development of the colony, but the peculiarities of tobacco cultivation—a labor-intensive activity requiring much intuitive

Table 9
Sources of income

Patron	Tobacco planting	Agricultural diversification	Marketing tobacco for others	Plantation management for others	Ownership of trading vessels	Commercial trade	Industry	Other businesses	Leasing land to tenants	Land speculation
John Banister III	Yes	—	Yes	Yes	Yes	—	Milling	—	—	Yes
Robert Beverley	Yes	Yes	—	—	—	—	—	—	Yes	—
Sarah Taliaferro Brooke	Yes	—	—	—	—	Yes	—	—	—	—
Carter Burwell	Yes	Yes	—	—	—	—	—	Ferry	—	—
Lewis Burwell III	Yes	—	—	—	—	—	—	—	—	—
John Carlyle	Yes	Yes	—	—	Yes	Yes	Mining, Milling	—	—	Yes
Charles Carter	Yes	Yes	—	—	—	Yes	Mining, Quarrying, Milling	Ferry, Tobacco warehouse	Yes	—
Landon Carter	Yes	Yes	—	—	—	—	Milling	Tobacco warehouse	Yes	—
Robert Carter I	Yes	Yes	—	—	Yes	—	Mining	Tobacco ware-house, Slave trade	—	—
Richard Corbin	Yes	Yes	Yes	—	—	—	Milling	—	—	—
William Fairfax	Yes	—	—	—	—	—	—	—	—	—
William Fitzhugh	Yes	Yes	—	—	—	Yes	Brewery, Milling	—	Yes	—
Benjamin Harrison IV	Yes	Yes	—	—	Yes	Yes	Milling	—	—	—
Thomas Jefferson	Yes	Yes	—	—	—	—	Mining, Milling, Nailery, Cloth weaving	—	—	—
Richard Henry Lee	Yes	Yes	Yes	Yes	Yes	—	Salt making	Slave trade	Yes	Yes

Name	C1	C2	C3	C4	C5	C6	C7	C8	C9	C10
Thomas Lee	Yes	—	—	—	Yes	—	—	Tavern, Ferry, Tobacco warehouse, Slave trade	—	Yes
George Mason IV	Yes	Yes	—	Yes	—	—	—	Ferry	Yes	Yes
John Mercer	Yes	—	Yes	Yes	—	Yes	Brewery, Milling	Tobacco warehouse	Yes	Yes
Mann Page I	Yes	—	—	—	—	—	Mining	Tobacco warehouse	—	—
Mann Page II	Yes	Yes	—	—	Yes	—	Mining	Tobacco warehouse, Slave trade	—	Yes
John Randolph II	Yes	—	Yes	—	—	—	—	Slave trade	—	Yes
William Randolph III	Yes	Yes	Yes	—	—	—	—	—	—	—
Alexander Spotswood	Yes	Yes	Yes	Yes	—	—	Mining, Quarrying	Tavern	Yes	—
John Tayloe II	Yes	—	—	—	—	—	Mining, Milling	—	—	Yes
John Thompson	Yes	—	—	—	—	—	—	—	—	—

skill as well as luck—also had an impact on the psychology of producers.[64] In an admirably concise turn of phrase, Benedict Leonard Calvert summarized the importance of tobacco in 1726: "In Virginia and Maryland Tobacco is our Staple, is our All, and Indeed leaves no room for anything Else."[65]

The domination of tobacco is reflected in the economic history of the architectural patrons in the study group; all twenty-five patrons engaged in tobacco planting. However, the extent to which each relied on tobacco as the chief source of wealth varied. Not only did several engage in more than one major occupation over the course of a lifetime, but a person's primary occupation was not always the most significant source of his income. Therefore, instead of trying to sort individuals by discrete occupational categories, we will examine the various means by which they tried to grasp the golden ring.

Agricultural diversification was a widespread economic strategy among architectural patrons.[66] Unlike the sugar plantations of the West Indies, the tobacco plantations of Virginia produced many of their own foodstuffs as early as the mid-seventeenth century.[67] Not only did Virginia grow sufficient food for its own consumption, but it also made enough to export. Nine years after Calvert's assertion that tobacco was Virginia's "All," John Custis wrote a letter divulging the way he ameliorated his tobacco cash crop: "as for those peas you call Italian beans wee call them black eyd indian peas and I make yearly hundreds of bushes [bushels] of them and ship them to the West Indies, [where] some times they answer well.[68] Throughout the colonial period, a few colonial planters attempted to introduce new cash crops such as mulberry trees for silk production, olive trees, or viticulture.[69] Tobacco, however, remained Virginia's single-largest export. Near the end of the colonial period, agricultural diversification became increasingly common, especially among more ambitious landowners.[70] The shift was noted by the anonymous author of *American Husbandry* (London, 1775), who claimed that among the colony's planters, "none of them depend on tobacco alone, and this is more and more the case since corn has yielded a high price, and since their grounds have begun to be worn out. They all raise corn and provisions enough to support the family and plantation, besides exporting considerable quantities; no wheat in the world exceeds in quality that of Virginia and Maryland.... It is no slight benefit to be able to mix tobacco planting with common husbandry; this is as easily done as can be wished, and is indeed the practice of the greatest planters."[71] The claim of the author of *American Husbandry* is borne out in the study group: fifteen architectural patrons engaged in at least one form of agricultural production other than tobacco planting. For George Mason IV of Gunston Hall, agricultural diversification may have been aimed chiefly at increasing the self-sufficiency of his plantations. For others, the purpose of diversification was additional cash revenue, either by selling within the colony or by exporting.

Efforts at agricultural diversification met with varied success depending on demand and the cost of production. Robert Beverley's hemp, Thomas Jefferson's sheep, and William Randolph III's potash were all disappointments, as were the several attempts at wine and silk production. The production of lumber, naval stores, cider, and brandy appears to have been more successful. The most lucrative form of agricultural diversification was the cultivation of small grain, particularly after midcentury, when poor harvests in Europe increased demand dramatically. In 1768, Landon Carter of Sabine Hall noted optimistically that Virginia "might become a kind of granary to most parts of Europe."[72] The shift to grain was not universal. Tobacco remained the largest export commodity of Virginia, and patrons such as Richard Corbin and Thomas Jefferson still relied on it as their primary cash crop. In 1760, Richard Corbin sold 191,630 pounds of tobacco on consignment, which, at 2s. 73d. sterling per pound, would have yielded him about £2,172 sterling in gross income.[73] A tax of 2s. per 500-pound weight would have reduced this to about £2,133 sterling, and various freight, handling, and commission charges decreased the sum further, by as much as 10 percent.[74] But whatever his final net income, the sheer volume of Corbin's tobacco transactions made him unusual among planters. According to historian Aubrey C. Land, only 2 percent of all producers in Maryland between 1750 and 1759 cultivated tobacco crops larger than 10,000 pounds.[75]

Some savvy planters recognized that the production side of agriculture, no matter how progressive or productive the planter, was not always sufficiently profitable. In 1751, John Smith of Virginia wrote to Edward Ambler, then in England, asking for Ambler's advice concerning educational and career opportunities for Smith's son Austin. Looking around for opportunity, Smith admitted, "I should be glad he would be fond of some business for planting alone is poor doings, but with other businesses it answers very well."[76] Seventy-five years later, Jefferson likewise acknowledged the limitations of depending entirely on agricultural production when he claimed that "a Virginia estate managed rigorously well yields a comfortable subsistence to its owner living on it, but nothing more."[77]

Maximizing marketing opportunities offered an alternative to relying on the production side of agriculture. To some extent, all successful planters had to be astute businessmen, for success required not only skillful cultivation but also an understanding of management and marketing methods. Over the course of the eighteenth century, British grammar schools increasingly taught the kind of accounting procedures necessary to keep track of hogsheads, commodity prices, and exchange rates, and those who attended grammar school in England may have learned commercial fundamentals as part of their formal instruction. For Robert Carter I, business knowledge came in the form of apprenticeship to Mr. Bailey in London. Others acquired such skills from relatives.

Apart from managing their own affairs, some planters exercised their business acumen in the broader economic field. At least five men marketed tobacco for other planters or small farmers, and two of these seem to have acted as resident agents for British mercantile firms. John Carlyle, Richard Henry Lee, and Thomas Lee served as business or plantation managers for relatives residing in England but owning property in Virginia. Seven men had part ownership of trading vessels. Many large plantation owners sold manufactured British goods to their smaller neighbors, especially before the establishment of the largely Scottish system of direct purchase supplanted the consignment or commission method of marketing tobacco.[78] Only a handful, however, engaged in commerce as a significant source of income, and only John Carlyle could be classified strictly as a professional merchant throughout his whole life.

The traditional image of the tobacco planter and the Virginia mansion is also modified by the twelve architectural patrons who were involved in extractive or manufacturing processes. Eight were engaged in iron mining,[79] William Fitzhugh and John Mercer invested in breweries, Charles Carter and Alexander Spotswood owned quarries, John Banister III and Thomas Jefferson owned commercial mills, Richard Henry Lee produced salt, and Jefferson established a nailery and cloth-weaving operation. At least eleven patrons possessed gristmills or sawmills, which existed not only to satisfy the needs of the patron's own plantations but also to provide additional income. The owner collected legally fixed fees, or tolls, when his neighbors used the gristmills, while lumber produced at sawmills was sold both in Virginia and abroad. The success of these ventures varied. While the iron mines of Alexander Spotswood and John Tayloe II turned a profit, the Frying Pan Company mine owned by members of the Carter and Page families was a complete failure. The commercial flour mill of John Banister III was the chief source of his fortune, but the brewery established by John Mercer added nothing but debt, as did the commercial mill, nailery, and cloth-weaving ventures of Thomas Jefferson. There were other ventures that promised, but did not always deliver, extra income to risk-taking architectural patrons. Four of them owned ferries, seven owned public tobacco warehouses, and at least two, Alexander Spotswood and Thomas Lee, owned ordinaries, or taverns. Five men sold slaves on consignment.

Patenting large tracts on the frontier afforded the owner with fresh land for future tobacco cultivation and also held out the possibility of profits through land speculation.[80] Rent paid in commodities or cash by the tenants who farmed these tracts was probably among the most widespread sources of additional income. At least nine men collected rents, but doubtless there were many others who leased portions of their property. The profitability of land speculation and leasing appears to have been greatest when the property was acquired before midcentury. During and after the French and Indian War, the process of acquiring a clear title to large tracts on the frontier beyond the Shenandoah Valley became more difficult, but nine patrons are known to have been involved in land speculation at this time either through joint stock land companies or acting as urban developers.

The practice of law offered yet another potentially profitable and steady source of income. In the same letter of 1751, John Smith passed on the following gossip to Edward Ambler: "I hear that my Coz. John has got the better of his Law scruples and determines to follow that business. I heartily wish him success in it and if he will be diligent there is nothing surer as to profit, our Country pays a great sum yearly to them and dayly increase."[81] Smith's evaluation of the law profession in Virginia is confirmed by other evidence. According to the historian A. G. Roeber, most lawyers at midcentury were able to earn at least £500 per annum by practicing in the county court system.[82] Both the high salaries of lawyers and the litigious nature of colonial society attracted an increasing number of men to the profession. Roeber calculates that from 1740 to 1750 there was one lawyer for every 500 Virginians, and from 1760 to 1770 the ratio decreased to one lawyer for every 338 Virginians.[83] By the eve of the Revolution, however, some lawyers experienced difficulty in collecting their fees, and the profession seems to have become less lucrative. Among the twenty-five persons in the study sample, four practiced law, but they also combined this occupation with other income-producing pursuits.

Some architectural patrons practiced other professions, not all of them lucrative. John Thompson, for example, was a Church of England clergyman by profession. The standard salary allotted to ministers from parishes amounted to 16,000 pounds of tobacco, which varied in worth, depending on type of tobacco, quality of the leaf, and European demand. His salary and the income from parish land set aside for his house and use, called glebe land, would have allowed him to live a respectably genteel life.[84] It would not have allowed him to build a mansion like Salubria. Like other Virginia ministers, Thompson purchased land of his own and earned additional income from planting. His big windfall came, though, when he married the widow of Alexander Spotswood and gained access to her property. Several men won other profitable positions within the colonial or United States government. Five patrons were officers in the colonial customs service, four served as chief executive of Virginia, two worked as clerk of the House of

Burgesses, Spotswood was named deputy postmaster general of British North America, Richard Corbin was appointed deputy receiver general, John Randolph II acted as attorney general, and Thomas Jefferson would one day serve as president of the United States. Yet none of these patrons engaged in politics as his sole occupation over the entire course of his life. Three men at one time or another worked as the land agent for the proprietor of the Northern Neck, the land between the Rappahannock and Potomac rivers. Those who occupied this choice job received profits from the office and, more importantly, were able to select and grant the best tracts in the Northern Neck to members of their own family or to associates.

Property Valuation

Clearly, architectural patrons had a voracious appetite for making money. But just how rich were these supposedly genteel planters? Evaluating the wealth of an individual in eighteenth-century Virginia is extremely speculative. Real estate mentioned in a will may not be listed by acreage, and inventories only rarely list tracts of land. Personal estate records, too, are often flawed. In Virginia, appraised inventories were not always required, and when they were, compliance was rarely uniform. John Tayloe II and Landon Carter specifically requested in their wills that no appraisal be made. The heirs of William Fairfax displayed only four slaves for appraisers to value.[85] Additionally, many of the court records of inventories have been lost or destroyed. Consequently, somewhat comprehensive appraised inventories exist for only six men (table 10). Among these, John Thompson's probate records offer the best focus for analysis and comparison because his inventory is appraised, appears to be complete and accurate, and contains a list of his landholdings. The value of Thompson's total personal property equaled £3,364 12s. 11d., or about £2,691 sterling, an indisputable mark of wealth. Again, according to Land, only 7 percent of testators in Maryland the 1760s possessed personal estates grossing more than £1,000 sterling.[86] Compared to estimates made by the economic historian Alice Hanson Jones, Thompson's personal property alone was about four times as large as the total physical wealth, including land, held by the average free adult male dying in Chesterfield, Fairfax, or Spotsylvania Counties in 1774.[87]

Enslaved human beings represented a large portion of the value of Thompson's personal property. The thirty-nine slaves he owned were appraised from between £10 and £85 current money and totaled £2,405 current money (£1,924 sterling). Enslaved human beings accounted for 71 percent of his personal estate, leaving nonhuman movable property worth £767 sterling. The fact that Thompson owned slaves was not unusual, for historians have estimated that, in the second half of the eighteenth century, between 51 and 78 percent of households possessed human chattel.[88] The

Table 10
Personal property valuations

Patron	Date property was valued	Personal property
Robert Beverley	September 1800	$104,230 (about £23,513 sterling) at two plantations £15,780 9s. 8d. (about £11,865 sterling) at three other plantations
John Carlyle	November 1780	£4,718 2s. 9d. (about £2,735 sterling)
William Fitzhugh	April 1810	$47,500 82s. (about £12,098 sterling)
Thomas Lee	September 1758	£1,453 7s. 6d. (about £1,076 sterling) not including slaves
Alexander Spotswood	January 1742	£1,139 7s. 10d. (about £949 sterling) including slaves
John Thompson	March 1773	£3,364 12s. 11d. (about £2,691 sterling)

number of slaves he owned, however, set him apart. According to Jones's analysis of 1774 probate records in Chesterfield, Fairfax, and Spotsylvania Counties, an average of 8.7 slaves were owned per household. Only 4.1 percent of all Virginia households possessed more than twenty-six slaves.[89] An average of eleven slaves could be found per household in Richmond County in 1783, with 11.4 percent of households owning more than sixteen slaves.[90] Thompson's slaves also appear to have been somewhat more valuable than average. The mean appraised worth of his thirty-nine slaves equaled about £49 sterling. By comparison, the average purchase price of a slave in 1773 to 1775 was about £44 sterling throughout the Chesapeake region, and only £33 sterling in 1774 in Chesterfield, Fairfax, and Spotsylvania Counties.[91]

Thompson's real estate is more difficult to assign value. Land prices varied considerably in colonial Virginia, depending on soil, location, and market pressure. In June 1752, Thompson paid £200 current money (about £156 sterling), or slightly more than 10s. sterling per acre, for the land on which his mansion was eventually constructed. In October 1764, he paid £28 5s. (about £18 sterling) for a single lot in Fredericksburg. By comparison, in 1769 and 1770 William Fitzhugh was able to command only slightly less than 5s. sterling per acre for the 8,997 acres he sold.[92] If an average of 10s. sterling per acre is used, then the 7,705 acres listed in Thompson's will would have been worth perhaps £3,852 10s. sterling. Real property, therefore, may have represented 59 percent of his total physical wealth.

The size of Thompson's landed estate amply demonstrates the economic distance between architectural patrons and the general population of colonial Virginia. In 1764, Thompson was assessed for 7,653 acres in Culpeper County. By contrast, data from Louisa and Goochland Counties in 1763 and 1767 show that of the 76 percent of households that owned, rather than rented land, the median number of acres possessed was 350. In 1768 in James City County, 70 percent of households owned land, with an average median size of only 210 acres.[93] Thompson may not have been the richest man, or the largest landowner among the architectural patrons in the study group, but he held far more capital in the form of land than the vast majority of his fellow Virginians.

The overall financial picture that emerges among patrons of Virginia's prodigy houses hardly matches an image of an indolent aristocrat disdainful of dirtying his hands with filthy lucre. Rather, something of the hustle, of looking out for the main chance in their financial activities emerges. Most assuredly, mansion owners did not lead lives of servile manual labor, but labor they did. Beneath a veneer of courtly manners and high-style architecture appear the remnants of an economic insecurity that manifested itself in diverse strategies for maximizing sources of income.[94] Not all of their economic ventures were successful, but it is clear that throughout the eighteenth century, patrons of genteel houses—from Robert Carter I and Alexander Spotswood in the 1720s to Richard Henry Lee and Thomas Jefferson in the early Republic—were seeking ways of expanding their economic base. Tobacco planting constituted the most prevalent occupation and source of wealth, yet none of the architectural patrons were content to rely on that commodity alone, and a few were able to obtain their riches through alternative endeavors such as the practice of law, or mercantile or proto-industrial occupations.[95] The mansions of eighteenth-century Virginia most accurately symbolize a broader economic success, not only because of the prevailing tobacco culture but also, to some extent, despite it.

The Larger British Context

Thompson and his architectural cohorts were definitely among an exceedingly small pool of colonials who could be called gentlemen. In Allan Kulikoff's estimation, the term "gentleman" could be applied to only 2 or 3 percent of the population. Similarly, Rhys Isaac has argued that only 2 percent of white adult males in midcentury Lancaster County could claim "unchallengeable status as gentlemen."[96] While men like Thompson were at the pinnacle of the colonial Virginia hierarchy, their status as high-ranking gentlemen within the wider scope of the British Empire was on shakier ground. It has been proposed that £500 per annum was required to move into the ranks of gentlemen in Virginia. In March 1771, Landon Carter recorded in his diary: "I find it has not for some years been less than £400 the year that has maintained my family in everything, tools, etc."[97] While that might have represented a princely sum in the colony, it did not approach the standards of wealth and income that defined the English, Scottish, or West Indian elite. Compared to the wealth of Englishmen, Richard Corbin's gross tobacco receipts of £2,172 sterling in 1760 would have placed him within the ranks of the lesser gentry with incomes of £1,000 to £3,000, not alongside the wealthy gentry with incomes of £3,000 to £4,000, nor among the great landlords with annual incomes of between £10,000 and £50,000.[98] Even the wealthiest Virginian fell short of accumulating the kind of wealth that could be made in the British West Indies. Robert Carter I's estate was not appraised, but if we generously assume his 200,000 acres to have been worth 10s. per acre, his 772 slaves and servants to have been worth £25 each, and add the £10,000 he purportedly held in cash, then his estate would have amounted to £129,300.[99] The estate of Peter Beckford of Jamaica, on the other hand, has been estimated as worth £283,696 in 1739.[100] Most Virginia architectural patrons, moreover, were far less wealthy than Robert Carter I. The value of John Thompson's personal property comes closer to that of a prosperous Glasgow bookbinder leaving an estate of £3,600 in 1745 than it does to a successful English tobacco merchant leaving an estate of £30,000 in 1785, or to a London aristocrat possessing hundreds of thousands of pounds sterling.[101]

As a whole, Virginia architectural patrons did not measure up to this broader scale of wealth that defined the English political elite. Instead, most fell into the category of the upper middle class.[102] Such economic differences in scale between the Virginia and British elites would be of minor importance if the colony had been a self-contained cultural entity. The comments of contemporary writers indicate, however, that the culture of the Virginia elite was anything but self-contained. Members of the Virginia elite were after all Englishmen, and their education, commercial connections, and system of law all repeatedly underscored England as the key cultural reference. Blessed with fortunes that were monumental by Virginia standards, these upwardly mobile members of the Virginia elite adapted the outward signs of the English elite, including fashions, manners, and aesthetic preferences. In fact, the members of the Virginia elite appear to have been more covetous of the accoutrements of status than their English economic counterparts. The author of *American Husbandry* (1775) alluded to the paradox of the style of living among Virginia's privileged class when he claimed that "in most articles of life, a great Virginia planter makes a greater show and lives more luxuriously than a country gentleman in England, on an estate of three or four thousand pounds a year."[103] Despite their immense wealth compared to fellow colonials, elite Virginians seemed anxious about their position and like other nouveaux riches found comfort in presenting and re-presenting outward signs of privilege. In *Letters from America . . . from 1769, to 1777,* William Eddis noted this curious theater of consumption: "I am almost inclined to believe that a new fashion is adopted earlier by the polished and affluent Americans, than by many opulent persons in the great metropolis."[104] Through consumption, elite Virginians attempted to emulate the genteel life of the English country gentleman and sought to create a society in which wealth, political power, and social standing was guaranteed at birth. To Englishmen like Eddis, though, aping the cultural practices of the British elite only made colonial elites look ludicrous. Nevertheless, it was the perspective of Britain that mattered most to the builders of Virginia's prodigy houses. The major source of perceived social and economic competition for architectural patrons was not the small landowner with a few slaves. Rather, in their attempts to optimize their wealth, Virginia architectural patrons were competing with each other and with the British gentry.

Taking the measure of architectural patrons must be approached from multiple viewpoints. From the perspective of a smart, hardworking, but poor academic like Fithian, "blind stupid fortune" had endowed Virginia's planters with disproportionate wealth that put them at the top of the social hierarchy and led them to imagine, erroneously, their own right to inherited privilege. From the perspective of the British social elite, on the other hand, successful Virginia planters must have looked like presumptuous strivers. From the perspective of the Virginia elite, their success in the colony must have seemed wonderfully fortunate, even providential. But it was not guaranteed and needed to be secured by advantageous marriage alliances, education, economic diversification, and perhaps by the creation and display of an elite house. The architectural patrons of Virginia's prodigy houses worked hard to convince themselves, as Fithian observed, that they were "much above other Men in worth."

"Reason Reascends Her Throne"

The Impact of Dowry

It is not likely that Anne Randolph had architecture in mind when she warned young women not to put their faith in romantic love when choosing a husband. Her hard-headed view of marriage, however, lies at the heart of one of the sub-rosa aspects of high-style houses, namely the influence of dowry money. In her 1788 letter to St. George Tucker, Randolph expressed her deep reservations about consenting to the marriage of her fifteen-year-old daughter. She specifically cautioned against the illusory nature of youthful infatuation that leads one to "think everybody perfect that we take a fancy to." Selecting the wrong husband was particularly dangerous because "a Woman's happiness depends entirely on the husband she is united to . . . the risk tho always great, is doubled when they marry very young." The excitement of courtship inevitably cools and they discover "foibles." If the couple fails to find "esteem and Friendship, they must be wretched, without a remedy." Unlike those who saw romantic attachment as liberating, Randolph argued for a more pragmatic liaison that would suffice when, as she said, "the delirium of love is over and Reason is allowed to reascend her Throne."[1] I would like to think that when reason did reascend her throne, she found comfort and reassurance in an elegant house—a house secured through her dowry.

Romantic love, what Randolph saw as mere youthful infatuation, was acknowledged as a part of a successful union in both England and Virginia, but, among the wealthy, the economic function of marriage remained an equal, even greater, component. As William Byrd II's sister-in-law bluntly put it in 1741: "Beauty without money seldom avails much in this present age."[2] Yet the historian Lawrence Stone viewed emotional attachment as a crucial component of what he called "affective individualism" in early modern England. He also proposed that it served to balance the severity of patriarchal control within nuclear families.[3] By the eighteenth century, another emotive concept—namely, romantic attachment—fed by drama and widely distributed novels such as Samuel Richardson's *Pamela,* created demand for a nonmonetary foundation for marriage.[4] And yet, parallel to these novel concepts of emotion, marriage continued to be viewed as a financial transaction, especially among propertied classes anxious to control their wealth from beyond the grave. Because marriage usually produces children and serves as a conduit through which to transfer property from one generation to the next, the arrangement of financially beneficial alliances proved a powerful antidote to the delirium of love. Fortunes were, after all, at stake. This tension between a romantic view of marriage and a more businesslike outlook offers a useful analytic tool for examining the question of women and architecture in eighteenth-century Virginia. More specifically, an examination of the wealth an elite woman brought to her marriage through her dowry may shed light on how Virginia prodigy houses were financed and how this wealth may have subtly altered the dynamics of legal patriarchy.

The question of the relationship between women and their houses is complex because, with few exceptions, while her husband was alive, he owned the house. Accepting the primacy of private property almost as an article of faith, architectural historians have interpreted residential building as a reflection of the character of that titleholder. Because men hold title and usually pass it on to their sons, there is a tendency to analyze houses in strictly patrilineal terms. However, by following dowry wealth, dower rights, and how these legal devices might have been connected to a prodigy house, an alternative matrilineal pattern can be discovered.

How many dowries were actually used for construction cannot be determined, but the inheritance laws and testamentary customs of colonial Virginia were such that marriage portions compel more than passing interest. An inquiry into dowry, among the other sources of wealth that made the erection of an elite dwelling possible, offers a useful tool of analysis. Not only does the search for patterns of inheritance tell us something about women and architecture, but it also serves to illuminate the overlapping spheres of meaning attached to the physical space of dwelling.

Evaluating the impact of dowry on the creation of a prodigy house can be seen as part of a larger project to determine how elite women in colonial and early republican Virginia influenced architecture. One approach would be to ask whether women participated in the physical labor, commissioning, or design of buildings. The answer would be that in early Virginia women impacted the built environment in all these ways.

At the most fundamental and morally compelling level, it is essential to begin by recognizing the innumerable and anonymous enslaved women who labored within these built environments as unskilled manual laborers. In his account book from the late 1760s, Jefferson coolly calculated the limits of strength and endurance of two enslaved adolescent girls and four boys who labored to excavate the cellar of Monticello in subfreezing temperatures.[5] Jefferson's easy exploitation of black females deeply contrasted with his attitude toward elite white females. Like many of his privileged male contemporaries, Jefferson convinced himself of the limited scope of activity and influence of genteel white women, which "fortunately for the happiness of the sex itself, does not endeavor to extend itself, in our country, beyond the domestic line."[6] Despite the official line toward proper elite feminine behavior and occupations, however, even privileged women could be engaged in the building process.

Occasionally, women acted as patrons of architecture and as financiers of public buildings. For example, Bridget Peirce, Susannah Randolph, Margaret Griffen, Tabitha Adams, Martha Todd, Anne Gough, and Elizabeth Dawson each served as both the proprietors and builders of public tobacco warehouses or wharves in the mid-eighteenth century.[7] Used for the official inspection of Virginia's principal export commodity, tobacco warehouses were rarely the substantial masonry buildings depicted on the cartouche of the 1747 Peter Jefferson/Joshua Fry map. Instead, they were usually rudimentary frame edifices. The one built by Bridget Peirce was described as "a House Thirty Feet in Length, Twenty Feet in Breadth, with an Eight Feet Shed on each Side and a Plank Floor of Twenty Feet Square."[8] The seven women recorded as builders acted not as the manual laborers who physically erected these structures, but rather as general contractors who financed or oversaw construction. Some of the women were widows carrying on the work of their late husbands. As one might expect, such industrious women were drawn primarily from the middle class, but among them was the widow of the late attorney general and speaker of the House of Burgesses, Susannah Randolph.[9]

Brooke's Bank, built by another widow, Sarah Taliaferro Brooke, represents one of the most significant examples of female architectural patronage in colonial Virginia. In her will of 1763, she was particularly careful to note "the mansion built by me," a forthright declaration of ownership on a legal document made not because she was proud, but because she was claiming control over its future use.[10] Brooke's architectural authorship of a prestige house is not unique in the English-speaking world. Among the more well-studied instances are Elizabeth Hardwick's building projects at Hardwick Hall, the Duchess of Lauderdale's remodeling of Ham House, and Anne Clifford's amazing castle-remodeling frenzy that successfully led to the legal recovery of her inheritance.[11]

More rarely do we have evidence that allows us to glimpse how women made decisions about specific parts of the built environment. After her husband's death, Maria Taylor Byrd managed the Westover plantation and maintained its architectural integrity. In 1761, she informed her long-absent son, William Byrd III: "I have the bricklayer now at work repairing the walls of both gardens. The bricks not being well burnt there wants a great deal to be done."[12] The letter suggests both Mrs. Byrd's ability to direct laborers and her capacity to judge the quality of materials.

At Mount Vernon, Martha Washington shaped interior space by opting for unostentatious but genteel ornament while George Washington was in Massachusetts preparing for war. On 15 October 1775, Lund Washington, a distant relative and manager of Mount Vernon, wrote to George that the plaster work in the dining room was almost complete and that work would soon commence in another room. Lund then wrote: "Mrs. Washington seems desirous that whatever is to be done to it may be at once [so] that she may get into it this winter. . . . She intends to talk to Col. Fielding Lewis . . . about it."[13] Fielding Lewis married George's sister, Betty, and shared with Washington the services of the anonymous artisan who decorated the Mount Vernon dining room and created the shallow, attenuated relief ornament in the Lewises' bedchamber ceiling in a neoclassical style associated with the eighteenth-century British architect Robert Adams. A month later, Martha had made her decision. According to Lund, "Mrs. Washington concluded to [make] the room intended for her chamber done quite plain, no ornaments upon the ceiling, the sides plain stucco."[14] Martha rejected the metropolitan style of her in-laws, and her aesthetic choice reveals a preference for convenience, expediency, and prudence in the face of British invasion over a display of wealth and fashion.

Sometimes women played a more collaborative role. An informal conversation at Nomini Hall may attest to a wife's de facto but not de jure collaboration in construction. In his 1774 diary, the resident tutor, Philip Vickers Fithian, recorded that his employers, Robert Carter III and his wife, Frances Anne Tasker Carter, "showed me their house, the original design, the present form, and what is yet to be done."[15] Fithian's choice of pronoun hints that ideas for remodeling came about because of dialogue between a companionate wife and husband. Such small domestic episodes of affective relations between spouses suggest that in day-to-day dealings—events hardly ever preserved in the historical record—a married woman could express her wishes and exert her preferences in architectural design. Fithian's diary entry certainly seems to undermine the patriarchal rhetoric of a wife's absolute submission to her husband. But intrafamilial emotional links did nothing to assuage the prevailing legal hobbling of women's property rights.

Understanding women's legal position vis-à-vis prodigy houses requires some knowledge of basic terms and concepts.[16] In order to exploit money trails and the descent of property as a methodological term of inquiry, we need first to become familiar with this broader legal context of the dowry, or dotal, system and have a clear picture of marriage rituals in colonial Virginia. Under English common law—and this is a key point in regard to women and their dwellings—all property of a married woman became the property of her husband, under a principle known as coverture. As Anne Randolph must have explained to her fifteen-year-old daughter, the thrill and gaiety of courtship would be replaced upon marriage by the sobering reality of legally and religiously sanctioned subjugation of the wife to the will of her husband. While a single woman, a feme sole, could own and control property, a wife, feme covert, lost any legal identity separate from that of her husband and had no ability to conduct business on her own. He controlled all profits accruing from her property and, under certain conditions, could sell it. As William Blackstone explained it: "By marriage, the husband and wife are one person in law: that is, the very being or legal existence of the women is suspended during the marriage, or at least is incorporated and consolidated into that of the husband."[17]

This basic powerlessness of females to hold possession necessarily affected inheritance patterns. Sons were usually given land and slaves. Until the practice was abolished by law in 1776, that land was often entailed from generation to generation upon the eldest son of the eldest son, etc., a provision intended to eliminate alienation of capital assets, that is, the sale of real property to people outside of the family.[18] Following a testamentary pattern established among the landed gentry in England, the eldest son in colonial Virginia received the largest portion of inheritance along with, significantly, the mansion house. Known as primogeniture, this rule of inheritance was more strictly enforced in land-poor England than in land-rich Virginia, where wealthy fathers and mothers strove to ensure that all their sons started their adult lives with a landed estate.[19]

Given that bequests of land to a daughter effectively meant alienating land, the wealthiest fathers were reluctant to give land or the slaves that were attached to that land to their daughters. Instead, fathers provided dowries, also called marriage portions, in the form of more liquid assets. Money or credit, however, may have held their own particular attraction insomuch as they could more easily and readily purchase imported building materials and skilled labor.[20] To what purpose the dowry or portion was applied remained the prerogative of the husband. Because he controlled all the couple's wealth, an improvident husband could fail to provide for his wife's maintenance if she should survive him, and even an elite woman could be pauperized.

Keeping this legal peril in mind, the perennially cranky Landon Carter of Sabine Hall withheld his daughter Judith's dowry when she married without his permission. Yet Carter's behavior was guided as much by a fatherly concern about the unpleasant reality of a married woman's legal status as by his imperious character. Carter continued to demonstrate his affective relationship with Judith by lending her some property after her marriage, but it was experience and legal knowledge that attached strings to the loan. He tried to explain his decision in a diary entry of 1774: "I had determined that whatever assistance she had from me everything should only be lent to her, to be returned by my Call, order, or appointment, how and when I should chuse. That I did not chuse to do it for her life because that would constitute A Property in her husband during that time, and might be removed for debt or otherwise. I know the family she married into . . . and that she might be made a beggar by whom she least expected."[21] Whether or not he correctly assessed his son-in-law, Carter knew well that romantic affection counted for nothing in protecting the property rights of married women after the delirium of love had passed.

Although the terms are related by their common Latin root for the verb "to endow," still the word "dowry" must be distinguished from "dower rights," that is, what wealth a woman could expect in case she became a widow.[22] Centuries-old English tradition provided a mechanism for some measure of support. If a husband died intestate, without a will, or if the widow were dissatisfied with the provisions in her husband's will, she had the right to claim her dower, or "widow's thirds," in court. In Virginia, a widow was allowed a life interest in one-third of her deceased husband's real property, and this third usually included the family's main dwelling house.[23] The general concept of "widow's thirds" was no colonial invention, but its legal definition varied over time and between regions. A widow's claim to one-third of her husband's real property—that is, land—was an Anglo-Saxon tradition reaching back to the seventh century AD.[24] In Virginia, her additional claim to a portion of personal property was established by statute law in 1664. Ideally, a woman's dowry and her reciprocal dower rights ensured that a widow would be maintained according to her status and quality. They served as a sort of life insurance policy. A more financially precise and secure form of dower rights could be determined via the creation of a jointure, that is, the establishment at the time of betrothal of designated property producing a fixed annuity for the widow, in lieu of her more customary one-third. For example, the 1743 will of William Byrd II specifies that his widow, Maria Taylor Byrd, was to have the yearly sum of £200 sterling in lieu of her dower.[25]

Play action in the game of dowry and dower rights in eighteenth-century Virginia commenced with the creation of romantic attachments at social events held at the homes of the well-to-do. Judging from the 1760 record of the courtship ritual of Robert Bolling and Anne Miller, graceful dancing, adept verbal flirtation, and passionate ardor figured prominently as critical tactical skills in courtship rituals in which adolescent girls were the center of attention by their swains.[26] Once serious emotional attachments were engendered, things got down to business quickly (fig. 71).[27] After a prospective suitor asked permission to pay his respects to a young woman, monetary negotiations between their fathers or guardians began. Marriage was understood as a matrimonial alliance between two families who provided the wealth to create a conjugal fund for the new household. Marriage agreements should not be confused with prenuptial contracts, which created a separate estate for a wife and gave her control over her own property. Prenuptial agreements rarely appear in the public records, and when they were written it was usually to protect the dower rights of a widow when she remarried.[28]

The aim of negotiating a satisfactory marriage contract was to balance, at least conceptually, the groom's portion of inheritance against a bride's dowry, which is why the word "dowry" is synonymous in records with marriage portion, or simply portion. The groom's father set out what he could give to his son at the time of marriage, and later at his death. Likewise, the bride's father announced how he would endow his daughter. Her wealth, or dowry, came to the groom around the time of the marriage, or upon the death of the bride's father, or it was divided and distributed at the two events. For example, in 1764 Thomas Walker of Castle Hill, Albemarle

Fig. 71. *Charles Concluding a Treaty of Marriage with the Daughter of the Nobleman,* engraving published by Carrington Bowles, London, 1787. (Colonial Williamsburg Foundation)

County, wrote a letter outlining his contribution to his son for the conjugal fund. He says: "My affairs are in an uncertain state; but I will promise one thousand pounds to be paid in 1766, and the further sum of two thousand pounds I promise to give him; but the uncertainty of my affairs prevents my fixing on a time of payment. The above sums are all to be in money or lands and other effects, at the option of my said son." Bernard Moore of King William County replied to Walker that although his financial affairs were also questionable, he would give an additional 500 pounds to what he had already promised as his daughter's share.[29] Walker's and Moore's hedging suggests that in negotiating an affinial connection, fathers played their cards close to the vest and that there was a dodgy line between generous and penurious settlements.

Among the colony's most elite families, determining jointure or even a less costly marriage settlement was a high-stakes game that offered the possibility of reshuffling the pecking order of social rank. Earlier in his life, William Byrd II had sought the hand of an English woman by promising in a letter to her father that he would settle his entire Virginia plantation upon her, including 43,000 acres and 220 enslaved men and women.[30] Apparently this was insufficient, and his bid for her hand failed. Subsequently, as a father of daughters Anne and Maria, Byrd stood on the other side of the table and probably demanded generous benefits to match his daughters' dowries. One prospective suitor for Anne's hand, Daniel Parke Custis (fig. 72), was rejected because his father refused to meet the demands of prospective in-laws. As William Byrd II's wife, Maria Taylor Byrd (fig. 73), who would later supervise the repair of brick walling, explained matter-of-factly in a letter of 20 November 1742 to the rejected beau:

> My Dear Mr. Custis I am heartily Concerned that we coud not bring your Father to agree to any Terms that were Reasonable; For without a Compliment I shoud (as you very well know) have preferd you to any other Match in the Colony. I here inclosed send you a Transcript, of what Mr. Byrd writ to Him, and likewise his Answer, that so you may descern the Sentiments of each Party. Miss Mina comes to pour Balm into your Wounds in her way to Sabine Hall.[31]

As a widower with four children, Landon Carter negotiated more successfully for the hand of Byrd's other daughter. Carter married Byrd's daughter Maria (fig. 74), who brought a handsome dowry of £1,500 sterling to the marriage.[32] We are, of course, not privy to the delicate conversations that occurred during negotiations between Byrd, Custis, and Carter, but I would like to suggest that fathers sought to ensure that their daughters, if widowed, and more importantly, their daughter's male heir, would inherit the prodigy house. Although there was no law compelling a husband

Fig. 72. John Wollaston, *Portrait of Daniel Parke Custis,* oil on canvas, 1755–57. (Washington-Custis-Lee Collection, Washington and Lee University, Lexington, Virginia)

to use his wife's property for any particular purpose, a father-in-law may have viewed his daughter's dowry as a means of providing her with shelter suitable to her station. In some cases, we do know that he negotiated with prospective in-laws so that the bride would have her portion, or "tithe," of dower in the mansion.

Unless title to real estate was transferred at the time of marriage, a record of the transaction need not have been entered into the colonial Virginia court. Unlike other early American colonies, early Virginia lawmakers had a more casual attitude toward private contracts.[33] Entry into the legal

Fig. 73. Unidentified artist, School of Godfrey Kneller, *Portrait of a Woman, called Maria Taylor Byrd,* oil on canvas, 1700–1725. (The Metropolitan Museum of Art, Fletcher Fund, 1925 [25.108]; photograph, all rights reserved, The Metropolitan Museum of Art)

and historical record in Virginia often occurred when things went badly, that is, when a private written agreement was contested, not fulfilled, or was placed in doubt because a father died intestate. At that point, it was brought before the House of Burgesses, a legislative body that also sat as a court of equity deciding cases on the basis of fairness. From the journals of the House of Burgesses we can extrapolate the usual procedure for marriage agreements from the context of those gone awry. One case recounts that William Robertson entered into an agreement with John Lidderdale setting forth that if Lidderdale married Elizabeth, Robertson's only daughter and heir, then Robertson would "settle upon" Lidderdale, Elizabeth, and any children the following: 330 acres of land in York County, a house and lots in Williamsburg, 2,800 acres in Hanover County, and 750 acres in Brunswick County. This was indeed a lavish wedding present. Despite its great value, the marriage agreement was not filed in court but was apparently stored in a safe place at Lidderdale's home, since we read that "the said William Robertson put into Writing, and signed; and delivered the same to the said John [Lidderdale]." Robertson died intestate, and Lidderdale went before the House of Burgesses seeking to gain control of the land on the basis of the private contract.[34]

Because marriage agreements, like that of Robertson and Lidderdale, were usually put into writing, signed, and delivered to the future husband,

Fig. 74. William Dering, *Portrait of Maria Byrd Carter,* oil on canvas, perhaps ca. 1744. (Courtesy of the College of William and Mary)

those contracts that went according to plan are often missing from the historical record, but some dowry data can be gleaned from testamentary evidence. Some fathers were quite explicit in revealing the entire extent of their daughter's dowry in a will. At other times, a will may declare a daughter's "fortune" without clarifying whether it referred to a marriage settlement or an additional inheritance. For example, John Grymes wrote in his last testament of 1747 that "whereas I have paid to Mr. Carter Burwell and to Mr. Mann Page respectively the sums of Twelve hundred and Fifty pounds Sterling I hereby declare the same to be in full of their Wives portions of my estate."[35] Landon Carter of Sabine Hall also clearly stated the extent of his daughter's marriage portion when he wrote, "Having paid one half (£400 Sterling) of my daughter Beverley's fortune, I direct the other half (£400 Sterling) to be paid."[36] On the other hand, the will of Peter Randolph simply says, "I give unto my dear daughter Ann Fitzhugh three hundred and fifty pounds current money," leaving the reader to speculate whether this was the full extent of her dowry.[37]

A woman's dowry may have significantly contributed to her husband's ability to build a mansion, including those owned by the twenty-five architectural patrons in the study group. The piecemeal character of the documentary evidence, however, means that the figures provided here should be approached cautiously; they represent only estimates rather than the exact size of a dowry. The total number of individual marriages among the architectural patrons in the study group equaled forty-one, but for sixteen of these alliances no estimation of the amount of wealth brought to a union can be determined.[38]

Evidence from the remaining marriages indicates that cash was the most popular form of wealth contributed by a wife. At least seventeen spouses brought money to architectural patrons. The dowries of women marrying for the first time ranged from £250 sterling going to Mann Page I of Rosewell to £2,000 sterling, which was the amount given to the wives of Richard Corbin of Laneville, Mann Page II of Mannsfield, and John Randolph II of Tazewell Hall. Anne Butler Brayne Spotswood (fig. 75), the decidedly unglamorous widow of former governor Alexander Spotswood, carried to her second marriage to Reverend John Thompson a heady jointure worth £2,750 sterling.[39] The average mean amount in dowry cash among the study group equaled about £1,115 sterling. Within the context of colonial Virginia, this would have been quite a prize and was somewhat more than twice the average total net worth of all testators in the older established counties of Virginia in 1774.[40]

A smaller number of marriage agreements in the study group provided dowries in the form of land or access to the profits from land. At least ten wives brought land to their husbands; sometimes they also contribut-

Fig. 75. Unidentified artist (English), *Portrait of Anne Butler Brayne Spotswood Thompson,* miniature, India ink on vellum, ca. 1724. (Virginia Historical Society, Richmond, Virginia)

ed cash. Real property varied in size from the profits from the 410 acres George Mason IV received from his father-in-law to the more than 11,000 acres Thomas Jefferson gained by marriage. Anne Butler Brayne Spotswood Thompson provided each of her two husbands with the profits from about 73 acres in England.[41] The average mean number of colonial acres amounted to about 3,890 acres with an average median of 3,396 acres.

This was not an inconsiderable amount of land when compared to the size of most plantations. For example, both Benjamin Harrison IV of Berkeley and Mann Page I of Rosewell operated and received the profits from plantations that were still technically owned by their father-in-law, Robert Carter I of Corotoman. Compared to figures from 1704 records of taxes paid to the Crown, known as the quitrent roll, Harrison's 2,870-acre tract in Henrico County was more than four times the size of the average plantation in that county, while Page's 5,346-acre tract in King and Queen County was more than thirteen times as large as the average plantation there.[42]

A husband required his wife's permission before he could sell land—a protection of her dower rights—but he retained control over the profits of her property as well as its diposition after his death. Some fathers-in-law, however, allowed a daughter's husband access to the profits without granting him outright ownership of the land. Robert Carter I's bequest of land to his daughter Anne and son-in-law Benjamin Harrison IV of Berkeley represents one such an arrangement. Harrison had rights to the profits from the land while living, but Carter entailed the land on Harrison's son, Carter Henry Harrison.[43]

One wonders how much construction these marriage portions covered. It has not been possible to calculate the total cost of a residence including the value of slave labor, but reasonable estimates have been made for public structures, where vestry and court officials more often recorded costs. Based on the vestry book records for three brick churches constructed in the 1730s, Dell Upton estimated an average per-square-foot price of 29s. Virginia currency (decimalized), or 5s. 10d.[44] The cost of Stratton Major church, begun in 1759, was somewhat higher: 6s. 6d. current money per square foot.[45] Including the expense of additional interior ornamentation at Pohick church, finished in 1774, the cost per square foot equaled 6s. 7d.[46] The cost of a brick public building, however, is not comparable to a multistoried brick dwelling. Additional interior load-bearing walls and multiple chimneys made a brick residence more expensive, but the most significant difference in cost was probably the degree and quality of interior and exterior ornamentation. Arlington, the Custis mansion on the Eastern Shore, was erected about 1670. Arlington was described by John Custis IV as a three-story brick building, measuring about 80 x 60 feet and costing £6,000.[47] If Custis's estimate is reliable, then Arlington would have cost 8 s. 4d. per square foot. The 1739 glebe house for St. Paul's Parish, presumably a much less luxurious residence, was built for only 4s. 8d. per square foot.[48] Admittedly, we are comparing apples and oranges, but the comparison does provide a glimpse of the possible impact of dowry funds.

Despite these variable costs, the average mean dowry in cash to architectural patrons, £1,115 sterling, could pay for a sizeable portion of a mansion. Maria Byrd's fortune of £1,500 sterling, worth £1,800 in current money in 1742, could have paid 121 percent of the debt incurred by Landon Carter in building Sabine Hall, a house containing 5,124 square feet and costing approximately £1,486 in current money if Upton's square-foot price of 29s. held in the 1740s.[49] Such an exercise, however, is no more than speculation. We do not yet have a clear picture of eighteenth-century construction prices. The value of the colony's paper money varied from county to county and often fluctuated monthly against the value of sterling, so that a reliable formulation of comparable building costs cannot be devised.[50] A dowry's measurable, proportional contribution to the overall cost of construction, therefore, remains unknown.

We can be assured, however, that for the groom, a generous dowry could dramatically improve his economic status. There was, though, something a bit tawdry about dowry negotiations, and the ambivalence with which the British elite confronted the conflict between marriage's affective properties and its economic consequences manifested itself in satire.[51] Tainted by the potential for gold-digging and its uncomfortable parallel to prostitution, dowry wealth became an easy target of tongue-wagging. In the process, an elite woman's identity and personhood were subsumed under her monetary value. In a wickedly snide letter of 1809 to her friend Rachael Mordecai, Sally Kennon wrote of "Bob Nelson's wedding; who was married yesterday, to a eight thousand pounder; a Miss Wilson."[52] The public press further displayed women as potentially valuable commodities. In the eighteenth century, the *Virginia Gazette* regularly reported the quality of marriage portions, or fortunes, as they were also called, in its social columns. Newspaper editors noted the conjoining of Mr. Beverley Randolph and Miss Betty Lightfoot, who is described as an "agreeable young lady with a fortune of upwards of five thousand pounds" and the nuptials of Ralph Wormeley "of fine Estate," and Sally Berkeley "a young Lady of great Beauty, and Fortune." The press also reported the more dubious match between William Carter, age twenty-three, and the widow Sarah Ellyson, age eighty-five, described as "a sprightly old tit with a three thousand pound fortune."[53] The last laugh might have been on William Carter, for widows who possessed property were far more likely than their blushing younger sisters to insist on prenuptial agreements.[54]

Standards of wealth, as measured by elite planter dowries, appear to be not far below those of the prosperous merchant classes of England. The largest dowries among the wives of the Virginia architectural patrons in the study group amounted to £2,000 sterling, but as we heard through Sally Kennon's gossip, Miss Wilson might have brought a dowry worth £8,000 pounds to her marriage. By comparison, one substantial London merchant gave his daughter £8,000 sterling, and William Shippen Jr. noted in 1759 that the *London Chronicle* had reported dowries of £10,000 and £15,000.[55]

English cultural production of the period recognized and mocked the tenuous link between dowry wealth and residential architecture. The conjoining of lucre and love lay at the crux of such moralizing literature as Samuel Richardson's tragic novel *Clarissa Harlowe*. It also served as the butt of satire. William Hogarth's 1742 pictorial series *Marriage à la Mode* narrates the sad outcome of a marriage of convenience between an impoverished, degenerate aristocratic family and a wealthy, social-climbing mercantile family of only gentry standing. In the first scene of the series, Hogarth depicts the signing of the marriage settlement (fig. 76). While the young couple obviously lacks romantic attachment, the groom's father, the Earl of Squanderfield, trades his ancient family tree for the rich merchant's profits. Where the dowry money is going to be spent is made clear in the background, where a bookkeeper comparing the architectural plans to the constructed Palladian house seen beyond the window discovers three columns on the ground floor and four above. Clearly, Hogarth intended to illustrate that the architectural patron lacked linguistic competency in fashionable architecture. It has been argued that Hogarth's contempt was

Fig. 76. William Hogarth, *The Marriage Settlement,* plate 1 from the *Marriage à la Mode* series, engraving by Gerard Jean-Baptiste Scotin, 1745. (Princeton University Library)

directed not only to marriage settlements but more directly to his personal enemy, William Kent, a principal designer of English Palladian architecture. Nevertheless, the combination of dowry money and academic-style architecture would have had to be recognizable to Hogarth's audience for the joke to work.[56]

A more serious example of pictorial evidence makes the same point: that the wealth a woman brought to a marriage could be entangled in architecture. An anonymous English painting, presently owned by Colonial Williamsburg and dated to the third quarter of the eighteenth century, appears to function neither as decoration nor as pure portraiture but rather as an artifact of an event, more serious in intent than the contemporary group portraits known as conversation pieces (fig. 77).[57] Formal analysis of the work repays the viewer not so much with aesthetic enjoyment as with clues to interpreting the image's lost documentary function. It is clear that, by virtue of her more bright pink dress and slightly larger scale, the woman on the left of the canvas serves as our central actor. The composition is divided between, on the left, the woman and a physically proximate young girl, likely her daughter, and on the right, an adult male with a young boy, likely his son, who holds a painting of a substantial framed house. Unfortunately the canvas was amputated beyond the boy. Positioned near the center, a clerk writes a new document that literally touches upon the subject of an older, once-sealed indenture. The inkwell and the position of the

Fig. 77. Unidentified artist (English), *Conversation Group,* 1775–1800. (Colonial Williamsburg Foundation)

woman's right hand suggest that she is about to sign the document, perhaps a prenuptial agreement. The most striking feature of the painting, however, is the pattern of gaze. All the actors look out at us as if to record their portraits, except the principal player, namely the woman on the left. She cares nothing for the viewer; she is mindful only of the house. Whatever the precise nature of the transaction, the painting records a meshing of the law, architecture, and a woman.

If a case can be made for the conjunction of a woman's portion on the one hand and creation of a prodigy house on the other, where is the proof in Virginia? Perhaps it was not just Hannah Ludwell Lee (fig. 78) but the persuasive power of her £600 sterling dowry that persuaded her husband to let her design Stratford Hall (fig. 79).[58] Thomas Lee's son Philip, believed that the functional accommodations at Stratford were the result of what he considered his mother's eccentric ideas. Later, Charles Lee recounted: "But admirable in every respect as the Stratford house was, I've heard that Colonel Philip used to complain of it and exhibit a picture of the house that his father had intended to build with the remark, 'See what it is to be ruled by a woman. I should have been now living in a house like this (showing the picture) had not my father been persuaded by his wife to put up this very inferior dwelling now over my head."[59] If Hannah was indeed responsible for the design of Stratford, it is tempting to think of her being inspired by her childhood home at Green Spring, outside of Jamestown (fig. 80), where the principal receptions rooms appear to have been located, as at Stratford, above the ground floor.[60]

Less speculative examples of the impact of the money a wife brought to a marriage also come to mind. Richard Taliaferro bequeathed the mansion he designed and built in the mid-1750s on the Palace Green in Williamsburg "to my Son in Law, Mr. George Wythe, and his wife, my Daughter Elizabeth" and their heirs.[61] The Richmond County mansion of Menokin, now only a ruin, also represents a bridal gift. In 1769, John Tayloe II of Mount Airy put his second daughter, Rebecca, and her new husband in possession of the 1,000-acre plantation known as Menokin. Construction seems to have started soon thereafter. John Tayloe claimed the land as his daughter's portion when he wrote in his 1773 will: "the deed I have made to my daughter Rebecca of the Menokin estate is to be reckoned in full for her fortune of the two Thousand pounds Sterling."[62] Yet he went on to stake a claim on the mansion by directing that the building was to be finished at the expense of his estate.[63] Tayloe's generous bequests of land and construction was unusual but not without precedent in colonial America. One of the more well-known houses literally built upon a daughter's wealth was the structure later known as the Old Feather Store in Boston. The land on which Thomas Stanbury built his house in 1680 was given to his wife,

Fig. 78. Attributed to Charles Bridges, *Portrait of Hannah Ludwell Lee,* ca. 1730 (Jessie Ball duPont Memorial Library, Robert E. Lee Memorial Association, Inc., Stratford Hall Plantation)

Susanna, in 1662. Susanna Walker Stanbury had received two urban lots from her parents upon her marriage for, as the deed claims, "divers considerations . . . and in particular, for the better livelihood & subsistence of our daughter."[64]

Menokin and the Stanbury House provide straightforward and incontrovertible evidence of the application of a woman's wealth toward the construction of an elite house, but other examples can be discovered by teasing out patterns from more circumstantial and complex records. By following the money through webs of kinship, legal papers, and architectural

Fig. 79. Stratford Hall, Westmoreland County, 1738. Land façade. (Photograph by author)

Fig. 80. Benjamin Henry Latrobe, *View of Green Spring House* (James City County), watercolor, 1796. (The Maryland Historical Society, Baltimore, Maryland)

projects, it becomes clear that dowry money and the assignment of dower rights served a critical function not only by cementing marriage alliances between wealthy families but also by strengthening the significance and power of female lines of descent through generations.

Take, for example, Robert Carter (fig. 81), his daughters, and their houses. Carter gave vast amounts of land to his sons, and each of the surviving sons built a monumental house, sometimes two houses. If we read all this building activity as signifying Carter's desire to demonstrate his family's prestige through construction, then we can also see that his dynastic ambitions were not limited to the male line of descent. In fact, we can trace the mechanisms by which Carter exerted his ambition through the female line. First, we examine Rosewell, a mansion built by Mann Page I after fire destroyed an earlier dwelling in 1721. Five years later, Page's father-in-law, Robert Carter, drew up his will. In that 1726 document, Carter promised £300 in money to his son-in-law if "the large brick house now building by Colo. Page in the room of the house that was unfortunately consumed by fire, shall be finished and completed during the life time of my said daughter Judith Page so that she shall come to enjoy it and to have her Tithe of Dower in it."[65] Although the mansion remained unfinished, Mann Page I complied with the bargain by specifying in his will: "I give and devise to my dear wife Judith the dwelling house . . . where I now live, and the mansion house now building."[66]

Circumstantial evidence connected to Berkeley not only indicates that a woman's dowry could significantly contribute to mansion construction, it also suggests Robert Carter's dynastic program of architectural prestige through matrilineal descent. More definitive documents demonstrate courtship and marriage customs among the Virginia elite. Benjamin Harrison IV's quest for the hand and money of Anne Carter started more than a year before their marriage. William Byrd II noted in his diary entry of 30 April 1721 that "Ben Harrison desired me to speak to Colonel Carter about his pretension to his daughter." Because Harrison's father was dead, Byrd agreed to act the role of go-between and recorded on 4 May 1721 that he "went to Colonel Carter and interceded with him for Ben Harrison and at last obtained leave for him to wait on the Colonel at Rappahannock."[67] On 3 October 1722, Robert Carter I wrote in his diary: "My daughter married to Mr. Ben Harrison."[68] He did not disclose the contents of his daughter's marriage settlement, but its value may have been impressive if we suppose reciprocity between dowry and dower. When she became a widow in 1745, Anne Carter Harrison was left by her husband "one equal third part of the net proceeds or profits of my whole estate during her Natural life, in addition to "the use and occupation of the Plantation whereon I now live, commonly called Berkeley, with all the Slaves, Property belonging to the Crop of the said Plantation, with all my household furniture of what kind so ever and house Servants, except my Cook wench Patty and her children and boy levy. . . . I also give to my wife the use of all my plate and kitchen Furniture as also the use of my flocks of Cattle, Hogs, horses and Sheep upon the said Plantation, all of which said gifts I give to the use of my said Dear Wife so long as she shall remain a widow or shall abide on or inhabit the said Plantation, with full power to Cut down and make use of any Timber." Harrison went on: "I also give to my wife my coach chariot, chair, Six horses and all Furniture thereto belonging as also all my Saddle horses, mares and Colts on the said Plantation, together with her Gold Watch and all Jewels now in her possession." Her obligation was to contribute 9,000 pounds of tobacco, about nine hogsheads, yearly to the other two-thirds of his estate, which was to be divided among their children until the eldest son achieved his majority.[69] Harrison explained his generosity in providing for his widow when he wrote: "my wife hath at all times behaved in a most dutiful and affectionate manner to me and all—always been assisting through my whole affairs, I therefore think proper to Give my dear wife as a small requital over and above the Thirds of my estate." Anne may have been the perfect wife, but Harrison and Byrd had also negotiated for her hand with her steely father, Robert Carter, who may have insisted on something more than a widow's third for his daughter.

Carter's urge to perpetuate his family name and influence through his daughter's progeny was behind his intent when he bequeathed land to his Harrison grandson, provided that he be christened Carter Harrison.[70] Was Anne Carter's dowry used to construct Berkeley? There is no direct statement attesting to that fact. But the plaque inscribed with the initials of Anne and Benjamin on the side exterior wall of Berkeley may signify more of an architectural conjoining of lineage rather than merely a Valentine of "the delirium of love" (fig. 82).

The mansion of Charles Carter, Robert's son, represents another instance where circumstances seem to point to the use of a woman's dowry for construction. The evidence is complicated and requires a patient read. Charles Carter (fig. 83), a widower with four young children, seems to have met William Byrd II's high dower rights expectations, as did his brother Landon Carter. In 1742, Charles married Anne Byrd (fig. 84) as his second wife, acquiring from Byrd a dowry of £1,500 sterling.[71] Within five years of Carter's marriage to Anne Byrd, he abandoned Stanstead, the house that he had built less than ten years earlier, and built the imposing mansion of Cleve. In 1757, Anne Byrd Carter died, leaving eight children, including two sons. That Charles Carter considered Cleve to be Anne Byrd's is suggested by the terms of his 1763 will. Recall that by colonial Virginia

Fig. 81. Unidentified artist, *Portrait of Robert Carter I,* oil on canvas, before 1723. (Shirley Plantation in Charles City, Virginia)

Fig. 82. Berkeley Plantation, Charles City County, 1726. Commemorative stone on west exterior wall. (Photograph by Robert T. Mooney)

custom, the father's eldest son inherited the most and best land, the biggest house, the most slaves. Carter's will, however, breaks with tradition. In that document, Carter seems to acknowledge Anne Byrd Carter's contribution by giving his most valuable mansion, Cleve, not to his heir-at-law, that is, his first son by his first wife, Charles Carter II, but by leaving it to Anne Byrd Carter's first son, John.[72] In other words, he seems to bequeath the house as if it had been hers.

Similar conclusions can be drawn from an examination of the life and will of Mann Page II (fig. 85). Mann Page II was the son and heir of the builder of the mansion Rosewell. Mann Page II and his first wife occupied Rosewell during the course of their married life and produced three children, including the eldest and heir-at-law, John. After Mann Page II's first wife died in 1747, he wed Anne Corbin Tayloe, who brought a dowry of £2,000 sterling.[73] In 1765, Page's heir-at-law, John, reached his majority and was placed in possession of Rosewell. Upon relinquishing Rosewell to his eldest son, Mann Page II and his second wife moved to Spotsylvania County and proceeded to build the dwelling called Mannsfield, known from an insurance policy plan (fig. 86), photographs taken shortly after the Civil War, and excavations. In his 1780 will, Mann Page II allowed his second wife to live at Mannsfield for her natural life, and in addition gave her half of the profits from the plantation, all the servants and furniture belonging to the house, a coach, horses, plus £200 annually. This was, as Page himself

Fig. 83. Unidentified artist, *Portrait of Colonel Charles Carter of Cleve,* oil on canvas, ca. 1725–30. (Colonial Williamsburg Foundation)

Fig. 84. William Dering, *Portrait of Mrs. Charles Carter* (Anne Byrd), oil on canvas, 1735–40. (Colonial Williamsburg Foundation)

noted, "over and above what the law allows."[74] What was more unusual and what seems to point to Anne Corbin Tayloe Page's financial contribution to the erection of Mannsfield were the events that were to unfold after her death. Rather than reverting upon her death to Mann Page II's heir-at-law, that is, to his eldest son, as would be expected, all of his land in Spotsylvania County, including the mansion, was left to her eldest son. Again, he appears to assign the house as if it had belonged to her.[75]

If one accepts the proposition that dowry money contributed financially to the erection of a domicile, then the next question might be, what difference does it make? Would the buildings have looked the same even without a woman's marriage portion? To understand just how crucial a dowry could be, we need to turn to England, to the famous country seat of Wilton. As a representative to the English court, Amerigo Salvetti forwarded

Fig. 85. John Wollaston, *Portrait of Mann Page II,* oil on canvas, 1750s. (Virginia Historical Society, Richmond, Virginia)

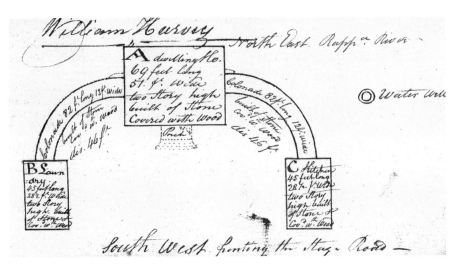

Fig. 86. Plan of Mannsfield from Mutual Assurance Society, declaration signed 1 February 1797. (The Library of Virginia)

gossip that might have proved beneficial to his employer, the Grand Duke of Tuscany. In 1626, he wrote that the "Duke of Buckingham this week contracted his little daughter who is four years of age, to the eldest son of the Earl of Montgomery, who is seven."[76] The potential groom was also the heir of Philip Herbert, the Earl of Pembroke. After an affective relationship started to develop between the young lady and another younger Herbert scion, a marriage ceremony was hastily arranged and took place in a small room at Whitehall Palace in 1635. By that year, the groom was sixteen and the bride thirteen. She brought with her a spectacular dowry of £25,000 in land and money.[77] In the year following the marriage, 1636, the elder Pembroke began a huge landscape and building campaign that, according to John Aubrey, was devised by Isaac de Caus with the advice and approbation of Inigo Jones. Unfortunately, after the ambitious building project had commenced, Pembroke's heir, the groom, died in Florence while on his Grand Tour. In accordance with the terms of the marriage settlement spelling out her jointure, Pembroke had the choice of either returning the dowry or paying the bereaved teenage widow £4,000 a year for the rest of her life. He briefly considered marrying off his next son to the same young girl, but after the Archbishop of Canterbury balked, Pembroke judiciously chose to return the dowry.[78] A mid-seventeenth-century sketch, found in the Harley Collection of the Society of Antiquaries of London, positions the house in relation to the new garden design and shows that work on the famous south façade was realized only on one side of Pembroke's new central garden axis (fig. 87).[79] Thus, the present Wilton represents only half of what was originally intended before the dowry disappeared. Wilton's history shows that dowry money, indeed, could affect design and that the application of dowry money to building finance was no colonial innovation but an established, though not highly publicized, English practice.

Not only could dowry money affect the appearance of a building, but it could alter the perception of the building. This modification, more psychological than material, is demonstrated by the history of Tazewell Hall, a mansion that once stood at the south edge of Williamsburg, Virginia (fig. 88). In 1751, Ariana Jennings married John Randolph II, bringing with her a dowry worth more than £1,000. Construction of the mansion in Williamsburg occurred that same decade. At the start of the Revolution, Randolph, who was a much-indebted Loyalist, fled with his wife to London, where he died intestate in 1784. Two years later, Ariana Jennings Randolph filed a petition with a commission of the English Parliament appointed to relieve the financial losses of Loyalists. During her testimony, she claimed that she "gave up certain Monies . . . in order that the Same should be applied to the Building of a dwelling house in the city of Williamsburg." She further stated that "in order to build it she gave up her right to the money settled on her on their marriage amounting to 1700 pounds sterling." Her son-in-law then testified that "the house for which claim is made was built with Mrs. Randolph's money left her by her father. . . . [T]his house was always considered as Mrs. Randolph's and always called hers."[80] Ariana was fudging a bit. Tazewell Hall was not confiscated but was deeded by John Randolph to his Virginia friends in an attempt to cover some of his debts. But Ariana's claim that her dowry money financed the construction of Tazewell Hall was probably correct, and in any case, the gambit would have been perfectly plausible to the well-to-do members of the British commission. While Tazewell Hall might have been recognized as her husband's by

Fig. 87. Unidentified artist, drawing of south façade of Wilton, 1640s. (Society of Antiquaries of London)

Fig. 88. Tazewell Hall, Williamsburg, 1758. Conjectural elevation. (Megan D. Roy after S. P. Moorhead)

the laws of patriarchal authority, it was recognized as hers by the laws of economics and that center of the public sphere, gossip.

Looking beyond Ariana's Revolutionary dilemma to the next century, we find an elite Virginia woman with opinions about domestic architecture that were specific, blunt, and wise. The evidence is important because unlike the colonial period, where little documentary evidence comes from women, we have a letter that gives voice to a woman who negotiated the issues of architecture on the one hand and the need to maintain the fiction of male domination on the other.

Elizabeth Barbour Ambler grew up at Frascati Plantation in Orange County, and by 1859 she was widowed.[81] In a letter of the same year, Elizabeth responded to her son and daughter-in-law's request for advice about the remodeling of Glen Ambler, a house located in Amherst County that no longer survives. Through her carefully couched wording, Elizabeth cleverly exerted her influence without overtly appearing to challenge male authority, in this case the authority of her son John over his own house. Elizabeth opened by demurring, "With regard to the improvement in the Glen Ambler house, I leave the matter entirely to your own judgment." She then proceeds immediately to give specific directions that are quite direct for someone who is leaving the judgment to others: "I think a room on the other side with a large cellar dining room would be ample room yet a while. I do not think you could have a stylish house, adding to the present house unless you built in front, a house that would hide the old one. You would have to change the windows and roof thereby losing the excellent garret rooms." She was acutely aware of the power of prestige houses to impart status not only to the first builders but to following generations when she advised: "Were I in your place, I would build such a house that would do for your own children in after times. You know when they go out into the world, they are mortified if every thing does not look nice about the homestead." Her role in the remodeling project is made clear in the next few sentences, namely, she is paying for it and she will occupy at least part of it. She framed her financial underwriting of the construction project as a reasonable contribution to her future old-age home, thereby maintaining her son's dignity and magnanimity and avoiding the appearance of his dependency. Elizabeth carefully described the implicit contract: "I thought I would appropriate then money from the present crop of wheat, corn and tobacco, and such of the personal property as was sold, to the building of the house, one half to be set down to you as an advancement, the other half I give because I think it nothing but right, as it would be built for my accommodation." Her largesse, however, came with strings attached, and over the top of the page, she added some last-minute instructions: "If you add a room on the other side I do entreat you make some plan to go into the dining room without going out of doors."[82] Clearly, she who paid the piper called the architectural tune.

Investigation into the role of dowry money and dower rights requires a reevaluation of the ways that prodigy houses have been interpreted as sites of social authority. If we construe the complex and admittedly only suggestive trail of inheritance and marriage portions as evidence of what we might call the matrilineal descent of at least some colonial Virginia mansions, what then are the larger implications? Did the money a woman brought with her result in any power, respect, or special esteem conveyed on the part of her husband? Judging the impact of dowry money is far from straightforward and depends on whether we look at the scene as a part of the patriarchal hegemony apparatus or unearth its counterhegemonic potential.

Of course, it needs emphasizing that a woman did not control her dowry; it usually passed from her father to her husband, who controlled his wife and all of her wealth. Thus, the extent to which a particularly large dowry permitted a woman any sort of personal leverage vis-à-vis her husband is at best a tenuous proposition. Are then dowry and the concomitant assignment of dower rights merely the legal mechanism enacted between two males haggling over the reproductive potential of a woman's womb, with a genteel house functioning as just one more bargaining chip? Were women simply passive bystanders in the negotiations over their bodies, who served at best as having "a very important role as mediators between kinship networks?"[83]

The significant economic advantage of a generous dowry may have rankled elite male Virginians who cultivated not only social superiority but defined the rank of gentleman as a position free of dependency. This much-vaunted sense of independence might have been compromised by relying on a conduit of wealth from their wives' families. Patriarchal ideology was therefore troubled and made more complicated by the influence of a wife's dowry. The somewhat shameful character of dowry money no doubt contributed to its historical erasure and created the necessary tension that lay beneath the surface of dowry humor. As much as gentleman patrons may have been loath to admit it, these houses embodied the dynastic ambitions of the bride and bride's family as well as the bridegroom's family.

A feminist analysis of architectural finance means that we can modify the iconographic meaning of Virginia's prodigy houses from serving solely as the emblems of the male owner's superior wealth and prestige to serving also as conveyances for the prestige of the female line, perhaps even female agency. In sum, instead of thinking of Virginia mansions as symbols of male authority and patriarchy, we also need to see them as icons of matrilineal descent and female security once the delirium of love was over and reason reascended her throne.

Chapter 4

"Each Rascal Will Be a Director"

Architectural Patrons and the Building Process

The Problem of Genteel Building in Colonial Virginia

William Fitzhugh wanted to save Nicholas Hayward from the hazards of good architecture. Writing from Virginia in 1687, Fitzhugh (fig. 89) warned his friend that if he anticipated moving his kin from London to the colony, he should not "build either a great, or English frame house, for labor is so intolerably dear, & workmen so idle & negligent that the building of a good house, to you there will seem insupportable." Fitzhugh knew whereof he spoke. His expertise, "especially in building & settling plantations" he boasted, came from directing the construction of his own wood-frame, thirteen-room house less than a decade earlier. Fitzhugh explained to Hayward that although his timber was free, his Virginia mansion had nonetheless cost a third more than one in London, and had taken three times as long to build. Tenants, he claimed, can easily construct their own "ordinary Virginia House" with their own physical exertion so their housing need not concern Hayward. However, if Hayward wanted "a very good house" for his relatives with not only "comfortable but creditable accommodations," then he would have to contract with British carpenters and bricklayers as indentured servants.[1]

Fitzhugh should have also informed Hayward that obtaining skilled and reputable immigrant craftsmen was difficult and expensive. Six years earlier, Fitzhugh had asked his London agent to send a carpenter and a bricklayer as indentured servants. Desperate for skilled builders, he offered "to advance something extraordinary for the procuration of them." Nothing about building in Virginia could be taken for granted so he felt compelled to remind his agent, "If you send in any tradesmen be sure to send in their tools with them."[2] While Fitzhugh did not complain about building materials or design, the labor force emphatically exercised him. Eighty years later, Fitzhugh's grandson, also named William, built Chatham. Did the same labor problems plague him?

Fig. 89. John Hesselius's copy of a seventeenth-century portrait of William Fitz-hugh, oil on canvas, 1751. (Virginia Historical Society, Richmond, Virginia)

Based on the comments of Thomas Jefferson, the answer would be yes. In his *Notes on the State of Virginia* (1785), Jefferson disparaged the architecture of Williamsburg as "rude misshapen piles." Save for the Capitol, he claimed that "no attempts are made at elegance. Indeed it would not be easy to execute such an attempt, as a workman could scarcely be found here capable of drawing an order."[3] Admittedly, Jefferson was measuring colonial architecture rather narrowly against published European authorities such as Andrea Palladio, James Gibbs, and Robert Morris. But his fastidious critique also shows that at the end of the colonial era, building tradesmen did not uniformly meet the standards of their clients, nor did they always take the lead in aesthetic innovation. Although Fitzhugh's chief concern in the seventeenth century was substantial timber-frame construction, while Jefferson's was the correct use of the Orders, each man points to the same problem in the colony: the lack of highly qualified craftsmen. They did not lament the absence of men capable of raising an ordinary building, but of men capable of creating what Fitzhugh said was "creditable" architecture.

The shortage of highly proficient building labor in the Tidewater became evident almost immediately after the colony was settled by the English and occurred well before the influx of large numbers of African slaves later in the seventeenth century. A single-crop tobacco economy led to dispersed farming and discouraged urban settlements that would have attracted practicing artisans. Many builders turned away from their trade to plant more profitable tobacco. In 1632, the colonial government passed a law stating that, unless he were lawfully dismissed or was not paid, a builder leaving a project incomplete was to be imprisoned for one month and fined £5 sterling in punitive damages, in addition to being held liable for compensatory damages.[4] Both colonial leaders and London authorities acknowledged the detrimental effects of dispersed development in Virginia. The authors of the "A Large and True Account of the Present State of Virginia," written in 1697, linked the shortage of craftsmen to Virginia's settlement pattern when they noted, "For want of Towns, Markets, and Money, there is but little Encouragement for Tradesmen and Artificers and therefore little Choice of them, and their Labour very dear in the Country."[5] It is against this background of a shortage of highly skilled builders that the owners of Virginia's prodigy houses struggled to create houses that would enhance and perpetuate their social rank. As the architectural historian Camille Wells has aptly put it, building a genteel dwelling was an ordeal.[6]

Modeling their expectations on British practice, as they did for everything from patterns of civilized settlement to the conventions of Grand Manner portraiture, elite Virginians hoped to rely on experienced professionals known as undertakers to oversee ambitious building projects. The colonial equivalent of the British master builder, or what we might now refer to as a general contractor, an undertaker was a man who could procure the proper building materials, locate and subcontract specialized craftsmen, marshal them into an efficient labor force, and see the project to completion.[7] He was also someone knowledgeable enough to monitor materials for flaws, watch out for shoddy construction, and ensure that the price charged accurately reflected the product. Englishmen would have expected a portion of journeymen joiners, carpenters, and masons to rise to the status of master builders. Master builders would then contract for, or undertake, an entire building project. A knowledgeable undertaker—or overseer, as he sometimes was called—was experienced in the logistics of coordinating materials and labor. That, at least, was the ideal.[8]

In the real world of colonial Virginia, undertakers were often overextended, tardy, or fell prey to political maneuvering. Undertakers could also be drawn from the wealthy planter class rather than the ranks of artisans. The prosperous Virginia planter Henry Cary Sr., for example, was named overseer for construction of the Capitol at Williamsburg in 1699 and later for the Governor's Palace. At least four Englishmen well trained in building craft, including the construction supervisor, Thomas Hadley, had been brought to Virginia only a few years earlier to work on another large-scale masonry building, the College of William and Mary. Yet these more qualified builders were passed over for the job.[9] It seems that Cary, whose building experience consisted of a small courthouse and a platform on a wooden fort, was not appointed solely on the basis of his architectural resumé, but because of the political clout of his brother Miles Cary II, a high-ranking member of the House of Burgesses who also held several profitable public offices.[10] Few complaints were raised over Cary's handling of the Capitol project, but his luck changed when Alexander Spotswood (fig. 90) arrived as lieutenant governor in 1710. Spotswood maneuvered Cary out of his position as overseer and proceeded to refashion the palace according to his own more metropolitan taste.

Construction contracting was then, as it still remains, prone to corruption and skimming. Nevertheless, a number of highly competent and reliable builders operated in eighteenth-century Virginia. Itinerant undertakers such as William Walker, Richard Bland, and James Skelton, who supervised construction of the second Capitol in the 1750s, succeeded in establishing reputations for reliable work in construction and in fact were referred to occasionally as architects. But the extant documents for public buildings also testify to many cases of careless workmanship, absenteeism,

Fig. 90. Unidentified artist (English), *Portrait of Alexander Spotswood,* miniature, India ink on vellum, 1720s. (Virginia Historical Society, Richmond, Virginia)

and duplicity. Even in the most competent hands, construction required close supervision by independent observers. When the Capitol in Williamsburg was rebuilt in 1751 following a fire, some of the best colonial builders were present: James Skelton as undertaker, and John Wheatly and Lewis Delony as carpenters. But substandard materials could still turn up and required the intervention of nonprofessionals. On 20 July 1751, John Blair noted in his diary that he "saw a bad Timb'r at Cap'l."[11] Putting up a large building required close supervision unexpected from modern clients.

Professional builders skilled at managing complex building campaigns, such as William Walker, were eagerly sought for both private and public building projects, and their reputations spread by word of mouth among potential patrons. In 1749, just before he died, Walker won the initial contract for rebuilding the Capitol at Williamsburg. Two years before, Walker had received final payment from Charles Carter for building Cleve. Carter may have known about Walker's expertise through Thomas Lee. Walker had worked for Lee in 1739 on constructing Stratford Hall. Although it certainly helped to have friends in high places—Lee was acting governor in 1749—it would appear that Walker won the Capitol contract because of his proven record of accomplishment and his ability to satisfy his clients' demands. As we shall see, not every undertaker was as skilled as Walker. Unfortunately, Walker died before construction of the Capitol commenced, further shrinking the pool of outstanding builders.[12]

Building the Prodigy House

Because of the shortage of highly skilled artisans and undertakers conversant in metropolitan building, as well as the lack of an established building materials industry, the owners of colonial Virginia mansions became actively engaged in the building process out of necessity. A close analysis of individual patrons in the study group shows that, from the early eighteenth century to the end of the colonial period, members of the native elite participated in the building process perforce.

In his work at Corotoman, Robert Carter I (fig. 91) set the pattern for eighteenth-century architectural patronage. Started in 1720 and destroyed by fire in 1729, Corotoman was a two-story brick dwelling with a two-story porch, or piazza, as Carter called it, across one elevation. This was a monumental building within the context of Virginia's built environment, and if anyone could afford to pay for convenience and quality, it was Carter, the largest landowner living in the colony. Yet Carter's letters and diary reveal that erecting a Virginia mansion was a lengthy, complex, and often frustrating endeavor. In the 1720s, Robert Carter I ordered paving stones from England, procured lumber from his own sawmills, purchased additional wood from his neighbors, and sent his workmen in small boats to gather oyster shells for mortar. His imported paving stones were tossed overboard in transit during a storm; his search for skilled builders also proved disappointing.[13]

Carter sought to build not just a very good house but also an extremely distinctive one in the Virginia landscape, and, as William Fitzhugh had done seventy years earlier, he contracted for skilled indentured labor. In theory, the owner would hold exclusive rights to the services of a skilled workman for a specified period of time, often as long as seven years, in exchange for providing passage to the colony, food, clothing, and shelter. In practice, results did not always live up to expectations. Such was the case with a Mr. Cole, an indentured joiner whom Carter had brought from England. Unhappy with Cole's performance, Carter refused to renew his contract in 1720, stating, "Such a tradesman I shall never want employ for."[14] Three years later, however, Carter had yet to find adequately trained workmen and asked his London agent to send a carpenter, joiner, brick maker, and bricklayer as indentured servants to the colony.

In addition to importing labor as indentured servants, Carter contracted with several local craftsmen, noting in his diary payments to a plumber, glazier, and brick maker. In one letter, Carter described how he compensated his workmen on the basis of the entire job, known as paying "on great," rather than on the price of each hundred square feet, known as contracting by squares. He admitted that, "doing the work by Squares . . . is a way I am not acquainted with I would make a Particular agreemt with him what he is to do and know the Certainty of what I must pay him for it."[15] Carter's experiences in building no doubt inspired his sons' desire for erecting extravagant dwellings. Landon and Charles Carter each built two substantial dwellings. Their experiences, however, were no easier than their father's.

Before Robert Carter's son Landon started to build Sabine Hall in 1738, he erected an earlier, now-lost mansion called Lansdowne. For this earlier house, Landon Carter hired one of his father's old bricklayers, Gregory Hinch, and another indentured servant, Ebenezer Balderton, whom the younger Carter had brought from England. In 1733, Landon Carter found it necessary to bail the disreputable Hinch out of jail. Landon's father had hired Hinch in 1724, but the bricklayer's problems with the law dated back at least two years. Either Hinch's talents as a bricklayer were exceptional, or skilled craftsmen, even those of mean character, were very scarce in the Northern Neck. In any case, Carter felt compelled to keep hiring Hinch.[16]

Landon Carter's indentured servant from England, Ebenezer Balderton, also proved disappointing. In 1738, as he commenced Sabine Hall, Carter took the joiner before the justices of the Richmond County Court, who concluded that "Ebenezer Balderton, Servant to Landon Carter Gent., does not understand the Trade for which he was bound, and sent into this

Fig. 91. Unidentified artist, *Portrait of Robert Carter I,* oil on canvas, ca. 1720. (National Portrait Gallery, Smithsonian Institution)

Country for." But, as was the case with Gregory Hinch, Carter found it necessary to rehire Balderton two years later.[17] Finally, in 1766, Carter had better luck. In that year he recorded in his diary that he employed "Buckland's two men," referring probably to the indentured servants owned by the talented builder, and former indentured servant himself, William Buckland.[18]

Charles Carter built his first mansion, Stanstead, in the 1730s, and it too is now lost. Both Stanstead and his brother's houses were ornamented with stone trim. By sharing laborers and materials, the brothers sought to minimize expenses, but this arrangement led to rather testy epistolary exchanges. In a letter of 1738, Charles tersely replied to Landon: "I can't spare the Masons above a month at farthest. I must finish my Steps before the frost. Your upper Story shall be done out of hand." The quality of the stone quarried by Charles Carter's workmen also proved to be a point of contention between them. Any attempt to imitate the stone country seats of England was hindered by the irregular and porous properties of the locally available stone, Aquia Creek freestone. Responding to complaints from his brother, Charles Carter grew defensive about his "Nasty Sorry Soft Stone."[19] Nevertheless, fashion took precedence over practicality, and Charles's later mansion, Cleve, was also embellished with the friable stone.

The impact of architectural patrons on the visual qualities of their prodigy houses is also illustrated by John Mercer's construction of Marlborough, started in 1746. Mercer acted as director of the works by procuring materials, coordinating labor, and determining design. Some of his efforts are recorded in an account book that survives; unfortunately, his mansion does not. Known only through rudimentary archaeological investigation and from an insurance policy sketch, the mansion was a one-and-a-half-story brick structure with an arcaded portico across its principal façade. Throughout six years of construction, Mercer obtained his own building materials by purchasing nails, specialized tools, lumber, oyster shells for mortar, and imported stone. Instead of contracting for indentured servants, he seems to have made agreements with a large number of self-employed craftsmen. In 1746 and 1747, he paid Thomas Anderson for making bricks but hired David Minitree to direct the bricklaying. In 1748, Mercer hired William Walker, who had worked earlier at Charles Carter's Cleve and Thomas Lee's Stratford Hall. Walker, in turn, directed the labor of the joiner William Monday (or Munday). But Mercer made separate agreements with skilled independent professionals: the joiner William Bromley and his Irish apprentice Mr. Paterson; the joiner Andrew Beaty and his apprentice; the plasterer Jacob Williams and his assistant Joseph Burges; the joiner George Eliot; the bricklayer Thomas Barry; and the stone carvers Job Wigley and William Copein.

In addition to procuring materials and labor, Mercer also determined the ornamental details of Marlborough by consulting the treatises and pattern books that illustrated what we refer to now as Anglo-Palladianism. In 1748, Mercer acquired an English translation of Palladio's *Four Books of Architecture* and other architectural handbooks by Edward Hoppus, William Salmon, and Batty Langley. Annotations made to his library list indicate that Mercer lent these books to his craftsmen, suggesting that Mercer was encouraging if not demanding up-to-date stylistic forms.[20] For some workmen unable to afford imported pattern books, access to Mercer's collection could introduce them to fashionable new forms to add to their repertoire of skills and designs.

Like Marlborough, Carter's Grove was the product of a planter taking on the obligations of an undertaker in his pursuit of genteel architecture (fig. 92). The main house was started in 1750 by Carter Burwell on land he inherited from his grandfather, Robert Carter I of Corotoman. In his account book, we find Burwell obtaining lumber, purchasing oyster shells with which to make mortar, paying for bricks made at Carter's Grove, and purchasing thousands of additional, ready-made bricks from his cousin Mann Page II. In February 1751, Burwell advertised in the *Virginia Gazette* for more oysters, and later the same year he placed a want ad for bricklayers "at the Rate of Four Pounds per Month." He bought plank, shingles, and lath, and spent £17 sterling for "sundry goods from England." For skilled labor, Burwell hired David Minitree, who had worked several years earlier at Marlborough, to take charge of the masonry walls, yet he contracted separately with other builders for different stages of construction and interior finish. Structural carpentry appears to have been supervised by John Wheatly, who was working on the second Capitol in nearby Williamsburg at the same time and was, perhaps, the man stretched too thin to notice the "bad Timb'r" found by John Blair. In 1752, Burwell contracted for the indentured services of the immigrant joiner Richard Baylis. Baylis, in turn, oversaw the work of six other craftsmen for the creation of the interior paneling. Yet while Baylis coached and judged the work of the six other joiners, he was, as an indentured servant, unable to take on the responsibilities of a subcontractor. Burwell paid the six joiners, presumably on the basis of Baylis's advice. When he paid the six men, Burwell did not follow his grandfather Robert Carter's practice of paying them "on great," but decided to contract their labor on a per diem basis. The complex relationship that emerges from the arrangements between Carter Burwell, his primary builders, and his secondary craftsmen in the account book illustrates how the building process at Carter's Grove was a collaborative effort, with aesthetic decisions distributed among a number of skilled craftsmen under the watchful eye of the owner.[21]

Fig. 92. Carter's Grove, James City County, 1750. River façade. (Photograph by author)

In contrast to John Mercer and Carter Burwell, Richard Corbin yearned to wash his hands of architectural cares. When fire destroyed his house on 15 March 1758, Corbin urgently needed to build a new dwelling to accommodate his temporarily dispersed family. After receiving a referral from John Robinson, the Speaker of the House of Burgesses, Corbin engaged Harry Gaines, whose family's business was building. The brick house Corbin commissioned from Gaines, called Laneville, no longer survives and is known only from brief written descriptions and a drawing on an insurance policy (fig. 93). The contract, however, does survive, and it stipulates that Corbin expected Gaines to "build and finish in the Neatest and best Manner a Brick House with a Cellar Under, Single Story and Dormers 52 feet by 20, which building was to be Compleated and fit to receive my Family in October." Interestingly, Gaines was "to find for this building all Materials of the best sort," with the exception of the most important item, the bricks. Those were to be supplied by Corbin. Gaines was not given free rein over construction but was "to observe and follow Such Instructions as he shoud receive." He may have been distracted by other building projects, but for one reason or another Gaines failed to make sufficient progress at Laneville. In a letter of 20 August 1758, Corbin complained bitterly about the man whom Robinson had recommended, claiming that Gaines had "almost failed and disappointed in every Instance: He has not imploy'd one good workman and the best that is [?] he cannot be certain of his Stay one day—had it not been for the Shells which you procured and others that have been brought upon my own acco't, not one Brick woud have been now laid and even with this assistance ⅔ of the Brick work woud have been now unfinished, if it had not been for the labor of my own People."[22] By default, Corbin took charge of procuring "materials of the best sort" that signaled a genteel house. He purchased sash pulleys for windows, and later £20 worth of nails. Evidently, the interior finishing dragged on, for in 1768 Corbin was ordering linseed oil and determining the dimensions for imported marble mantelpieces himself.

The entire process of building a house that signaled aesthetic distinction could be so vexing that some patrons wondered if the display of wealth, status, and taste was worth the extraordinary effort. This was precisely the sentiment expressed by John Carlyle, who built his mansion in the early 1750s using that notoriously porous Aquia Creek freestone that Charles Carter had referred to as his "Nasty Sorry Soft Stone." Carlyle (fig. 94) deputized an indentured servant, Teba Wilson, to take charge of "Carting Materiales for My Building."[23] But midway through construction, rain caused such severe damage to the exterior stone walls that Carlyle was obliged to order them dismantled and rebuilt. Shortly after, Carlyle

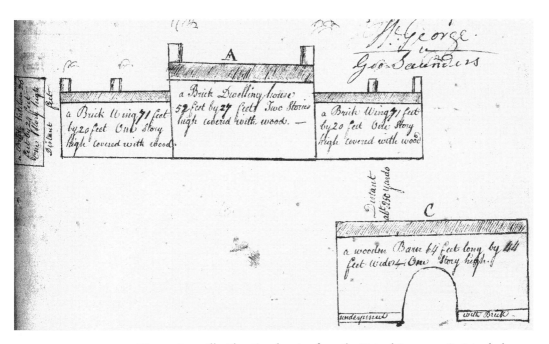

Fig. 93. Laneville. Elevation drawing from the Mutual Assurance Society, declaration signed 10 March 1802. (The Library of Virginia)

Fig. 94. John Hesselius, *Portrait of John Carlyle,* oil on canvas, ca. 1765. (Courtesy of Carlyle House Historic Park, Alexandria, Virginia)

summed up the frustrations of probably more than one architectural patron by proclaiming, "Its A Pleasure to build in England but here where we are obliged To Doe Everything With one's own Servants & these Negroes make it Require Constant Attendance & Care—& So much Trouble that If I had Suspected it would have been What I have met with, I believe I should have made Shift with A Very Small house."[24] Did Carlyle disdain local builders because of their actual lack of skill, or because the colonial elite increasingly gravitated toward British cultural production? By turning to imported workmen for the construction of their genteel dwellings, were architectural patrons simply displaying the social-climbing conceits of a pretentious colonial elite?

Richard Henry Lee's attitude toward Virginia's builders sheds light on these questions (fig. 95). Here was a man who, by 1767, could distinguish the relative merits of the paintings of Joshua Reynolds and Benjamin West, a man who raised subscriptions for a portrait of William Pitt and promoted the work of its artist, Charles Willson Peale, by asserting that "there is much propriety in encouraging American Artists in America."[25] Yet in the same year, Lee begged his brother, who was a London merchant, "[You] cannot imagine how much I am hurt for want of a good ship joiner who understands something of the house joiners business—I therefore entreat you will not cease trying until you furnish me with such a person."[26] Surely Lee's request was not caused by an underlying lack of pride in the artisans of his native land. Rather, it seems he was unable to find a competent carpenter.

Fig. 95. Charles Willson Peale, *Portrait of Richard Henry Lee,* oil on canvas, ca. 1795–1805. (National Portrait Gallery, Smithsonian Institution; Gift of Duncan Lee and his son, Gavin Dunbar Lee)

Apart from making his elder and richer brother happy, Richard Henry Lee appears to have found little reward in architecture and preferred that another person take charge. The names of the builders that Lee employed to construct Chantilly have not been discovered, and we have references only to Lee hiring an itinerant Irish sawyer in 1786 and "Mr. Moxley's 2 carpenters" to construct a garden enclosure.[27] But in 1770 Richard Henry Lee made inquiries concerning the cost of repairing the late seventeenth-century house at Green Spring, the James City County plantation owned by his brother William. Reporting to his brother who lived in London, Richard Henry Lee related that the well-regarded undertaker Richard Taliaferro had offered to "make a thorough repair [for] £500." William was reluctant to spend such a large sum on a house he did not inhabit and directed his brother to simply stabilize the structure and build an income-generating mill. At that point, Richard Henry Lee turned the job over to the plantation overseer at Green Spring, Cary Wilkinson. In a letter of 1772, Richard reported on the project's progress: "We have desired Cary to get some bricks ready, and sustain it [Green Spring] as well as possible, so soon as he has done with the new mill.[28] Unlike other architectural patrons, Lee exhibited little care or interest in closely superintending the building process, and when possible, he was more than willing to hand the job to someone else.

For George Mason IV (fig. 96), that perfect someone materialized when he contracted in 1755 for the labor of William Buckland, a London-trained specialist in ornamental woodworking. By the time Buckland arrived at Gunston Hall, the plan and elevation of the mansion had already been largely determined (fig. 97). He persuaded Mason to make some changes, including enlarging the Venetian frontispiece into a porch, adding the ogee porch on the garden façade, and building a secondary stairway that facilitated private communication between Ann Eilbeck Mason's bedchamber and the children's room on the second floor. Buckland's chief role consisted of directing the design and execution of an elaborate, textbook demonstration of fashionable interior woodwork and exterior porch decoration. So successful was Buckland's performance that, once his indenture expired, he soon garnered private and public commissions from other members of the Tidewater elite in Virginia and Maryland. Buckland was an ambitious man adept at marshaling an efficient and talented workforce consisting of his own indentured servants, James Brent and William Bernard Sears, and, eventually, trained slave labor. From ornamental design, Buckland moved into architectural design and construction.[29] Procuring Buckland in England was fortuitous, but not all of Mason's experiences in building were as pleasant. In 1756, Mason asserted in court that his bricklayer, Thomas Spalding, had failed to execute the work for which he had been indentured four years earlier.[30]

Fig. 96. Dominic W. Boudet, *Portrait of George Mason IV* (after lost portrait by John Hesselius), oil on canvas, 1811. (Virginia Museum of Fine Arts, Richmond; Gift of David K. E. Bruce; Photo: Ron Jennings, © Virginia Museum of Fine Arts)

Fig. 97. Gunston Hall, Fairfax County, 1752. Principal façade. (Photograph by author)

While a detailed account of the building process at Gunston Hall has not been discovered, a letter written in 1763 reveals that George Mason IV paid close attention to the mechanics of construction. He recalled, "When I built my House I was at pains to measure all the Lime and Sand as my Mortar was made up and always had two Beds, one for outside-work ⅔ Lime and ⅓ Sand, the other equal parts of Lime and Sand for Inside work." After explaining where to find the most suitable sand, Mason cautioned, likely from disagreeable experience, "I wou'd by no means put any Clay or Loam in any of the Mortar, in the first place the mortar is not near so strong and besides from its being of a more soft and crumbly nature, it is very apt to nourish and harbor those pernicious little vermin the Cock-roaches."[31] Such close attention to the unglamorous aspects of construction suggests that Mason received pleasure from directing the building process. Like his younger colonial cohort, Jefferson, the master of Gunston Hall seems to have been bitten by the architecture bug.

Unlike Richard Henry Lee, Mason approached architecture with relish. His son remembered that Mason, with the labor and expertise of "his carpenters and sawyers built and kept in repair all the dwelling houses, barns, stables, ploughs, harrows, gates etc. on the plantations & the out houses at the Home house."[32] Even as an old man, Mason directed construction for the house of one of his sons. In 1792, the same year he died, he ordered "a hundred feet of cypress scantling for the columns, railes, balusters etc. of the piazzas and steps to your brother Thomson's house" from John Brent of Norfolk. Brent, however, neglected to send the lumber up the Potomac, and Mason grew impatient: "I have lately got all the shingles, which with all the weather boarding are ready to put up. The house will be raised next week, and I am in danger of having the building stopped, and half a dozen workmen upon my hands, doing nothing, for want of this small quantity of cypress scantling, without which the piazzas can't be raised."[33] Although delays such as this typically plague construction projects, Mason's frustration could, presumably, have been avoided by hiring a knowledgeable undertaker skilled in the logistics of building. But Buckland had died in 1774, other qualified undertakers were scarce, and Mason, like his uncle before him, John Mercer, seemed eager to take up the challenge of genteel architecture.

Jefferson's intellectual engagement with the building process is well known because he left extensive documentation of his building activities. In addition to procuring structural lumber and decorative wood, he directed workmen who carted limestone for mortar up the mountain at Monticello, where bricks were made on site. For skilled labor, Jefferson preferred either to contract for a short period of time or to pay for a specific job or quantity of materials, and he rarely employed a worker for more than a year. He hired a dizzying array of craftsmen, among them the brick makers George Dudley, William Pond, and John Brewer; the bricklayers Stephen Willis and Randolph Johnson; and the carpenters Humphrey Gaines, Joseph Neilson, and Joseph Price. In 1778, Jefferson made a separate agreement with William Rice for the creation of stone columns, but the contract allowed Rice to use "the labor of my two stone-cutters."[34] As other Virginia architectural patrons did, Jefferson became frustrated with the slow pace of building and the inability of workmen to create accurately his idealized and numerically specific architectural plans. Like Robert Beverley, who requested his English agent John Blackhouse to "procure me a House Joiner," Jefferson asked his own London agent to "procure me an architect," the term he used in lieu of undertaker.[35] No supervising architect arrived at Monticello, and Jefferson continued to act as undertaker, directing his own slaves and contracting with local workmen. Seen within the context of the pattern of architectural patronage in eighteenth-century Virginia, Jefferson becomes less unique for his active role in the building process and more remarkable for his graphic representation and his aesthetic choices.

Slaves as Builders

In exploiting slave labor for the construction of Monticello, Jefferson was following a path well traveled by other architectural patrons. Not only did human chattel provide the largest share of unskilled labor, but many slaves were also highly skilled and valued for their construction craftsmanship. By the early 1720s, the presence of knowledgeable slave artisans was noticeable. In *The Present State of Virginia* (1724), Hugh Jones described their specialized work: "Several of them are taught to be sawyers, carpenters, smiths, coopers, etc. and though for the most part they be none of the aptest or nicest; yet they are by nature cut out for hard labour and fatigue."[36] Closer examination of the documentary record, however, indicates the contrary: some African builders demonstrated far more competence than Jones recognized.

Among his 749 slaves, Robert Carter I owned at least thirteen black men with special skill in carpentry and sawing. Guy, Ben, Jacob, Will, Frank, and others complemented Carter's white indentured servants: two carpenters, two bricklayers, and one glazier.[37] Of the black workers, four carpenters and two sawyers were settled upon the Falls Quarter, inherited by his son Charles Carter. In his will, Charles Carter publicly acknowledged his indebtedness to one of these skilled slave mechanics, although he was unwilling to grant the man his freedom: "I also desire that my negro man, Benjamin Boyd, may be well used and maintained with good clothes and sufficient meat and bread, and be employed as an overlooker in repairing my Mills, Machines and buildings of my Manor of Cleve, and in consideration of his great fidelity that he be paid annually during his life five pounds Current money out of the profits of my Estate at Cleve."[38] With less affection, but with similarly revealing dependence, Richard Corbin admitted his reliance on his enslaved builders in a complaint we have already encountered: "⅔ of the Brick woud have been now unfinished, if it had not been for the labor of my own People."[39] Colonial Virginians became accustomed and dependent on slaves to erect and maintain utilitarian plantation structures. In 1759, for example, Corbin wrote to his manager telling him that he was sending "my two carpenters Mack and Abraham to Mosse's Neck to build a good barn, mend up the quarters and get as many [barrel] staves and heading as will be sufficient for next years" tobacco hogsheads.[40] But bondsmen were also capable of creating the more aestheticized components of a planter's domain.

While William Buckland probably directed the interior ornament in John Tayloe's Mount Airy, skilled slave craftsmen likely had a hand in building other parts of the mansion, specifically the impressive and attractive stone walls (fig. 98).[41] In 1764, Landon Carter made a reciprocal arrangement to exchange the labor of "Colo. Tayloe's Stone Cutter Ralph" for that of "my man Jammey who is to work at the Colonel's when he goes to Walling in his Plantations." Two years later, Jammey was to execute brickwork for Carter's son John.[42] A 1774 description of one runaway slave shows the versatility of one of Tayloe's slaves. The advertisement in the *Virginia Gazette* for the capture of this "Billy or Will" also provides a white man's endorsement of the enslaved black man's skills: "From his Ingenuity, he is capable of doing almost any Sort of Business, and for some Years past has been chiefly employed as a Founder, a Stone Mason, and a Miller, as Occasion required."[43] William Fitzhugh also divulged his dependence on the skill of an enslaved craftsman in building Chatham when he advertised in 1769 for a runaway who was "by trade a good house carpenter and joiner."[44]

Adeptness in construction served the master but could be turned against him, too. Skilled slaves followed orders, but by taking the initiative in building and displaying architectural competence, they could also undermine their master's authority. On 2 June 1771, Landon Carter (fig. 99) complained in his diary, as he was wont to do, that "there is no making my Carpenters understand me." According to Carter, he had ordered his enslaved builders to erect a simple log structure requiring minimal labor, skill, materials, and time. Ignoring his instructions, the African American carpenters erected a fully framed building displaying more sophisticated "plates, posts and sill." Instead of simply repairing the roof, they built an "intire new set of new rafters." After being ordered not to create good architecture, the carpenter, Guy, perhaps the son of Robert Carter I's carpenter

Fig. 98. Mount Airy, Richmond County, 1760. Detail of stonework. (Photograph by author)

of the same name, "spent a week more in doing it his way." While Carter expressed frustration and contempt for his bondsmen, at the same time he acknowledged his black carpenter's spirit of creative resistance through architecture when he concluded in his diary: "Thus it is each rascal will be a director."[45]

Considering the uncertainties of hiring an undertaker or contracting with an indentured servant, the architectural patron and his skilled slaves probably comprised the most reliable, albeit an unjust, building team. It was certainly the most economically efficient arrangement from the master's point of view. Wages for free skilled builders were consistently higher, almost twice as high, in Virginia compared to England. In 1757, Peter Fontaine claimed that a "bungling carpenter" in Virginia commanded 2s. sterling per day. In the same year, an English building craftsman received only 1s. 4d. per day. By 1774, the Englishman's wages had risen to 1s. 9d., but, according to John Harrower, a sober and conscientious journeyman bricklayer could earn no less than 4s. sterling per day in Virginia.[46] Hiring Harrower's kind of bricklayer for three hundred days could cost £60 sterling, whereas the most valuable slave in John Thompson's 1773 inventory was appraised at £85 current money, or £68 sterling. An architectural

Fig. 99. John Hesselius, *Portrait of Landon Carter,* oil on canvas, early 1750s. (Courtesy of R. Carter Wellford)

patron clearly profited by owning the labor of a skilled slave for life rather than an indentured servant for seven years. Yet owners continued to procure indentured servant craftsmen from abroad. Perhaps because of the racial taboo against taking advice from dark-skinned people, or because of a fundamental fear of encouraging leadership in slaves, architectural patrons failed to credit black builders with architectural abilities.

All in all, erecting a "creditable" dwelling in colonial Virginia was never a seamless endeavor. Acquiring the sort of building materials that signified gentility, such as sash glass, required access to suppliers in Britain, but the most vexing part of creating their prodigy houses was the scarcity of trained, reliable undertakers available and willing to take charge of construction. Architectural patrons who had the money and the connections to contract for British laborers risked a lengthy obligation to an incompetent, slothful, or drunken ne'er-do-well. Men such as William Buckland and Richard Baylis represent the happy exceptions, and otherwise excellent undertakers, such as Harry Gaines, seem to have been stretched too thin. By necessity, the owners of Virginia mansions became involved in the building process. Bearing in mind John Carlyle's wry reflection upon his own difficult building campaign, it is a wonder that any sane person would take part in another architectural project again. Yet they did.

Shaping Public Architecture

Despite all the difficulties related to the construction of their prodigy houses, architectural patrons continued to shape the built environment by engaging in public building projects. Construction of their house did not represent an isolated architectural event for most of them. Because of the political offices they held, elite Virginia men were often called upon to make decisions concerning public buildings. These public projects ranged from simple, cheap, wooden tobacco warehouses to complicated, costly, and aesthetically significant brick parish churches and county courthouses. Men selected by the local vestry of the established Church of England to serve as vestrymen, for instance, were responsible for constructing and repairing parish churches, glebe buildings, vestry houses, and sometimes poorhouses. Men appointed as justices of the peace to the county court guided the erection of courthouses, prisons, bridges, and public tobacco warehouses. Burgesses elected from each county and councilors appointed by the lieutenant governor made decisions concerning the colony's major structures, including the Capitol and the Governor's Palace, although such large building campaigns occurred less frequently. Some of these projects, such as the erection of wooden prisons or stocks, were quite ephemeral and needed frequent replacement. Courthouses constructed of wood could last several decades, but the creation of new counties often required the relocation of courthouse sites. Brick courthouses, while not as expensive as brick churches, could be utilized for several generations; indeed some have lasted for centuries.

In order to appreciate how the architecture patrons in the private domain came to affect buildings in the public domain, we must recognize the collaborative process by which public buildings were erected. Undertakers were not selected by the government and then given relatively free rein concerning questions of design, materials, and construction.[47] Along the path to completion, critical decisions were made by the entire governmental body, which determined the site, general building program, construction standards, and quality of materials; the building committee, which advertised for bids, contracted with an undertaker, and appraised the work; the undertaker, who was often in charge of materials and labor; and finally, individual craftsmen who made decisions about the execution of specific parts of the building.

Although the building process for public structures was broad-based, it was not indicative of the will of the people, for, with the exception of burgesses, public officials were not selected by popular vote.[48] Neither can the process be described accurately as autocratic; nonelected vestrymen and magistrates were, in the end, answerable to taxpayers. If a site proved inconvenient, or a building project became too financially burdensome, disgruntled members of the community could, and did, petition the colonial government at Williamsburg for redress. Although most of the grievances concerned location, complaints about the expense of, and practical need for, public structures also came before the General Assembly. It behooved vestries and county courts to keep extravagant building projects in check. Within bureaucratic bodies, various factions and jealousies ensured that no one member benefited at the expensive of others. Ambitious men like Alexander Spotswood who were perceived as erecting public edifices solely for their own convenience and aggrandizement eventually encountered opposition, even from their social peers. This informal system of constraint meant that most parish or county buildings were far from grandiose in terms of scale and expense, though not all were plain, utilitarian shelters devoid of beauty.

Ideally, religious and secular public buildings, like their domestic counterparts, would be supervised by an undertaker. Not surprisingly, clients of public building projects also encountered problems dealing with undertakers. Not all the difficulties were related to the number of workmen available. In fact, more men in the colony were acquiring at least the rudimentary skills in the building trades. By the mid-eighteenth century, the number of men skilled in the building trades seems to have increased. Between 1701 and 1730, the courts of nine Virginia counties recorded indentures for 354 carpenter apprenticeships and 60 joiner apprenticeships.[49] This increase in the labor force is reflected in the number of men hired as builders. From 1731 to 1774, the vestry of St. Mark's Parish employed twenty-two workmen for building projects. Some of these men appear to have been little more than handymen hired to do custodial work, such as tarring roofs. Others were vestrymen who contracted for entire buildings. But even with the abundance of craftsmen willing to undertake the parish's construction needs, nonprofessionals stepped in as undertakers and resolved problems.

The four decades of building projects related to St. Mark's Parish demonstrate an uneven, but not atypical, pattern in regard to undertakers. David Kinked, probably from Albemarle County, had successfully built the parish a vestry house in 1733 and a church at Southwest Mountain in 1737. On 27 May 1741, he received the contract for additions and repairs to the glebe house, the term used to designate the home of the resident minister. The alterations to the glebe house included the addition of a 12-foot study, chimney, cellar, one additional window, and the glazing of all windows. In September, Kinked also won the contract for a new church at Tenants Old Field. Neither project was completed in a timely manner, and the vestrymen eventually brought suit against Kinked. The glebe addition may even have never been started. On 27 March 1744, the vestry ordered a new set of specifications for a 20 x 26 foot addition and this time found it expedient to allow the minister, John Thompson, to act as undertaker. The addition was completed by November 1751.[50]

Occasionally, St. Mark's Parish had better luck with undertakers. Thomas Covington built a barn and stable at the glebe in 1742, a church at Buck Run in 1753, and an addition to the Little Fork church in 1761. Thomas Brown had erected the church at Little Fork in 1750, and Captain William Brown enlarged the Buck Run church in 1769. After Thompson's death in 1772, the vestry decided to construct a new glebe house. Although the churchwardens were ordered to advertise for bids in the *Virginia Gazette,* the contract was awarded, not to an itinerant undertaker, nor to one of the experienced local builders, but to James Slaughter, a vestryman whose previous work for parish building projects was limited to putting windows in the Little Fork church in 1768. During the time Thompson served as minister, the parish's building campaigns included three new churches; three new vestry houses; additions and repairs to four standing churches; and three additions and repairs to the glebe.[51] Because he had a personal stake in these projects, Thompson's architectural activities should not be construed as representative.

Nevertheless, in large and small ways owners of prodigy houses influenced public architecture. Surviving documents, imperfect as they may be, offer insight into the ways the native elite participated in the public building process. In 1771, for instance, Richard Henry Lee, as churchwarden of Cople Parish, advertised for bids on a 28-foot addition to the parish glebe house.[52] Although Mann Page II was not a vestryman of St. George's Parish, Spotsylvania County, in 1768 he was named one of the managers of a lottery to raise money for a new church and organ.[53] John Banister III served on the vestry of Bristol Parish starting in December 1764, and during his tenure, the parish made additions to the glebe house in 1765; built a new church in 1769; engaged Colonel Richard Bland, Banister's in-law, to enlarge a brick church and enclose its yard in 1769; repaired the glebe house and enlarged other churches in 1770; and constructed a new glebe house in 1772.[54] As vestryman, John Mercer contracted in 1745 with William Walker for the construction of a new church in Overwharton Parish. Mercer was also serving on the vestry when the Aquia church was built from 1751 to 1757, with Mourning Richards as undertaker and William Copein as stone carver. Both Walker and Copein worked for Mercer at Marlborough.[55] Earlier, in 1732, Mercer had built a public tobacco warehouse for the county at Marlborough.[56] William Randolph III was a member of the Henrico Parish vestry during a period when they built a new glebe house in 1751, with "Colo. Bland" serving as undertaker, and repaired the existing churches at Curle's and Richmond in 1751.[57] While there is no record of Carter Burwell's appointment to the vestry of Bruton Parish, on 11 October 1744 he was named a trustee by the House of Burgesses to supervise repairs to be made to the wings of the Bruton Parish church, that is, to the portion of the building that had been paid for by the colony in 1711, not by the parish. In 1751, as he was erecting Carter's Grove, Burwell was called on by the vestry of the parish to contract with an undertaker for an enlargement of the Bruton church, an addition that was built from about 1752 to 1754. In 1748, as burgess, Carter Burwell was named to the committee for rebuilding the Capitol after its destruction by fire. Seven years later, Burwell was again named to a building committee, this time to supervise construction of a brick wall around the ammunition magazine.[58]

Occasionally, the documentary record allows greater insight into the ways Virginia's native elite shaped public architecture. Again we see Robert Carter I engaging in promoting prestige architecture and setting a pattern that would continue through the colonial period. County court records reveal that Robert Carter I's interest in what Fitzhugh called "creditable architecture" began more than twenty years before the construction of Corotoman. Carter wanted to create public architecture that was distinguished by permanent building material, refined surfaces, and sophisticated ornamentation. On 11 November 1698, the Lancaster County Court, of which Carter was a member, decided to erect a new courthouse, which no longer survives. At the following meeting, on 24 November, the county clerk recorded the specifications for a new courthouse. It was to be a one-and-a-half-story brick building measuring 30 feet long and 20 feet wide, with a lower floor–to-ceiling height of 10 feet. In addition to four windows on the ground floor, the upper story, reached by stairs, was to be illuminated by windows in the brick gable ends. Double doors were to mark the entrance, and the interior walls were to receive plaster. According to the agreement, smaller details, such as rails, banisters, and seats, were to "be left to ye discretion of ye undertakers." The justices also ordered the construction of a 16 x 12 foot brick prison to be located adjacent to the courthouse.

The specifications concluded by naming Carter as the undertaker for both projects, for which he was to be paid a total of 45,000 pounds of tobacco in three yearly installments.[59]

Carter probably built the prison first, and, about a year later, the justices allowed certain changes to be made to the original courthouse specifications, changes most likely proposed by Carter himself. On 14 December 1699, Carter pointed out to his fellow justices that the thickness of the walls and ceiling joists would have resulted in a cramped interior. The dimensions therefore were increased to "33 foot long & 23 foot wide," with the ceiling raised to 11 feet. Next, he added an antechamber to the principal façade, described as a "porch to be built 10 foot square inside 9 foot pitch ye roofe to be left to ye descretion of ye undertaker." In place of a wooden floor, both the courthouse and the porch were "to be laid with paving stone." Last, Carter enriched the ornamental articulation of the building. The courthouse was now "to have mondelion eves and ye dores windows & mondelions to be laid in oyle, and ye Kings Arms to be left to ye descretion of ye undertaker." In adding ceremonial accessories that traditionally encouraged deference to civic authority, Carter created something more than a convenient place to adjudicate the law.[60]

Given the fairly humble level of county courthouse building in the Tidewater at the end of the seventeenth century, Carter's Lancaster project constitutes an ambitious foray into academic public architecture. By comparison, the Charles City County courthouse in Maryland was built of wood frame supported by posts in the ground. The interior was heated by a wooden chimney canted away from the building so that it could be pulled down in the almost inevitable event of fire.[61] The permanent brick exterior walls of the Lancaster courthouse, its genteelly plaster-covered interior walls, generous fenestration, and wide doors were meant to signal the court's and the county's permanent and secure position in the colonial landscape. These features were comprehensible to all who saw the building. Carter's decision to include a reference to the classical language of architecture, namely a modillion cornice, and to display the emblematic sign of the king's authority required a somewhat more sophisticated visual reader who had linguistic competence in academic design.

Carter's inspiration for the more refined quality of Lancaster County's public buildings may have come from a variety of sources: the old statehouse at Jamestown; the new and as yet unfinished College of William and Mary in Williamsburg, where he was serving as both speaker of the House of Burgesses and treasurer of the colony in 1699; architectural dialogue with the well-traveled Governor Francis Nicholson; or perhaps even from his own memories of English building from his student days in London. In any case, Carter was contributing features of high-style architecture to a county building at a time when those features were largely confined to major buildings owned by the colony. His building experience, as well as political influence, probably led to an even larger project. On 26 August 1702, Carter, in his capacity as councilor, was named to a committee to adjust "all matters relating to ye capitol."[62]

About a quarter century later, and not too long after he built Corotoman, Carter spearheaded another project that linked an unusually high standard of public architecture with his family's prestige. In his will of 1726, Carter bequeathed £200 sterling toward construction of a new house of worship for Christ Church Parish, Lancaster County (fig. 100). His gift was given with a proviso that the chancel in the new church "be preserved" as the location of a "commodious pew" and as a place of burial for his family. Carter, however, may have contributed building materials in addition to the £200 sterling. His will further stipulated that "the bricks that are new made and burnt shall be appropriated to the building of the said Brick church or as many thereof as will perfect the building, and likewise the bricks that shall be made and be there at my decease, and if my son John shall have occasion to make use of any of the said bricks, then he be obliged to make and burn as many more for the use aforesaid." While the church may have been funded initially by Robert Carter I, it was finished in 1735 by his son John.[63]

As if following his father's example, Landon Carter seems particularly attuned to shaping the colonial built environment by imposing an academic character upon conventional vernacular building. During the period Landon Carter served as justice, the Richmond County Court constructed a number of utilitarian structures, including two bridges in 1740 and a public tobacco warehouse in 1742, for which Carter was named undertaker. A more aesthetically ambitious design opportunity arrived in 1748. In August of that year, the justices of the Richmond County Court, including both Landon Carter and John Tayloe II, decided to build a brick addition to the courthouse, costing £130 current money, and they named Carter undertaker.[64] Carter did not proceed immediately with construction, but instead must have spent time persuading his fellow justices to drop the idea of an addition and embark on an entirely new scheme. On 6 March 1749, the court made a new agreement "for the Building of a New Court house according to the plan Lodg'd, instead of Repairing the old one," for which Carter was now to receive £300 current money. Carter's courthouse measured about 52 feet long and 40 feet wide. Enclosed within the rectangular building was an apse-shaped judge's bench at the north end opposite the entrance. Along each of the longer sides was an arcade about 10 feet wide and 34 feet long. Neither the use of the polygon-shaped or curved interior end nor the use of an arcade was unique. Curved apsidal ends could be

Fig. 100. Christ Church, Lancaster County, ca. 1732–35. (Photograph by author)

found in the first Capitol at Williamsburg, and arcades were frequently employed in European and colonial civic structures such as city halls and marketplaces.[65] The construction of two arcades for the Richmond County building, however, was unusual, and so too was a feature Carter added to the interior during construction. On 6 November 1749, the justices agreed to spend an additional £20 current money and let Carter "Build a Roman Arch in the new Courthouse According to the Plan Lodg'd."[66] How this arch was incorporated into the interior is not explained in the order book, but it was likely over the center of the apselike judge's bench, creating a convincing basilican arrangement that enhanced the stature of those below.

Landon Carter's classical references were no accident. He knew his ancient architectural precedents and could cite them as well as case law. Years later, he bragged about the bridge design he had persuaded the county to adopt, which, he claimed, had been derived "from Vitruviusis [*sic*] bridge over the Rhine in Julius Casar's [*sic*] days."[67] The bridge is not found in Vitruvius but discussed in book 3, chapter 5 of Palladio's *Four Books of Architecture*. The addition of a "Roman Arch" to the Richmond County courthouse may have represented Carter's adaptation of a design motif from book 3, chapter 19, specifically the left side of plate 18 described as "the profile of the place, made to place the tribunal opposite to the entrance."[68] Carter wisely chose not to attempt to copy to an entire Roman basilica. Rather, he selected an emblematic feature emphasizing the stature of the justices and suggesting divine approbation for their deliberations. Such references to specific architectural books are rare in eighteenth-century Virginia architecture and were meaningful to those few men who valued the prestige of classical precedent.

John Carlyle's public architecture projects in Alexandria also amplified his prestige and wealth by enhancing the urban and commercial environment in which he operated. The same year he began to build his mansion, Carlyle was appointed a justice of the peace of Fairfax County and was named to a committee to build a 16-foot-square brick addition to the county's existing courthouse farther inland from the Potomac at Spring Fields. Soon, however, he, William Fairfax, and other town inhabitants began to campaign for the relocation of the county's court sessions to Alexandria, pledging £30 toward a new courthouse in 1751. In 1752, he served on committees for construction of a county bridge and repairs to a public tobacco warehouse. The following year, Carlyle was on yet another committee for the erection of a new wharf at Alexandria, one that would be built at the county's expense, but would no doubt also prove advantageous to his own commercial shipping ventures. On behalf of the county, he later agreed with workmen to make improvements to the yard surrounding the courthouse and to build a clerk's desk.[69]

Utilitarian, though not necessarily minor, structures would hardly warrant the application of the kind of experience Carlyle had gained by building his own mansion. He was, however, able to bring that more complex and aestheticized knowledge to bear in his work for the Church of England. As a Presbyterian, Carlyle could not serve as vestryman, but as a leading citizen of Fairfax County, he was entrusted in 1751 with management of a lottery to raise money for an early Anglican church for the town of Alexandria.[70] When James Parsons, the undertaker for the second church in Alexandria, now known as Christ Church, failed to fulfill his contract in 1772, Carlyle took over as undertaker and finished the church—which was based on a design purchased from James Wren—the following year.[71] Two years later, as an elder in the Presbyterian congregation, Carlyle advertised for bids for a Presbyterian meetinghouse in Alexandria and may have served as its undertaker.[72]

Because church construction was second only to that of prodigy houses in terms of expense and complexity, how architectural patrons altered design in religious structures provides important clues for judging their architectural competence. Richard Corbin's influence on public buildings began more than a decade before he erected Laneville. In 1745, he was appointed to the vestry of Stratton Major Parish. During the next few years, the vestry ordered additions and repairs to the glebe house, and construction of several new utilitarian buildings on the glebe. Corbin became more directly involved in parish projects in 1759. In August of that year, the vestry ordered the new churchwardens, including Corbin, to "give Publick Notice that a New Church is to be Built in this Parish" and to "receive Planns from Undertakers & agree for Building of the Same." The following February the vestry decided to erect the new church upon a spent tobacco field belonging to Corbin. The vestry also agreed with the undertaker, Harry Gaines, whom Corbin had employed previously, to build a 80 x 50 foot brick church costing £1,300 current money. As one of two overseers appointed by the vestry, Corbin was instructed in 1760 to "see Over the Building of the Church." Two years later the building was unfinished. In September 1762, the vestry altered the original design, deciding that the "Pillars mention'd in the Agreement . . . will be of but little service," and directed Gaines to eliminate them. At the same vestry meeting, Gaines was yet again hired to build a new brick house for the meetings of the vestry. Gaines died in 1767, and the church was finally finished the next year by William Muir. In October 1768, the glebe buildings were remodeled, and in 1774 Corbin was once more on a building committee, this time to determine what further glebe repairs were necessary.[73]

Corbin's impact on Stratton Major Parish architecture was made within the context of a corporate body, namely the vestry. His expertise was no doubt valuable in keeping a watchful eye on undertakers, but he was not running the show by himself. Design decisions were the purview neither of a single artistic personality nor of a socially prominent vestryman. Moreover, fairly dramatic design alterations were made over the course of construction, namely, the design that the vestry had received from undertakers in 1759 was altered by eliminating specified interior columns four years later.

George Mason IV's record of public architecture provides one of the most insightful glimpses into the working of building committees and their control over the design process. Perhaps the recording secretary of Truro Parish wrote more ably, but the transcript of building deliberations shows that vestrymen, Mason included, displayed a lively engagement with the aesthetics of architecture. Appointed to the vestry in 1749, Mason was named to a committee to inspect the parish's new glebe house by 1753, just after he began to build Gunston Hall. The next year, a report by this committee found much fault with the work of the undertaker, Thomas Waite. The vestry were "of opinion that none of the bricks of the first two kilns are fit to be put into the Walls of the Glebe House but that what is done be pulled down & done with good bricks." They further wanted the cellar windows rebuilt with either ring oak or locust. Several more years passed with the vestry prodding Waite to complete the glebe building. Eventually they dismissed Waite and in 1759 contracted with William Buckland, whose indenture with Mason at Gunston Hall had just ended.[74]

Mason and the vestry seem determined to create a showpiece at the parish's new church at Pohick, but the vestry minutes pertaining to this building also make it clear that a number of men contributed to its final design. The plans for the church were created by James Wren and William West, who were each paid 40s. in 1769 for their efforts. Management of the project was handed to Daniel French, a wealthy planter and member of the parish, who had contracted to undertake church construction for "£877, Virginia Currency." His work, in turn, would be checked by a committee, of which Mason was a member, that would "View & examine the Building from time to time as they or any three of them shall see fitting, to whom the undertaker is to give notice when the different Materials are ready." The agreement that French signed was unusually particular in its specifications and included an "Alter-Piece [sic] to be twenty feet high and fifteen feet wide and done with wainscot after the Ionic Order." But already the vestry was making changes to the Wren and West drawings in the contract. French was to execute the church in a "Sufficient and Workmanlike manner, and agreeable to the Plan thereof hereunto annexed, except with this Alteration in the West end of it, that instead of the door, there shall be a Window; and instead of the two windows, there shall be two Doors opposite the two Isles." By mid-1771, the exterior was substantially complete, but at that point someone started to complain about the visual details. On 8 July, the vestry ordered corrections:

> Whereas it appears that the Dimentions of the Alterpiece mentioned in the Articles with the undertaker for building the New Church, are not according to the proportions of Architecture, the undertaker is authorized and desired to make the Same according to the true proportions of the Ionic order.

The exterior corner quoins were judged "coarse grain'd and rather too soft," and the vestry ordered French to paint them with lead white oil paint. The color of the rubbed brick on the sides of the windows did not match the color of the rubbed brick arches above the windows, and they too were ordered painted. Daniel French died sometime before May of the following year. As French's executor, Mason completed the Pohick church, and it was under Mason that additional interior work was performed. On 4 June 1773, the vestry allowed Mason to remove two pews so that a baptismal font could be installed permanently. Taking the unusual step of specifying the precise model the carver was to use, the vestry instructed William

Copein to "make a stone Font for the Church according to a Draught in the 150th plate in Langleys Designs being the upermost on the left hand."[75]

On 24 February 1774, the vestry officially received the church Mason completed. Mason also presented the vestry with a bill "for Sundry Alterations in the said Church and other work done thereto not inserted in the Undertakers Articles," totaling £116 19s. 10½d. current money. Charges included a substantial amount of "carved work" worth £58 19s. executed by Gowan Langfier, William Copein and William Bernard Sears, who had proved his worth to Mason twenty-five years earlier at Gunston Hall.[76]

The Role of the Patron

The picture that emerges from a close examination of ways that architectural patrons participated in public and private building projects is complex, and at odds with the image of the consummate and authoritative professional architect that was to emerge in the mid-nineteenth century. In terms of public buildings, officeholders frequently made architectural decisions for a number of reasons, including the state of the building industry, their obligations to taxpayers, their personal ambition, or even an individual delight in creating "creditable buildings." Some officials were more involved than others in the building process, but very few dominated the aesthetic character of a public structure. More often an officeholder's role was limited to determining whether and where to build and how much to spend. A smaller number served on building committees, and a few had the management skills and access to skilled and unskilled laborers that allowed them to affect design and construction more directly by acting as undertaker. Rarer still are those individuals who sought to act as the sole arbiters of architectural taste. In short, none of the patrons in this study can be designated as the equivalent of the modern design-architect, traversing the countryside providing the final word in plans and elevations to acquiescent corporate clients. While peripatetic undertakers did exist during the colonial period—William Walker, Richard Bland, and the Carys come to mind—they too were subject to the instructions or censure of political bodies. At any point in the building process, corporate clients could intervene to correct the proportions of an Ionic pilaster, eliminate a structural column, or alter the arrangement of interior spaces.

The diffuse nature of the public building process implies two things. First, the development of colonial architecture was not the product of a few avant-garde artistic minds. Second, it was generally understood that architectural competence extended beyond those whose livelihood depended on the building trades. Knowledge of building and the ability to judge design were not vested solely in professional builders but extended to individuals who comprised the governmental bodies—that is, to members of the elite classes.

In terms of private architecture, the surviving evidence reveals that Virginia architectural patrons contributed to all aspects of the building process for their own prodigy houses, that is, to its materials, labor, and design. Even those patrons who hired an undertaker could not avoid all responsibilities. Many seem to have fulfilled the function of undertaker themselves and provided the unifying force underlying the erection of a mansion. In the absence of a more orderly, competitive building industry, colonial Virginia patrons contributed to the design of their mansions in ways that were direct, often frustrating, and absolutely necessary. Because of a shortage of reliable, qualified professionals knowledgeable in the design elements of academic architecture, those colonial patrons who coveted fashionable dwellings had no choice but to become entangled in building. Nowhere in the extant documentary record do we find evidence of architectural patrons relinquishing control over the building process. On the contrary, it was recognized that architectural competence extended beyond those whose livelihood depended on the building trades, more particularly it extended to the owners of Virginia's prodigy houses. In sum, it was not those men who occasionally dabbled in architecture who were unusual. Rather it was those not actively participating in design who were exceptional.[77] From Robert Carter I in the early eighteenth century to Thomas Jefferson in the late eighteenth century, architectural patrons provided building materials, sought out skilled artisans, and collaborated in the design of their own prodigy houses. Appropriating Landon Carter's complaint, we can apply his phrase to the architectural patrons of Virginia prodigy houses: "Thus it is, each rascal will be a director."

The Social Limits of Architecture

Yet the patron's role need not be exaggerated to make the point. There were limits to his knowledge, experience, and status that made individual skilled workmen necessary partners in the entire enterprise. Specialized skills critical to an academic decorative scheme, such as laying ornamental brickwork or carving interior paneling based on the classical Orders, were clearly beyond the owner's ken. It was one thing for George Mason IV and his fellow vestrymen to select a plate from an expensive book; it was something altogether different for William Copein to know how to put hand and chisel to stone to imitate that plate. Ironically, the more academic the design, the less elite patrons could rely on their own resources.

Distinct social limitations also restricted a patron's participation in architecture. Whereas indentured men like William Buckland could ascend professionally and socially to join the ranks of polite society, and whereas men of gentlemanly rank could on occasion serve as undertakers, the sons of families of quality soon discovered that they could only descend socially by becoming specialists in the building arts. Laboring as an artisan with skilled hands was entirely out of the question for elite men. This prohibition became painfully evident to one architectural patron when he apprenticed his son to a master carpenter. In 1766, John Mercer and members of his family were pilloried in the *Virginia Gazette* because of Mercer's opposition to the Stamp Act. One son in particular became a target of ridicule because he had once briefly been engaged in a "vile art" by learning the skills of a "faber-carpenter" as a young man. Showing off his social superiority, the writer made a point of using the Latin word for smith, or carpenter, *faber*. Mercer went to his son's defense and cleverly sought to exact public revenge by charging his son's defamer with class prejudice. His mocking indictment of this adversary's social snobbery bears close analysis because his voice reveals conflicting pride and embarrassment, both unresolved admiration for and prejudice toward those men who could make manifest what William Fitzhugh might have called "creditable architecture."

Mercer first explained that his son's interest was encouraged by one of the builders of Marlborough, William Bromley, whom Mercer claims "was the best architect that ever was in America." Deciding that men of mechanical ability were "more beneficial members of society" than men who improved themselves by attending "ordinaries, horse races, cock matches, and gaming tables," Mercer apprenticed his son to Thomas Waite, "master carpenter and undertaker," who worked for Truro Parish. Careful to show the masterful status of his son, Mercer also noted that he gave his son four male slaves to receive instruction in carpentry, so that his son could eventually set up his own business. At the time, "I received the compliments of the Governour, several of the Council, and many of the best Gentlemen in the country, for having set such an example, which, they said, they hoped would banish that false pride that too many of their countrymen were actuated by." But Mercer's brother, a captain in the British army then quartered in Alexandria, considered carpentry beneath the dignity of a gentleman and "found means to make his nephew uneasy." The elder Mercer, too, was "incessantly teazed, by those who well knew their interest over me, until I was brought to consent very reluctantly that he [Mercer's son] should quit the plumb and square . . . but it seems that vile art of a carpenter is a blemish not to be effaced."[78] Apprenticeship itself was not the problem, for some of Virginia's wealthiest planters, including Robert Carter I and William Byrd II, had been apprenticed to merchants. Nor was facility in handicraft repugnant. John Locke had approved of "Gardening or Husbandry in general, and working in Wood, as a Carpenter, Joyner, or Turner, these being fit and healthy Recreations for a Man of Study, or Business." But Locke also limited manual arts as "the Recreations of one, whose chief Business is with Books and Study."[79] The real social barrier lay in the equivocal status of the building profession in colonial Virginia, with its unresolved demands for facility in both theory and practice. Earning a living through *techne,* even at a highly skilled level, was an unacceptably base source of income to men ranked as gentlemen, and the architecture profession in Virginia had yet to shed its craft associations. Eighteenth-century Virginia was coming to terms with tensions that had been played out between humanists and guild members in quattrocento Italy, master builders and gentlemen architects in Britain—namely, resolving the relative merits of intellectual and physical exertion in what was fundamentally a collaborative process.[80] Competence in the building arts was perfectly legitimate among the Virginia native elite as long as the hand did not tarry too long upon the plane and lathe.

Chapter 5

Learning to Become "Good Mechanics in Building"

The Problem of Architectural Literacy

In 1748, the Virginia spinster Martha Jaquelin wrote to her young nephews then studying at Wakefield Academy. Jaquelin came from a politically powerful family wealthy enough to pay for her portrait when she was a young woman (fig. 101). Despite its stylized limner conventions, the portrait captures the independent spirit communicated through her letter. After relating in a rather breezy manner which of their chums had died of a recent epidemic of smallpox, she admonished her nephews to study diligently and went on to cajole one boy, "We hear Jack, you are grown a nice drawer pray let me have some of your Performance. I promise you A Guinea for your Trouble, and that I think pretty good pay."[1] Jaquelin's bid was good pay indeed, and her letter not only conveys the affectionate and indulgent love of an aunt to her beloved nephews but reveals how some upper-class Virginians acquired a modicum of drawing skill and indicates how that skill was encouraged. Her animated letter provides a rare glimpse into the complex way that Virginia's native elite gained knowledge about architecture.

In order to collaborate effectively with professional builders in the construction of their prodigy houses, Virginia's wealthy planters faced two problems: first, what design features were important to emulate, and second, how to create them. Acquiring the arbitrary aesthetic design values of eighteenth-century architecture and the specialized knowledge necessary to materialize them did not come about by accident. Virginia's prodigy houses comprised a set of visual features that set them apart from less aesthetically self-conscious vernacular buildings. By contrast, high-style architecture was terribly self-conscious and was deliberately intended to display a body of knowledge that was considered crucial to know; crucial, that is, among the privileged few. This body of knowledge, an architectural theory if you will, consisted of a relatively limited number of visual preferences rooted in Renaissance aesthetic values: symmetry of elevation and plan;

proportional relationships between parts and of parts to whole; references, albeit abbreviated ones, to ornament derived from the classical Orders; and allusions to design elements that, however remote, had their origins in the prestige architecture of Britain. Eighteenth-century Virginia planters had to learn to admire symmetry and to prize classical pilasters and entablatures like those at Stratford Hall (fig. 102). They also had to learn that the exuberantly curved gable ends and elaborately articulated chimney stacks seen at Bacon's Castle (1665) were no longer worthy of emulation. Creating high-style architecture in eighteenth-century Virginia required owners to acquire a set of aesthetic principles that were distinct from traditional colonial building practices. The question then is, how did Virginia's native elite acquire this high-style or academic architectural competency?

Fig. 101. Attributed to Nehemiah Partridge, *Portrait of Martha Jaquelin,* oil on canvas, ca. 1722. (Virginia Museum of Fine Arts, Richmond; Lent by the Ambler Family; © Virginia Museum of Fine Arts)

Fig. 102. Stratford Hall, Westmoreland County, 1738. Detail of pilaster and entablature in Great Hall. (Historic American Building Survey, Prints and Photographs Division, Library of Congress)

There is no single, clear answer. No systematic process of conveying architectural values existed for ambitious and wealthy Virginians. Instead, the means of acquiring architectural competence was piecemeal, synthetic, and more often accomplished within private rather than public domains. However, information teased out from extant documentary fragments such as Jaquelin's delightful epistle to her nephews points to six identifiable sources of architectural information. These sources also reveal that the acquisition of architectural literacy, like the acquisition of Latin grammar, served as a sign of elite prestige and was manipulated and displayed in an attempt to inscribe social privilege permanently into a fluid social environment.

Formal Education

Formal education contributed to the architectural education of future mansion owners in three specific ways: it gave them access to a body of literature in which aesthetic appreciation and style was validated; it inculcated numeracy; and, occasionally, it provided them with drawing ability. A cursory glance at the schooling of the scions of elite planters, however, shows that little of the curricular content was aimed at visual education. Instead, mastery of the written word in English and Latin stood as the objective of formal education.

Members of Virginia's native elite were keen to give luster to their nouveau riche status by polishing their linguistic skills. In a letter of 1776 concerning his son's schooling in England, Robert Beverley of Blandfield sketched the curriculum he considered fundamental to the formation of his son and heir:

> He has but little classical knowledge, and therefore my wish is, that he should be placed under some able clergyman as a private tutor, who may give him some idea of the Latin language, of history, and geography, and in short any other accomplishments requisite to form a Man of the World. . . . [He should] make himself acquainted with modern Languages, which I find by experience to be absolutely necessary in the polite and active scene of life.[2]

Beverley emphasizes the written word, Latin grammar, modern languages, the lessons to be learned from history, and a sense of the larger world. Neither theology, science, visual art, nor architecture represented a part of Beverley's ideal curriculum.

Anxious colonial fathers such as Richard Ambler put great stock in acquiring a historical perspective of the world, but he also wanted his sons to communicate in a fashionably metropolitan rather than a markedly provincial mode of expression. In a letter of 1749, Ambler urged his sons at the Wakefield Academy to study history, "which I much approve, as it will enlarge your knowledge and make you acquainted with Men and Things which happen'd in Ages long since passed." Ambler continued to advise them that "if you'd read the Spectator deliberately you will observe a great beauty and correctness in the stile." Rich colonial Virginians like Ambler purchased the *Tatler* and the *Spectator* throughout the century. From the *Spectator,* elite Virginians such as Robert Carter III and his family not only acquired clues about writing style but absorbed information about gentlemanly deportment, current landscape design, and London aesthetic trends.[3]

We witness the influence of English literature in the writing of William Byrd II, who owned one of the most impressive colonial libraries. In the *Spectator*, no. 37 (12 April 1711), Joseph Addison described the country seat of the character Leonara as "situated in a kind of Wilderness, about an hundred Miles distant from London, and looks like a little enchanted Palace." Addison's description of a country seat amid a rugged setting seems the likely inspiration for Byrd's 1732 description of Germanna, the remote colonial mansion of former governor Alexander Spotswood that today retains a portion of its rustic environs (fig. 103). Byrd dubbed the mansion an "enchanted Castle" and drew a literary image suspiciously similar to Addison's picturesque passage. According to Addison, Leonora's "woods are cut into shady Walks," and "the Springs are made to run among Pebbles, and by that means taught to murmur very agreeably." According to Byrd, at Germanna there was "a Shady Lane to the Landing," and along the way he drank "some very fine Water that issued from a Marble Fountain, and ran incessantly." Both Addison and Byrd end their literary episodes with a joke at the expense of a woman.[4] It is doubtful that "enchanted Castle" can be construed as a descriptive term. Indeed, Byrd used the same term in 1735 in an apparently facetious reference to the ancient, reviled, but occasionally risible Fleet Ditch debtor's prison in London.[5] Moreover, the phrase's pedigree goes back further than Byrd and Addison. In his essay "Of Building," Francis Bacon referred to the "Enchanted Pallaces of the Poets" as a way of condemning houses that put fanciful design before practical function.[6] Through polite literature by writers such as Bacon and Addison, Virginia's native elite acquired aesthetic models and linguistic templates with which to order the colonial built environment.

Rather than imparting specific classicizing designs through a specific course of study, a quality education gave the Virginia pupil access to literature that imparted the patina of cultural literacy. This broader range of literature, namely history, classical and modern authors, courtesy manuals, and travel and antiquities guides generated a desire to demonstrate one's worth through building. Even young Virginia women who were barred from grammar school, such as Frances Baylor Hill, reaped knowledge about architecture if they had access to the beguiling literature of privilege. At the end of the eighteenth century, Hill would record in her diary her rapt fascination with "a disription [*sic*] of the most magnificent building that ever I read or heard off, there was one in particular spoken of call'd the Kings hunting palace it had in it 1500 rooms all beautifully furnish'd and another that had 800 which was as elegantly fited out as the one before mentioned."[7]

Though literate Virginians could often read portions of the *Gentleman's Magazine* in William Park's *Virginia Gazette*, only a lucky few subscribed to the prestigious journal. Fewer still had their names mentioned in its columns. When Robert Carter I died, for example, his wealth and prestige

Fig. 103. Landscape at Germanna, Spotsylvania County. (Photograph by author)

warranted an obituary. Philip Ludwell Lee, eldest son of the builder of Stratford Hall, was an avid reader and penned his mother's obituary, which was published in the May 1750 issue. The *Gentleman's Magazine* included illustrations of British architecture, and in later issues of 1750 Lee could have studied an illustration of the interior of Wren's St. Stephen, Walbrook church with its domed roof supported on a grove of sixteen elegant Corinthian columns. He could have also perused a view of Florence, and the elevations of eight city gates into London.[8] But while the most privileged among Virginia's native elite might have seen such stylish models, they did not imitate them. By reading fashionable English literature, wealthy young Virginians learned a more abstract but equally valuable lesson: the concept of artful rhetorical gestures in building as well as literature.

Although knowledge of classical authors and modern literature was the hallmark of the most polished education, additional fields of study were requisite for elite cultural literacy. Pragmatic skills were also necessary to make a "Man of the World" and for negotiating the colonial Virginia building process. Formal education also provided an elite Virginian with practical accounting skills useful in operating a successful plantation. Merchant-oriented training became an increasingly important component of formal gentry education in early modern Britain, and classroom drill was occasionally supplemented by apprenticeship. William Byrd II, for example, acquired his business acumen in mercantile establishments in Holland and London.[9] According to the historian J. A. Bennett, mid-sixteenth-century educators exploited a well-known architectural metaphor, namely a sure foundation, to argue that mathematics was the sure theoretical basis of knowledge.[10] Interestingly, to make the argument meaningful, these early modern educators assumed that their audience would have fully understood the role of foundations in the building process. In other words, a certain level of architectural competency on the part of those able to purchase books about mathematics was assumed.

By the eighteenth century, the new importance of numeracy in a capitalistic economy was reflected in the education offered to the sons of the upwardly mobile. A 1766 advertisement for Reverend B. Booth's Academy near Liverpool claimed that students would learn not only English, Latin, Greek, and writing, but arithmetic, merchants' accounts, geography, navigation, astronomy, surveying, mathematics, drawing, and perspective. Similarly, the 1769 curriculum at the Academy at Leeds included English, classics, modern languages, and penmanship, but also arithmetic, merchants' accounts, mathematics, geography, "experimental philosophy," and astronomy.[11]

The commercial numeracy absorbed by the sons of colonial planters would prove advantageous in estimating crop yield, freight charges, and exchange rates between local money and pounds sterling. And, in the absence of a sufficient number of building contractors, patrons exploited the same skills to estimate materials, and contract with carpenters, masons, and joiners in conducting ambitious domestic or public building campaigns. Successfully creating genteel architecture in Virginia required close attention to pecuniary details that we more readily associate with hard-boiled merchant capitalists, not polite or stereotypically languorous planters.

Formal education occasionally included some instruction in drawing. Facility in graphic representation, however, was viewed as a convenient and practical skill for members of the emerging commercial elite, not as the foundation of future artistic achievement. The evolution of drawing from craft to liberal art is a well-known Renaissance story with its origins in fifteenth-century Italy. By the late seventeenth century, instruction in the graphic arts was considered a proper and beneficial component of an English gentleman's education, but secondary to classical literature. The ability to draw was encouraged, for instance, in Henry Peacham's *Complete Gentleman,* a text found in a number of colonial libraries. John Locke, too, approved of drawing as a gentlemanly embellishment. Concurring with the advice given in Castiglione's 1528 *Book of the Courtier,* a copy of which was owned by Robert Carter III, Locke saw drawing as

> a thing very useful to a Gentleman in several occasions; but especially if he travel, as that which helps a Man often to express, in a few Lines well put together, what a whole Sheet of Paper in Writing, would not be able to represent, and make intelligible. How many Buildings may a Man see, how many Machines and Habits meet with, the Ideas where of would be easily retain'd and communicated, by a little Skill in Drawing; which being committed to Words, are in danger to be lost, or at best but ill retained in the most exact Description? I do not mean that I would have your Son a perfect Painter; to be that to any tolerable degree, will require more time, than a Young Gentleman can spare from his other Improvement of greater Moment. But so much insight into Perspective, and skill in Drawing, as will enable him to represent tolerably on Paper any thing he sees, except Faces.[12]

Locke's qualified endorsement of drawing encouraged some wealthy Virginians to learn drawing as a gentlemanly accomplishment. While he resided in London in 1717, William Byrd II hired the watercolor artist Thomas Albin "to teach me to draw." Albin also instructed Byrd in art appreciation and collecting. In the spring of 1718, "Mr. Albin then came to bring some prints." Byrd, it should be noted, was learning to draw as an adult in his forties. His grammar school education at England's Felsted School, his apprenticeships with Dutch merchants, and his legal training at the Middle Temple in London left little time for fine arts classes.[13] Attitudes toward the utility of drawing in genteel education, as the art historian Ann Bermingham has shown, were altered by the imperatives of the commercial revolution.[14]

When schools taught drawing it was not to train professional artists but to provide a supplementary tool useful to other, specifically mercantile vocations. As we have already seen, certain English grammar schools, such as that run by Richard B. Booth, and the Wakefield Academy, did provide instruction in surveying, drawing, and perspective. Martha Jaquelin was happy to encourage her nephew's emerging graphic talent, but the goal of Wakefield Academy was not to nurture a sophisticated level of amateur artistry. The prescribed curriculum of grammar school education was liberal and utilitarian in content, not professional. In short, there is no evidence to suggest that knowledge of the building arts represented a significant educational objective in grammar schools, nor that drawing instruction was attuned to architectural design.

While drawing instruction at Booth's Academy or at Wakefield was directed to pragmatic problem solving, it still represented a privileged endeavor. The specialized tools that would have been manipulated by Locke's hypothetical pupil to depict buildings, machines, and "habits" would in themselves have marked the user's gentlemanly status. Such instruments were precious, expensive objects that could be purchased only by the wealthy, and their marketing was part of the new didactic emphasis on numeracy. How-to books about drawing, such as Carrington Bowles's 1760 figure-drawing manual, were also costly and were seldom purchased, even by wealthy Virginians.[15]

If drawing comprised a significant part of an eighteenth-century English gentlemanly education, there is very little to show for it in Virginia. To be certain, the Carter tutor at Nomini Hall, Philip Vickers Fithian, recorded that he drew a design at the request of one of his young female charges and made "my Scetch of Nominy-Hall" for another. In a less representational though more spatially complex exercise, the young woman Frances Baylor Hill of Hillsborough Plantation had to think in terms of two- and three-dimensional design when she "drew a patron" (pattern) or cut out fabric for the caps, aprons, and "vandike" collars she sewed at the end of the century. More than eighty years before, Governor Francis Nicholson established his reputation in design by devising plans for Annapolis and Williamsburg. Nicholson's work in the New World was sufficiently well known and valued among the English intelligentsia that Humphrey Ditton dedicated his 1712 textbook entitled *Treatise on Perspective* to the former governor of Virginia, Maryland, New York, and the Carolinas. Evidence supporting the knowledge of drafting, however, is extremely rare, and even references to drawings in written documentation are infrequent.[16]

Thomas Jefferson's drawings offer insight into an elite gentleman's drawing expertise, but they may not represent the drafting abilities of his planter cohorts. Jefferson's unusually voluminous body of extant drawings shows him adept at employing both simplified graphical modes and more elaborate scaled drawings. He made loose, freehand sketches as well as more carefully executed elevation drawings of Monticello I (figs. 104 and 105).

Jefferson's use of graph paper after 1784, his adoption of the pencil, and the evolution of his orthographic style provide some insight into his development as a draftsman, but because he did not date his drawings, the sequence of many of his drawings remains tantalizingly conjectural.[17]

George Washington drew simple outline diagrammatic plans with only a few spare lines. Such a minimal mode of representation fits easily within colonial surveying practices wherein surveyors such as Washington, who received instruction in surveying from his older brother and who was heir to his father's surveying instruments, platted real estate with single straight lines.[18] This does not mean that Washington's earlier drawing exhibited either a naïve or amateurish understanding of architectural representation. On the contrary, the same visual economy was employed by professional colonial builders and can be seen in Richard King's 1719 plan for the Swan Tavern in Yorktown as well as in Richard Munday and Benjamin Wyatt's 1739 plan for the Daniel Ayrault House in Newport, Rhode Island.[19]

Though few architectural drawings survive, we do know that they were used by patrons and craftsmen alike in colonial Virginia. One needs to be cautious and sensitive to the dual meaning of the word "plan" when it appears in public records. A plan could refer to a description, a set of specifications, or to the graphic representation of the intended building. In 1710, the Bruton Parish vestry received a "platt or draught" from Alexander Spotswood of his proposed church design, a phrase intended to indicate a drawing.[20] Spotswood's platt represented an image of a T-shaped church, minus the eastern addition and tower built later in the century. As we know from the comments of Governor William Keith of Pennsylvania, Spotswood was a gifted mathematician whose talent in geometry presumably informed his ability to draw a two-dimensional plan. Like those few drawings that survive from colonial Virginia, the sketch was probably very simple.

Two-dimensional plans, in conjunction with detailed specifications, were made both before and after an undertaker was engaged. For example, on 8 August 1759, the Stratton Major Parish vestry ordered the churchwardens to "give Publick Notice that a New Church is to be Built" and further ordered a meeting the next February "in Order to receive Planns from Undertakers & agree for Building the same." It was only at the February meeting that precise specifications were recorded in the vestry book, indicating that the design was the undertaker's.[21] The design process for the James City County courthouse differed. After the Common Council of the town of Williamsburg "had determined to build a commodious brick Courthouse," they instructed prospective contractors that the "plan of the above courthouse may be seen at Mr. Hay's, at any time."[22] A more skilled draftsman might be engaged for the production of a higher-quality drawing. On 3 December 1771, the St. Mark's Parish vestry ordered the churchwardens

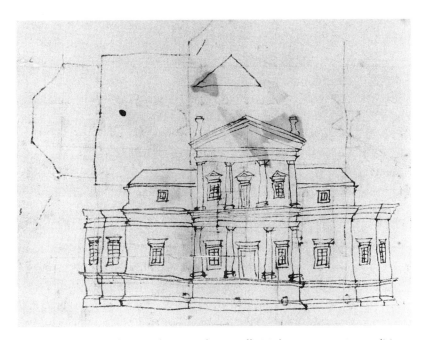

Fig. 104. Thomas Jefferson, *Elevation of Monticello I,* ink on paper, 1769–70. (Monticello/Thomas Jefferson Foundation, Inc.)

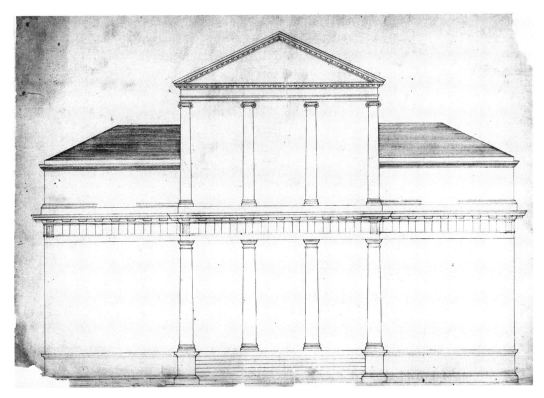

Fig. 105. Thomas Jefferson, *Elevation of Monticello I,* ink on paper, ca. 1771–72. (Elizabeth D. Moyer and Stevens M. Moyer)

to "Prepare Plans for the Building a Glebe House and Exhibit them to the vestry on Easter Tuesday next." Six months later, the vestry named one of their own, James Slaughter, to serve as undertaker, but they paid Peter Taliaferro "three Pounds for a plan."[23]

An associate who knew how to communicate graphically could also lend a hand to a building project. Although John Blair was a wealthy and powerful planter, not a professional draftsman, he obliged his friend John Custis IV (fig. 106) in this way. Lacking the skill that would convey his ideas to craftsmen, Custis enlisted Blair's help in drawing a plan for the house Custis wanted to provide for his illegitimate mulatto son. Custis's will clarified the relationship between design concept and graphic representation when he promised his son "a handsome strong convenient dwelling house according to the dimensions I shall direct and a plan thereof drawn by my said friend John Blair Esquire."[24] In other words, Custis determined design, and Blair served as draftsman. Custis chose well. Blair's surviving diary reflects the mind of a man who took special pride in his architectural experience and competence.[25]

No matter what the level of drawing sophistication, graphic representation did not constitute an absolute prerequisite for communicating design between patron and builder. Before carefully delineated orthogonal projections became standard professional practice in the mid-nineteenth century, specifically written descriptions and verbal instructions functioned as reliable ways for colonial Virginians to create serviceable, even elegant, buildings. The architectural historian Catherine W. Bishir characterized the generalized building terms found in building contracts as comprising a social compact between parties who understood a more precise meaning. For most colonial buildings, these linguistic conventions sufficed.[26] A 1775 Augusta County, Virginia, building contract for a frame house sketches only the essentials: "thirty two feet long and eighteen feet wide from outside to outside to be eight feet from floor to floor to be covered and weatherboarded with clapboards two Tire of joists to be laid and the whole job to be finished in a workmanlike manner."[27] The contract assumes a certain shared understanding of technological terms such as "two Tire of joists" and a common meaning of what level of skill represented a "workmanlike manner."

Virginia's professional undertakers and craftsmen were not dependent on graphic representations to demonstrate or achieve a respectable edifice built according to local and regional standards. But Virginia's native elite desired houses that far surpassed local and regional standards. From his research on early Virginia courthouses, Carl Lounsbury speculated that drawings may have been more imperative if patrons wanted to convey new design concepts to builders inclined to follow traditional practices.[28]

Fig. 106. Charles Bridges, *Portrait of John Custis IV,* 1735–45 (after an earlier portrait of 1725), oil on canvas. (Washington-Custis-Lee Collection, Washington and Lee University, Lexington, Virginia)

Because so few drawings of domestic buildings survive, it is impossible to know if they served a similar function as a vehicle for innovation in residential architecture.

Plantation Management

The second conduit by which elite colonial Virginians acquired their architectural education was through plantation management. Even if they hired overseers, prudent and profitable planters supervised all aspects of plantation operations carefully, not only tobacco cultivation, but grain, livestock, and food production. Most of these agricultural endeavors required buildings or enclosures, and it was the owner who ultimately ordered, supervised, and decided upon their form, construction, and maintenance. From the few surviving diaries, account books, and letters of the architectural patrons in the study group, it is clear that they actively sought to increase their income by making capital improvements to their plantation properties. Robert Carter I, for instance, needed to find storage facilities for the huge quantity of cider he produced. His son Landon Carter experimented with grain-drying bins and heated lambing houses.

A number of architectural patrons in the study group supplemented their tobacco income by trying to diversify their economic base, a strategy often requiring purpose-built structures. John Mercer and Richard Corbin built private tobacco warehouses. John Carlyle erected a warehouse in Alexandria, and Thomas Lee built a transport landing along the Potomac at Stratford Hall. At least fifteen architectural patrons in the study group possessed gristmills or sawmills, a major capital investment often requiring specialized and expensive equipment from England. When Richard Corbin realized he had made errors in calculating the dimensions of millstones he ordered, he was greatly relieved to learn he could send correct specifications before the next shipment sailed.

Some planters took greater personal interest in capital improvements to their property than others, but failure to keep a rein on plantation operations and expenditures could and in fact did lead to financial disaster and social embarrassment. For example, John Mercer attempted to expand his economic base by building a brewery, and decided to focus his attention on that endeavor. He later justified his single-mindedness by claiming, "My rule has always been that every thing I attempted ought to be set about in earnest & not carried on by piecemeal my business & [law] practice prevented my superintending it, without which I am now satisfied no business will prosper." In order to devote all his energies to the brewery project, Mercer delegated the rest of his plantation affairs to hired overseers, who "were supplied with everything they demanded, as I neither wanted money or credit." He later discovered that his quarrelsome overseers had left his agricultural operations in complete disarray.[29] Mortified by the sorry state of his affairs, he felt compelled to explain his financial misadventures in the *Virginia Gazette*. Mercer's public mea culpa, directed to his creditors, supports the historian T. H. Breen's concept of the psychological weight of tobacco cultivation, namely that a planter's sense of self-esteem was intimately tied to his agricultural abilities.[30] Depending on their ultimate financial return, building projects could either enhance or diminish that sense of worth.

Granted, there was little need to know the difference between Doric and Ionic Orders when it came to constructing a tobacco warehouse, gristmill, or brewery. But with personal prestige as a planter at stake, there was great incentive in knowing what species of wood was durable, what framing system was efficient, and what a proposed structure would cost in labor and materials. Wise planters would have calculated exchange rates, insurance charges, and shipping costs for imported items such as millstones. Prudent planters would also avoid diverting slave labor to activities such as sawing during months of peak agricultural production. All of this experience was brought to bear when constructing a mansion. Knowing local building practices was essential. Without it even the most exalted members of Virginia's colonial hierarchy could find construction daunting. Lieutenant Governor Alexander Spotswood, who had ample experience in British military campaigns but no experience in managing a Virginia plantation, explained his inability to estimate the cost of finishing the Governor's Palace by claiming that "it was very Difficult to make Computations in this Country."[31]

Some architectural patrons honed their practical construction-management skills during the construction of houses built prior to their more famous mansions. At least seven and possibly ten men erected or made substantial repairs to residences that antedated their primary mansion. We know very little about these lost earlier dwellings, but we can surmise that Charles Carter brought knowledge he gained from building Stanstead to the construction of Cleve. His brother Landon also learned from Lansdowne before he built Sabine Hall. Alexander Spotswood went through his paces in colonial building practice when he haggled with the colonial General Assembly for money to finish the Governor's Palace in a style he considered befitting the dignity of his office. He brought that knowledge to bear when building his large country seat on the edge of the frontier, the setting of which would later be described by Byrd à la Addison. Whereas the Governor's Palace represented the pinnacle of academic style, the earlier houses built by Robert Carter I, Charles Carter, John Mercer, and Landon Carter probably expressed more modest features. Nevertheless, the experience patrons gained in building their earlier dwellings would prove valuable in constructing their later, more extraordinary mansions.

Virginia's native elite sowed and reaped practical knowledge about construction when they collaborated on civic or religious building projects. By virtue of their position in offices such as justice of the peace or vestryman, they had greater opportunities to learn how to contract with craftsmen, and how undertakers succeeded and profited or failed when coordinating the complex management of building. Wealthy planters had learned enough about building through plantation management that their construction competency was evident to nonnative Virginians by the second quarter of the eighteenth century. It was, in fact, an identifying characteristic of prestige landowners. Hugh Jones noted in 1724 that "the Virginia planters readily learn to become good mechanics in building, wherein most are capable of directing their servants and slaves."[32]

It would be a mistake, however, to ascribe too much importance to practical plantation construction practices. It was one thing to have the technical and organizational knowledge necessary for putting up tobacco barns or even substantial dwelling houses, and quite another to have the aesthetic competence, or desire, to append a modillioned cornice to a house, a Roman arch to a courthouse, or corner quoins to a church. Between the two kinds of endeavors lay the intervention of outside, non-Virginia design factors.

Travel

The third factor contributing to the architectural education of colonial planters is just one of these outside influences, namely travel through England. Encouraged by an expanding post road system, sightseeing in rural as well as urban England became more feasible for moneyed tourists in the eighteenth century. In 1776, Mrs. Libbe Powys noted in her travel journal that 2,324 visitors had registered their names at the gatehouse of the famous English country house Wilton in the previous year. According to the historian William L. Sachse, very few American travel diaries failed to record "visits to great piles like Windsor, Blenheim, Chatsworth, or Wilton."[33]

Travel outside of the colony represents one of the characteristics that most sharply distinguished elite Virginia planters from their poor and middling neighbors, and a substantial number of the twenty-five architectural patrons in the study group traveled abroad before construction of their mansion. Of the seventeen individuals for whom the historical record is somewhat complete, two, William Randolph III and Thomas Jefferson, went to Europe after construction of their mansions. A significant number of patrons in the study group, fourteen, spent time in England, Scotland, or Ireland before they built their Virginia dwelling.[34] Travel to Britain, therefore, offers an attractive explanation for the infusion of metropolitan design values into vernacular building conventions in British North America. To what extent this travel experience influenced the architecture of gentility represents a more challenging question.[35]

Travel held a significant place in the education of English gentlemen in the early modern period. Consequently, wealthy Virginians valued travel for its ability to impart social and cultural distinction. Conventional English wisdom stressed the pragmatic rather than the aesthetic benefits of travel. In essay 18, Francis Bacon recommended a broad sightseeing itinerary wherein visits to courts of justice, churches, monasteries, libraries, and warehouses comprised a program meant to improve the character and general enlightenment of the elite traveler.[36] In Locke's famous phrase, travel was "commonly thought to finish the Work, and compleat the Gentleman." In his *Some Thoughts Concerning Education* (1693), Locke touted the advantages of travel as a means of acquiring foreign-language skills and as serving as "an Improvement in wisdom and Prudence, by seeing men, and conversing with People of Tempers, Customs, and Ways of Living, different from one another, and especially from those of his Parish and Neighborhood."[37] The recommendations of David Fordyce in his *Dialogues Concerning Education* (1745) expanded on Locke's pragmatic agenda. Fordyce recommended that students study

> chiefly the natural, political, and commercial state of countries: let him inspect their manufacturers, magazines, arsenals, work-houses, and their special regulations; examine their natural produce and foreign import, the price of their markets, the rise, fall, and revolutions, or [*sic*] their trade.[38]

For Locke and Fordyce, the arts had a proper place in a man's foreign travels, but the principal aim of travel was more businesslike. The English diarist John Evelyn thought otherwise. His journeys were more specifically focused on design, and his travel through Italy eventually led to his 1664 translation of Roland Fréart de Chambray's French architectural treatise. Snidely referring to Locke's pragmatic generalized notion of gentlemanly travel and comparing it with his own focused architectural fieldwork, Evelyn ridiculed "the entertainment of travelers who go not abroad to count steeples, but to improve themselves."[39]

Bacon and Locke circulated far more widely in Virginia than Fréart de Chambray so it is hardly surprising to discover that the journeys of elite Virginians were not dedicated to the close study of buildings. Financially prudent fathers and guardians of colonial boys only reluctantly underwrote travel. Richard Ambler, for example, prohibited his sons at Wakefield Academy from spending money on pleasure excursions, but conceded that later,

> when you come to be further advanced in years and shall have inclination to enquire into Trade and Commerce it may then be necessary to vissit defferent parts of England in order to make acquaintance, which may prove usefull in the future part of your lives, when you come to settle here in your own Country.

Three years later, when Edward Ambler finished his schooling, his father did allow him to travel through England, but here too the chief purpose was business, not aesthetic enrichment:

I would have you make your observations on what is remarkable, but always be mindfull to keep good Company, such will be able to assist you in making prudent observations, let not the business of Husbandry be below your notice when you happen to fall into conversation with skillfull Farmers.[40]

For the eminently practical Ambler, whose fortune derived from levies on tobacco exports and who constructed the remarkably aestheticized Custom House at Yorktown, other education priorities trumped a systematic study of architecture (fig. 107).

Nevertheless, some colonial students did take in the architectural wonders of England and not just those found in London. Grammar schools at Wakefield, Leeds, and Beverley in Yorkshire were popular with elite colonial Virginians because the cost of living in the northeast of England was substantially less than in London. Fashionable urban architecture was built in locales beyond London and Bristol, and classicizing country houses could be found throughout England.

No student travel journal has been located for the patrons in the study group, but the 1759 diary of William Shippen Jr. of Philadelphia proves that some students from well-endowed colonial families combined formal instruction with aesthetic enrichment. Shippen wedged his architectural expeditions into spare moments of his medical studies. On 19 August

Fig. 107. Custom House, Yorktown, 1720. (Valentine Richmond History Center)

1759, he visited "Sir John Shaw's Seat" at Eltham, designed by Hugh May, a building that shared some affinity to Virginia prodigy houses in its brick building materials and hipped roof. In his judgment, "there are many fine Rooms and elegantly furnished with some fine pieces of Painting and Tapestry" at Eltham. Two days later Shippen traveled to Hertford to see "Mr Braceys Grotto very neat and elegant indeed," and on 2 September he remarked that "Woodford which is situated on an Eminence commands very extensive Prospects." The next day, Shippen "walked 2 mile to Wansted to see Lord Tinley's Seat which is a Mere pallace fitter for a King than nobleman" and was also awed by its landscape design. In November, he "Went to see St. Pauls, whispering Gallery etc, etc, till 2," and on Christmas Day, he noted that he "went in the afternoon to Chelsea College and see all the Curiosity of it."[41] According to Hugh Jones's 1724 account of Williamsburg architecture, Christopher Wren's 1682 Chelsea College served as the inspiration for the design of the College of William and Mary, but it is unlikely that Shippen studied architecture by the comparative method. His side trips did not constitute a cohesive survey of the most up-to-date monuments of mid-eighteenth-century English architecture, and his brief recorded comments do not reflect the same depth of critical analysis as those of Thomas Jefferson.

Nevertheless, Shippen's diary provides great insight into how colonial visitors appraised the built environment. First, the diary shows that Shippen was attuned to trends in English landscape theory, and his remarks indicate that his taste had been informed by other sources, perhaps poetry, prose, or travel guides.[42] Second, he was aware of the association between high social rank and grand residences. Third, he was attracted to Wren's famous buildings but also took note of things like the "whispering Gallery" and "all the Curiosity of it" rather than its use of the Orders, its spatial monumentality, or its triple-shell dome structure. Finally, Shippen was impressed by luxurious interior furnishing within houses, but he did not pay much attention to, or at least did not write about, specific planning and elevation features. If young Virginians had similar experiences during their education in England, they returned, not with particular models to be copied in their entirety, but with more general and somewhat vague reminiscences of the kind of housing and accoutrements befitting people of quality whether they be ennobled or not.[43]

The impact of student travel was limited to Great Britain. With the exception of Richard Henry Lee, no native Virginia architectural patron is known with certainty to have taken the Grand Tour of the Continent before construction of his or her house. Alexander Spotswood, on the other hand, was born in Tangiers and spent time in Germany, France, and the Low Countries as an officer in the British Army. That few Virginians undertook the Grand Tour is not surprising. Like education, travel was tremendously expensive. Sons of the British nobility are known to have spent from £1,000 to £3,000 per year on their Grand Tour, which often lasted as long as five years. But even more frugal expeditions could cost £100 per annum.[44] Apart from Alexander Spotswood and Richard Henry Lee, a Virginia patron's firsthand knowledge of European architecture was limited to what could be seen in the British Isles.

Compared to dependent students, adult colonial tourists who controlled their own purse could conceivably take greater advantage of travel than minor students. But what they gained in financial freedom, they lost in time for journeys to England were made not for leisurely sightseeing but for pressing business and political purposes. The comments of South Carolinian Henry Laurens likely echoed the lament of other adult colonial travelers. Writing in 1748, Laurens regretted that he would not be able to benefit culturally from his English experience: "I promised this voyage should polish me and make me quite polite; but really I believe my time will be so taken up with business that I shall return just the fellow that left you in September last."[45] Laurens's experience may have represented the norm for wealthy adult visitors to England.

Even when colonial adults had time to take in the sights, what they viewed was probably a combination of utilitarian, artistic, and entertainment curiosities. Again, no travel journal or diary prior to construction has been located for the architectural patrons in the study group, but William Beverley's tour through England may represent the abbreviated, distracted, and perhaps typical adult tourist itinerary. Beverley journeyed to England in part to place his son Robert, who would eventually build Blandfield, in grammar school. Architecture was not beyond the elder Beverley's attention for he noted in his diary on 7 August 1750, the same day his party debarked at Beaumorris, Wales, that they "went on shoar with ye Capt. to ye Town & after we had refresh'd our selves we walk to view L'd Buckley's gardens, ye scituation of ye house was pleasant & romantic." Like Shippen's, Beverley's words suggest a prior acquaintance with eighteenth-century aesthetic theory, particularly regarding landscape design. On 20 August, Beverley, in the company of William Fairfax of Belvoir and "Mr Rich'd [Henry?] Lee" of Chantilly, went to "Leeds to see the cloath market," probably Ralph Thorsby's famed building where merchants bargained for textiles. Next Beverley and his companions "kept on & call'd ye York raceground where we saw ye race." The following day, "We view ye Cathedral" at York. At the end of the month, he "Viewed ye Minster" at Lincoln and also "Viewed Chatsworth" which he judged a "noble house." By October, Beverley was in London and was now accompanied by John Carlyle. He noted on 23 October 1750 that "we all dined at Majr F[airfa]x's house which is beautiful & had a kind entertainment & he carried us to ye play house Covent Garden & where yt Conscious Lovers was acted." Two days later, he left the metropolis and spent the night at the prehistoric ruins of Stonehenge. Beverley spend much of his time in England visiting relations and friends and in finding suitable yet affordable living accommodations for his son. But Beverley faced problems far more pressing. First, he had some trouble coming up with ready cash, and second, he was trying to counter the political machinations of Governor William Gooch, who was attempting to remove him from the Virginia Council.[46] While Beverley's diary points to an unmistakable interest and enjoyment in architecture, it also demonstrates that colonial tourists visited certain sites for reasons other than aesthetic appeal or because they could serve as architectural models for Virginia's prodigy houses. Certainly the cathedrals at York or Lincoln had no impact upon eighteenth-century Virginia church architecture. What was viewed along the way was a fortuitous mix of Gothic, Anglo-Dutch, Baroque, Anglo-Palladian, and industrial structures, some of which had little relation to building styles that were erected in Virginia.

Theoretically, travel could have allowed wealthy colonial visitors such as Beverley and Shippen to absorb current English fashions and imitate them in Virginia, thus expressing their superior status and social distance from the vernacular building practices of their neighbors. But the direct aesthetic impact of British architectural monuments on the fourteen architectural patrons who lived abroad is hard to prove. The richness of Rosewell's exterior articulation, including its refined brickwork and daring side elevation fenestration, definitely point to design influences outside of Virginia norms for genteel housing (fig. 108) Instead, Rosewell's exterior elevation design fits more closely within the Baroque and Mannerist features associated with the work of the English architects William Talman and Thomas Archer.[47] Mann Page I had access to the most fashionable ideas circulating in Britain, having attended Eton and then St. John's at Oxford. But despite the great exertion of numerous architectural historians, no English model has been convincingly identified as the prototype for Page's magnificent mansion.[48]

Men who lived in the British Isles in their youth might exhibit, one would imagine, their formative cultural experience in the mansions they built. But at Belvoir or Salubria (fig. 109), both built by immigrants, one is hard-pressed to see any greater concession to specifically English standards than to the taste of elite Virginians and the abilities of their builders. The use of stone at John Carlyle's elegant townhouse in Alexandria, for example, has been interpreted as reflecting the patron's origins in northwest England, where the principal building material was stone. Mann Page II also built his mansion, called Mannsfield, of stone (fig. 110). He, however,

Fig. 108. Rosewell, Gloucester County, 1726. (Virginia Historical Society, Richmond, Virginia)

was a fourth-generation Virginian, and no record of him ever having traveled abroad has been discovered.[49]

In terms of style, the clearly articulated Anglo-Palladianism massing exhibited in the design of John Randolph's Tazewell Hall, Richard Henry Lee's Chantilly, John Banister's Battersea, and Thomas Jefferson's Monticello I attests to the owner's familiarity with au courant taste in English architecture. Randolph, Lee, and Bannister are each known to have attended school in England and may have seen examples prior to building in Virginia, but the most vocal proponent of Palladian architecture, Thomas Jefferson, did not.

For some architectural patrons, the impact of their early travel was expressed through the dim light of memory. As a young apprentice to the merchant Arthur Bailey, Robert Carter I spent time in Mile End, a socially ascendant suburban neighborhood east of London popular with nouveau riche mariners and merchants.[50] Forty years later, in 1720, Carter built

Fig. 109. (*Opposite, top*) Salubria, Culpeper County, 1763. (Photograph by author)

Fig. 110. (*Opposite, bottom*) Mannsfield, Spotsylvania County, 1767. View of western dependency after the destruction of the mansion in the Civil War. (Virginia Historical Society, Richmond, Virginia)

Corotoman, which burned in 1729 and is known through archaeology undertaken in the 1970s (fig. 111). Yet, despite this temporal distance, modern archaeology at Carter's lost mansion demonstrates long-remembered architectural ambition. Not content with homegrown colonial features, Carter built a mansion with projecting side towers that alluded to examples of English Baroque architecture he probably saw as a youth (fig. 112).[51]

If the journeys of Shippen and Beverley are representative of the experiences of other rich and influential Virginians, we are left then with a conundrum. While a significant number of Virginia architectural patrons traveled to England, they did not necessarily copy what they saw. The greater influence of travel may rather have been the opportunity to see the realization of building styles with which they were already familiar through print sources. It is hazardous to put too much store in the impact of travel on shaping the design features of prodigy houses. Travel in Britain probably reinforced the association in the mind of the patron between architecture and social status, and may have provided a rather heterogeneous collection of half-remembered architectural motifs. The constraints of travel could

Fig. 111. Corotoman, Lancaster County, 1720. Aerial view of excavations. (Virginia Department of Historic Resources)

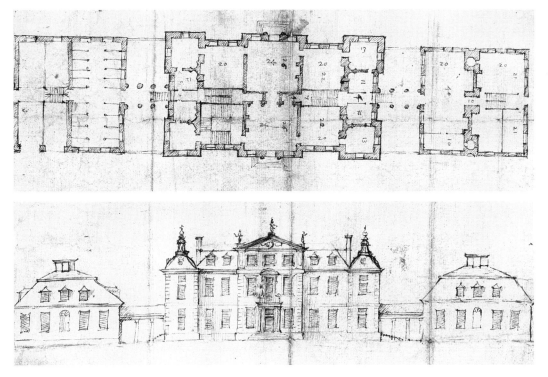

Fig. 112. Attributed to Christopher Wren or William Talman, *Plan and Elevation for an Unidentified Country House,* ca. 1690s. (The Warden and Fellows of All Souls College, Oxford)

not have afforded the patrons with a thorough and systematic exercise in architectural theory. Nor is there any evidence, either physical or documentary, that patrons viewed the most famous English buildings with the aim of copying those structures with any kind of exactitude. On the contrary, the British gentry houses that the architectural historian Daniel D. Reiff proposed as closer analogues to Virginia mansions received no comments by colonial tourists.[52]

What wealthy tourists did comment on, however, was likely a product of their prior expectations. Colonial Virginians did not arrive in England as architectural babes-in-the-woods. Patrons traveled to England with their taste in architecture already informed, sources that led Shippen to seek out "Mr Braceys Grotto" and Beverley to pronounce Chatsworth "a noble house." It is hard to ignore the significant number of architectural patrons who traveled to England. It is equally important to concede that the greatest benefit of travel to wealthy Virginia tourists was to see the concrete realization of building values they were already acquainted with through literature, criticism, and other printed material.

Architecture Books

Few aspects of Virginia's colonial architectural history have undergone as much revision as our understanding of the role of books. Publications specifically about building, especially those with illustrations, have frequently been cited as the primary conduit of architectural fashion and building knowledge from England to the colonies. Writing in 1922, S. Fiske Kimball claimed that "the adoption of the new style came about in America in the same way in which it did . . . in England, through the making of its form universally accessible to intelligent workmen, or even laymen, by means of books."[53] Kimball's confident assertion inspired generations of both scholarly and popular writers to search for the illustrated model behind the elevation design, planning principles, and interior ornamentation of scores of colonial buildings.

Other architectural historians evaluated print sources more cautiously. Writing in 1952, Hugh Morrison warned readers that "handbooks were used less for plans of buildings or elevations of whole facades than they were for details." He also wisely told his audience that "carpenters and joiners of the colonies departed freely—and usually intelligently—from their sources." Marcus Whiffen likewise conferred only a qualified endorsement of the influence of architectural books and acknowledged that examples of direct borrowing were extremely rare. Yet the myth of the pattern book as the prevailing influence on polite colonial design remained very attractive to historians and historic house museum docents alike. One writer in the 1980s went as far as to proclaim that books were the "true architects" of the mansions of the Chesapeake region.[54] In 1984, Dell Upton discounted pattern book influence more emphatically. In its place, he emphasized the role of competent colonial craftsmen in a well-established building industry that had developed its own classicizing architectural vocabulary without constant recourse to pattern books.[55]

The documentary record supports this revised assessment of the pattern book influence, although it must be stated at the outset that the evidence is complex and often contradictory. On the one hand, we have John Ariss's advertisement in the *Maryland Gazette* on 22 May 1751, which reads in part: "By the Subscriber (lately from Great Britain) Buildings of all Sorts and Dimensions are undertaken and performed in the neatest Manner . . . either of the Ancient or Modern Order of Gibb's Architect."[56] To be effective as an advertisement, the message had to be comprehensible to readers familiar with Gibbs and who would value Ariss's ability in reproducing features from Gibbs's luxury quarto engraved plates. On the other hand, surprisingly few references to architecture books can be found in the documentary record of most architectural patrons. In short, it is difficult to assign published sources as the principal conduit of architectural competence among Virginia's native elite.

Among the twenty-five architectural patrons in the study group, only five are known with any certainty to have owned books offering advice on the design of the built environment. One rare piece of evidence of architecture book ownership can be glimpsed in connection with Alexander Spotswood. Unfortunately, the appraisers of his property did not list his library—which he bequeathed in his will of 1740 to the College of William and Mary—by title. Among the very few books to survive the several fires at the college, however, is one noted as his gift: the first volume of Piganiol de la Force's *Description des chateaux et parcs de Versailles, de Trianon, et de Marly* (Amsterdam, 1715).[57] Spotswood also owned a book called "Evelyn's Gardening," a volume thought to have been Jean de la Quintine's treatise, which was translated into English by John Evelyn in 1693 and published as *The Compleat Gard'ner.*[58]

This last volume was lent in 1726 to John Mercer, who recorded it in his book list. In March 1748, Mercer purchased four other architectural publications, which have been identified as Edward Hoppus's *The Gentleman's and Builder's Repository on Architecture Displayed* (2nd ed., 1738); William Salmon's *Palladio Londinensis* (1st ed., 1734); Giacomo Leoni's *The Architecture of A. Palladio in Four Books* (1st ed., 1715–20); and Batty Langley's *The City and Country Builder's and Workman's Treasury of Designs* (1st ed., 1740).[59] Significantly, Mercer bought these Anglo-Palladian publications at the time the exterior of his mansion, Marlborough, was already taking shape, so whatever influence they exerted, it was exercised in decorative details rather than exterior design.

The library at Sabine Hall has survived, and many of the titles have been identified as belonging to Landon Carter, including M. Loriot's *A Practical Essay on Cement, and Artificial Stone, justly supposed to be that of the Greeks and Romans* (1774).[60] Carter's architectural holdings probably comprised additional, more influential titles that have subsequently left the collection. A translation of *The Four Books of Architecture* by Palladio probably served Carter with the inspiration for his design for a "Roman Arch" in the interior of the new Richmond County courthouse in 1749.[61] In a diary entry of 30 July 1770, he claimed credit for the design of a new bridge for the county: "The plan was my own taken from Vitruviusis [*sic*] bridge over the Rhine in Julius Caesar's days."[62] Carter drew his inspiration for the bridge probably from a bridge over the Rhine described in Palladio's third book.[63]

Carter's Grove also indicates the way architectural patrons selectively employed pattern books. When Carter Burwell bought an edition of William Salmon's *Palladio Londinensis, or, the London Art of Building* in 1751, he had already started construction of the main building, and the offices to each side were probably finished. He was looking to books, in other words, not to make his exterior but his interior stair hall conform to English taste (fig. 113). Nevertheless, there is no wholesale copying of Salmon's text at Carter's Grove.

Thomas Jefferson's acquisition of architecture books began, he claimed, when he purchased his first volume outside the gates of the College of William and Mary as a student. The immense and immensely expensive libraries he assembled over the course of his lifetime have been the subject of much scholarship.[64] Analysis of his early 1770s sketch designs for Monticello I and of his accompanying annotations demonstrate that he was well acquainted with the works of Andrea Palladio, Claude Perrault, and James Gibbs. But the books he possessed as a youth were lost in the 1770 fire at his parents' home in Albemarle County, Shadwell. And, because Monticello I was obliterated in 1796, when he built the house seen now, the relationship

Fig. 113. Carter's Grove, James City County, begun 1750. Stair hall. (Cook Collection, Valentine Richmond History Center)

between what he actually constructed in the 1770s and his book-inspired drawings remains speculative. Jefferson might not have realized his ambitious paper plans for Monticello I completely. But even in its incomplete form, the Marquis de Chastellux recognized Jefferson's architectural erudition as compared to that of his colonial cohorts when he noted that Monticello I "resembles none of the others seen in this country; so that it may be said that Mr. Jefferson is the first American who has consulted the Fine Arts to know how he should shelter himself from the weather."[65]

Sharing among relatives may account for a wider circulation of architecture texts. For instance, many of Robert Carter I's books may have been lost in the fire that destroyed Corotoman in the winter of 1729. However, the inventory of his elder brother, John Carter II (died 1690), notes, "Joachym Scughim of Architecture," a title that was probably one of the translated English editions of Joachim Schuym's Dutch version of Vincent Scamozzi's treatise on the Orders, to which was appended practical construction advice.[66] When Charles Carter built, he seems to have had access to this book. He also may have used a volume cited by his brother John (died 1743) in a letter of 26 August 1738 as the "Builders Dictionary," which was likely Richard Neve's *The City and Country Purchaser, and Builder's Dictionary*, first published in 1703.[67] John Carter II's library also included Charles Estienne and Jean Liebault's *Maison rustique, or, The Countrie Farm*, translated by Richard Surflet (1600), revised edition by Gervase Markham (1616). Surviving books from their father's library included John Evelyn's *Sylva, or a Discourse of Forest Trees* (1664), which, starting with the second edition of 1670, included a discussion of landscape design.[68] Through these books, Charles Carter acquired a working vocabulary of classical architectural features, and accounts with his brother John in 1738–39 mention the work of stonemasons for a "Pedestal, Architrave & Cornice for two chimneys."[69]

Mann Page I's knowledge of environmental design may have been increased though his access to the library of his first father-in-law, Ralph Wormeley II (died 1701). Wormeley owned a book listed in his inventory as "the country ffarme," identified by Betty C. Leviner as Estienne and Liebault's *Maison rustique*; and the "ffrench Gardiner," identified as a translation by John Evelyn, published as *The French Gardiner: instructing how to cultivate all Sorts of fruit-trees and Herbs for the garden . . . translated into English by Philocepos* (1658).[70]

The titles of George Mason IV's book collection at Gunston Hall do not survive, but one might reasonably imagine that he had access to the substantial number of architectural books owned by his uncle John Mercer of Marlborough. Mason's linguistic competency in architectural vocabulary suggests a familiarity with pattern books but also more theoretical texts. His endorsement on the back of William Buckland's indenture, wherein he praises Buckland as "a complete Master of the Carpenter's and Joiner's Business both in Theory and Practice," is telling. By pairing the opposing terms "theory" and "practice," Mason echoes books such as the 1703 edition of Joseph Moxon's *Mechanick Exercises,* wherein the author distinguishes between "those Workmen who understand the Theorick part of Building, as well as the Practick."[71] In showing off his learning, Mason also flattered those who read his endorsement: presumably they, too, could discern between theory and practice and would judge Buckland's work accordingly.

Codes of gentlemanly conduct that equated magnanimity with nobility would have encouraged lending among friends of similar social status. It would be foolish to place too much emphasis on the hypothetical circulation of books among associates, but some possibilities make more sense than others. For example, the inventory of Benjamin Harrison IV is not extant, so we will never know what Harrison owned. After his father died, his close neighbor William Byrd II took a paternal interest in the young man and helped negotiate Harrison's marriage into the Carter family. With such a personal affiliation between neighboring families, it is difficult to imagine that Byrd did not allow Harrison access to his library and print collection.[72] Byrd, however, records no such event in his diaries. Speculation about borrowing, moreover, fails to account sufficiently for the lack of a convincing number of architecture books found in the documentary record.

Apart from documentary evidence, the record of physical evidence also fails to support the argument that pattern books served as the sole means by which Virginia's native elite became adept in architectural design. If architectural patrons had access to pattern books, they rarely directed their builders to copy them for the elevations or plans for their prodigy houses. No doubt, similarities exist. The H-shaped plan fashionable in Elizabethan and Jacobean England can indeed be related to the plan of Stratford Hall, but that does not necessarily mean that Thomas Lee or his wife, Hannah Ludwell Lee, had access to Stephen Primatt's *City and County Purchaser and Builder* (1667), where an H-shaped plan was recommended and illustrated.[73] No direct copy exists, and when general design principles of English high-style architecture were adapted, they were mediated and amended by regional concepts of convenience and social standards.

Yet one cannot ignore the influence of published sources on patrons and artisans altogether for in some cases the influence of published book illustrations is unmistakable. Almost every student of American architectural history can recall John Tayloe's Mount Airy for its tidy correspondence to a published source (fig. 114). While Tayloe's inventory and so any record of his architectural books is lost, the front and garden façades and arrangement of main house and offices linked by curved hyphens are unambiguously copied from several plates in James Gibbs's 1728 *A Book of Architecture, Containing Designs of Buildings and Ornaments* (fig. 115). Mount Airy's affinity to this famous Anglo-Palladian book, however, makes it atypical. No other composition matches its correspondence to a published source.

Other Virginia mansion designs also found their roots in Anglo-Palladian ideals, but their relation to specific plates in the considerable body of mid-eighteenth-century English architecture publications is far less obvious. Tazewell Hall, Chantilly, Blandfield, Battersea, and Chatham exhibit either pedimented projections, or three- or five-part compositions that are characteristic of Anglo-Palladianism. Many also exhibit a widening of the central interior space so that it functions not only as a corridor but as a social space. The roots of the centralized saloon lie ultimately in Palladio's interest in re-creating a Roman atrium space and inserting it into a villa in the Veneto. But the owners of Virginia's mansions need not have known the origins of such a motif. Their dwellings are best described, as Calder Loth put it, as paralleling, rather than as copying designs found in books by James Gibbs, Robert Morris, or translations of Palladio.[74]

Turning from elevations and plans to ornamental details, one also finds several well-known but exceptional examples drawn directly from book sources. The riverfront doorway at Westover, a mansion not included in the study group, is another memorable but unrepresentative example (fig. 116).

Fig. 114. Mount Airy, Richmond County, 1760. South façade. (Photograph by author)

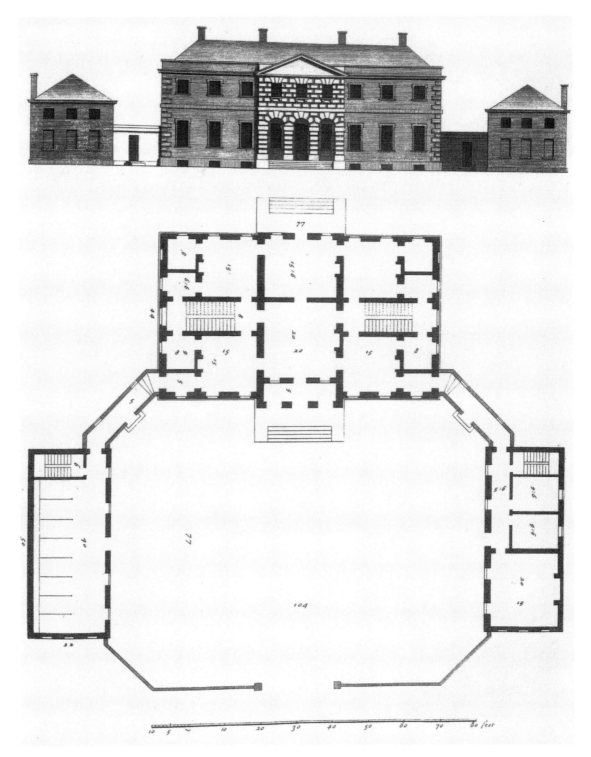

Fig. 115. James Gibbs, *A Book of Architecture, Containing Designs of Buildings and Ornaments* (London, 1728), plate 58. (From the collections of The Rare Book & Special Collections Library, The University of Illinois, Urbana-Champaign)

The frontispiece with its swan's neck pediment has clearly been created by a worker who either knew or had been directed to plate 26 of Salmon's *Palladio Londinensis* (fig. 117). Likewise, the chimneypiece in the dining room of Mount Vernon can be connected assuredly to Abraham Swan's *British Architect* (1st ed., 1745), while the Venetian window in the banquet hall was drawn from Batty Langley's *The City and County Builder's and Workman's Treasury of Designs* (1st edition, 1750).

Fig. 116. Westover, Charles City County, 1750. South façade frontispiece. (Photograph by Robert T. Mooney)

Fig. 117. William Salmon, *The Composite Order,* plate 26 in *Palladio Londinensis, or, the London Art of Building,* 2nd ed. (London, 1738). (From the collections of The Rare Book & Special Collections Library, The University of Illinois, Urbana-Champaign)

Far more common are interiors that bear resemblance to book sources only in parts. Architectural historians, for instance, have assigned no less than six separate publications by Abraham Swan, Thomas Chippendale, Batty Langley, and Robert Morris to the interior ornamentation of George Mason IV's Gunston Hall. In the chinoiserie decoration of the parlor, S. Fiske Kimball saw the influence of three distinct published sources among the many decorative details:

Such a scalloped cresting occurs frequently in the "Chinese" designs in Chippendale's first edition of 1754: notably on his "China cases," Pls. CVIII. CIX, and CX. The main cornice of the Dining Room, with its shallow uncarved ogee modillions, seems to come from a figure in Swan's *Designs,* 1758, Plate 53, "Bloc Cornices." On the other hand, suggestions for the frieze panels here, as for the Drawing Room windows, seem to come from William Pain's *Builder's Companion,* 1758.

Kimball imagined Buckland, an indentured servant earning £20 a year, bringing his own British books to Virginia and exploiting them creatively by combining elements from diverse sources. Kimball credited the books listed in the talented joiner's inventory as the primary inspiration for design, saying that "it was chiefly from among these books that came many motifs found in Buckland's works."[75] Buckland's inventory, however, was made in 1774, when he had established himself as a prosperous contractor with an impressive workshop of skilled craftsmen and slaves working for him. In 1755, his salary as an indentured laborer amounted to only £20 sterling, plus food, drink, lodging, and washing, making it difficult for him to afford books. Although currency comparisons are notoriously difficult in colonial Virginia, Fithian's salary as a tutor at Nomini Hall in 1773 was £35 sterling, and he found it necessary to barter and economize.[76]

Two alternative explanations for the virtuoso decorative performance of decorative details at Gunston Hall invite consideration. First, Mason might have directed his talented but impoverished servant toward published sources that Mason knew through his own collection or that of his uncle. Second, and much more plausibly, Buckland had acquired a sophisticated repertoire of high-style ornamental details during his seven years apprenticeship to his uncle James Buckland, a joiner in the artisan neighborhood of Holborn, London. Buckland may have had no need for constant recourse to published instructions to execute up-to-date architectural embellishment.

Even that notorious bibliophile Jefferson acknowledged the limited role of architecture books. In December 1804, James Oldham, the joiner responsible for many of the elegant doors and window sashes at Monticello II, wrote to Jefferson from Richmond asking him to procure a copy of Palladio's *Four Books of Architecture.* Oldham no doubt wanted to exploit Palladio's treatise to attract the silk-stocking trade to his new business in Richmond by offering the sort of prestige designs his former employer had so valued. Jefferson's reply of 24 December 1804 from the new federal city of Washington has much to tell about the limited availability of architecture books in the early nineteenth century and the scope of their influence:

> In answer to yours of the 17th desiring me to procure a Palladio for you either here or at Philadelphia, there never was a Palladio here even in private hands

till I brought one: and I scarcely expect it is to be had in Philadelphia; but I will try both there and at Baltimore. The late Mr. Ryland Randolph of Turkey Island had one, which is probably in the hands of whoever has his books, and as probable not of use. Mr. David Randolph could probably give you information respecting it, and whether it can be bought. The chance of getting one in America is slender. in the meantime, as you may be distressed for present use, I send you my portable edition, which I value because it is portable. you will return it at your own convenience. it contains only the 1st book on the orders, which is the essential part. The remaining books contain only plans of great buildings, temples, etc. Accept my salutations.[77]

In Jefferson's estimation, Palladio was a rare volume, important for its clear instructions concerning the orders but not a source for entire buildings in the colony. As much as he admired Palladio, Jefferson seems to be admitting the entire treatise was unsuitable for craftsmen like Oldham and his likely customers. Yet, Jefferson mentions only Palladio. Insurance records depicting Ryland Randolph's house on Turkey Island with a typical representational economy of single lines suggest that a number of Jefferson's peers found inspiration in other Anglo-Palladian books (fig. 118).[78]

For wealthy Virginians and the skilled craftsmen they hired, books on architecture were rare prestige possessions, valued but not essential to polite building. Such books made their greatest impact on decorative details and rarely served as models for entire houses. Ownership of pattern books was far from widespread, and, with the exception of Jefferson's later collections, architectural books do not seem to have constituted a major portion of a gentleman's library.[79] Print sources were occasionally consulted in the aesthetic decision-making process but were only one of several factors contributing to a patron's knowledge of design and construction. Aesthetic information was conveyed in other more elusive ways that do not lend themselves to written documentation, namely informal conversations among social peers.

Conversation among Gentlemen

The fifth and perhaps most effective way that members of the planter elite acquired their architectural knowledge was through informal social interaction with their peers. Conversation and correspondence among the Virginia gentry disseminated aesthetic values and preserved the exclusivity of knowledge within a closed group of social and economic cohorts. Like insider trading among financial elites or pig latin messages among schoolchildren, the conversations of gentlemen provided a way of sharing exclusive privileged information that was effective only if it excluded others. And, like the seemingly inconsequential anecdote, casual conversation can be laden with coded significance. All gossip is political, and even the most quotidian exchanges can relay important messages about status and expected behavior. These are just the sort of dialogues that are usually missing from the extant record and the most elusive to reconstruct.

Robert Carter III's assiduous pursuit of knowledge through personal contacts and self-improvement underscores the important role of the conversation of gentlemen among the Virginia elite. In his memoir, John Page stated that Carter squandered his educational opportunities in England and returned to Virginia "inconceivably illiterate." Thomas Hudson's exquisite portrait of Carter in fancy dress costume points to the young man's priorities. Page then explained how Carter sought to rectify his misspent youth:

> In a course of years, after he had got a seat at the Council board, [he] studied Law, History, and Philosophy, and although his knowledge was very limited, and his mind confused by studying without the assistance of a tutor, he conversed a great deal with our highly enlightened Governor Fauquier, and Mr. Wm. Small, the Professor of Mathematics at the College of Wm. and Mary, from whom he derived great advantages.[80]

Carter's personal pursuit of knowledge was not unique. In the same manner, Jefferson acquired the intellectual polish that seems to have been absent

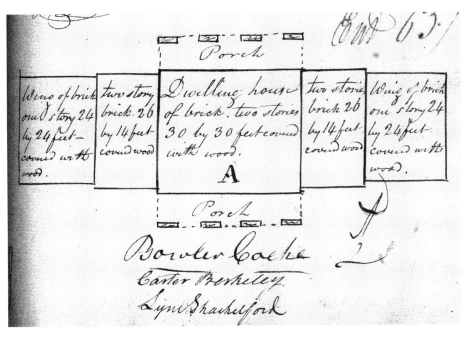

Fig. 118. Plan of Ryland Randolph's house on Turkey Island from Mutual Assurance Society declaration made by Bowler Cocke on 10 March 1806. (The Library of Virginia)

from the formal course work at the College of William and Mary. In his autobiography of 1821, Jefferson praised his tutor in law, George Wythe, who

> introduced me to the acquaintance and familiar table of Governor Fauquier, the ablest man who had ever filled that office. With him, and at his table, Dr. Small and Mr. Wythe, his *amici omnium horarum* [friends of all hours], and myself, formed a *partie quarée,* and to the habitual conversations on these occasions I owed much instruction.[81]

Note the composition of the company at Fauquier's table. While there were certainly differences of power among those present, this was no exchange of liberal ideas between men of varying classes at the public sphere of the coffeehouse. Both Carter and Jefferson enjoyed and acquired knowledge that could not be accessed by less exalted members of the colonial community. With the exclusive character of elite dialogue in mind, we can see how casual exchanges of information could serve as significant and exclusive conduits of architectural values.

For example, when Edmund Jenings advised John Tayloe II on the design of Mount Airy, he directed Tayloe's attention to environmental concerns, particularly to the dampness of northeast rooms; the need to accommodate large families and frequent guests; and, at the same time, recommended "Porticoes before the wings." But, as to the dimensions of the "whole or any part," Jenings left that to Tayloe's "Discretion" without mentioning any model or author.[82]

The benefits of wealth and status were not limited to verbal instruction but included visual demonstration as well. In April 1771, Robert Beverley wrote to his London agent, Samuel Athawes, requesting the selection of wallpaper for Blandfield. Beverley referred to a type of paper that he had seen probably in the ballroom of the Governor's Palace in Williamsburg:

> I have been some Time employed in Building an house, & I am desirous of fitting it up in a plain neat Manner, I w[oul]d willingly consult the present Fashion, for you know that foolish Passion had made its way, Even into this remote Region. I observed that l[or]d B[outetourt] had hung a room with plain blue Paper & border'd it with a narrow stripe of gilt Leather, w[hi]ch I thought had a pretty effect.[83]

Like a shop window, the Governor's Palace interior tantalized ambitious planters with novel architectural fashions and engendered a desire to possess or re-create them. Beverley's models were not drawn from print sources or directly from the English models he saw as a student in England but from current examples displayed in the architectural spaces of his social peers and superiors. Rather than citing an illustration from a pattern book to direct his agent's purchase of mantelpieces, Beverley ordered "Chimney Pieces of the Grey Marble, perfectly plain." He desired the reserved style of mantelpiece, not because they were illustrated in a book he had seen but, as he explained to his agent, because he had seen "several . . . imported here [in] late Years." Beverley clarified his aesthetic priorities when he added, "I am told they are cheap & I think them infinitely neater than the Embossed or figured ones."[84]

The owner of Blandfield may have acquired some of his taste in architecture from his father-in-law, Landon Carter. While Blandfield was under construction in 1770, Carter "rode to see Beverley's [new] building just raised to the surface of the earth." Carter scrutinized the design and judged the proportional relationship between the main block and the dependencies faulty. It is difficult to believe that the irascible Carter would not have said to Beverley what he wrote in his diary: "I wish both front[s] are not spoiled for I find there is to be a building at each end which goes no higher than the first story."[85] Although he failed to use the more sophisticated term, "proportion," Carter must have persuasively conveyed his aesthetic critique to his son-in-law; Beverley raised the dependencies to two stories (fig. 119).

The Craftsman's Knowledge

Acquiring knowledge of metropolitan fashion or even conforming to the prevailing taste of one's peer group is not the same as being able to reproduce it. There were definite limits to the extent of an architectural pa-

Fig. 119. Blandfield, Essex County, 1769. View of main house and dependencies. (Photograph by author)

tron's expertise, and executing the design ideals they coveted often proved daunting.

Conservative colonial craftsmen competent in vernacular styles were unable to satisfy the needs of wealthy planters demanding more unique fashion. At one point, Jefferson asked his English factor to procure for him an "architect"—not to design the first version of Monticello, but to execute Jefferson's demanding specifications. Nothing came of Jefferson's request. Significantly, Monticello I was never finished.

George Mason IV, on the other hand, was extremely fortunate in finding William Buckland to direct the embellishment of the interiors at Gunston Hall. Buckland arrived in Virginia in 1755 armed with the knowledge of current styles and the ability to organize other workmen, including the equally talented James Brent, who carved the woodwork. Buckland seems to have shared his ideas, perhaps even instructed his master, George Mason IV, on architectural matters. As Carl Lounsbury has shown, the sketches discovered behind paneling at Gunston Hall suggest an architectural dialogue between an influential planter and a respected and knowledgeable craftsman (fig. 120).[86]

After finishing his indenture to Mason, Buckland went on to work for other wealthy colonials in Virginia and Maryland.[87] His artistic talent and his business acumen provided a comfortable income by the 1770s, and he celebrated his social ascent by commissioning his portrait by the best painter in Annapolis, Charles Willson Peale (fig. 121). Unlike almost every other Virginia craftsman, Buckland's career is well documented and his aesthetic authority well established. Other builders whose voices have fallen silent may have shared their knowledge as well while they collaborated in the design of Virginia's colonial buildings. Specialized building tradesmen, therefore, served as the sixth and last conduit of the architectural education of Virginia patrons.

Not every colonial Virginian, of course, had the sort of connections and wealth that allowed Mason to procure an indentured, well-trained joiner to create the frontispiece at Gunston Hall or enjoyed the social rank that allowed Beverley to see how the governor had decorated his ballroom. Indeed, all of the conduits of architectural education described above were sharply distinguished by the fact that they were unavailable to poor or even middling colonists. Like the acquisition of rare plant material, an elegant suit of clothes, or the correct use of a Latin phrase, knowledge of high-style architecture served as an external sign signifying personal accomplishment and worth. Virginia's elite was, after all, not a titled aristocracy and, with ambitious former indentured servants able to commission expensive portraits, the social hierarchy could hardly be characterized as calcified. Fash-

Fig. 120. Unidentified draftsman, courthouse sketches discovered at Gunston Hall in 1983 (Colonial Williamsburg Foundation; Courtesy of Carl R. Lounsbury)

Fig. 121. Charles Willson Peale, *Portrait of William Buckland,* oil on canvas, 1774 and 1789. (Yale University Art Gallery, Mabel Brady Garvan Collection)

ion facilitated a new ordering of the colonial hierarchy, which is why Peter Collinson warned his fellow botanist John Bartram in 1737 that wealthy Virginians looked "more at a man's outside than his inside."[88] Like other elite commodities, elite Virginia planters eagerly pursued their architectural education in an attempt to inscribe social privilege permanently into a fluid colonial social environment.

Chapter 6

Epistemologies of Female Space

Early Tidewater Mansions

The Problem of Female Domestic Space

At a moment of supreme self-satisfaction in 1726, William Byrd II of Virginia (fig. 122) boasted to his scholarly British correspondent Charles Boyle, the 4th Earl of Orrery, that "Like one of the patriarchs, I have my flocks and my herds, my bondmen and bondwomen, and every sort of trade amongst my own servants, so that I live in a kind of independence of everyone but providence."[1] Byrd's words stand as a succinct metaphorical summary of colonial patriarchy, with its construal of divine approbation for his authority, prosperity, and male agency. He knows and understands his plantation at Westover from a male-centered, or androcentric, point of view. Because of the sheer volume of his documentary legacy as well as his vivid literary style, Byrd's claims, like those of the similarly garrulous Virginia diarist Landon Carter, have significantly impacted scholarship on colonial architecture. Taking direction from the preponderance of literary evidence written by men such as Byrd, Carter, and Jefferson, the interpretation of Virginia's early mansions has acquiesced to a male-centered perspective that accepts these grand dwellings as the architectural analogue to Byrd's ideology.

Byrd proffered historians a seductively persuasive explanation of the meaning of Virginia's prodigy houses: expressions of male power. From an androcentric standpoint, the colony's colonial mansions fostered as well as reflected the patriarchal hegemony of the tobacco planter elite.[2] This unmasking of planter motivation concerning architecture has served well to destabilize earlier romanticized and uncritical notions of the colonial period. Yet, anyone who has read Byrd's diary also knows how insecure his Old Testament idyll was. His own accounting of his privileged life shows that he routinely experienced petty vexations and more serious challenges to his presumed authority not only at the hands of his black slaves but from the white women of his household. Byrd's own words undermine patriar-

Fig. 122. Studio of Sir Godfrey Kneller, *Portrait of William Byrd II,* oil on canvas, 1700–1704. (Colonial Williamsburg Foundation)

chy and the androcentric perspective that has served as the dominant story of Virginia's colonial mansions.

In this chapter, I offer an alternative to Byrd's androcentric understanding of his domestic environment by examining the ways elite women viewed their mansions from a female-centered, or gynocentric, perspective. What factors influenced a woman's perceptions of architectural space? Did women conceive of their mansion as primarily a male-dominated setting wherein male authority was acted out on an architectural stage? Or did women, as Byrd's domestic troubles suggest, go about the business of domestic life expressing their own will, work, and agency within a space that was conceptualized from a female point of view? Does the production of space generate only one relationship of power?[3]

The problem of female space within the Virginia mansion goes beyond architectural questions; it requires venturing into abstract philosophical concepts about female ways of knowing, that is, female epistemology. The historical issue is really twofold: first, how did women know domestic space, and second, how can we as historians know, or at least glimpse, their knowledge of space? In other words, how can we reconstruct a gynocentric standpoint, a term defined as a depiction of the world "in relation to female or feminine interests, emotions, attitudes or values"?[4]

Architectural features themselves yield little. The physical plan and material ornamentation of eighteenth-century Virginia mansions do not communicate overtly gendered forms. Quantity and quality of detail and finish of door moldings or mantelpieces speak frankly about rank and class, but are more taciturn about gender. Without specific evidence that is reliably denoted in room-by-room probate inventories, many historic house museum curators are forced to guess about room use and the sex of those using it most frequently.

In place of the building fabric, documentary evidence offers more reliable clues toward the reconstruction of a gynocentric perspective, but unfortunately first-person records written by women during the colonial period, especially early in the eighteenth century, rarely survive. Lower literacy rates and cultural biases that once discouraged the preservation of female writing have resulted in a silencing of women's speech in the historical record. Absent such voices from the past, a material culture approach offers an alternative means of shedding light on the question of how elite women used, knew, and embodied domestic space. Specific gender-laden items of material culture, such as particular pieces of furniture or ceramic assemblages, once located spatially within the house through an analysis of selected probate inventories, can serve as stage marks allowing us to position and envision female social performance on the stage of the colonial Virginia mansion. To that end, forty-five transcribed room-by-room inventories from elite Tidewater households, recorded between 1742 and 1810 and assembled and transcribed by scholars at Gunston Hall, stand as the core of evidence for this material culture approach to gendered space. The much larger entire Gunston Hall probate inventory database is particularly valuable because it has been sorted by social and material class, meaning that the forty-five inventories used here are all of a similarly elite household status. Classified by the Colonial Williamsburg historian Barbara Carson, the Gunston Hall inventory database designated the most privileged households in the Tidewater region by the owner's ability to serve at least twenty guests with specialized dining utensils, namely knives, spoons, and that more modern addition, the fork. Biases in the sample, of course, exist. Late eighteenth- and early nineteenth-century households appear too frequently in the classification, as do more materially sophisticated urban examples from Annapolis.[5] Imperfect as the elite-status probate inventory sample is, it—along with diaries, other print material, additional Virginia probate inventories, and costume history—provides vital clues toward a mental mapping of gendered behavior and movement within and around the colonial Virginia mansion. They allow us to imagine what the historian Kathleen Brown calls the "choreography of domestic life."[6]

It bears emphasizing that the evidence presented here is not marshaled in order to propose separate spatial spheres for elite colonial men and women, much less distinct rooms of female seclusion or confinement. There was no eighteenth-century equivalent of the male *andronitis* and female *gunaikonitis* that may have been part of ancient Greek domestic planning. Nor can one identify a colonial Tidewater parallel to the *gynaceum,* female-only space that might have characterized Byzantine architectural interiors.[7] Compared to more coeval eighteenth-century examples, Virginia mansions also seem less gender segregated. No Tidewater male planter, for instance, voiced his disapproval of an overtly feminized colonial domestic space in the same way that French male writers disparaged the boudoir, the female-dominated room adjacent to the bedchamber of a French suite of private rooms.[8] It would be inappropriate, therefore, to dichotomize domestic space in a colonial Virginia mansion strictly according to gender. Adult men, women, and often children, servants, and domestic slaves all moved through the mansion. Even a diurnal segregation in the use of room space is difficult to prove. But while rigid spatial division of residential buildings finds little proof in the historical record, more conceptual patterns of architectural space based on the distinct experiences of men and women do emerge from the documentary evidence.

This more conceptual understanding of the epistemology of gendered space has already been explored by a handful of scholars, and this chapter builds upon their foundations. The architectural historian Mark R. Wenger and the sociologist Jessica Kross, for example, have each addressed questions about architecture and gender in the colonial mansion. Kross argued that the mansion's contrasting androcentric and gynocentric areas facilitated the creation of multiple public spaces that allowed a freer exchange of ideas. She also was among the first scholars to point to the binary opposition of a man's library or study with a woman's bedchamber. She saw the male library or study as a site that architecturally underscored the identification of literacy and reason with the construction of the male gender.[9]

For his part, Wenger focused on the development of the androcentric dining room, the site of the midday meal, with its ritualized, male-dominated behavior.[10] Women shared in the meal, but conventions of gentility encouraged their retreat following the meal. The author of one eighteenth-century conduct book regarded it as vulgar if "at dinner-time the women seldom leave the company, till the last bowl or bottle, but stand the fumigation of tobacco, the most shocking obscenity and ribaldry of a whole afternoon."[11] Published guides to polite conduct fail to offer an entirely reliable picture of actual behavior, but on at least one occasion we find prescriptive literature paralleled in practice. Philip Vickers Fithian, a Princeton-trained tutor employed at Nomini Hall in 1773–74, noted in his diary that "when we had dined, the Ladies retired, leaving us a Bottle of Wine & a Bowl of Toddy for companions."[12] Fithian, though, may have been a bit too reticent in his description of the afternoon's events once the ladies left. According to Wenger's research, the colonial dining room was soon "bathed in the effluvia of male fellowship" produced by copious amounts of alcohol, pungent smoking, sputum, and urine.[13] Overtly expressed and repetitively enacted behavior by men in a designated room can easily lead one to consider the dining room a male-centered space, even though women were present and often presided over meals a short time before more ribald dramas commenced. While in a literal, physical sense the male domination of the dining room is only diurnal, in a conceptual sense the dining room has been assigned as the primary site of elite male bonding.

With this androcentric perception of space acting as a contrasting foil, we can distinguish a parallel mental map of the domestic territories where elite Virginia females expressed their duties, work, leisure, and individual agency. The pattern coalesces into four specific loci within the Virginia mansion: the bedchamber; the parlor or other designated site of female-directed conviviality; the kitchen; and the garden. Because the bedchamber was most closely associated with a woman's body and her role in the heterosexual reproductive economy, it lies at the core of a female epistemology of the Virginia colonial mansion.

The Bedchamber

The bedchamber within a colonial Virginia mansion functioned as the primary site of authority for elite matrons and can be seen as a sort of female command and control center. Moreover, because of the bedchamber's long associations with marriage, sanctioned sex, childbirth, and legitimate inheritance of property, this architectural space is laden with potent generational associations.[14] But imagining the bedchamber as a site of female agency, real or symbolic, poses a challenge. The bedchambers of elite Virginians, like those of their less exalted fellow colonists, were sleeping rooms that, with a few temporal exceptions, were shared by husband and wife.

Readers more familiar with the architectural planning practices of eighteenth-century Parisian *hôtels particulier*, with separate sequences of *antichambre, chambre, cabinet* (or *boudoir*), and *garde-robe* for husband and wife, may find the single shared bedchamber in colonial Virginia contrary to elite decorum.[15] Yet there is no strong documentation for routinely segregated married adult male sleeping quarters within polite households in colonial America. The diary of Samuel Sewall of Boston offers some insight into British colonial practices. Written between 1676 and 1729, Sewall's diary indicates that the only time he abandoned the marital bedchamber was when his wife was giving birth or was very ill. He refers to their bedchamber variously as "my Wife's Bedchamber" and "our chamber." His diary entries also demonstrated that the shared bedchamber was emotionally central to family life.[16]

The diary of William Byrd II offers frank insight into the intimate practices of the colonial bedchamber and beyond. Though Byrd did not make reference specifically to his wife's bedchamber, his use of pronouns and phrases such as "we went to bed about 10 o'clock" and "as soon as we were in bed my wife complained of great pains in her belly" make it clear that elite colonial spouses shared a common bed and bedchamber. Byrd also noted that this domestic space was the routine site of sexual intercourse, an act he referred to as having "rogered" his wife, or giving her a "flourish." Hence, he wrote that "I rose at 8 o'clock, having first rogered my wife," and "I rogered my wife when we got to bed." The spatial boundaries of sexual behavior were flexible at Westover, however, and Byrd recounted with satisfaction that "In the afternoon my wife and I had a little quarrel which I reconciled with a flourish. Then she read a sermon in Dr. Tillotson to me. It is to be observed that the flourish was performed on the billiard table." Byrd also recorded the day he "rogered his wife on the couch." Based on Byrd's remarkable candor, we may surmise that for elite men and women, for whom matters of decorum were of no little concern, routine sexual relations were associated with the bedchamber, but could also occur in more novel domestic architectural settings.[17]

Elite Virginia women shared their bedchambers with other members of the family on occasion. When their mother was crushed to death by a large clothes press, the children of William Byrd III stayed with their grandmother, then a widow. One slept with her in her bed, and the other two slept in another bed in the same room, gaining grandmotherly consolation and comfort from her close presence.[18] It is this proximity to a woman's body that imbued bedchambers with potency.

Apart from sleeping, sex, childbirth, and death rituals, Virginia women also utilized their bedchambers for more solitary moments away from the eyes of the numerous mansion occupants. At Nomini Hall, the mistress of the plantation, Frances Anne Tasker Carter, thought of the bedchamber she shared with her husband, Robert Carter III, as a personal retreat. The plantation tutor, Philip Vickers Fithian, noted in his journal that during a daytime thunderstorm, a fearful Carter sought refuge in this bedchamber. Literate women could use bedchambers as a place to read and write. Martha Washington, for example, seems to have worked on her correspondence in her chamber because she bequeathed her "writing table and the seat to it standing in my chamber" to her granddaughter. Wealthy Virginia women, however, could read and write in other rooms of the mansion, though significantly no evidence can be found of Washington using her husband's study or library, the British equivalent of the French *cabinet*. Neither were their intellectual pursuits confined to any colonial equivalent of the French *boudoir,* the fashionable and distinct female room designed for pleasure, reading, or the delights of the imagination. Frances Anne Tasker Carter (fig. 123) was pictured by Fithian, in a memorable diary image of her, as "lying in the long room among the Books on the Couch." Her not-so-private leisure occurred in the room usually used for dancing lessons and notably not in "Mr. Carter's study." The picture of a well-dressed, reclining gentlewoman quietly enjoying the paraphernalia of intellectual stimulation is an attractive one, to be sure, but one that demands caveat. Her immersion in the republic of letters was made possible by the unpaid labor of 184 enslaved souls in addition to a paid staff that took care of most of her domestic chores.[19] Gentility came at a tremendous cost.

A sharper image of female agency inside the bedchamber can be drawn by examining three examples. For example, the mothering function of an elite woman's sleeping room is revealed at Gunston Hall, the mid-eighteenth-century mansion of George Mason IV and his wife, Ann Eilbeck Mason (fig. 124). One of her children, John Mason, wrote a reminiscence of life at Gunston Hall in 1832 in which affectionate memories of his mother are intimately associated with the character of domestic architecture. John refers to the space as "my Mothers Chamber," although it was the bedroom of both his mother and father (*A* in fig. 125). He remembers the orderly arrangement of children's clothes in the chest of drawers kept in this room as well as the closets on either side of the chimney, one for his mother's seasonal clothes and the other for safekeeping valuable dining items (fig. 126). He honors his mother's memory by reference to a common exhortation to virtuous housewives, namely the wise stewardship of the household's material wealth. Similar small closets on either side of the fireplace survive in the bedchamber at the Jacob Faulcon House, Surry County, dated by dendrochronology to about 1765 (fig. 127). The dwelling represents a

Fig. 123. John Wollaston Jr., *Portrait of Mrs. Robert Carter III* (Frances Anne Tasker Carter), oil on canvas, 1755–58. (Colonial Williamsburg Foundation)

Fig. 124. Dominic W. Boudet, *Portrait of Ann Eilbeck Mason* (after lost portrait by John Hesselius), oil on canvas, 1811. (Virginia Museum of Fine Arts, Richmond; Gift of David K. E. Bruce; Photo: Ron Jennings, © Virginia Museum of Fine Arts)

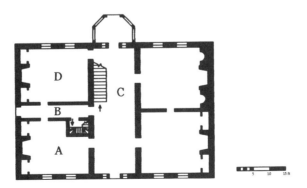

Fig. 125. Gunston Hall, Fairfax County, 1752. Plan of first floor; scale bar equals 15 feet. *A* = Ann Eilbeck Mason's bedchamber; *B* = secondary passage with small service stairs; *C* = central passage with main stairs; *D* = Little Parlor. (Megan D. Roy after Fiske Kimball and Mark R. Wenger)

genteel though much smaller and less richly embellished house than Gunston Hall. Nonetheless, the presence of arched closets on either side of the fireplace in the so-called "Blue Room" indicates a more widespread demand for bedchamber furnishings that conveniently stored and protected increasingly availabile luxury goods.

Ann Eilbeck Mason's maternal authority was also manifested in other ways, some of which are facilitated via architecture. According to her son, she taught her children their prayers by having them kneel before her with their hands folded upon her lap. Her body served as a sacred space that mediates between earthy and heavenly realms. Changes made to Gunston Hall's plan after initial construction, specifically the insertion of a secondary small stair (*B* in fig. 125), facilitated the use of her chamber as a site for maintaining physical and emotional closeness between mother and child. John recalled climbing into her bed and drinking sweet tonics in the morning. He may have been brought in the arms of a slave from an upstairs room to his mother's downstairs chamber via a small corridor that bypassed the richly embellished public stairway in the large central passage (*C* in fig. 125). In this way, the architectural plan of Gunston Hall would have created a meaningful spatial relationship, a concept that Edward T. Hall referred to as "proxemics."[20] But while the architectural design in and around Ann's bedchamber supported her mothering role, the intimate bond between mother and child did not necessarily extend to breastfeeding. As in Europe, breastfeeding one's own progeny was a sensitive and contentious issue. Fithian, for instance, was flabbergasted to learn that gentry children, including several of Frances Anne Tasker Carter's children, had been breastfed by black women slaves.[21]

John Mason's memories of his mother are colored, of course, by the growing sentimentality about motherhood in the early nineteenth century. By contrast, his reminiscences of his father are notably impersonal and political in nature. He does say, however, that when his father was engaged in a lengthy writing project, he appropriated what he called the "little Parlor" (*D* in fig. 125) as a study, causing the family to eat elsewhere and temporarily establishing a male intellectual domain beyond the reach of women and children.[22]

Brooke's Bank, the Virginia mansion built by Sarah Taliaferro Brooke, illustrates a female patron's remarkable understanding of the bedchamber as a female space of refuge and also authority (fig. 128). On 19 August 1763,

Fig. 126. (*Opposite, top*) Gunston Hall, Fairfax County, 1752. View of Ann Eilbeck Mason's bedchamber. (Courtesy of Gunston Hall Plantation)

Fig. 127. (*Opposite, bottom*) Jacob Faulcon House (Smith's Fort Plantation), Surry County, ca. 1765. View of bedchamber. (Photograph by author)

Brooke wrote her will, in which she attempted to control the future use of the mansion she had built after her husband died in either 1734 or 1735. In this document, she particularly notes "the mansion built by me." More than expressing pride in her own architectural patronage, the language was intended to clarify legally her ownership over the house, not as an heir but as creator. By claiming the dwelling as her own, not part of her late husband's property, she was laying the foundation for attempting to control its interior use after her death. More specifically, she tried to provide her unmarried daughter with protected domestic space, her bedchamber:

> My will is that my son William or whosoever shall be the legal occupant of the dwelling house built by me permit my said daughter to have the free and full use and occupation of the room and closet . . . and that during the time she may remain single, and if my son or other legal occupant shall disturb my said daughter or not permit her to live peaceably in the said room and closet and to have the free use of the same, so that my daughter should be obliged to leave the place, in that case my will is that my son or his representative do forfeit and pay to my said daughter the sum of two hundred and fifty pounds current money to be raised by the sale of my estate or other wise.

Notably, Sarah did not challenge Virginia's legal tradition by ignoring her son's claim to property via primogeniture. Instead, she tries to subvert the law through the terms of her will by bequeathing a legal territory, a safe haven, within the mansion for her unmarried daughter. Brooke's choice for that safe haven is significant. She did not select the parlor or any of the more public spaces, but a bedchamber. While the daughter's place of legal refuge would be restricted technically to a bedroom and closet, Sarah effectively gave her broader movement, because if access were to become difficult and she were "obliged to leave," her brother would have to pay a hefty fine. As a widow for some twenty-nine years and no doubt experiencing firsthand the legal hobbling of females, Sarah tried to protect her unwed daughter with a safe domestic seat of authority.[23]

Martha Dandridge Custis Washington's (fig. 129) shaping of her bedchamber at Mount Vernon reveals how elite colonial women understood both the practical functions and potent symbolism of architectural space. Her new second-story bedchamber (*A* in fig. 130) was shared by both husband and wife, but was known as "Mrs. Washington's room" and functioned as the site from which she supervised domestic activities.[24] Like Ann Eilbeck Mason's room at nearby Gunston Hall, Martha's bedchamber included two closets, one for her wardrobe and another for expensive table linen (*B* and *C* in fig. 130).[25] And, like Ann's, Martha's bedchamber had a small private stairway (*D* in fig. 130). At Mount Vernon, however, the steps led not to children's bedrooms but down to George's first-floor study, from which he supervised agricultural activities (*E* in fig. 130). The stair allowed

Fig. 128. Brooke's Bank, Essex County, 1751. View from southwest. Addition to left and porch on right not original. (Photograph by author)

communication between male and female domestic loci that was hidden from the eyes of numerous and constant visitors who made the mansion a public rather than private site for virtually all of their married life.

Martha understood the symbolic implications of her own domestic space and its power to shape perception of its inhabitants. We can witness this in the actions she took after George died in her bedchamber on 14 December 1799. She proceeded to close her personal site of authority not for just a decorous period of mourning but until her death in 1803.[26] Instead of removing to one of the more sumptuously decorated bedchambers in the mansion, she relocated to a smaller, recently improved attic bedchamber, simply though genteelly finished with plaster and wood trim (*F*). Notably, her attic chamber had no dressing table. The bureau dressing table made by the Williamsburg cabinetmaker Peter Scott and sold to Martha's first husband, Daniel Parke Custis, in 1754 remained in the closet of her bedchamber on the second floor.[27] If Martha were in the court of Versailles, we might even say, in the parlance of the French court, she had renounced the rouge.[28] She seems to acknowledge and encourage the concept that it was her second-floor bedchamber where George expired, and not the study where he managed the plantation, which would become sacred ground. The apotheosis of George Washington had begun even before his death, and by erasing herself from the bedchamber Martha fashioned the room as a *martyrium* for her husband, complete with a symbolic bed of state.

Fig. 129. Charles Willson Peale, *Portrait of Martha Dandridge Custis Washington,* oil on canvas, 1795. (Independence National Historical Park)

Martha's reconfiguration of her domestic environment underscores the symbolic importance that was attached to expensive furnishings such as beds and case pieces like her dressing table. Purchasing highly specialized tables or complex assemblages of textiles and stuff for a bed demonstrated not only one's affluence but a particular insider's knowledge of how to spend money, what Cary Carson refers to as "the owner's superior ability to squander his wealth."[29] Certain of these costly pieces constructed polite gender roles as well.

The bedchamber came to function as a focus of rituals that were central to the creation of self-esteem among elite Virginia women. Dressing tables and their accompanying objects are key in forming elite behavior in early Virginia as well as in England and France. The artful and fashionable enhancement of facial features comprised an important element in the self-esteem of young elite females in Virginia, but it was an activity that could lead to disaster or conflict. Fithian noted that Nancy Carter, after experimenting with makeup, went too far and "clipt off her Eye-Brows." Many years earlier, William Byrd II and his first wife, Lucy Parke Byrd, quarreled over her desire to pluck her brows.[30] Although dressing tables

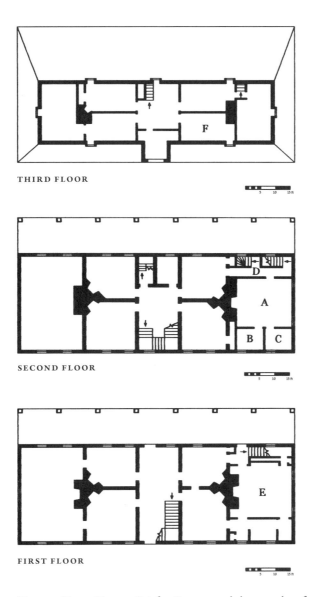

THIRD FLOOR

SECOND FLOOR

FIRST FLOOR

Fig. 130. Mount Vernon, Fairfax County; scale bar equals 15 feet. Plans showing the building after additions of 1770s. *A* = Martha Washington's bedchamber; *B* and *C* = closets; *D* = secondary passage with stairs; *E* = George Washington's study; *F* = Martha Washington's chamber as widow. (Megan D. Roy after plan by Mount Vernon Ladies' Association)

and mirrors were used by men for shaving and wig placement, they came to be associated with makeup and women, and therefore became emblems of tiresome accusations of female deception.[31] The female toilette could be executed by one woman alone, but could also be performed with a select coterie of intimate friends. Cleverly described by the art historian Mimi Hellman, the manipulation of dressing table equipment and the selection of objects on the table provided French women with a scenario in which to display refined motion and delicacy in taste before peers and servants.[32] According to William Byrd II, his first wife, Lucy Parke Byrd, spent three hours dressing with her friends.[33] The location of dressing tables in bedchambers underscores that architectural space as functionally feminine. But where were those bedchambers? The dressing tables give up some ambiguous information.

In the forty-five inventories examined, fifty-nine dressing tables are identified specifically as such. Stratford Hall possessed four in 1776, and Berkeley also had four in 1791. All but two or three of the dressing tables in all the inventories were found in bedchambers. In those inventories where the bedchamber containing the table can be located with some measure of certainty, twenty were placed on the ground floor and twenty-nine on the floor above, suggesting that elite Tidewater planters felt some indecision about whether to display expensive, prestige furniture such as the bed and dressing table on the more public first-floor level, or to withdraw them to a more physically remote and private upstairs room where the politics of access could be heightened.

The migration of the principal bedchamber to a place above the ground floor can signal significant gender meanings. As Alice Friedman has shown, the late sixteenth-century Hardwick Hall, built by the noblewoman Bess of Hardwick, circumvented the authority of the male-associated hall on the ground floor by architecturally privileging an alternative site of authority in the High Great Chamber on the third story, which was intended for, but never used by, Queen Elizabeth. Hardwick and her builder reoriented the axial relationship of the old hall to conform to fashionable new ideas about symmetrically planned rooms derived from Andrea Palladio's *Four Books of Architecture,* but she adapted Italian ideals to her own social and gender imperative. In fact, Hardwick's manipulation of the principal reception space becomes more complex when compared to the traditional building practices of English yeomen, where upper rooms continued to be used for grain storage and chambers of lesser status, as they often were in Italian Palladian villas.[34]

The location or, more precisely, the elevation of the bedchamber as an important marker of status and gender not only reflects the increasing specialization of rooms but also testifies to a measure of tension between traditional ideals about display and more modern notions of privacy in early modern European culture. In seventeenth-century New England as well as in the Upper South, the best bed was often in the parlor, a semipublic space reserved for the parents and entertaining. As polite architecture in the Tidewater became more multicellular and multistoried, though, wealthy planters made individual choices about the placement of the most expensive bedstead. A consistent pattern for the location of the principal bedchamber does not emerge, and the documentary evidence is ambiguous. We do know that Ann Eilbeck Mason's room was on the ground floor, and according to Dell Upton's study of vernacular planning practices, this was the location preferred by most Virginians wealthy enough to inhabit multiroom houses.[35] But at the Governor's Palace and at Nomini Hall and in the enlargement of Mount Vernon in the 1770s, the principal bedchamber was on the second floor. Similar to traditional English urban housing, the best chamber of Elizabeth and Moses Myer's prestige house in Norfolk, Virginia, was on the second floor.[36] A number of bedchambers might be found in a grand house, and this can make our analysis more difficult. In April 1709, Byrd wrote that "my wife and I had another foolish quarrel about my saying she listened on the top of the stairs, which I suspected, in jest." A number of entries in Byrd's diary imply that he and his wife shared a bedchamber and that this room was located on the second floor.[37] Byrd's anxiety over his wife's eavesdropping, however, suggests another dynamic in elite female topography: namely, that a woman's superior position at the top of the stairs, presumably near her second-story bedroom, afforded her a measure of seclusion and privacy but also surveillance that made male inhabitants wary.

Norms for genteel behavior concerning the use of furnishings such as dressing tables were disseminated through personal, textual, and graphic sources, all of which were then adapted to the customs and limitations of the colony. Women who had lived in cities and towns in England such as Katherine Russell, Governor Spotswood's mistress; Anne Butler Brayne, who later became Spotswood's wife; Maria Taylor Byrd, William Byrd II's second wife; or the English governess at the Fauntleroy Plantation who made a splash with her exaggerated corset stays, all advertised metropolitan dress, social behavior, and their proper theaters.[38]

Widely circulated texts among the wealthy such as the *Spectator* provided sources of information for elite female performance and where it should be performed. The *Spectator,* originally published from 1711 to 1714, was extremely popular throughout the eighteenth century in the southern colonies, and eight of the Tidewater inventories mention this periodical by name.[39] Even before Fithian arrived from Princeton to act as tutor to the Carter children, the eldest daughter was reading the *Spectator,* and during his time at Nomini Hall, Fithian also enjoyed it.[40] In addition to providing models of witty expression, the essays occasionally give clues about gendered behavior and material culture.

Starting around midcentury, novels too offered instruction in the fashionable manners of urban England or provided a familiar mirroring and justification for previously established colonial manners.[41] After reading the *Spectator* and more didactic aphorisms such as "she speaketh and her servants fly; she pointeth and the thing is done" in *The Economy of Human Life,* Frances Baylor Hill poured over Fanny Burney's *Evelina,* learning patterns of polite conversation, the proper use of rouge, and how to avoid appearing "bumpkinish." Burney's novel might have taught her about fashionable behavior in drawing rooms, taking tea at public entertainment venues such as Ranelagh, visiting Vauxhall, and promenading through public parks.[42] Such descriptive texts provided glimpses into exciting urban concourse that most Virginians would never experience.

Imported prints may also have instructed Hill in the ways of elite female behavior. With the exception of portraits, few paintings were produced by colonial artists. Tidewater elites did vary the decoration of their dwellings with prints purchased from English and local merchants, and this kind of visual avenue conveyed potent social information.[43] No doubt the subject of visual imagery occasionally eluded or went unappreciated by some viewers. The appraisers of the estate of Governor Botetourt, for example, may have recognized the specific religious subjects depicted in three of the governor's paintings but listed them simply as "3 large Roman Catholick Pictures." Even those more attuned to biblical narratives, such as the Princeton-trained theological student and Virginia tutor Philip Vickers Fithian, used a descriptive shorthand by simply referring to "Scripture Prints."[44] How John Tayloe I, father of the patron of Mount Airy, came to own a set of engravings after Peter Paul Rubens's *Marie de Medici* cycle of paintings from the Luxembourg Palace in Paris is a greater mystery.[45]

Prints that ornamented the walls of genteel colonial rooms offered convenient opportunities for polite conversation. William Byrd II, for instance, entertained Governor Spotswood's companion, Mrs. Russell, in his library, where he "showed her some prints."[46] The subjects of many of the framed prints that embellished the walls of Virginia mansions are unknown because most probate inventories use such frustratingly vague phrases as "sundry prints in gilt frames," but a variety of print subjects are known to have been imported to the colonies. These include Robert Furber's flower and fruit series, topographic views, and pictures of famous race horses; some religious subjects; and engraved portraits, from which the colonial elite learned lessons about comportment and dress—what the art historian Margaretta Lovell has aptly called "body rhetoric."[47] At Nomini Hall, the dining room was decorated with serial prints of "twenty four of the most celebrated among the English Race-Horses, Drawn masterly, & set in elegant gilt Frames." Serial subjects such as the elements, seasons, and satirical mezzotints known as "drolls" often presented scenes in which figures pose in physical space.[48] Less serious and didactic than either portraits or religious scenes, such drolls may have been what John Custis meant when he ordered, in 1717, "good Commicall diverting Prints" to hang in "the passage" of his secondary house in Williamsburg.[49]

Some English prints were actually copies after the work of French painters such as Nicolas Lancret and François Boucher, and thereby made elite French conduct accessible to a small number of provincial settlers.[50] The subject matter of most of the prints in the forty-five inventories will be forever unknown, but three appraisers mentioned Hogarth by name, and two of those specified the *Marriage à la Mode* series.[51] In prints such as the *Countess's Morning Levée* (fig. 131) and in various *Spectator* essays, elite

Fig. 131. William Hogarth, *The Countess's Morning Levée,* plate 4 from the *Marriage à la Mode* series, engraving by Simon François Ravenet, 1745. (Princeton University Library)

Virginia women witnessed cosmetic rituals that were ridiculed as vain and simultaneously valorized as metropolitan. The images praise by faint damnation.[52]

Other Sites of Conviviality

Like dressing tables, the location of tea tables, by virtue of their feminized character, helps to define centers of female activities and space within the Virginia mansion. Tea was introduced to England by the mid-seventeenth century but was made fashionable in court life in 1662 by Catherine of Braganza, the Portuguese queen of Charles II.[53] By the second decade of the eighteenth century, wealthy and fashion-conscious Virginians were purchasing noticeable quantities of tea and coffee, and their increasing consumption was mirrored in ceramics ownership.[54] Starting in midcentury, more middling Virginians aspiring to gentility could purchase these items at a local retail store.[55] In both England and the colonies, entertaining family and visitors with cups of sweetened tea functioned as a vehicle for displaying the ability to buy the valuable commodity and its costly equipage: a tea caddy for storing the leaves, a kettle for heating water, a pot for steeping the leaves, perhaps a coffeepot, a milk or cream pot, sugar bowls, teacups, saucers, teaspoons, sugar tongs, and a slop bowl for refuse.[56] With the possible exception of the teakettle, all was arranged in an orderly manner on a specially designed table. In 1774, almost 50 percent of colonial inventories list tea equipment, and although tea drinking was an increasingly popular activity, it continued to be associated with gentility.[57] For the truly rich, such as the Mason family at Gunston Hall, the glamour of tea and its ability to confer social distinction were expressed more exclusively by using two silver tea sets made in London and imprinted with the Mason crest.[58] Requisite graceful gestures and witty verbal exchange, accompanied by a familiar ease with the accoutrements of wealth, all extended the social profits accruing to visually delightful tea services such as the Mason family's.

Usually scheduled for breakfast and again in the late afternoon, tea drinking was a heterosocial event, yet because women controlled the tea equipment and the act of pouring, the activity became culturally associated with women. Public coffeehouses, on the other hand, became closely linked with men.[59] Because of the gendered character of tea drinking, British men in the early eighteenth century feared and ridiculed it. Defamation included a warning in the *Spectator* that teenage boys risked emasculation by too frequently attending tea.[60] Benjamin Franklin understood the social desirability of tea tables as markers of status for women. In a 1727 letter to his sister explaining his choice of present, he sought to mitigate his poverty by disparaging the value of a tea table, saying that "the character of a good housewife was far preferable to that of being only a pretty gentlewoman."[61]

Opponents of the Townshend Acts effectively cajoled colonial women into boycotting tea by flattering them, but a much earlier English print of about 1705 already reveals a deep and troubling fear of a woman-centered and woman-controlled social event (fig. 132).[62] Entitled *The Tea Table,* the image depicts well-dressed women seated on expensive, matched chairs in a well-appointed room. On the left, the allegorical figure of Scandal drives Truth and another figure out of the room. To the right, curious men furtively peek in at the window and anxiously listen for information.[63] An attentive homunculus lurks in the shadows under the table. Not surprisingly, a mirror, a traditional symbol of vanity, adorns the room. For men of sense, the conversation at the tea table lacked epistemic authority, wasted resources, and was a conversation they did not control.[64]

The design of tea tables contributed to their function as actors in a female-centered performance. Dimensions, materials, forms, and ornamental details all responded to stylistic changes in England and to colonial Virginia preferences, but one is struck by how small and delicate the tables appear. One example, dating between 1725 and 1745 and attributed to Peter Scott, of a Virginia-made, Queen Anne–style tea table illustrates this physical delicacy (fig. 133). The table features attenuated cabriole legs

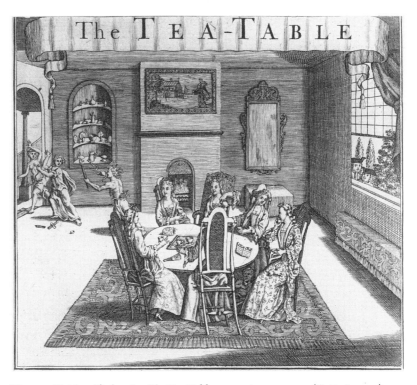

Fig. 132. Unidentified artist, *The Tea Table,* engraving, ca. 1705. (Getty Images)

Fig. 133. Peter Scott, tea table, Williamsburg, 1725–45. (Colonial Williamsburg Foundation)

and small pad feet, and measures only 26¾ inches high, 29½ inches wide, and 19⅜ inches deep.[65] Freestanding kettle stands were even smaller. Because furnishings were normally placed against walls when not in use, their movement toward the middle of the room—center stage, if you will—at tea time heightened the theatrical act. Comparing the size of tea furniture to women's apparel further demonstrates their performative character.

Until the late eighteenth century, the skirts of informal yet fashionable attire had considerable width and mass, while hoops of more formal, court attire attained their broadest ovoid dimensions in the 1740s. Even the more narrow informal gowns worn by gentry women in the mid-1770s for formal teas had voluminous girth.[66] A quilted petticoat (what we would today call a skirt) with small side hoops could measure about 26 inches in depth, 39 inches in width, and have an elliptical circumference of about 104 inches at the hem.[67] Similar petticoats were owned by Jenny Washington and Priscilla Hale in 1774 and were described by the tutor Fithian with an attention to detail that contradicts a supposedly male disdain of female frippery.[68]

Reflective, polished surfaces of the wood of tea tables complemented the soft sheen of fine textile petticoats worn by the women in attendance. But movement around tea tables required forethought and grace; a misjudged swish of a skirt or an abrupt gesture by a woman whose upper body was made erect and stiff by stays could upset a table loaded with ceramics.[69]

Tea tables supported on a tripod base, also known as claw tables, accommodated more fabric under the tabletop and became popular toward mid-century—that is, at the time when petticoats, gowns, and hoops were widest—and one is tempted to think that fashion in clothing and furniture worked in tandem. Tripod tea tables were slightly larger, averaging about 29 inches tall and 30 inches in diameter, and may have been more convenient, but a woman had to be conscious of her physical movements when navigating around any tea table and might require practice.[70] A child's tea table, constructed of sturdy oak, found in the Richmond, Virginia, home of Dr. Nicholas Flood and inventoried in 1776, suggests how genteel parents encouraged playful practice in social graces from an early age.

Because of the importance of tea drinking as a women-centered activity, the location of the tea table serves to establish a key indicator of female space within the Virginia colonial mansion. In the forty-five inventories evaluated, fifty-seven tea tables are listed by that specific name, and, as was the case with dressing tables, there are instances of more than one per household. Probate records relating to Bacon's Castle (1665) show that no tea tables are mentioned in a 1711 inventory, but four are listed in 1728.[71] Most tea tables (twenty-five out of the fifty-seven tea tables) were positioned in the principal reception rooms on the more public ground floor, but nine were found in bedchambers on the upper floor, underscoring the use of bedchambers as sites of social exchange. The architectural connection between tea drinking and places of conviviality among one's most intimate or privileged associates finds its analogue in elite English conventions as well. In the late seventeenth century, Elizabeth Lauderdale, Duchess of Dysart, kept her tea table, writing cabinet, books, tea, and sweetmeats in a small room on the ground floor referred to in Ham House inventories as a "private closet."[72] The practice had its parallel in Virginia. William Byrd II, for example, records in 1710 that after dinner at the governor's residence, "I went to make a visit to Mrs. Russell in her chamber and drank some tea with her. Then we went down." For Byrd, success at the politics of access was expressed by penetrating the privileged architectural space of his governor's mistress; for Katherine Russell, social negotiation and political power was exercised by granting or denying access to her bedchamber.[73]

Tea drinking was not the only heterosocial event in which women participated. In addition to attending numerous dances, Byrd noted that he "played billiards with the ladies" and "played cards with my own wife."[74] None of these activities, however, were as closely identified with female agency. Therefore, situating the tea table within the mansion helps us to pinpoint more accurately rooms that were important to elite women. When we look to the evidence, it is clear that the names of the room where this key symbol of female agency was located varied. At Nomini Hall, Frances

Anne Tasker Carter presided over the tea table in a ground-floor room that Fithian called "a dining room where we usually sit." The study inventories indicate that only six tea tables were located in dining rooms, whereas twenty-nine were listed in a space referred to as a parlor, hall, drawing room, or great room. This division suggests that the primary elite female social performance, tea drinking, usually was separated spatially from the most ceremonious room, namely, the dining room. It was separated temporally as well. Several opportunities and architectural spaces existed for conviviality between men and women in the Virginia mansion, but it appears that more informal events contributed to a freer exchange of information between wealthy gentlemen, gentlewomen, and people of somewhat lesser social standing. Fithian notes the following schedule: breakfast at 8:30 AM, dinner between two and three in the afternoon, tea (after the Townshend Acts, coffee only) in the late afternoon, and supper around 8:30 PM. After breakfast, Fithian and Frances Anne Tasker Carter "had a long conversation on religious affairs—Particularly on differing Denominations of Protestants." He could talk with "the Ladies" on the topic of "Fashions," and he held his own at coffee with Robert and Frances Anne Tasker Carter when the discussion turned to philosophy, eclipses, telescopes, and the solar system. The less formal setting of evening supper also led to postmeal exchanges of ideas on topics including slavery, death, and contemporary manners.[75]

Polite practices shifted according to the social significance applied to a social event. Fithian acknowledged the dual character of elite behavior when he noticed how Frances Anne Tasker Carter was routinely polite and informal, but was "also well acquainted . . . with the formality and Ceremony which we find commonly in high life."[76] The degree to which the event was considered "high life" served as the gauge of its relatively androcentric character. It was the occasion, therefore, and not necessarily the architecture that signaled male or female empowerment.

The Kitchen

Nineteenth-century notions of domesticity are not applicable to the elite of early Virginia, and the kitchen, which is pictured even today as a typical female domain, was a socially insignificant space for privileged females in the Tidewater. Their role in the kitchen was, as most foodways historians agree, supervisory.[77] To be sure, high-quality food and its proper presentation before guests may have been important to an elite woman, but concern for the appearance of a table did not necessarily translate into labor in the kitchen. She was distanced from the kitchen both physically and in terms of her responsibilities there. Rather, it was the black slave who, under the direction of the white mistress, would come to occupy the kitchen and take charge of cooking for rich planters. Because the relationship between women and cookery is historically a powerful one, the frequent absence of the elite white female from the plantation kitchen needs detailed examination.

We can see how minimally invested elite women were in kitchens by examining the value of the items inventoried there compared to the value of the tableware stored in the main house.[78] Probate records indicate that more precious comestibles, particularly tea and spices, were not stored in the kitchen but in rooms where white owners had greater oversight. For example, according to the 1750 inventory of Leroy Griffin of Richmond County, tea, coffee, and sugar containers were all located in a bedchamber. Evidence of a black presence in the kitchen comes from food itself, and the regional distinctiveness of southern cooking is well known. Traveling through Virginia in 1732, the Englishman William Hugh Grove found worth noting the presence of foods that today we would associate with African American cuisine. According to Grove, "the Gentry at Their Tables have commonly 5 dishes of plates, of which Pigg meat and greens is generally one."[79] According to scholars of American foodways, enslaved cooks in elite households incorporated and adapted traditional African cuisine into traditional English fare, which in turn was altered by the influence of French cuisine, especially sauces.[80] A picture of the withdrawal of white elite women from kitchen labor can be drawn from anecdotal evidence and cookbooks.

Fithian offers some of our best information about the relationship of the wealthiest colonial women to household labor. As a New England Presbyterian ministerial candidate, he was predisposed to look askance at Virginia gentry behavior but eventually was seduced by the orderly comfort he enjoyed at the plantation of Robert Carter III. Fithian attributes the gentility of life at Nomini Hall to the oversight of Frances Anne Tasker Carter. When he became ill, he noted that she "sent me over coffee for Breakfast" and "sent the waiting Man to Know if I was better."[81] The verb specified her commanding role. She dispatched; she did not convey.

The 1797 diary of Frances Baylor Hill, a young woman living at Hillsborough, further shows how genteel women engaged in domestic labor. Hill routinely sewed entire garments for herself and her family, finished a three-year-long counterpane project, reluctantly learned to knit stockings, occasionally washed and ironed fabric, and visited sick slaves with her mother; she rarely mentions cooking. When she did exert herself in the kitchen, she baked biscuits and created sweet treats such as pies and tarts rather than entire meals. Frances reenacted little of the work of her British social cohort of a century earlier, Elizabeth Pepys, who according to her husband, Samuel, was preoccupied in "making her tarts and larding her pullets till 11 a-clock."[82] Hill's other culinary skills seem to come from observation rather than hands-on experience. She notes, for instance, that she "staid in Cellar to see a few Hogs cut out & salt'd."[83]

A disinclination to prepare meals does not mean that elite women were entirely indolent, although Hill does undertake a fairly rigorous party schedule. Productive manual labor for elite Virginia women was concentrated in the needle arts, and garment construction was expected of genteel ladies not only as a matter of economy but also because it was deemed a suitably genteel way of occupying time. For example, Maria Taylor Byrd, meddling in her son's marriage to Elizabeth Hill Carter, writes to him complaining that his wife "orders her underclothes to be made and ruffled in England. I cant help but think, she had better make them her-self, it would be some employment for her."[84] Productive work was executed by elite women, but in architectural settings that did not require extended contact with servants and slaves.[85]

The ideal relationship of the elite mistress and the spaces of food preparation is described in Mary Randolph's 1824 *The Virginia Housewife,* a book that, although postcolonial, might be seen as building upon the practices of her youth in the eighteenth century. Note that although the content is devoted to recipes, preservation, and even butchering procedures, the title is not *The Virginia Cook* or *The Virginia Cookbook* but refers to the woman who supervises the household. The preface and introduction to the 1829 edition describe the perfect system to which her readers should aspire. Randolph envisions the ideal housewife as a manager, not a cook. Her system aims for minimal contact between mistress and servant and therefore minimal time spent in the kitchen. According to Randolph, decisions about cooking the midday dinner meal should be made according to a strict morning regimen. While the servants are eating their own breakfast, the mistress is to spend the time "washing the cups, glasses, etc., arranging the cruets, the mustard, salt-sellers, pickle vases, and all the apparatus for the dinner table." This is the only hands-on labor Randolph allows her. Recipes are supposed to be well known, even memorized, by the mistress, but not executed by her. The ideal mistress knew what ingredients were needed for each dish for that day's dinner because "we have no right to expect slaves or hired servants to be more attentive to our interest than we ourselves are." The ideal mistress would "have" all the ingredients "measured to the cook," and the proper quantities should "pass in review before her" because when "the mistress gives out every thing, there is no waste; but if temptation be thrown in the way of subordinates, not many will have the power to resist it." The wise conservation of wealth was not the only benefit of such a routine. Randolph claims that her system would reduce to one hour the time the mistress would need to spend on housework, hence freeing her from the "horrible drudgery of keeping house all day long."[86]

Hannah Glasse's *The Art of Cookery, Made Plain and Easy,* first published in London in 1747, addresses this supervisory relationship between mistress and cook. The earliest American edition was published in Alexandria, Virginia, in 1805 but retains the original English introduction, where Glasse states: "I have both seen, and found by experience, that the generality of Servants are greatly wanting [in cookery], I therefore have taken upon me to instruct them in the best manner I am capable and I dare say, that every Servant who can but read, will be capable of making a tolerable good Cook." The American edition includes a small but meaningful alteration in the next section. While the earlier edition remarks on the ineptness of the "lower sort," the American edition aims to "instruct the ignorant and unlearned . . . in so full and plain a manner that the most ignorant Person, who can but read will know how to do Cookery well." Presumably, the intention was not to insult the book buyer by implying her ignorance, and so the 1805 edition may signal that by the end of the eighteenth century, a cook who could read on her own was indeed a desirable servant in Virginia. The more frequent scenario, though, was vividly described by Isaac Jefferson, a slave at Monticello whose mother, Ursula, labored as washerwoman and pastry cook: "Mrs. Jefferson would come out there with a cookery book in her hand and read out of it to Isaac's mother how to make cakes, tarts, and so on."[87]

Slave cooks increasingly came to replace white women in the elite plantation kitchen; in doing so, they came to exercise a certain degree of power vis-à-vis their masters and fellow laborers. Highly valued in inventories of slaves and by their owners, slave cooks were also in a position, by virtue of their access to foodstuffs, to reallocate surreptitiously small amounts of much-needed nutrition to family and favorites. Cooks were not necessarily female, nor were all enslaved. Two male cooks worked at Stratford Hall: the indentured servant Richard Mynatt, who departed in 1754, and the slave Caesar.[88] At Westover, there were three slave cooks, one male and two female; while at Mount Vernon in 1808, there were also three cooks, two male and one female.[89] The white historical record has preserved some of the cooks' names. At the Governor's Palace in Williamsburg, Sukey Hamilton, a slave, cooked for Governor Francis Fauquier. At Monticello, food was prepared by James Hemings, a literate slave who was trained in French cuisine while in Paris with Thomas Jefferson in the 1780s. After 1809, fancy cooking at Monticello was created by Edith Fossett, a slave who was taught French cooking in Washington, D.C.[90] At Jefferson's Bedford County retreat, Poplar Forest, the cooking and housekeeping was the domain of his slave Hannah, who in a letter of 15 November 1818 in her own hand informed her owner that "your house and furniture are all safe as I expected you would be glad to know."[91] Lydia Broadnax may also have been somewhat literate inasmuch as her master, George Wythe, is known to have taught some of his slaves to read. Following the death of Wythe's wife in 1787, he freed Broadnax, but she continued to work at his Williamsburg mansion as his housekeeper.[92]

Ownership of a slave cook served as a sign that a planter was wealthy enough to shift capital from fieldwork to housework, that is, to labor expended for the comfort of white inhabitants. Few Virginians could afford to redirect their expensive human property in this way, and in the eighteenth century domestic slaves signified a highly desirable luxury that was out of reach for middling planters. Whereas middle-class or artisan-class families may have been able to purchase tea equipage and partake in genteel social events, not many had the means to own a specialist in cookery. It is estimated that an average slave owner in 1800 diverted only 5 percent of his slaves to domestic labor, whereas truly wealthy planters may have diverted 25 percent.[93] Fewer slaves worked as domestics earlier in the eighteenth century. Of the approximately seven hundred slaves owned by Robert Carter I, his 1732 inventory lists only one white indentured male servant, John Foulton, and one black female slave, Criss, as cooks.[94]

The fashion for black domestic servants was not an indigenous Tidewater development dependent on purely economic factors. Portraits of British aristocrats with black pages, seen, for instance, in Peter Lely's *Elizabeth Murray, Countess of Dysart* (ca. 1651), and the presence of rich West Indies planter families who returned to England with Caribbean slaves transformed black servants into exotic, attractive novelties among the English upper class.[95] Possessing a black domestic slave distinguished those who had knowledge of the beau monde from those who were merely prosperous.[96]

Over time, cooking became more closely linked to black skin and slave status and hence encouraged the removal of elite white women from the Tidewater kitchen. The act of pushing up your sleeves and kneading dough side by side with a black woman engendered a practical equality that corroded the fiction of white supremacy that underpinned slavery. Like the segregated use of cornmeal for black people and fine wheat flour for white people at Nomini Hall, a distinctive division of female labor according to race and status was facilitated by architecture.[97]

Site planning of secondary outbuildings in early Virginia underscored the physical and social distance of an elite woman from kitchen labor. Unlike its New England counterpart, the Virginia mansion did not incorporate a kitchen into the main dwelling house. Instead, the kitchen, as well as the smokehouse, dairy, and a small number of slave quarters, were erected as separate freestanding buildings at a distance sufficient to ensure that heat, smoke, and odors did not affect the more genteel residence. In 1686, a French traveler, Durand de Dauphiné, found this ensemble ap-

proach to domestic planning remarkable and compared a wealthy plantation complex to "a fairly large village."[98] By comparison, in England the
incorporation of the kitchen into the body of the house was a development
dating from the second half of the sixteenth century, and one that eventually found its class-dividing solution in placing the kitchen on a level lower
than the ground floor.[99] Distances between kitchens and the main block
of the Virginia mansion varied. At Carter's Grove, 24 feet separated the
kitchen wall from the side wall of the main block (fig. 134).[100] At Stratford
Hall, slaves walked about 75 feet between the kitchen door and the door
into the warming kitchen on the lower service level of the main house (fig.
135).[101] At Hillsborough, Frances Baylor Hill noted she "staid in the Cellar
to see a few Hogs cut out & salt'd," suggesting that some food preservation
was occurring below the main house.[102] At Nomini Hall, kitchen servants
worked within the context of other places of hard, unpleasant labor: the
washhouse, stable, and coach house.[103] But among these outbuildings, the
kitchen was the most important to plantation owners, and its status was
signaled by its often whitewashed finish. The kitchen was not as genteel as
the main house, but distinctly better than the bare wood of a barn.[104]

Fig. 134. Carter's Grove, James City County, 1750. View from south of main house
and dependencies. Photograph after 1879. (Cook Collection, Valentine Richmond
History Center)

Fig. 135. Stratford Hall, Westmoreland County, 1738. View from the door of the warming kitchen in the main house to the kitchen. (Photograph by author)

For most wealthy women, domestic duties focused on supervising the productive labor of others and knowing what and when and who to command in order to facilitate the running of a plantation. Their jobs, therefore, approached that of the housekeeper in an English aristocratic household.[105] A few gentry women, however, increased their distance from the kitchen by hiring white housekeepers. In doing so, they moved closer to the one-hour ideal envisioned by Randolph. At Nomini Hall, Frances Anne Tasker Carter left routine chores to an older housekeeper, Miss Stanhope.[106] At Belvidera, Sarah Taliaferro Daingerfield was shielded from household tedium by Lucy Gaines, who, like the tutor John Harrower, ate with the planter and his immediate family. When Gaines quit, Lucy Holmes was interviewed and quickly hired, suggesting a plentiful supply of white women eager to work as housekeepers for the wealthy.[107] To be sure, there is always the possibility that we are not seeing elite women in kitchens because men are not there to record their presence or because it was so unexceptional and routine that no one noted it. But the available evidence points to a different conclusion, namely that an elite woman's time in this architectural space was as minimal as they could manage. For black slave cooks and for poor and middling white women, kitchens were key sites. For wives of wealthy planters, kitchens were on the periphery of the cognitive map of their own space in the colonial Virginia mansion.

The Plantation Landscape

Outside of the domestic buildings, a number of socially significant spaces for elite females can be identified, particularly the landscape adjacent to the mansion. Both formally designed gardens and the less controlled landscape beyond provided genteel women extended spaces of sociability. The wealthiest women living in the Tidewater experienced formal gardens like that restored at Carter's Grove (fig. 136) that were planned according to geometric principles and that consisted of orderly beds of vegetables, herbs, and flowers and perhaps descending terraces enclosed by wooden fences or masonry walls. Such highly controlled gardens in turn gave way to a much less tidy plantation landscape of cultivated plots, abandoned scrubby fields whose soil was spent from tobacco planting, and woods, creating an awkward juxtaposition that Peter Martin described as the "colonial paradigm of the wilderness."[108]

Fig. 136. Reconstructed garden at Carter's Grove, James City County. (Photograph by author)

The landscape at Nomini Hall afforded Frances Anne Tasker Carter, Fithian, and other members of the household with not only a source of nourishment and ornament but a place to display socially significant behavior (fig. 137). Fithian noted the mixed character of social performances in the garden when he recorded that he "walked through the Garden—The whole Family seem to be now out Black, White, Male, female, All enjoying the cool evening." For those with access to the world of British letters, however, the pleasures of nature had leapt the fence by the mid-eighteenth century. Wealthy landowners in Virginia as well as England acquired a taste for a vision of nature less manipulated by artifice. Fithian glimpsed elite women exercising their linguistic competency in fashionable British landscape and aesthetic theory: "At five with Mrs. Carter & the young Ladies I took a walk; She shewed me from a high Hill several beautiful Prospects." Perambulations through unkempt plantations reenacted British aesthetic values that well-read participants would have been able to rehearse from texts such as the *Spectator* and James Thomson's *The Seasons*. Like performances at the dressing table or tea table, engagement with nature was an acquired skill.

Elite Virginia women expressed the freedom of the garden in several ways, some marked by greater female physical motion and social inclusion. In 1774, Mrs. Daingerfield and a female friend planned a "picnic" attended by her husband, his friend, the Daingerfield children, and their Scottish tutor, John Harrower. While strolling through the pasture, Fithian met "Miss Stanhope, Priss, Nancy, Fanny, and Betsy Carter. They walked to the Mill; there they entered a boat and for exercise and amusement were rowed down the river quite to the granary and then went to angling."[109] Gardens also acted as sites where women challenged male control. Byrd noted that he was angry at his first wife, Lucy Parke Byrd, for climbing over the palisade fence surrounding the garden when she was five months pregnant and, in his aggrieved mind, endangering a potential male heir. In this instance, the garden at Westover offered not an enclosure of purity but an opportunity for women to countermand male authority by the physical actions of their bodies.

The plantation landscape also provided opportunities for women to exercise their intellects by supervising work associated with plants and animals. Fithian noted the distinct amusements of his employers: "when we returned about Candlelight, we found Mrs. Carter in the yard seeing to the Roosting of her Poultry, and the Colonel in the Parlour tuning his Guitar."[110] Frances Anne Tasker Carter proudly showed Fithian her poultry and sheep and "observed, with great truth, that to live in the Country and take no pleasure at all in Groves, Fields, or Meadows; nor in Cattle, Horses, and domestic Poultry, would be a manner of life too tedious to

Fig. 137. E. Maund, *Nomony Hall* (Nomini Hall), Westmoreland County, watercolor, before house burned in 1850. (Courtesy of Thomas Lee Arnest of Nomini Hall)

endure." But the enjoyment elite women took in horticulture and animal husbandry did not translate into strenuous labor. Carter gave her orders to Mr. Gregory, the white indentured servant who acted as the head gardener, and to two slave "gardeners by Trade, who are constantly when the weather will any how permit working in it." She "ordered the Gardiner to sew Lettice and Plant Peas." Her pleasure controlling nature was formed at a young age. Her father, Benjamin Tasker, seems to have been part of a small coterie of wealthy Annapolis men who pursued a passion for plants, trees, and enhancing architecture. With the leisured men of Annapolis or John Randolph in Williamsburg, Carter shared an intellectual passion for a subject exercised in a space that was not overly burdened with strict gender associations. For women who took pride in their work, however, these spaces held special significance as places of affirmation.[111]

Imagining a mental map of important elite female spaces beyond the immediate curtilage of the mansion becomes more difficult. Traditional English cultural values identified virtuous women with domestic seclusion.[112] Genteel women of course were not confined, but their appearance at public events was often met with finger-wagging male disapproval in the eighteenth-century British world. Male critics probably knew from their own behavior how women's bodies became objects of scrutiny in public places such as ferry crossings or church. Byrd thought his evaluation of a woman worth a diary entry in 1709: "When I came to the ferry I saw Mistress Mary Eppes, a pretty girl and capable of impression." Church services also availed Byrd with opportunities to judge women including, he noted, "Mrs. H-M-L-N, a very handsome woman."[113]

From a female perspective, exciting parties rather than perfunctory church services figure more prominently. Young Frances Baylor Hill's keen interest in these heterosocial events is conveyed by her careful description of the events, food, and location. Hill took particular delight in attending a "Barbacue" that included dining under an arbor in mixed company, music, dancing, eating watermelon, and a side trip to another plantation for tea. By contrast, Hill says next to nothing about the slave quarters: "went to see all the sick negroes." She did record the affecting impact of the death of Phill: "his wife was greatly distress'd I never was sorry'r for a negro in my life."[114] For privileged young women like Hill, significant public space was not located at the market or in the courthouse, but was found at other mansions.

Conclusion

An inventory of the most important loci of elite female activity reveals insight into female agency, the tension between the conflicting modern ideals of privacy and display, and the distancing between those who produced and those who consumed. Seen from a gynocentric point of view, the Virginia mansion does not represent a frozen set of aesthetic forms underscoring male values, but a more malleable and evolving stage where female values and imperatives were performed parallel to and sometimes in contradistinction to male claims of patriarchal omnipotence.

The Virginia prodigy house, therefore, can be understood as encompassing a complex, overlapping web of intertwined significant male and significant female spaces. For the poor or middling burdened with greater physical labor, the pattern of important domestic space would look far different, but for elite Virginia women, significant architectural space focused on the bedchamber, places of conviviality where social performances were enacted, and more distanced places where they exerted control over the labor of others.

The overtly feminized character of the American domestic setting that emerged so clearly in the nineteenth century did not yet serve as the normalized vision of private architecture. Most genteel men's work had not been removed from home. Nor had the accompanying doctrine of female domestic domination been articulated by writers such as John Ruskin or Catherine Beecher and Harriet Beecher Stowe. For the native elite in eighteenth-century Virginia, the mansion served as the stage for both male and female identity formation and performance. The success of the so-called cult of domesticity in the next century makes more sense, however, when seen against the previous age. When women took control of the domestic stage in the nineteenth century, they were not radically altering the ways that they knew their architectural environment. Writers and popular culture were legitimatizing and throwing a dramatic spotlight on the ways that elite females understood from their own gynocentric perspective. A mental map of significant genteel female architectural space existed before the nineteenth-century cult of domesticity but had been overshadowed by the more historically visible patriarchal fantasies of men like Byrd.

Chapter 7

Political Power and the Limits
of Genteel Architecture

Claiming Power

Perk up your ears at almost any art or architectural history conference these days, and you can hear the following proclamation: buildings are instruments of power. In fields ranging from Etruscan to modern American architecture, scholars insert such phrases as "a design meant to demonstrate the power of," "serves to authenticate power," or "by building he hoped to join the ranks of." Sometimes the speaker—and I admit to having used similar phrases—boldly claims a direct causal relationship between construction of an impressive building and the subsequent achievement of status and prestige. In other instances, only a modest, suggestive link connects the two in a loose fashion. Whether it is expressed overtly or more subtly, scholars of various methodological persuasions confidently, and often uncritically, assert an association between impressive architecture and its ability to either impart or convey power. For architectural historians, this is indeed an attractive theory. It invests the subject of our life's research with potent historical purpose and agency far surpassing the connoisseur's more narrow aesthetic focus. Exposing and destabilizing the wicked machinations of the ruling class is heady stuff.

But what exactly is the nature of the relationship between architecture and power? If prodigy houses of eighteenth-century Virginia served to create, maintain, and perpetuate authority, what kind of power did they create? In this last chapter, I measure the impact of constructing and owning a prestige house against one gauge of power, public office holding, and explore additional, complex relations between architecture and power. There is no disputing the association between Virginia's eighteenth-century classical architecture and the wealthiest, educated, privileged, and politically influential members of colonial elite, but the dynamic between architecture and power is not one of cause and effect.

Political Offices and Architectural Patrons

A simple comparison between the date of construction of each mansion in the study group and the dates of accession to political offices by their owners shows the tenuous relationship between the two (table 11).[1] It underscores the danger of overestimating the political benefits likely to result from genteel building. Some of the offices through which power was exerted comprised the following list: militia officer, vestryman, justice of the peace, burgess, councilor, and lieutenant governor.

All of these positions of authority, except that of burgess, were appointive. Sitting county justices of the peace named new justices to fill vacancies, and by the end of the seventeenth century, local parish vestrymen named new vestrymen to fill openings.[2] Potential new council members were recommended by the lieutenant governor and approved by the Crown. The lieutenant governorship was an appointment made by the Lords of Trade and Plantations and also required Crown permission. With the exception of election to the House of Burgesses, politically ambitious planters needed to adhere to the political and social values of men who controlled a preexisting political entity. They had to convince their social superiors, not their social inferiors, of their worthiness. Only the office of burgess required that a man appeal popularly to the white, male, and landowning electorate.

The architectural patrons in the study group were, as a whole, politically potent individuals. Listed according to the highest political office held before the American Revolution, Alexander Spotswood served as lieutenant governor; six were appointed to the Council; John Randolph II was appointed attorney general; and twelve others were elected to the House of Burgesses. For three architectural patrons—Robert Beverley, John Carlyle, and John Mercer—political success ended at the rank of justice of the peace. Only two individuals held no public office, and this occurred not because they lacked political ambition, but rather because law and custom eliminated them from office holding. As a woman, Sarah Taliaferro Brooke was barred from voting and office holding. As a minister of the Church of England, John Thompson was strongly discouraged but not technically prohibited from holding public office. Although the correlation between success in the political arena and the ability to construct a genteel residence is high, it is difficult to prove that building a high-style dwelling directly influenced future political status. The data require a close analysis.

MILITIA OFFICER

Military authority represents one measure of power, and my detailed analysis begins with appointment to the rank of county militia officer. In eighteenth-century Virginia, as in Europe, military command was viewed not as a function of specialized training or experience but as the duty and privilege of the upper class by virtue of their presumed superior capabilities.[3] Lacking titled nobility, the colony selected its county militia officers from among individuals who could corroborate their honor with the next best thing: external evidence of status.

In times of peace, the duties of county militia officers were largely ceremonial and often sporadic, but even when the threat of war was immediate and local, the outward show of status was a necessary qualification for military command. In 1757, in the midst of the French and Indian War, Fielding Lewis was recommended for the rank of county lieutenant of Spotsylvania County, not only on the basis of his personal leadership potential but also because of his wealth. The recommendation was made because "Col. Fielding Lewis, a gent. of fortune and character in the county and much esteemed by the people, who I make no doubt would readily exert themselves under such a Gent. in case of a sudden call to the defense of our frontier."[4] In reality, militia officers may have had little notion of the rudiments of warfare. When John Banister III of Battersea was selected to lead a volunteer unit during the Revolution, he was singularly unprepared for the task and had to resort to a quick read through military treatises borrowed from a relative.[5] Leaving aside the ludicrous image of the refined mill owner feverishly pouring over his books on the brink of British invasion, military rank was not a position of authority lightly dismissed, and its feudal associations continued for generations to convey prestige in the South.

As military command was the prerogative of those exemplifying superior status, not talent, and because the refined features of prodigy houses express wealth and status, one might expect a close correspondence between the owners of Virginia mansions and those holding high rank in the county militia. By and large this hypothesis is true. Out of the twenty-three patrons eligible to serve in the military, only five men are not known to have ever held rank as militia officers. Among the eighteen men for whom the date of highest military commission can be determined, seven acquired this rank before their dwelling was constructed, eight after, and three at about the same time. Although status and wealth were necessary prerequisites for a military position, it seems that proof of superiority was not always expressed through the construction of a fashionable dwelling.

VESTRYMAN

Appointment to the parish vestry gave officeholders the opportunity to exercise control over the local population at more regular intervals than did military command.[6] Because the Church of England was the established religious body in the colony, vestrymen were charged with levying taxes payable in tobacco for the construction and/or maintenance of church

Table 11

Political offices held by study group patrons

Patron	Building date	Militia officer	Vestryman	Justice of the peace	Burgess	Councilor	Offices of power and profit
John Banister III	1767	1775	1764	1769	1765	No	1762
Robert Beverley	1769	No	Unknown	1768	No	No	No
Sarah Taliaferro Brooke	1751	—	—	—	—	—	—
Carter Burwell	1750	1751	Unknown	1737	1742	No	No
Lewis Burwell III	1725	1728	1725	1726	1736	No	1728
John Carlyle	1751	1749	No	1749	No	No	1749
Charles Carter	1746	1752	1738	1730	1736	No	1729
Landon Carter	1738	1742	In 1740s	1734	1752	No	No
Robert Carter I	1720	1699	Unknown	ca. 1690	1691	1700	1699
Richard Corbin	1758	1753	1745	1735	1749	1750	1762
William Fairfax	1741	1742	1755	1734	1742	1744	1749
William Fitzhugh	1769	No	Unknown	Unknown	1772	No	No
Benjamin Harrison IV	1726	1726	Unknown	1726	1736	No	No
Thomas Jefferson	1770	1770	Unknown	1766	1769	No	No
Richard Henry Lee	1758	1755	Before 1771	1756	1758	No	1761
Thomas Lee	1738	By 1720	By 1720	1714	1726	1733	1713
George Mason IV	1752	1756	1749	1747	1759	No	1749
John Mercer	1746	No	1730	1748	No	No	No
Mann Page I	1726	1715	Unknown	Unknown	No	1714	1727
Mann Page II	1767	No	1779	1743	No	No	No
John Randolph II	1758	Before 1761	Unknown	1762	1769	No	1767
William Randolph III	1751	Unknown	1748	1748	1746	No	No
Alexander Spotswood	1721	1693	No	No	No	No	1710
John Tayloe II	1760	Before 1752	1743	1742	No	1756	1759
John Thompson	1763	—	—	—	—	—	—

buildings, the relief of the poor, and administrative expenses. It was also a group that exerted control over morals, church attendance, and conformity in liturgical practices. Due to the absence of a resident bishop in the colony, vestrymen usually exercised control over the appointment of their ministers.[7] Two men among the vestrymen, known as churchwardens, served in a more executive capacity by handling day-to-day matters. Potentially, vestrymen could shape the character of the parish by the decisions they made about building, taxation, and the enforcement of religious standards. Vestrymen were elected only when a parish was first established. After that the vestry became a self-perpetuating body, and a special act of the General Assembly was required for new elections.[8] Appointment to this political body meant that you were recognized as adhering to the ideals of the men already on the vestry.

Out of the twenty-three patrons able to hold political office, sixteen are known to have been appointed as a vestryman of a Virginia parish. Among those nine whose first date of appointment is either known or can be surmised with some certainty, six were named to the vestry before erection of their mansion, William Fairfax after, and the appointments of Lewis Burwell III and William Randolph III came at about the same time. While this is too small a group from which to draw solid conclusions, appointment to a local vestry appears to have been influenced by factors other than possession of a dwelling exhibiting sophisticated classicizing features.

JUSTICE OF THE PEACE

The extant records are somewhat more complete for the next step along the path of political power: appointment to the county court as a justice of the peace. Justices of the peace served as judges in these county courts, and their authority surpassed that of vestrymen insomuch as they could order fines and physical punishments short of execution.[9] Of the twenty-three men in the study group able to hold public office, twenty served as justice of the peace. Among these, the date of appointment was either recorded or can be placed somewhat securely for fifteen. Eleven men were named justice of the peace before erection of their mansion, three at about the same time, and one, John Randolph II, shortly after he built Tazewell Hall. Appointment to the county commission of peace, therefore, was influenced by factors independent of having built a genteel house.

BURGESS

Election to the House of Burgesses, however, may be a different story. Becoming a burgess meant participating in a colonywide, rather than local, arena of power. It was, moreover, a political body whose power increased throughout the eighteenth century.[10] Whereas at least eight justices of the peace served on each county court, and twelve men acted as vestrymen, the House of Burgesses was comprised of only two men from each county, plus one each from Jamestown, Williamsburg, Norfolk, and the College of William and Mary.[11] Election to the House of Burgesses, therefore, signaled inclusion within a smaller and more elite political category, and it is significant that a large proportion of the architectural patrons in the study group did serve as burgesses. Out of the twenty-three individuals allowed to hold public office, seventeen were elected to at least one session of the House of Burgesses. Comparing the first date of service in the House of Burgesses to the assumed date of construction, eight men were elected burgesses before they built their residence, six won the office after construction commenced, and for three men, construction and election nearly coincided. The numbers are more balanced here than they were for appointment to the vestry or county court. Perhaps some small and middling landowners were sufficiently impressed by a large, formal dwelling to vote for its owner and send him to the House of Burgesses. But once elected, ownership of a prodigy house was not enough to ensure reelection. Gaining and maintaining elective office required active campaigning in addition to representing the will of constituents.[12] In his diary, Landon Carter confessed that his reluctance to mingle with colonial plebeians cost him his election: "I can well remember when I was turned out of the House of Burgesses. It was said that I did not familiarize myself among the People and because two elections after it was proved by my son's going amongst them and Carrying his election."[13] Carter had lost his bid for reelection in 1768, more than twenty years after Sabine Hall was built. If his house had convinced voters of his superiority at one time, its luster had faded by 1768. Tactics less high-minded than architectural gentility also swayed voters: in 1765 Theodorick Bland Sr. attributed John Banister's (Battersea) election to the House of Burgesses to "swilling the planters with bumbo," that is, rum.[14]

COUNCILOR

By comparison, a man need impress no more than a handful of powerful planters and the lieutenant governor in order to win appointment to the highest and most prestigious office attained by any native Virginian, that is, councilor. Acting as the upper house of the General Assembly with the lieutenant governor as presiding officer, the Council functioned as the supreme judicial body of the colony and heard capital cases. In addition, members of the Council served as advisors to the governor and hence performed in an executive role. Councilors were appointed for life by the Crown after being nominated by the lieutenant governor. In the eighteenth century, the Council numbered no more than twelve men at any one time. This was a very select and powerful group indeed, and out of the twenty-three potential officeholders in the study group, only six were appointed to the Council. By comparing the date of appointment to the date of construction, we find that only one architectural patron, William Fairfax, was elevated to the Council after he erected his mansion. The other five persuaded the lieutenant governor and the king's advisors with qualities other than their ability to build a fashionable dwelling.

Mann Page I's vertiginous political ascent is particularly worth noting. Page entered Eton College in 1706 and St. John's College, Oxford, in 1709. After returning to Virginia, he was promptly appointed to the Virginia Council in February 1714, at the age of twenty-three. Seven years later, after his house was destroyed by fire, he commenced to erect Rosewell, an extravagantly lavish building that was one of only two known three-story mansions built in colonial Virginia. For Page, architecture was unnecessary to achieve high political office.

OTHER OFFICES OF POWER AND PROFIT

While the positions of militia officer, vestryman, justice of the peace, burgess, and councilor represent the most well-known political offices in Virginia, colonial government was replete with opportunities to exert personal authority. The office of attorney general was held by one owner, John Randolph II, after he built Tazewell Hall, while both the positions of treasurer and Speaker of the House of Burgesses were occupied by Robert Carter I well before he started construction of his new house at Corotoman. Power was also exercised by those who held offices of profit, which were appointments that provided not only political influence but also legally sanctioned monetary gain in order to encourage the assiduous collection of taxes and duties. Of the twenty-three architectural patrons able to hold public office, five were named either collector of customs or naval officer: four before and one, Lewis Burwell III, after they erected their dwelling. Three men held clerkships during their political careers: two were appointed before construction, while William Randolph III was named at about the same time. Two other offices of profit were won following construction: Richard Corbin became deputy receiver general of Virginia after he built Laneville, while Alexander Spotswood was appointed deputy postmaster general of North America after he started building the mansion at Germanna.

Appointment as feoffee, or trustee, of a town also conveyed political authority. The responsibilities of these municipal officials included the selling of lots, regulation of streets and public facilities, and, in some cases, the laying out of the town plan. Town trustees, therefore, not only influenced the physical conditions of a community but also could determine who received the choicest lots and urban amenities. Ten architectural patrons served as town trustees, while John Randolph II acted in a similar capacity as a member of the Williamsburg Common Council. Among these, four were appointed before they built their mansion, an equal number after, and three at about the same time. Six mansion owners in the study group were selected as Visitors of the College of William and Mary: two were appointed before they began their mansion, three after, and one, Richard Corbin, at about the same time.

Inherited Power and Privilege

Based on the information from the twenty-five architectural patrons in the study group, construction of a prodigy house was not a prerequisite for holding powerful political office. Many mansion owners who were politically ambitious impressed their superiors, or the electorate, with evidence of their wealth, status, and personal worth beyond that exemplified by their possession of a high-style residence. A much more significant factor for their political success was the political status of their fathers. Only two of the sixteen men serving as vestrymen did not have fathers who held the same or higher office, and those two were recent arrivals to the colony, William Fairfax and John Mercer. Of the twenty architectural patrons acting as justices of the peace, three, who were also immigrants, did not have fathers who held the same or higher office.[15] Only one of the seventeen men elected to the House of Burgesses did not have a father who was a burgess or held a higher position, and he, William Fairfax, was also an immigrant.[16] Four of the six councilors in the study group had fathers who also were councilors. The two exceptions, however, were not appointed entirely on their own merit, but probably because of the political influence of other near relatives, an uncle and a father-in-law.[17] While prior paternal office holding seems the critical factor in political advancement, there was no guarantee that a son could match his father's record of accomplishment. Nine native architectural patrons rose to the same level of political authority as their fathers,[18] but nine others fell short.[19] Only one native, Richard Corbin, exceeded his father in political station. There also seems to have been a point beyond which a patron's family connections and wealth were ineffectual in the wider context of the British Atlantic Empire. Members of the native elite continually campaigned among their benefactors in the English political establishment for choice political positions, but the selection process was often beyond their control. No native Virginian, for instance, ascended permanently to the rank of lieutenant governor. The prestige, preferment, and arrogance of the British military over the colonial elite created a deep animosity to British authority. Byrd was both disappointed and rankled when he was informed in 1710 that "that no one but soldiers should have the government of a plantation."[20]

Elite Architecture and Liberal Democracy

Eighteenth-century Virginia mansions do not appear to have been constructed as emblems of a specific political ideology relating to political independence. Fourteen of the architectural patrons in the study group were alive in 1765, long enough to have formed an opinion concerning the political rights of the colony after the passage of the Stamp Act. The political position of John Thompson is unknown, but among the other thirteen, ten may be classified as American Revolutionaries, either because of their outspoken support of independence, participation in the Revolutionary government, financial support of the colony during the war, or anti–Stamp Act activities.[21] The remaining three are classified as Loyalists.[22]

Comparing the patron's political stance to the stylistic characteristics of his mansion, a clear relationship between architecture style and political ideology does not emerge. The more academically correct, Palladian features that began to appear in the massing of elite houses after midcentury are found in the dwellings of Revolutionaries such as Thomas Jefferson and John Banister III, but also in the mansions of Loyalists such as John Randolph II and Robert Beverley. There is no easily identifiable Whig or Tory style among wealthy planters. If the use of classical motifs such as pediments and porticoes, columns and pilasters can be interpreted as a political ideology, then that ideology transcends the specific issue of an independent America and a republican form of government.[23]

Alternative Expressions of Power and Authority

Two general observations result from the preceding analysis of architecture and office holding. First, for the great majority of men in the study group there was a close correlation between possessing a fashionably metropolitan house and holding positions of political authority. Second, it can not be proved convincingly that building such a dwelling led to attaining those political offices. Some mansion owners, such as Sarah Taliaferro Brooke and John Thompson, were never permitted political advancement. The ethnic origins of John Mercer and John Carlyle served as a bar to political preferment. Yet, all four engaged in the politics of aesthetic display. If high-style architecture functioned as a tool with which to acquire power, then that efficacy was not overtly manifested in office holding. What then can we make of architecture and power?

Office holding represents only one gauge of power. Other indicators, such as the acquiescence of others to specific policies or personal prestige before one's social inferiors, cohorts, and superiors, may actually be more potent and desirable. Just as there are various ways of measuring power, so too are there diverse means of architecturally expressing the claim to that power and authority. And for Virginia's native elite, the presumption of authority was made before multiple audiences.

Elevation design and ornamental details expressed aesthetic sophistication to a peer audience of culturally literate, wealthy planters. Plans and the politics of access, on the other hand, could be performed before Virginians without insider knowledge of metropolitan fashion. The action of selectively displaying, distancing, or hiding either a person or object constitutes an ancient and universal method of creating the mystique or aura of value, superiority, and desire. Architectural historians have argued that the increasing specialization of rooms—entrance passageways, parlors, bedchambers, and rooms for ritualized formal dining—all served to distance the owners and their guests from those people considered beneath the dignity of social intercourse. Like the ceremonial route that served as the social foundation of seventeenth-century Roman palace planning, movement within the Virginia prodigy house signaled status. Successful entree to the remote object of desire required deference and acquiescence to the will of those most remote, be it a cardinal of the Catholic Church or the owner of a large plantation and his family.[24]

On the exterior, Virginia's architectural patrons and their builders also artfully manipulated design in order to create the mystique of prestige. At Germanna, Alexander Spotswood planted an avenue of cherry trees between his mansion and a chapel, which linked, both literally and psychologically, his personal authority to that of the Church of England. At Gunston Hall, George Mason IV planted a grove of trees in front of his mansion with so much mathematical precision that a visitor at his threshold perceived only six trees standing before him. Like the carefully groomed patterns of Versailles' meticulously planted flowerbeds, the perspectival sleight of hand in Gunston Hall's landscape was intended to prove the superior intellect of the master and his authority to rule even nature. At Mount Airy, Dell Upton discovered a pattern of physical barriers and opening vistas that enhanced the impression of the Tayloe family's reserved remoteness, a regal presence beyond the ken of everyday Virginians.[25] Some visitors as well as middling and poor landowners and tenants were, no doubt, awed by the theatrical effects of a manipulated landscape. Germanna's German mine workers were less entranced with Spotswood's architectural and landscape tableau. They demonstrated their dissatisfaction with Spotswood, the terms of their indentured servitude, and a church they found inconveniently located, and perhaps theologically incompatible, by burning it down less than ten years after the governor had it built.[26]

For their part, black slaves and white servants were neither hoodwinked by the contrivances of architectural or landscape design nor bound by the rules of spatial interior hierarchy. Upton, again, has convincingly argued that domestic servants transgressed the rules and routes that guided white guests through and around mansions, and has revealed how the scope of their labor required them to disregard the parade of honor implicit in the hierarchy of white-owned rooms. Slaves and indentured servants needed more than a modillioned cornice to keep them in their place. By means as overt as escape and physical resistance, or by means more subversive such as word play, the ridiculing imitation of Caucasian hairstyles, or the mocking reuse of cast-off clothing, slaves undermined the myth of white planter superiority, though at some peril.[27]

William Byrd II could fantasize that he was the biblical patriarch of his Virginia flock at Westover, but his brutal behavior against his slaves and servants betrayed his imagined idyllic world. When a "negro woman" challenged his authority in 1709 by unsuccessfully attempting to drown herself, Byrd ordered a bit, an iron instrument of restraint and punishment, put in her mouth. After running away again, she was tied up but managed to escape once more. In 1710, her suicide attempts seem to have succeeded. Even within Byrd's immediate household, servants gave ample proof of their resistance. Byrd's maid, Jenny, whose race is unknown, also tried to end her life by running into the river, "but came out again of herself and was severely whipped for it." Byrd might have believed that he was fulfilling his rights and duties as patriarch in his methods of chastising a young servant he called "my boy Eugene," who may have been Jenny's son. In June 1709, Byrd noted in his diary that "Eugene was whipped for running away and had the [bit] put on him." Later that same year, "Eugene was whipped for pissing in bed and Jenny for concealing it." When a second whipping did not cure Eugene's bedwetting problem, Byrd tried another approach to assert his authority: "I made him drink a pint of piss." The actions of Byrd and his servant serve as a potent reminder of the violence and desperation woven into the fabric of colonial Virginia's refined gentility.[28]

Before their peers and superiors, Virginia's native elite anxiously displayed architectural refinement in an attempt to demonstrate that they were, as Fithian put it, "exalted as much above other Men in worth & precedency."[29] We occasionally glimpse their insecurity. Behind a façade of planter arrogance, Byrd fussed like a nervous dinner party host in anticipation of a visit from Governor Alexander Spotswood and made sure that "all things were put into the best order" at Westover. When the governor's cousin came, Byrd was delighted to find that "Mr. Graeme was pleased with the place exceedingly."[30] Byrd showed his plantation to Graeme to prove his worth within the larger Atlantic colonial elite. The same motive lay behind his actions when he sent Peter Beckford of Jamaica a drawing of Westover and an idyllic description of Virginia country life.[31] Three other men also attempted to display their personal and political authority through architecture. In the early eighteenth century, Alexander Spotswood used building projects as a way of exerting British colonial authority. In the late eighteenth century, Thomas Jefferson displayed his superior sense of academic design to argue a new government's legitimacy. In the early nineteenth century, William Henry Harrison constructed a prodigy house in Indiana in an attempt to graft the Virginia economic and social system onto the American frontier.

Spotswood, Architecture, and British Authority

No other colonial architectural patron approached the design and construction of a prodigy house with as much experience as Alexander Spotswood (fig. 138). Prior to building his mansion at Germanna, Spotswood worked to shape at least five major buildings he hoped would reflect his own authority as well as that of the Crown. Born on 12 December 1676 at the British garrison at Tangier, Spotswood descended from an important Scottish family that had suffered political and economic decline during the English Civil War. Nothing is known about his education either at the British outpost where he lived until his father died when he was about six, or after he returned to England. His father, Robert, who worked as the surgeon at the garrison, however, sought the intellectual prestige of the new scientific intelligentsia by authoring an article, "A Catalogue of Plants within the Fortifications of Tangier, in 1673." The article, which was published posthumously in the Royal Society's *Philosophical Transactions* of 1696, suggests that Spotswood learned the value of cultural capital at an early age. Though his education remains a mystery, he claimed that it did not include any part of the practical commercial apprenticeships that many rich colonial planters, including Robert Carter I and William Byrd II, had served. Before planters who would later challenge his authority, he professed an aristocratic disdain for trade and attempted to create a lofty social distance from his colonial enemies whose wealth and position he pointed out was dependent on hard-nosed tobacco trade. Striving for prestige based on a more ancient road to privilege, namely military service, Spotswood claimed that "for my own part, as I never had any education in ye way of merchandize, I think it below the dignity of one of her Matys. Governors, to be a Trader."[32]

Spotswood's military resumé was indeed impressive. Commissioned in 1693 when he was seventeen years old, Spotswood served in the Earl of Bath's regiment in Flanders. In 1696, he was promoted to lieutenant and by 1701 was serving as lieutenant quartermaster under Lord Cadigan. During the War of Spanish Succession, Spotswood was raised to captain and finally to lieutenant colonel. He was wounded at the 1704 Battle of Blenheim, and captured at the 1708 Battle of Oudenaarde. His release was negotiated though the offices of the victor of Blenheim, John Churchill,

Fig. 138. Charles Bridges, *Portrait of Alexander Spotswood,* oil on canvas, 1735–36. (Colonial Williamsburg Foundation)

the Duke of Marlborough. On 11 September 1709, Spotswood retired from active military duty and was rewarded for his service with stunning speed. His commission as lieutenant governor under the titular governor, George Hamilton, Earl of Orkney, was signed less than six months later, on 18 February 1710.[33]

Fueled with ambition, Spotswood arrived in Virginia eager to implement instructions from the Crown that were intended to check the increasing presumptive power of the planter elite. Among the policies Spotswood sought to impose on the colony were the creation of a state monopoly of Indian trade to enrich the Crown; correcting and perfecting tax rolls to increase Crown revenue; creating an independent supreme judicial body separate from the Council; and exercising control of the Virginia colonial agent in London.[34] In the larger conflict of imperial authority versus local elite planter control, architecture was to play an important role.

During his years in office as lieutenant governor, Spotswood strove to impose a kind of permanent, high-style architecture at the capital that would underscore the permanence and presence of British colonial authority. His predecessor, Francis Nicholson, fought for the same symbolic presence in Virginia and elsewhere in the British North American colonies. Like Nicholson, Spotswood faced either ambivalence or outright opposition from a native elite whose interests lay in their own aggrandizement.

One of his first tasks was to see to the rebuilding of the College of William and Mary, a monumental building first proposed in 1693, in use by 1700, and destroyed by fire in October 1705. Money to rebuild was only conferred from the Crown to Virginia in June 1709, and in December a contract was signed with the undertaker, a Mr. Tullitt, who would also work for William Byrd at Westover. In a letter of 1716, when the college was once again operable, Spotswood indicated that it was the college, meaning the president of the institution, Reverend James Blair, who "resolved to prosecute the original design of this foundation" rather than alter the reconstructed building. Hugh Jones, on the other hand, who was a Spotswood appointee, apologist, and perhaps lackey, was more inclined to emphasize his mentor's role. In what is perhaps Jones's most famous statement, he claimed that "the Building is beautiful and commodious, being first modelled by Sir Christopher Wren, adapted to the Nature of the Country by the Gentlemen there; and since it was burnt down, it has been rebuilt, and nicely contrived, altered, and adorned by the ingenious Direction of Governor Spotswood; and is not altogether unlike Chelsea Hospital."[35]

Before the reconstruction of the College of William and Mary, however, Spotswood embarked on three other new building projects: a new Bruton Parish church, an addition to the gaol for the incarceration of debtors, and the construction of a brick magazine to safely store the implements of military power.

Spotswood's interest in constructing a new church big enough to accommodate the religious obligations of government officials in a dignified manner when the House of Burgesses was in session began only five months after his arrival in Virginia. By 1 March 1711, Spotswood was pressing for a functionally efficient T-shaped design that departed from conventional Virginia church planning while still incorporating a familiar decorative detail borrowed from the earlier Bruton Parish church, curved gable ends.[36] According to the vestry minutes, church leaders "received from the Honble. Alexr. Spottswood, a platt or draught of a Church (whose length 75 foot, and bredth 28 foot in the clear, with two wings on each side, whose width is 22 foot,) which he Laid before the Vestry for approbation—Adding further, that ye Honble. Ye Governor proposed to the Vestry to build only 53 of the 75 foot, that he would take care for the remaining part."[37] Spotswood expected a significant financial contribution toward the grand new church from elected colonial legislators. The House of Burgesses was less enthused. After a year of arguments, insinuations, and alterations to the plan, Spotswood told the recalcitrant burgesses that he would "Diminish the Wings projected for the Publick use in the Parish Church of Bruton Since I perceive you will be Contented with less Room therein."[38] In December 1713, new estimates were made for materials and labor needed for the wings. Two years later, the church began functioning for services but was not shingled until 1717.[39] The wings remained unfinished until 1727.[40]

Spotswood's efforts to construct a debtor's prison and the magazine in the colonial capital seems to have encountered none of the same controversy. Begun in November 1711, the now-lost debtor's prison was remarkable at the time it was built because of its unusual roof, described in the 1722 second edition of the historian Robert Beverley's *The History of Virginia in Four Parts,* as "flat roofed anew; a very useful Invention of the present Governor also."[41] Spotswood procured funding for the construction of a magazine in November 1714. Unlike the debtor's prison, the magazine still stands. The House of Burgesses empowered Spotswood to "order and direct the building" and to locate it "at such place as the lieutenant-governor shall think proper." Located in the center of town along the principal street, Spotswood's polygonal plan for the town's magazine remains a central focal point in the urban fabric. It quite literally embodied the military power of the regime that Spotswood represented.

Spotswood's effort to invest the architectural design of the Governor's Palace with British imperial authority proved more contentious. Though an official residence for the lieutenant governors had been proposed in the seventeenth century, and land had been procured in 1701, it was not until

1705 that the colonial government passed an act to appropriate £300 for its construction, determined building materials and dimensions, and appointed a substantial planter and the undertaker for the Capitol, Henry Cary Sr., to build the palace.[42] The government failed to raise sufficient funds for what its members must have seen as an unnecessary expense and was unable to meet the payroll of construction workers. When Spotswood arrived in February 1710, he found a shell of a house and a General Assembly disinclined to raise the money to finish it. During the honeymoon period of his administration, Spotswood persuaded the government to appropriate more than £2,000 for completing the house and perhaps changing its plan. But the plan also included adding symmetrical outbuildings and creating a lavish garden comprised of ornamental parterres, informal park land, and a canal.[43] He also mounted a campaign to oust Cary and take control of the project personally. Byrd notes, for instance, that in February 1711 he walked with Spotswood "to the house that is building for the Governor where he showed me abundance of faults and found great exception to the proceeding of the workmen." The following February, Cary was fired by members of the government after they were "informed of divers Mismanagements in the building the Govrs. House." While he still received funds for rented lodging until 1716, Spotswood took direct charge of the building campaign and, according to Byrd, of "looking over the workmen." Spotswood introduced an ornamental display of military power at the palace, and Byrd noted on 29 October 1711 that he saw "several of the Governor's contrivanences, and particularly that for hanging the arms." The following month, Byrd found the governor in the palace "putting up the arms." Ornamental arrangement of arms appeared in England during the Restoration and could be found at Windsor Castle and the Tower of London, but Spotswood may also have seen one at the King's Guard Chamber at Hampton Court.[44] While his display of swords and armor was a blatant and obvious display of potential military might, Spotswood was also displaying his cultural authority by exhibiting an intimate knowledge of the center of British command. Spotswood used language for the same effect when he told John Custis that he needed to cut down some trees on the latter's property. As a completely unimpressed Custis related, Spotswood wanted to "make an opening, I think he called it a visto."[45]

Eventually, Spotswood would come to regret his decision to take personal responsibility for construction. As relations between the governor and the General Assembly deteriorated on issues of Indian trade, perfected tax rolls, and control of the judiciary, wealthy planters tried to obstruct the creation of a building that symbolized the superior taste and political power of the king's representative at the expense of their own authority. In the late teens, influential planters checked the governor's architectural ambitions by failing to fund construction sufficiently and by demanding a strict accounting of his disbursements and design plans. Not surprisingly, civil discourse disintegrated. When asked by the House of Burgesses in May 1718 if the mansion was complete and what further sum might be required to finish it, Spotswood replied curtly: "It is not finsht and I don't know how much it will take."[46] In response to a site inspection, Spotswood said that he would deal only with members "as declare they are for treating me with decent good manner" because some members were "apt to speak to me in their usual rude Terms."[47] By November 1720, Spotswood wanted no more of the Palace, saying that "this has given me a greater Trouble than I ever intended. . . . Whereupon you'l Excuse me if I decline all future Concern in these Works."[48] Members of the General Assembly were only too happy to discharge Spotswood from the project. They paid his balance of £460 2s. 9½d. and, ironically, engaged the overseer Henry Cary Jr., son of the original overseer, to finish the house.[49]

By 1720, however, Spotswood was absorbed in a different exercise in prestige architecture, namely the creation of his immense country house complex at Germanna at the fringes of the colony. In fact, his scheme for creating a country seat where he could control mining and manufacturing and benefit from frontier trade started within three months of his arrival in the colony. Barred from granting himself land, Spotswood may have granted land to cronies who then later transferred it back to the governor. He arranged for the immigration of three groups of German Protestant miners and their families in 1714, 1717, and 1719 as indentured servants and settled them within a shabby fort in a bend in the Rapidan River. Spotswood astutely mounted a public relations campaign to promote his mining venture. In 1716, he organized an exploratory expedition over the Blue Ridge Mountains. Participants came to be known as the Knights of the Golden Horseshoe for the gold souvenir Spotswood allegedly gave to the well-born members of the expedition. Cunningly evoking a medieval romance, Spotswood's adventure was celebrated by later novelists and historians. William Byrd II, however, saw through his enemy's strategy and dubbed the pseudo-event and its self-congratulatory drinking party in the mountains, the "Knights of the Rum Cask."[50] Spotswood enlisted the aid of his appointees to tout his project. On 16 November 1720, William Byrd II recorded in his diary that Spotswood "Showed us the [draft] of the upper part of the country." Later that same month, Byrd noted that he "went to church where Mr. Jones gave us a sermon about the mountains. . . . About 3 o'clock we went to church and Mr. Jones gave us another sermon on the same subject."[51] Hugh Jones, who was educated at Jesus College, Oxford, had arrived in Virginia in 1716 and served as the mathematics professor at the College of William and Mary and would later act as the chaplain of the

House of Burgesses.[52] Jones was richly rewarded for his campaign from the pulpit. On 1 March 1721, Jones was granted 5,000 acres in the part of Essex County that two months later was to become Spotsylvania County.[53] By December 1721, however, he had left Virginia for London, where the following year he would write *The Present State of Virginia*.[54]

In addition to cleverly acquiring land, labor, and publicity, Spotswood exploited the culture of display. At a site that very few Tidewater planters would see in the 1720s, Spotswood began to erect a mansion intended to surpass the dwellings of his colonial opposition and to create perhaps an alternative site of political authority well beyond Williamsburg. Construction of his mansion was underway by 1721.

In a letter of 25 March 1721, Robert Carter reported that "the Governor is gone to Germanna, pursues his iron mine strenuously. There is mighty talks about it, how 'twill succeed must be left to time." The same month, Byrd and his neighbor began to gossip about Spotswood's successor as governor.[55] The following July, Spotswood apologized for missing an important communication at Williamsburg with the excuse that he "was employed on the Frontiers of this Government."[56] Spotswood had disclosed his overall architectural plan to Jones, who wrote in 1722 that Spotswood "is building a church, court-house and dwelling-house for himself; and with his servants and Negroes he has cleared plantations about it, proposing great encouragement for people to come and settle in that uninhabited part of the world, lately divided into a county."[57]

The Germanna site is now a wooded, gently sloping hillside (fig. 139), but archaeological investigation indicates that Spotswood designed a mansion complex comprised of a main dwelling house and four formal dependencies arranged to create a forecourt on the south or upper side of the hill (see fig. 61 on p. 74). The dependencies were linked to the main dwelling house by means of covered walkways, and the overall length of the complex measured approximately 210 feet. Spotswood constructed the walls of his mansion with a stone core faced with brick. The mansion's plan remains conjectural, although the presence of a massive chimney stack with four corner fireplaces in the center of the building suggests that the core of the house was divided into at least four major heated rooms.[58] Unearthed fragments of glazed and rubbed brick and carved sandstone for classical ornaments such as columns and molding indicate Spotswood's efforts to build a house with a high degree of aesthetic finish.[59]

As Jones noted, Spotswood envisioned a more monumental composition that would have complemented the visual potency of his house. In its November 1721 session, the General Assembly provided £500 current money for the construction of a church, courthouse, prison, pillory, and stocks for the new county of Spotsylvania, "where the governor shall appoint

Fig. 139. Germanna archaeological site looking east. (Photograph by Robert T. Mooney)

them."[60] Spotswood chose to have these structures erected at Germanna. In August 1722, the first meeting of the Spotsylvania County Court took place in Spotswood's house, and Byrd later tells us that Spotswood located the "Chappel about a Bow-Shot from the Colonel's house, at the End of an Avenue of Cherry Trees."[61]

Work on the mansion was interrupted when Spotswood was forced to return to England to defend his shady land dealings and misappropriation of use of public building funds; accusations of corruption continued to hound him later.[62] Yet when Byrd visited his old enemy in 1732, he found Spotswood's frontier mansion a paragon of refined and sophisticated design. The house was embellished with costly mirrors and surrounded by an artfully romantic rustic landscape.[63] The inventory of Spotswood's movable property serves as a checklist for what the cultural critic Pierre Bourdieu called the habitus of the social class in which Spotswood operated. Matched fabric ensembles, japanned tea and card tables, twenty-six prints, and an oil painting of the *Woman Taken in Adultery* all testify to Spotswood's absorption into the culture of display that he sought to create on the edges of the Piedmont.[64] Spotswood was smart, and he was cunning. And he successfully held on to much of his property even after legal challenges. But his use of aesthetically superior architecture did not convince Virginia's native elite to follow his policies. Indeed, his cultural pretensions alienated wealthy planters, who on the one hand eagerly sought British fashion while at the same time strenuously resisted British administrative control.

An undated letter containing clues in its text that indicate it was written sometime between May 1721 and September 1722 reveals the extent to which Spotswood's architectural ambitions exacerbated his political and legal problems. Dispensing with any feigned politeness, the anonymous writer divulges the sort of personal jealousies and scandalous gossip that male writers attributed to women at the tea table. First, the anonymous author points out Spotswood's dissatisfaction with the burgesses of the colony and his plan to call for new elections. Then Spotswood's problems with the Council are recounted at length, specifically noting that Mann Page I, "who was once an Extraordinary Favorite is sudenly become coole." Spotswood's aims are unmasked by the writer, who noted that "whilst he is representing to the Lords of Trade how advantageious it would be to Secure those Passes threw the Mountins that he has only his private Intrest in View by his Improveing that part of Virginia." The author passed along reports that Spotswood "is Building a very Fine house there & has Incourage'd Artificers of all Sorts to People his New Town which I hear is regularly lay'd out in Streets and Squares and a pretty many houses are allready Built." The writer was more confident in his assessment of the potential economic benefit of Spotswood's mansion complex: "This is Certain that by having a Setlement so considerable & so far back to the Westw'd they will be able in a manner to Command the Indian Trade at Pleasure." The letter, though, contained more than idle gossip. By implying that Spotswood was constructing a locus of political power to compete with Williamsburg's fading glory, the writer warned the native elite establishment that: "In the whole Wm'sBurgh Seems to have seen its best Days & it will not be otherways whilst so powerfull a Rivall as Germanah is growing, for the Govern'r declares that whenever he is obliged to Quit the Governm'nt That he will still be an Inhabitant of Virginia which is Demonstrable Enough by the Cost he is at In making Spotsilvania agreeable to his Humour."[65] The threat was real enough that Virginia's planter elite mounted a successful campaign before British officials and had Spotswood removed from office in 1722.

By 1726, all the Germans who had worked for the former lieutenant governor as indentured servants had moved to land of their own and were replaced by slave labor for the operation of the iron mines and furnaces.[66] As Byrd noted, by 1732 the original fortification had fallen into ruins, and in the same year the county seat was removed to Fredericksburg in order to be more convenient to a greater number of the Spotsylvania County inhabitants.[67] Spotswood had convinced no one, neither his social cohorts nor his indentured servants, that architecture, even aesthetically superior architecture, justified corruption or exploitation. As a tool of social hegemony, Germanna failed to produce any sort of false consciousness.

Jefferson and the Critique of Pure Architecture

Jefferson may not have been aware of Spotswood's futile attempts to enhance his own prestige or that of the colony he tried to control. Jefferson (fig. 140) did, however, recognize the potential of architecture—particularly his own knowledge of classical architecture—as a persuasive means of influencing others, most especially the Europeans of distinction whose esteem he wished to garner.

Thomas Jefferson's *Notes on the State of Virginia,* written in the early 1780s before his stay in France, represents another example of how elite Virginians attempted to exploit architectural design. The pertinent section on architecture is entitled "Colleges, Buildings and Roads" and is found in Query XV: "The only public buildings worthy [of] mention are the Capitol, the Palace, the College, and the Hospital for Lunatics, all them in Williamsburg, heretofore the seat of our government. The Capitol is a light and airy structure, with a portico in front of two orders, the lower of which, being Doric, is tolerably just in its proportions and ornaments, save only that the intercolonnations are too large. The upper is Ionic, much too small for that on which it is mounted, its ornaments not proper to the order, nor proportioned within themselves. It is crowned with a pediment, which is too high for its span. Yet, on the whole, it is the most pleasing piece of architecture we have."[68] In contrast to Jefferson's self-consciously aesthetic analysis, the Princeton-trained visitor Ebenezer Hazard's description of the Capitol simply noted that "In the "Front of the Building is a Portico & Balcony, each supported by four Pillars."[69]

The Capitol to which each man referred is no longer extant. The present reconstruction on the site was modeled after the first Williamsburg Capitol, which burned in 1747. Jefferson and Hazard described the second Capitol, which was used from about 1753 until the seat of state government was removed to Richmond in 1780. Only drawings made from memory give us an idea of the design of this little-known building that had disappeared by the mid-nineteenth century (fig. 141).[70] Huge by the standards of Virginia's public buildings, the second Capitol's projecting double pedimented portico also made it very unusual, perhaps unique in the colony. The cost of construction would have represented a significant expenditure of the colony's revenues. For Virginia, this was indeed high-style architecture.

The double portico feature is loosely inspired by Palladio's villa elevations, such as the central section of the Villa Pisani. But the more important

Fig. 140. Charles Willson Peale, *Portrait of Thomas Jefferson,* oil on canvas, 1791–92. (Independence National Historical Park)

Fig. 141. A. Bollett, *The Old Virginia Capitol* (the second Capitol at Williamsburg), engraving. (Colonial Williamsburg Foundation)

aesthetic reference is to fashionable English interpretations of Palladio and Serlio. The transformation of their designs into a distinctly English idiom can be seen in such influential buildings as Inigo Jones's Prince's Lodgings at Newmarket (1619), or John Webb's Amesbury Abbey (ca. 1660). Dutch interpretations of Palladio, seen, for example, in Jacob Van Campen's Mauritshuis (1633), also had a potent effect on proportional character, roof pitch, and ornament of fashionable English houses after 1650. The salient characteristics of this Anglo-Dutch interpretation are the simple massing, hipped roof, and (often astylar) references to a temple-front portico.[71] The designers of the second Capitol may or may not have had access to published illustrations of Palladian architecture, but it was this northern European version of Palladio that lay at the root of Williamsburg's second Capitol's design.

Jefferson chose to criticize this American adaptation of an iconic English Palladian building type not on its overall design concept, which he admired, but rather on the finer points of its execution. In doing so, he reveals to his readers that: (1) he knows the names of the Orders—the basis of all good architecture; (2) he knows the appropriate ornaments, such as volutes and moldings, associated with each order; and (3), and perhaps most important, he judges beauty on proportions of height, width, and intercolumniation. In other words, he exhibits before his audience his erudition in classical architecture. He shows that he has not merely picked up a fashionable feature here or there, but that he also understands the fundamental principles of classical design. Further, he flatters his audience in assuming that they will know what intercolumniation is and that they too have access to Palladio.[72] And to whom is he showing off?

Jefferson did not write his *Notes on the State of Virginia* for an American, much less a Virginia, audience. According to the advertisement for the book, the questions he addressed in the book were proposed "by a foreigner of Distinction, then residing among us."[73] *Notes on the State of Virginia* was written for the benefit of the intelligentsia in Europe, members of the educated elite who were curious about the New World and who might find reasonable compatibility with Americans as intellectual equals, not frightening radicals. By critiquing the Ionic Order in Virginia, Jefferson was intellectually engaging a knowledgeable class of European men and women familiar with the rules of classical architecture. His purpose was not to control poorer Virginians or slaves but to converse on the finer points of architectural design in order to demonstrate that the provincial elite was honest enough to recognize its cultural limitations, and wise enough to know where to look for authoritative answers. He argues here, as elsewhere in the *Notes on the State of Virginia,* that an independent America can measure up to the standards of aristocratic Europe and "can produce her full quota of genius."[74] In terms of architecture, he is enormously flattering to his Continental readers.

William Henry Harrison and the Architecture of the Virginia Aristocracy

Given the esteem in which Jefferson was held both in America and abroad by those who valued his intellectual achievement and aesthetic refinement, it is not surprising that, as we look beyond the colonial era, we find other Virginia architectural patrons using high-style building design in an attempt to enhance and secure their own power, prestige, and concept of the social order. The architectural patronage of William Henry Harrison shows how the Virginia gambit of claiming power through architecture persisted as white settlement moved west. It also suggests how it was undermined by a new architectural myth.

Harrison (fig. 142) descended from the family in the study group whose roots go back the farthest in Virginia history. He was born at Berkeley in 1773, attended Hampden-Sidney College for only one year, briefly studied medicine, then embarked on one of the most reliable paths to power, a military career. His record and no doubt his family connections led to his appointment by President John Adams in 1798 as secretary of the Northwest Territory. After Adams named him governor of the Indiana Territory, which comprised both Indiana and Illinois, Harrison moved to the territorial capital with his family and assumed office in January 1801. Harrison was not yet twenty-eight years old. Like other elite Virginians had done in the previous century, Harrison then set out to justify the power he had already acquired.

As a way of proving his worthiness to rule, Harrison started to construct Grouseland, a Virginia prodigy house in Vincennes, the former French settlement and new territorial capital. The two-story brick mansion (fig. 143) is believed to have been the first brick house in the region. Much of the mansion's original appearance is presently unknown. Its size and its use of permanent materials and aesthetic refinements, such as a stringcourse, however, clearly indicate that it was meant to be an overt declaration of superior architecture. The attenuated curved stairway in the central passageway fits well within the standards of the most fashionable architecture found back East, and the polygonal walls projecting toward the Wabash River side of the house recall architectural forms favored by his mentor, Thomas Jefferson (fig. 144). As was the case with other Virginia prodigy houses, Harrison's house contrasted dramatically to the roughly fashioned log dwellings of his fellow American settlers. Grouseland also would have stood out from traditional French colonial buildings in Vincennes, houses characterized by sturdy but not classicizing vertical log construction.

Fig. 142. Rembrandt Peale, *Portrait of William Henry Harrison,* oil on canvas, ca. 1815. (National Portrait Gallery, Smithsonian Institution; Gift of Mrs. Herbert Lee Pratt Jr.)

Harrison's importation of high-style design into the Indiana frontier was not limited to his own house; he sought to impose fashionable design on the territory's urban character as well. Here, too, he was attempting to win approval by making claim to exceptional intellectual and aesthetic sensibilities and by flattering his political and social superior. In 1802, he wrote to Thomas Jefferson about his design for the plan of Jeffersonville, a new town along the banks of the Ohio. Harrison's ideas were based on Jefferson's checkerboard plan in which every other block was left open as green space. Much in the same way Jefferson had done in *Notes on the State of Virginia* almost twenty years earlier, the young governor wanted to show off his cultural sophistication. On top of a basic grid of square blocks, Harrison added a web of diagonal streets—probably inspired by L'Enfant's plan for the new national capital—that clipped off the corners of each town block.[75] Jefferson was not impressed by the hybrid scheme,

Fig. 143. Grouseland, Vincennes, Indiana, begun 1801. Main façade. (Photograph by Robert T. Mooney)

Fig. 144. Grouseland, Vincennes, Indiana, begun 1801. Bowed side elevation. (Photograph by Robert T. Mooney)

and neither were most of Jeffersonville's inhabitants. Within the context of frontier Indiana, Harrison's plan for Jeffersonville appeared to settlers as an impractical waste of profitable land. His mansion in the territorial capital also presented to the eyes of passing Vincennes inhabitants what must have seemed like an outlandish architectural statement. Neither aesthetic proposition persuaded them to accept Harrison's political objectives.

As territorial governor, Harrison pursued a plan to re-create the political and social environment he had enjoyed as a youth in Virginia, namely, an immensely wealthy planter class supported by chattel slavery. To that end, he showed preferment in naming Virginians to territorial office and labored persistently to undermine the terms of the 1787 Northwest Ordinance that outlawed slavery. Yeoman farmers, both from the North and the South, expressed their opposition to Harrison and his policies in the frontier press. More than simply venting their anger over his favoritism and stand on slavery, however, they identified the broader ideology behind his specific political agenda and architectural excesses. Small farmers vilified Harrison and his favorites as the "Virginia aristocracy" and the enemies of the middling landowner.[76] In elections at the end of the decade, white male voters effectively staunched his scheme to re-create the Virginia social landscape in Indiana. Harrison's use of aesthetically superior architecture as an instrument of political authority had failed. He was luckier the next time he built a genteel house.

At the end of the War of 1812, Harrison resigned his military commission and abandoned his prodigy house at Vincennes. He moved to property in North Bend, Ohio, that he had purchased from his father-in-law in 1796. He proceeded to improve an existing log dwelling piece by piece with additional rooms and by cladding the exterior walls with clapboard. By the time he was finished, the North Bend log dwelling was transformed into a main block linked to flanking dependencies by short wings (fig. 145). Although the polygonal projection of the Vincennes parlor had disappeared, a nineteenth-century plan of the North Bend dwelling indicates that it was even more capacious than Grouseland. Yet, at the core of the main block lay a Virginia two-room, center transverse passage plan (fig. 146).

Ironically, it was the log house that Harrison hid under a cloak of respectable clapboard and Anglo-Palladian massing that became a focal point

Fig. 145. (*Opposite, top*) *William Henry Harrison House at North Bend, Ohio,* illustration from James A. Green, *William Henry Harrison, His Life and Times,* 1941.

Fig. 146. (*Opposite, bottom*) Mrs. Hendryx, *William Henry Harrison House at North Bend, Ohio,* illustration from James A. Green, *William Henry Harrison, His Life and Times,* 1941.

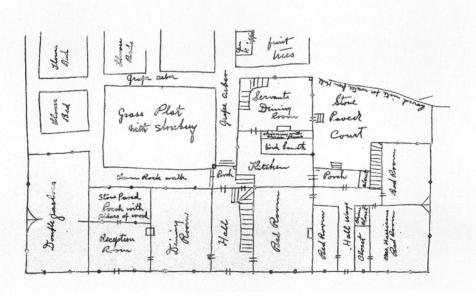

in his presidential campaign of 1840.[77] When Harrison was ridiculed as a coarse rube living in a crude log cabin, his supporters turned his opponents' attacks to their advantage. Though Harrison remained anti-abolitionist, he shrewdly dodged taking a public stand on the issue of slavery and ran with a states' rights southerner, John Tyler. Harrison campaigned and won on the basis of his military exploits over Indians at Tippecanoe and embraced the nongenteel cultural politics of the "log cabin and hard cider."

Even though the North Bend house had been transformed into a paragon of gentility, the log dwelling that lay at its core proved more politically potent to Harrison than his Virginia prodigy house at Vincennes. By 1840, the model that equated superior aesthetics with superior worth and worthiness to rule was dead. Spotswood's experience more than one hundred years before suggests that it was never an efficacious ploy. In building two houses, the scion of the Virginia native elite learned to exploit a new architectural iconographic mythology: the builder of a vernacular house was as straightforward, honest, and worthy of trust as the building itself. Both models were attractive illusions.

Conclusion

Like the performance of a child prodigy who manifests a brilliant display of musical genius, Virginia prodigy houses encapsulate an early and spectacular ascent of a relatively small coterie of wealthy landowners intent on sustaining their success and new authority. Unlike many child prodigies, who eventually succumb to mediocrity or a disinterested public, Virginia prodigy houses have retained their hold on the historic and aesthetic imagination of later Americans. Members of the Virginia native elite understood superlative houses like Mount Airy (fig. 147) as not only reflecting their newly achieved power and wealth but as cultivating its perpetuation. The wealthiest Virginians' strategy was to distance themselves, the material culture they surrounded themselves with, and the design of their dwellings far from poor, middle-class, and even prosperous inhabitants.

The mansions the eighteenth-century native elite erected as part of this project of distancing were characterized by great size, permanent building material, and a language of reserved classical architecture. Elevation design drew inspiration but did not copy the housing of high-ranking British elites. Exterior and interior ornament emphasized accomplished craftsmanship calculated to signal the wealth and exclusive cultural capital that lay behind their creation. Rooms within accommodated both the stylistic proclivities and social imperatives operative not only in Virginia but in the wider European Atlantic world. Far from superfluous or cosmetic, design was a pivotal component of the rhetorical and ideological arguments to which their owners ascribed. As an emblem intended to display the owner's superior aesthetic sensibilities, a Virginia prodigy house was addressed to an audience that understood and appreciated it as a demonstration of personal worth. It was a game played best among those who chose to believe in the rules.

The typical member of the native elite who engaged in this game and embarked on building a monument to his family's relatively new-wrought status was almost always a male who represented the third or fourth generation of his family to live in Virginia. His ancestors would have arrived in the colony in the middle of the seventeenth century not as tenants, but likely as middle-class immigrants, bringing financial or social capital that

Fig. 147. Mount Airy, Richmond County, 1760. North façade. (Photograph by author)

allowed them to ascend relatively quickly to the top of the colonial hierarchy. Although likely to survive well into his fifties, an architectural patron would have built his mansion in his mid-thirties, only after the death of his father and after having gained control over his inheritance. Marrying a woman from a similarly prominent family by age twenty-five, again after the death of his father, the patron eventually would have fathered about six or seven surviving children, who, in turn, would go on to marry into the same circle of families of quality. Living in a spacious and comfortable house likely added about ten years to his life. Unfortunately, his splendid house failed to ensure the survival of his young children, so that he left about the same number of offspring as less affluent colonial landowners.

Architectural patrons were exceptionally well educated compared to their fellow colonial inhabitants. They were both cognizant of their fortunate circumstances and eager to prove their worth by exhibiting a body of knowledge unavailable to others. Wealth in itself was not sufficient. Rather, wealthy Virginians believed that they needed to display their worth through erudition. The wealth that built prodigy houses was identified with a tobacco economy. Tobacco planting, however, was significantly ameliorated by more diversified economic conduct, such as milling, mining, and land speculation—actions more allied with the emerging industrial revolution than with traditionally more genteel land-based revenue.

Architectural patrons did not come by the emblems of their aspirations easily. They shouldered much of the responsibility of creating their mansions by procuring building materials, locating skilled builders, and collaborating in design. Those planters who desired more fashionable architecture, particularly fashionable interior architecture, occasionally resorted to importing artisans from England. In the building process, reputable and skilled building professionals—the brick maker, the bricklayer, and especially the joiner—appear to have been the most pivotal figures in creating the prodigy house.

Mansion-building members of the native elite gleaned the practical skills and aesthetic proclivities that occasioned the design of their prodigy houses via diverse means. Almost all of the ways they acquired knowledge of metropolitan architectural fashions, however, were beyond the means of average or even prosperous Virginia inhabitants. While none of the architectural patrons in the study are known to have read Alberti before Jefferson purchased an Italian copy sometime after 1785, their actions confirm that they would have understood Alberti when he claimed that there are "some sure rules of art and proportion, which whoever neglects will make himself ridiculous."[1] As to those without access to education, travel, books, wealth, and examples of fashionable architecture, affluent architectural patrons in the colony would concur with Alberti that it is a "common thing with the ignorant to despise what they do not understand."[2] Recondite knowledge of architecture functioned, like Latin, as proof of social precedence. As Jefferson said, it showed so much.

Elite women figure more prominently in Virginia's prodigy houses than their husbands and fathers would have been inclined to admit. Through their wives' dowry wealth, male members of the native elite, like their British counterparts, acquired the liquid assets that enabled them to construct houses on a level of magnificence that they might not have attempted with only their own resources. In the sensitive and complicated balance between dowry and dower right, Virginia's mansions represented security and a measure of empowerment that descended through, and perhaps was exerted through, the female line.

Though fettered by laws and customs prohibiting women from owning a prodigy house while their husbands lived, elite women exercised agency by fashioning distinct patterns of space filled by activities and objects important to their sex. Patterns of female behavior were accommodated and ameliorated within prodigy house design even at the same time that these activities were disparaged by male-controlled literary and print media. Functions within prodigy houses signaled the removal of elite women in

Virginia from productive labor on the plantation and can be seen as presaging the cult of domesticity that was only to take hold in middle-class America in the next century.

Wealthy colonials fashioned houses that attempted to parallel the prized features of the residential buildings of the British elite, whom they emulated in terms of material culture and built forms, and whose social structure they attempted to replicate. Prodigy houses were not responsible for the rise of the Carters or the Harrisons, but they did represent a vision of privilege through birth that some of their contemporaries such as the Germanna Germans and Fithian found unconvincing if not offensive. If privileged colonial Virginians built their mansions solely for the purpose of forging permanent political authority, the outcome of their effort was mixed. Violent repression of enslaved Africans, the powerful impact of money, and the manipulation of the political system proved more persuasive than architectural design in perpetuating the authority of the native elite. By the mid-nineteenth century, their power would be eclipsed by violent conflict, capitalism's industrial revolution, and soil exhaustion, none of which could be overcome by intercolumniation or symmetrical planning. In some cases, moreover, such as Rosewell or Monticello, the construction of prodigy houses undermined the wealth and security their owners were striving to perpetuate.

Despite the unpleasant social class hierarchy that lay at the foundation of Virginia's prodigy houses, they have perennially held the attention of many Americans who have admired their design rather than the source of the money that built them. The visual appeal of Virginia's prodigy houses persists, I believe, because of, rather than despite, the failure of their first owners to establish a permanent oligarchy based on inherited privilege and signaled by superior architecture. Prodigy houses stand as dreams that fortunately did not come true.

Appendix

Sources for Study Group Data

Data for the study group were drawn from the books and articles listed below. Information is alphabetized by the name of the mansion, accompanied by the name of the county in which it is located, the date when construction was started, and the person who paid for its construction. Mansions typically required more than a year for construction, and therefore dating to a single year is subjective. Additional sources for the information below can be found in Barbara B. Mooney, "'True Worth Is Highly Shown in Liveing Well': Architectural Patronage in Eighteenth-Century Virginia" (Ph.D. diss., 1991, University of Illinois, Urbana-Champaign).

Battersea, originally in Dinwiddie County (presently in St. Petersburg), 1767, John Banister III

Dating: Timbers felled in winter of 1767–68, Jack Heikkenen, *Report on Battersea*, Colonial Williamsburg Foundation (hereafter CWF). I have selected 1767 for the beginning of construction.

Ancestry: Willie Graham and Mark R. Wenger, "Battersea: A Historical and Archaeological Study," 1: 1, 6, CWF (prepared for the Friends of Battersea Committee, Historic Petersburg Foundation, Inc., 1988); Joseph Ewan and Nesta Ewan, *John Banister and His Natural History of Virginia, 1678–1692* (Urbana: University of Illinois Press, 1970), xvii–xviii, xxii; William Byrd, *The Secret Diary of William Byrd of Westover, 1709–1712,* ed. Louis B. Wright and Marion Tinling (Richmond: Dietz Press, 1941), 389; Louis Des Cognets Jr., comp., *English Duplicates of Lost Virginia Records* (Princeton: privately printed, 1958), 30, 32, 42; Bristol Parish Register, 36, 57, Library of Virginia (hereafter LVA); John S. Bassett, ed., *The Writings of Colonel William Byrd of Westover in Virginia Esqr.* (1901; repr., New York: Burt Franklin, 1970), 325; *Executive Journals of the Councils of Colonial Virginia* (hereafter *EJC*), ed. H. R. McIlwaine et al., 6 vols. (Richmond: Virginia State Library, 1925–66), 5:387; William W. Hening, ed., *The Statutes at Large, Being a Collection of All the Laws of Virginia,* 13 vols. (1819–23; repr., Charlottesville: University Press of Virginia for the Jamestown Foundation of the Commonwealth of Virginia,, 1969), 6:485; Thomas C. Barrow, *Trade and Empire: The British Customs Service in Colonial America, 1660–1775* (Cambridge: Harvard University Press, 1967), 263.

Vital Statistics: Bristol Parish Register, 34, LVA; "List of Obituaries from Richmond, Virginia, Newspapers," *Virginia Magazine of History and Biography* (hereafter *VMHB*) 20 (1942): 283; Graham and Wenger, "Battersea," appendix 4:4, CWF.

Marriage: "Mumford and Munford Families," *Tyler's Quarterly Magazine* 3 (1921–22): 177; H. W. Krafft, comp., "Amelia County Marriage Bonds, 1735–1755," *William and Mary Quarterly* (hereafter *WMQ*), 1st ser., 19 (1910–11): 174; Charles Campbell, *History of the Colony and Ancient Dominion of Virginia* (Philadelphia: Lippincott, 1860), 725; "Personal Notices from the Virginia Gazette," *WMQ,* 1st ser., 11 (1902–3): 96; 12 (1903–4): 25; "Some Colonial Virginia Records," *VMHB* 11 (1903–4): 164–65.

Progeny: Graham and Wenger, "Battersea: A Historical and Archaeological Study," appendix 4:1–4, CWF; Julian P. Boyd et al., eds., *The Papers of Thomas Jefferson,* 33 vols. (Princeton: Princeton University Press, 1950–2007), 7:98; 14:458, 592; "John Cameron's Register of Marriages for Bristol Parish," in *Cumberland Parish, Lunenburg County, Virginia, 1746–1816, Vestry Book,* ed. Landon C. Bell (Richmond: William Byrd Press, 1930), 310; Campbell, *History of the Colony,* 725; "Some Colonial Virginia Records," 165; "Selections from Campbell Papers," *VMHB* 9 (1901–2): 69.

Education: C.E.A. Bedwell, "American Middle Templars," *American Historical Review* 25 (1920): 684.

Sources of Income: Charles Campbell, ed., *The Bland Papers: Being a Selection from the Manuscripts of Colonel Theodorick Bland, Jr. of Prince George County Virginia,* 2 vols. (Petersburg: Edmund and Julian C. Ruffin, 1840), 1:37, 59, 70; C. G. Chamberlayne, ed., *The Vestry Book and Register of Bristol Parish, Virginia, 1720–1789* (Richmond: privately printed, 1898), 199; John Ferdinand Dalziel Smyth, *A Tour in the United States of America,* 2 vols. (1784; repr., New York: Arno Press, 1968), 62; *Virginia Gazette* (Pinckney), 15 June 1775; *Journals of the House of Burgesses* (hereafter *JHB*), ed. H. R. McIlwaine et al., 6 vols. (Richmond: Virginia State Library, 1905–15), 10:78; *Virginia Gazette* (Purdie and Dixon), 16 January 1772.

Public Office: *Virginia Gazette* (Dixon and Hunter), 18 November 1775; Bristol Parish Vestry Book, 166, LVA; "Justices of the Peace of Colonial Virginia, 1757–1775," *Bulletin of the Virginia State Library* 14 (April-July 1921): 95; *JHB,* 10:158; 11:3, 79, 135, 181, 221; 12:3, 113, 143; 13:3, 67, 163.

Belvoir, Fairfax County, 1741, William Fairfax

Dating: William Fairfax purchased land in November 1741, [Fairfax Harrison], *Landmarks of Old Prince William: A Study of Origins in Northern Virginia* (1924; repr., Berryville, Va.: Chesapeake Book Co., 1964), 55n.

Ancestry: Fairfax Harrison, "The Proprietors of the Northern Neck, Chapters of Culpeper Genealogy," *VMHB* 34 (1926): 19–64; Virginia D. M. Pearson, "The Lord Proprietors of the Northern Neck," *Northern Neck of Virginia Historical Magazine* 27 (1977): 2945–59; Richard Wheatly, "The Fairfaxes of Yorkshire and Virginia," *Magazine of American History* 13 (1885): 217–36.

Vital Statistics: *Encyclopedia of Virginia Biography,* ed. Lyon G. Tyler, 5 vols. (New York: Lewis Historical Publishing Co., 1915), 1:156; Kenton Kilmer and Donald Sweig, *The Fairfax Family in Fairfax County: A Brief History* (Fairfax, Va.: Fairfax Office of Comprehensive Planning, 1975), 28; "Notes from Colonial Virginia Newspapers," *VMHB* 16 (1908): 208; Fairfax County Will Book B-1, 1752–1767, 171–74, LVA.

Marriage: Edward D. Neill, *The Fairfaxes of England and America in the Seventeenth and Eighteenth Centuries* (Albany: Joel Munsell, 1868), 70; [Harrison], *Landmarks of Old Prince William,* 340–41 n. 46; Andrew Burnaby, *Travels in North America,* ed. Rufus R. Wilson, 2nd ed. (1798; repr., New York: A. Wessels, 1904), 207–8; "Fairfax Family Letters," *Essex Institute Historical Collections* 68 (1932): 169–70;

William Byrd, *Another Secret Diary of William Byrd of Westover, 1739–1741, With Letters and Literary Exercises, 1696–1726,* ed. Maude H. Woodfin and Marion Tinling (Richmond: Dietz Press, 1942), 153 n. 1.

Progeny: Burnaby, *Travels in North America,* 209–13; C. E. Schulz, *Belvoir on the Potomac* (Fort Humphreys, Va.: n.p., 1933), 2–3; *Encyclopedia of Virginia Biography,* 1:163–64, 232; Wheatly, "Fairfaxes of Yorkshire and Virginia," 229–32 passim; "Fairfax Family Letters," 171; "Diary of a Little Colonial Girl," *VMHB* 11 (1903–4): 212.

Education: Burnaby, *Travels in North America,* 207; Neill, *Fairfaxes of England and America,* 48.

Sources of Income: [Harrison], *Landmarks of Old Prince William,* 259, 272, 340–41 n. 46; Harrison Williams, *Legends of Loudoun; An Account of the History and Homes of a Border County of Virginia's Northern Neck* (Richmond: Garrett and Massie, 1938), 35; Burnaby, *Travels in North America,* 199; George H. S. King, "The Land Agents in Virginia of the Proprietors of the Northern Neck," *Northern Neck of Virginia Historical Magazine* 4 (1954): 294.

Public Office: *JHB,* 8:375; Pohick Church Vestry, *Minutes of the Vestry: Truro Parish, Virginia, 1732–1785* (Lorton, Va.: Pohick Church Vestry, 1974), 71; *EJC,* 4:331; 5:45, 103, 140; 6:28, 33; *JHB,* 7:77; [Harrison], *Landmarks of Old Prince William,* 407.

Berkeley, Charles City County, 1726, Benjamin Harrison IV

Dating: Commemorative stone over west door dated 1726.

Ancestry: William G. Stanard, "Harrison of James River," *VMHB* 30 (1922): 408–12; 31:108–81.

Vital Statistics: Stanard, "Harrison of James River," 30:408–12; 31:108–81; 32:102; Hening, *Statutes at Large,* 3:538–39; "Will of Benjamin Harrison, of Surry County," *WMQ,* 1st ser., 10 (1901–2): 109–10; *EJC,* 3:537–38; Gerald S. Cowden, "Spared by Lightning: The Story of Lucy (Harrison) Randolph Necks," *VMHB* 89 (1981): 295.

Marriage: Diary of Robert Carter I, 3 October 1722, microfilm, University of Virginia Library (hereafter UVA).

Progeny: Stanard, "Harrison of James River," 32:102, 299; 33:313–14; 34:183, 186–87, 285–87; 41:162–66; Gerald S. Cowden, "The Randolphs of Turkey Island: A Prosopography of the First Three Generations 1650–1806," 2 vols. (Ph.D. diss., College of William and Mary, 1977; repr., Ann Arbor: University Microfilms International, 1988), 1:173; 2:587.

Education: Byrd, *Secret Diary,* 20; Lyon G. Tyler, "Education in Colonial Virginia," *WMQ,* 1st ser., 6 (1897–98): 80.

Sources of Income: Stanard, "Harrison of James River," 32:97–98; Des Cognets, *English Duplicates,* 288, 298; Jon K. Kukla, *Speakers and Clerks of the Virginia House of Burgesses, 1643–1776* (Richmond: Virginia Historical Society [hereafter VHS], 1981), 106; Benjamin B. Weisiger, comp., *Charles City County, Virginia, Court Orders 1687–1695, with a fragment of a Court Order Book for the Year 1680* (Berryville, Va.: Virginia Book Co., 1980), 185, 187, 194–95, 209–11; Byrd, *Another Secret Diary,* 146.

Inheritance: Byrd, *Secret Diary* 226, 261; *JHB,* 4:272; "Will of Benjamin Harrison, of Surry County," 110–11.

Public Office: "Carter Papers," 5 *VMHB* (1897–98): 418; William Meade, *Old Church-*

es, *Ministers and Families*, 2 vols. (Philadelphia: Lippincott, 1857), 1:319; Des Cognets, *English Duplicates*, 32, 44; "Virginia in 1726," *VMHB* 48 (1940): 143; *JHB*, 6: ix; 7:vii.

Blandfield, Essex County, 1769, Robert Beverley

Dating: Jack P. Greene, ed., *The Diary of Colonel Landon Carter of Sabine Hall, 1752–1778*, 2 vols. (Charlottesville: University Press of Virginia, 1965), 1:362.

Ancestry: John McGill, *The Beverley Family in Virginia: Descendants of Major Robert Beverley (1641–1687) and Allied Families* (Columbia, S.C.: R. L. Bryan, 1956), 1–7, 534.

Vital Statistics: McGill, *Beverley Family*, 534–35; Campbell, *Bland Papers*, 1:xiii, 149; Essex County Will Book 15, 1792–1800, 543–54, LVA; Essex County Will Book 16, 1800–1806, 4–5, LVA; McGill, *Beverley Family*, 535; William G. Stanard, "The Beverley Family," *VMHB* 20 (1912): 332.

Marriage: George H. S. King, *Marriages of Richmond County, Virginia, 1668–1853* (Fredericksburg: privately printed, 1964), 18.

Progeny: King, *Marriages of Richmond County*, 18.

Education: "Diary of William Beverley of 'Blandfield' during a Visit to England, 1750," *VMHB* 36 (1928): 27–35, 161–69; J. A. Venn, comp., *Alumni Cantabrigienses: A Biographical List of All Known Students, Graduates and Holders of Office at the University of Cambridge, From the Earliest Times to 1900*, 10 vols. (Cambridge: Cambridge University Press, 1940), 1:254; Bedwell, "American Middle Templars," 685.

Sources of Income: Robert P. Thomson, "The Merchant in Virginia, 1700–1775" (Ph. D. diss., University of Wisconsin, 1955), 246; Beverley Fleet, *Virginia Colonial Abstracts*, 34 vols. (Baltimore: Genealogical Publishing, 1961), 4:93; Essex County Will Book 15, 1792–1800, 543, 552, LVA; "Will of William Beverley," 298.

Inheritance: "Will of William Beverley," 298.

Personal Property Valuation: Essex County Will Book 16, 1800–1806, 15–36, LVA.

Public Office: Meade, *Old Churches, Ministers and Families*, 2:391; "Justices of the Peace of Colonial Virginia," 88, 126.

Brooke's Bank, Essex County, 1751, Sarah Taliaferro Brooke

Dating: "Brooke's Bank," National Register of Historic Places Inventory Nomination Form, 1971, Virginia Department of Historic Resources (hereafter VDHR); *APVA Bulletin* (1996), 13–14.

Ancestry: St. George T. Brooke, "The Brooke Family in Virginia," *VMHB* 10 (1902–3): 199; 12:104–6; William B. McGroarty, *Taliaferro Family Chart* (Falls Church, Va.: n.p., 1928); *EJC*, 3:543; John B. C. Nicklin, "The Taliaferro Family," *Tyler's Quarterly Magazine* 11 (1929–30): 12–13.

Vital Statistics: Brooke, "Brooke Family," 12:104, 106; Essex County Will Book 12, 1762–1775, 113–14, LVA.

Marriage: Brooke, "Brooke Family," 12:104–6.

Progeny: Brooke, "Brooke Family," 10:199, 444.

Education: Essex County Deed Book 21, 1735–1738, 363–65, LVA.

Sources of Income: Ralph E. Fall, ed., *The Diary of Robert Rose* (Verona, Va.: McClure Press, 1977), 3, 424; *JHB*, 7:98; Hening, *Statutes at Large*, 6:18.

Inheritance: Brooke, "Brooke Family," 12:104; "The Taliaferro Family," *WMQ*, 1st ser., 20 (1911–12): 270.

Carlyle House, Alexandria, 1751, John Carlyle

Dating: James D. Munson, *Colo. John Carlyle, Gent., A True and Just Account of the Man and His House* (Alexandria: Northern Virginia Regional Park Authority, 1986), 35–37, 42.

Ancestry: Mary Kate Black, "My Dear Brother: John Carlyle of Alexandria As Revealed in Letters to George Carlyle," *Northern Virginia Heritage* 6 (October 1984): 3; Richard H. Spencer, "The Carlyle Family," *WMQ*, 1st ser., 18 (1909–10): 208–9.

Vital Statistics: [Harrison], *Landmarks of Old Prince William,* 385; Munson, *Colo. John Carlyle,* 1, 3; Fairfax County Will Book D-1, 1776–1782, 203–7, LVA.

Marriage: Munson, *Colo. John Carlyle,* 30; Black, "My Dear Brother," 3–4.

Progeny: Munson, *Colo. John Carlyle,* 30, 113; Black, "My Dear Brother," 4–5.

Sources of Income: Munson, *Colo. John Carlyle,* 1, 3, 14, 33–35 81–83, 92–94, 97, 114; Hening, *Statutes at Large,* 7:22; *JHB,* 8:375; 9:357; *Virginia Gazette* (Hunter), 19 July 1754; Willard F. Bliss, "The Tuckahoe in the Valley" (Ph.D. diss., Princeton University, 1946; repr., Ann Arbor: University Microfilms International, 1984), 56.

Inheritance: Lois Mulkearn, ed., *George Mercer Papers Relating to the Ohio Company of Virginia* (Pittsburgh: University of Pittsburgh Press, 1954), 2–3; [Harrison], *Landmarks of Old Prince William,* 556; Munson, *Colo. John Carlyle,* 111.

Personal Property Valuation: Fairfax County Will Book D-1, 1776–1782, 368–93, LVA.

Public Office: Munson, *Colo. John Carlyle,* 16, 37, 48–74, 85; *EJC,* 5:279, 390; Black, "My Dear Brother," 5.

Carter's Grove, James City County, 1750, Carter Burwell

Dating: *Virginia Gazette* (Hunter), 7 February 1751 ; Mark R. Wenger and Carl R. Lounsbury, "Carter's Grove," in *The Early Architecture of Tidewater Virginia,* ed. Carl Lounsbury (Williamsburg: CWF, 2002), 101.

Ancestry: "Burwell Records," *WMQ,* 1st ser., 14 (1905–6): 259; George H. Burwell, "Record of the Burwell Family," in *Carter Hall and Some Genealogical Notes on the Burwell Family of Virginia,* ed. Stuart D. Brown Jr. and Ann B. Brown (Berryville, Va.: Virginia Book Co., 1978): 1–3, 17; John L. Blair, "The Rise of the Burwells," *VMHB* 72 (1962): 311, 328; Everard K. Meade, "The Children of Major Lewis Burwell II of Gloucester County in the Ancient Colony of Virginia," in *Carter Hall and Some Genealogical Notes on the Burwell Family of Virginia,* ed. Stuart E. Brown Jr. and Ann B. Brown (Berryville, Va.: Virginia Book Co., 1978), 24, 26.

Vital Statistics: "Burwell Records," 259; Meade, "Children of Major Lewis Burwell II," 30; Mary A. Stephenson, *Carter's Grove Plantation: A History* (Williamsburg: Colonial Williamsburg for Seatlantic Fund, 1964), 259–64.

Marriage: *Virginia Gazette* (Parks), 6 January 1738.

Progeny: George H. Burwell, "Sketch of Carter Burwell (1716–1756)," in *Carter Hall,* 79–80; Burwell, "Record of the Burwell Family," 10–11, 21.

Education: Diary of Robert Carter I, April 1724, microfilm, UVA; *A Provisional List of Alumni, Grammar School Students, Members of the Faculty, and Members of the Board of Visitors of the College of William and Mary in Virginia, from 1693 to 1888* (Richmond: Division of Purchase and Printing, 1941), 10.

Sources of Income: Pat Gibbs, ed., "Carter Burwell Account Book, 1738–1756," n.d., 12, 43, 47, and passim; Bliss, "Tuckahoe in the Valley," 45.

Inheritance: Stephenson, *Carter's Grove*, 211; *JHB*, 7:368; "Carter Papers," 6:20.

Public Office: "Diary of John Blair," *WMQ*, 1st ser., 7 (1898–99): 135; George C. Mason, *Colonial Churches of Tidewater Virginia* (Richmond: Whittet and Shepperson, 1945), 18–19; *EJC*, 4:413; 5:391; *JHB* 7:vii, ix; 8:vii; Letter of Governor Robert Dinwiddie to the Lords Commissioners of Trade and Plantations, 29 January 1751, P.R.O./C.O.-5/1328, photocopy, University of Illinois at Urbana-Champaign.

Chantilly, Westmoreland County, 1761, Richard Henry Lee

Dating: Jeffrey M. O'Dell, "1972 Excavation at the Chantilly Manor House Site," *Archeological Society of Virginia Quarterly Bulletin* 28, no. 1 (September 1973): 5.

Ancestry: Frederick W. Alexander, *Stratford and the Lees Connected with Its History* (Oak Grove, Va.: privately printed, 1912), 47; Cazenove G. Lee Jr., *Lee Chronicle: Studies of the Early Generations of the Lees of Virginia*, ed. Dorothy Mills Parker (New York: New York University Press, 1957), 55, 67; Ludwell L. Montague, "Richard Lee, The Emigrant, 1613?–1664," *VMHB* 62 (1954): 8–9, 11, 13; Ethel Armes, *Stratford Hall: The Great House of the Lees* (Richmond: Garrett and Massie, 1936), 1–12, 18–20, 25.

Vital Statistics: Oliver P. Chitwood, *Richard Henry Lee: Statesman of the Revolution* (Morgantown: West Virginia University Library, 1967), 7; Edmund Jennings Lee, *Lee of Virginia, 1642–1892* (Philadelphia: privately printed, 1895), 123; Westmoreland County Deeds and Wills 19, 1794–1799, 29–33, LVA.

Marriage: Ethel Smither, "Richard Henry Lee," *Richmond College Historical Papers* 1 (1915): 42; James C. Ballagh, *Letters of Richard Henry Lee*, 2 vols. (New York: Macmillan, 1911–14), 1:40

Progeny: "Descendants of Col. Richard Lee, of Virginia," *New England Historical and Genealogical Register* 26 (1872): 63–64; Lee, *Lee of Virginia*, 206–8, 320, 323–24, 327–28.

Education: Ballagh, *Letters of Richard Henry Lee*, 1:1; Lucille Griffith, ed., "English Education for Virginia Youth: Some Eighteenth-Century Ambler Family Letters," *VMHB* 69 (1961): 14.

Sources of Income: Ballagh, *Letters of Richard Henry Lee*, 1:39–40, 42–43, 52–55, 103, 123, 2:559; Lee, *Lee Chronicle*, 60–62; Armes, *Stratford Hall*, 111; Chitwood, *Richard Henry Lee*, 9; "Early Letters of Arthur Lee," *Southern Literary Messenger* 29 (1859): 67; Richard Henry Lee Account Book, 1776–1794, microfilm, Huntington Library; Paul C. Nagel, *The Lees of Virginia: Seven Generations of An American Family* (New York: Oxford University Press, 1990), 81, 84; Thomas P. Abernethy, *Western Lands and the American Revolution* (New York: Appleton-Century, for the Institute for Research in the Social Sciences, University of Virginia, 1937), 47.

Inheritance: Lee, *Lee of Virginia*, 121–23.

Public Office: Armes, *Stratford Hall*, 95; *Encyclopedia of Virginia Biography*, 2:21; *Virginia Gazette* (Rind), 5 September 1771; *EJC*, 6:18; *JHB*, 8:x; 9:viii; 10:4, 32, 46, 64, 170, 202, 226, 314; 11:4, 80, 136, 182, 222; 12:4, 114, 144; 13:4, 68, 164; Hening, *Statutes at Large*, 7:427, 431.

Chatham, Stafford County, 1769, William Fitzhugh

Dating: *Virginia Gazette* (Rind), 5 October 1769.

Ancestry: William G. Stanard, "The Fitzhugh Family," *VMHB* 7 (1899–1900): 197–99, 317–18, 425; Henry A. Fitzhugh, "The Foundations of the Fitzhugh Family in Virginia," *Magazine of Virginia Genealogy* 22 (November 1984): 10; Richard B.

Davis, ed., *William Fitzhugh and His Chesapeake World* (Chapel Hill: University of North Carolina Press, 1963), 9–10; George H. S. King, *The Register of Overwharton Parish, Stafford County, Virginia, 1723–1758, and Sundry Historical and Genealogical Notes* (Fredericksburg: privately printed, 1961), 225.

Vital Statistics: "Marriage Bonds in Lancaster County," *WMQ*, 1st ser., 6 (1897–98): 107; George H. S. King, *The Register of Saint Paul's Parish, 1715–1798, Stafford County, Virginia, 1715–1776; King George County, Virginia, 1777–1798* (Fredericksburg: privately printed, 1960), 48; George H. S. King, *King George County, Virginia Will Book, A-I, 1721–1752, and Miscellaneous Notes* (Fredericksburg: privately printed, 1978) 236; Ronald W. Johnson, "Chatham, Fredericksburg, and Spotsylvania County Battlefields Memorials: Preliminary Historic Resource Study," 1982, 52, National Park Service (hereafter NPS); Fairfax County Will Book J-1, 1806–1812, 244–48, LVA.

Marriage: King, *Register of Overwharton Parish*, 225.

Progeny: King, "Fitzhugh of Chatham," 107; Stanard, "Fitzhugh Family," 8:95, 430; Meade, *Old Churches, Ministers and Families*, 2:195–96.

Education: Ralph Happel, *Chatham: The Life of a House* (Philadelphia: Eastern National Park and Monument Association, 1984), 10.

Sources of Income: Courtland Davis, "Ravensworth," *Historical Society of Fairfax County Bulletin* 3 (1954): 20–22; Donald Jackson, ed., *The Diaries of George Washington,* 6 vols. (Charlottesville: University Press of Virginia, 1976), 3:205; Gerald Karr, "Historic Structure Report, Architectural Data Section, Chatham, Fredericksburg and Spotsylvania County Battlefield Memorial National Military Park, Virginia," 1982, 7, NPS; Johnson, "Chatham," 8–9; Mutual Assurance Society of Virginia, policy no. 47, 6 May, 1796, LVA; John C. Fitzpatrick, ed., *The Writings of George Washington,* 39 vols. (Washington, D.C.: U.S. Government Printing Office, 1931–44): 36:390.

Personal Property Valuation: Fairfax County Will Book J-1, 1806–1812, 284–95, LVA.

Inheritance: King, *King George County Will Book A-I, 1721–1752,* 236; Johnson, "Chatham," 15.

Public Office: Meade, *Old Churches, Ministers and Families,* 2:183, 192; King, *Register of Saint Paul's Parish,* xxxiii; *JHB,* 13:3, 67, 163.

Cleve, King George County, 1746, Charles Carter

Dating: Charles Carter payment to William Walker, 21 May 1747, Box 8, Minor Collection–Carter Family, James Monroe Law Office Museum, Fredericksburg. I am indebted to Carl Lounsbury for sharing his discovery of this document.

Ancestry: C. A. Jones, *John Carter I of Corotoman, Lancaster County* (Irvington, Va.: Foundation for Historic Christ Church, 1977), 1, 19, 88.

Vital Statistics: Fairfax Harrison, "The Will of Charles Carter of Cleve," *VMHB* 31 (1923): 39; Jones, *John Carter I,* 89; King George County Will Book 1, 1752–1780, 169–210, LVA.

Marriage: Lyon G. Tyler, "Berkeley Manuscripts," *WMQ*, 1st ser., 6 (1897–98): 135–36; Harrison, "Will of Charles Carter," 40–41, 44; Bassett, *Writings of Colonel William Byrd,* 447.

Progeny: Harrison, "Will of Charles Carter," 51, 57 n. 21, 58 n. 22–23, 59 n. 25–27; "Some Carters of Cleve, King George County and Their Descendants," *VMHB* 46 (1936): 343–45.

Education: Harrison, "Will of Charles Carter," 39; Louis B. Wright, ed., *Letters of Robert Carter, 1720–1727, The Commercial Interests of a Virginia Gentleman* (San Marino, Calif.: Huntington Library, 1940), 26, 83.

Sources of Income: Harrison, "Will of Charles Carter," 52, 65; Robert L. Hilldrup, "A Campaign to Promote the Prosperity of Colonial Virginia," *VMHB* 67 (1959): 415; Hening, *Statutes at Large,* 4:531; Peter V. Bergstrom, *Markets and Merchants: Economic Diversification in Colonial Virginia, 1700–1775* (New York: Garland, 1985), 84–85, 187; Hening, *Statutes at Large,* 8:218; *JHB,* 6:286, 297.

Inheritance: "Carter Papers," 5:413–14; 6:1, 5, 16; Hening, *Statutes at Large,* 8:25, 218–22.

Public Office: King George County Court Order Book, 1751–1765, pts. 1 and 2, 96, LVA; G. MacLaren Brydon, "A Sketch of the Colonial History of St. Paul's, Hanover, and Brunswick Parishes, King George County, Virginia," 1916, typescript, photocopy, 23, 66, LVA; Meade, *Old Churches, Ministers and Families,* 2:184–86; *EJC,* 4:210, 216, 311, 331; 5:392; *JHB,* 6:ix, 195, 208–9; 7:vii, ix; 8:vii, ix; 9:vii; 10:3, 31, 45, 63, 169, 201, 225, 313.

Corotoman, Lancaster County, 1720, Robert Carter I

Dating: Wright, *Letters of Robert Carter,* 15–16.

Ancestry: Hening, *Statutes at Large,* 8:218; *JHB,* 6:286, 297; William W. H. Warner, "The Early Carters of Corotoman," *Northern Neck of Virginia Historical Magazine* 20 (1970): 2014–24.

Vital Statistics: Jones, *John Carter I,* 5–6, 19, 88; Meade, *Old Churches, Ministers and Families,* 2:121; "Carter Papers," 6:7, 8, 13, 18, 21.

Marriage: Thomas R. Harrison, "Which of 'King' Carter's Two Wives Was Mother of Anne Carter, Wife of Benjamin Harrison of Berkeley?" *Virginia Genealogical Quarterly* 16 (1978): 51.

Progeny: Harrison, "Carter's Two Wives," 49–51; Jones, *John Carter I,* 89, 92; "Marriage Bonds in Lancaster County," 107; Hening, *Statutes at Large,* 5:300–303, 8:215–17; "Virginia Council Journals," 32:20

Education: Jones, *John Carter I,* 68. Alan Simpson, "Robert Carter's Schooldays," *VMHB* 94 (1986): 161–88.

Sources of Income: Edmund Berkeley Jr., "Robert Carter, Colonial 'King,'" *Northern Neck of Virginia Historical Magazine* 12 (1962): 1120, 1129–30; Diary of Robert Carter I, microfilm, UVA; Greene, *Diary of Colonel Landon Carter,* 2:1038–39; Des Cognets, *English Duplicates,* 260, 285, 293; Hening, *Statutes at Large,* 4:267; Simpson, "Robert Carter's Schooldays," 174; King, "Land Agents," 292–94.

Inheritance: Jones, *John Carter I,* 18, 35, 67–72.

Public Office: Berkeley, "Robert Carter," 1119–20; *EJC,* 2:14, 93, 123; 4:113; Des Cognets, *English Duplicates,* 35–41, 249; "Virginia in 1726," *VMHB* 48 (1940): 146–52 passim; Meade, *Old Churches, Ministers and Families,* 2:117; George C. Mason, "The Colonial Churches of Northumberland and Lancaster Counties," *VMHB* 54 (1946): 239; Hening, *Statutes at Large,* 3:198; 4:238.

Germanna, Spotsylvania County, 1721, Alexander Spotswood

Dating: Wright, *Letters of Robert Carter,* 36.

Ancestry: Charles Campbell, *Genealogy of the Spotswood Family in Scotland and Virginia* (New York: privately printed, 1868), 12; Leonidas Dodson, *Alexander*

Spotswood, Governor of Colonial Virginia, 1710–1722 (1932; repr., Ann Arbor: University Microfilms, 1969), 3; *Encyclopedia of Virginia Biography,* 1:58.

Vital Statistics: Robert A. Brock, ed., *The Official Letters of Alexander Spotswood, Lieutenant-Governor of the Colony of Virginia, 1710–1722,* 2 vols. (Richmond: Virginia Historical Society, 1882), 1:1; Edith Eliot, "General Roger Elliot, Half Brother to Governor Alexander Spotswood," *VMHB* 13 (1905–6): 95–99; *EJC,* 5:20; Orange County Will Book 1, 1735–1743, 131–37, LVA.

Marriage: "Letter of John Benger, 1762, in Regard to the Brayne Estate in England," *VMHB* 2 (1894–95): 339–42.

Progeny: Campbell, *Genealogy of the Spotswood Family,* 19–20, 23, 25–27.

Education: Brock, *Official Letters of Alexander Spotswood,* 1:4; Lester J. Cappon, ed., "Correspondence of Alexander Spotswood with John Spotswood of Edinburgh," *VMHB* 60 (1952): 212.

Sources of Income: Lester J. Cappon, *Iron Works at Tuball: Terms and Conditions for Their Lease as Stated by Alexander Spotswood on the Twentieth Day of July 1739* (Charlottesville: University of Virginia, 1945), 3, 9–13, and passim; Dodson, *Alexander Spotswood,* 298, 300; Cappon, "Correspondence of Alexander Spotswood," 226, 229; George Reese, ed., *The Official Papers of Francis Fauquier, Lieutenant Governor of Virginia, 1758–1768,* 3 vols. (Charlottesville: University Press of Virginia for the Virginia Historical Society, 1980), 3:1181; Bassett, *Writings of Colonel William Byrd,* 366; Orange County Will Book 1, 1735–1743, 132, 134, LVA.

Inheritance: Eliot, "General Roger Elliot," 96–97.

Personal Property Valuation: Orange County Will Book 1, 1735–1743, 181–87, LVA.

Public Office: Dodson, *Alexander Spotswood,* 5; Cappon, "Correspondence of Alexander Spotswood," 222; *EJC,* 3:247; 4:20.

Gunston Hall, Fairfax County, 1752, George Mason IV

Dating: Gunston Hall, Historic American Building Survey (hereafter HABS), 1982, 4; "Chronology of George Mason's Land, Business and Trade Affairs," 1990, photocopy, Gunston Hall Library.

Ancestry: Pamela C. Copeland and Richard K. MacMaster, *The Five George Masons: Patriots, and Planters of Virginia and Maryland* (Charlottesville: University Press of Virginia, 1975), 2, 18, 19, 49, 50, 73; Kate Mason Rowland, *The Life of George Mason, 1725–1792,* 2 vols. (New York: Putnam's, 1892), 1:375

Vital Statistics: Copeland and MacMaster, *Five George Masons,* 56; "The Recollections of John Mason," unabridged transcript by Terry Dunn, Gunston Hall Library, Lorton, Va., 7; Fairfax County Will Book F-1, 1791–1794, 95–120, LVA.

Marriage: Rowland, *Life of George Mason,* 1:159; "Recollections of John Mason," 29, 37 n. 42.

Progeny: "Recollections of John Mason," 27, 35; Copeland and MacMaster, *Five George Masons,* 95–96, 100, 115, 235–37.

Education: "Miscellaneous Notes, Prince William County," *WMQ,* 1st ser., 9 (1900–1901): 241; Copeland and MacMaster, *Five George Masons,* 75.

Sources of Income: *Dictionary of American Biography,* s.v. "Mason, George"; Beth Mitchell, *Beginning at a White Oak: Patents and Northern Neck Grants of Fairfax County, Virginia* (Fairfax, Va.: n.p., 1977), 211–12; Willard F. Bliss, "The Rise of Tenancy in Virginia," *VMHB* 58 (1950): 431; Hening, *Statutes at Large,* 4:363; 5:252; 6:19; Rowland, *Life of George Mason,* 1:55; Copeland and MacMaster, *Five*

George Masons, 87, 153, 199; "Chronology of George Mason's Land, Business and Trade Affairs."

Inheritance: "Chronology of George Mason's Land, Business and Trade Affairs."

Public Office: Helen Hill Miller, *George Mason: Gentleman Revolutionary* (Chapel Hill: University of North Carolina Press, 1975), 64–65; Joseph Horrell, "George Mason and the Fairfax Court," *VMHB* 91 (1981): 420–21; Pohick Church Vestry, *Minutes of the Vestry,* 55; *EJC,* 5:231; *JHB,* 9:vii; Copeland and MacMaster, *Five George Masons,* 152; [Harrison], *Landmarks of Old Prince William,* 663.

Kingsmill, James City County, 1725, Lewis Burwell III

Dating: *EJC,* 4:184, 443; *JHB,* 6:258; Hening, *Statutes at Large,* 4:535; Lyon G. Tyler, "Bruton Church," *WMQ,* 1st ser., 3 (1894–95): 180.

Ancestry: Lyon G. Tyler, "Inscriptions on Old Tombstones in Gloucester County," *WMQ,* 1st ser., 2 (1893–94): 220, 231; Blair, "The Rise of the Burwells," 304, 311; Meade, "Children of Major Lewis Burwell II," 24.

Vital Statistics: Tyler, "Inscriptions on Old Tombstones," 2:221; Louis B. Wright, *The First Gentlemen of Virginia: Intellectual Qualities of the Early Colonial Ruling Class* (San Marino, Calif.: Huntington Library, 1940), 114–15; *JHB,* 7:78, 81; L. Y. Lipscomb III, "Lewis Burwell III of Kingsmill, York County, Virginia," *VMHB* 55 (1947): 173.

Marriage: *Virginia Gazette* (Parks), 3 October 1745.

Progeny: Lipscomb, "Lewis Burwell III of Kingsmill," 174; Meade, "Children of Major Lewis Burwell II," 32; Burwell, "Record of the Burwell Family," 3.

Education: Ann Camille Wells, "Kingsmill Plantation: A Cultural Analysis" (master's thesis, University of Virginia, 1976), appendix B:12; Wright, *First Gentlemen of Virginia,* 114–15; Richard B. Davis, "Arthur Blackamore: The Virginia Colony and the Early English Novel," *VMHB* 75 (1967): 25.

Sources of Income: *EJC,* 4:184; 5:139; William M. Kelso, *Kingsmill Plantations, 1619–1800: Archaeology of Country Life in Colonial Virginia* (San Diego: Academic Press, 1984), 199–200; *Virginia Gazette* (Dixon and Nicolson), 24 February 1781, quoted in Kingsmill, 1940, HABS.

Inheritance: Lipscomb, "Lewis Burwell III of Kingsmill," 174; Hening, *Statutes at Large,* 4:534–37.

Public Office: Kelso, *Kingsmill Plantations,* 44; Tyler, "Bruton Church," 180; W. A. R. Goodwin, *Historical Sketch of Bruton Church, Williamsburg, Virginia* (Petersburg: Franklin Press, 1903), 29; *EJC,* 4:184, 413; 5:139; *JHB,* 6:ix; 7:vii.

Laneville, King and Queen County, 1758, Richard Corbin

Dating: Letters of 20 April 1758, 26 April 1758, 20 August 1758, Richard Corbin Letterbook, microfilm, CWF.

Ancestry: William G. Stanard, "The Corbin Family," 29 *VMHB* (1921): 374–82, 520–22; Return J. Meigs, *The Corbins of Virginia* (n.p., 1940), 7, 9; cf. Fleet, *Virginia Colonial Abstracts,* 6:48.

Vital Statistics: Elizabeth C. Johnson, "Colonel Richard Corbin of Laneville," *Bulletin of the King and Queen County Historical Society of Virginia,* no. 22 (January 1967): 2; Fleet, *Virginia Colonial Abstracts,* 4:63–66.

Marriage: *Virginia Gazette* (Parks), 29 July 1737.

Progeny: Stanard, "Corbin Family," *VMHB* 30 (1922): 85, 312, 314–15, 318.

Education: *Provisional List,* 14.

Sources of Income: Stanard, "Corbin Family," 30:80–81; Richard Corbin to Messrs. Capel and Osgood Hanbury, 17 February 1760; Richard Corbin to Mr. Hanbury, 22 July 1762; Richard Corbin to James Buchanan and Co., 30 June 1764; Richard Corbin to John and James Taylor, 10 March 1768, Richard Corbin Letterbook, microfilm, CWF; Richard Corbin Tobacco Book, microfilm, CWF; Robert A. Brock, ed., *The Official Records of Robert Dinwiddie,* 2 vols. (Richmond: Virginia Historical Society, 1883), 1:390; Reese, *Official Papers of Francis Fauquier,* 2:1020, 1057 n. 4.

Inheritance: Stanard, "Corbin Family," 29:375, 377, 380, 520; tax assessment, 1778, Richard Corbin Papers, microfilm, CWF.

Public Offices: *Calendar of Virginia State Papers and Other Manuscripts, 1652–1781, Preserved in the Capitol at Richmond,* 11 vols. (Richmond: R. F. Walker, Superintendent of Public Printing, 1875–93), 1:247; C. G. Chamberlayne, ed., *Vestry Book of Stratton Major Parish, King and Queen County, Virginia, 1729–1783* (Richmond: Division of Purchase and Printing, 1931), 60, 62–63; *JHB,* 7:ix; *EJC,* 4:348–49, 434–35; 5:190, 316; 6:229.

Mannsfield, Spotsylvania County, 1767, Mann Page II

Dating: William A. Crozier, ed., *Virginia County Records: Spotsylvania County, 1721–1800* (New York: Fox, Duffield, 1905), 260; James Hunter to Richard Corbin, 26 February 1768, Richard Corbin Papers, microfilm, CWF.

Ancestry: [John Page], "Governor Page," *Virginia Historical Register* 3 (1850): 142–43; "Virginia Council Journals," *VMHB* 32 (1924): 37, 45.

Vital Statistics: "Marriage Bonds in Lancaster County," 107; Richard C. M. Page, *Genealogy of the Page Family in Virginia,* 2nd ed. (New York: Jenkins and Thomas, 1883), 60–61; Spotsylvania County Will Book E, 1772–1798, 387–90, LVA.

Marriage: Page, *Genealogy of the Page Family,* 61–63.

Progeny: Meade, *Old Churches, Ministers and Families,* 1:339; [Page], "Governor Page," 142; Page, *Genealogy of the Page Family,* 63–64.

Education: Courtlandt Canby, "A Note on the Influence of Oxford University upon William and Mary College in the Eighteenth Century," *WMQ,* 2nd ser., 21 (1941): 246 n. 5; *Provisional List,* 31.

Sources of Income: Hening, *Statutes at Large,* 5:137, 142, 325; 7:601; *Virginia Gazette* (Purdie and Dixon), 13 June 1766, 28 April 1768, 16 June 1768; *Virginia Gazette* (Rind), 2 March 1767, *Virginia Gazette* (Royle), 4 November 1763; *Virginia Gazette* (Rind), 13 April 1769; *JHB,* 10:149.

Inheritance: "Virginia Council Journals," 32:39–42, Hening, *Statutes at Large,* 5:277–84; 7:480–83; 8:161, 445–47; "Carter Papers," 5: 416, 427; 6:19.

Public Office: St. George's Parish Vestry Book, 1746–1817, n.p., LVA; *EJC,* 5:121, 391.

Marlborough, Stafford County, 1746, John Mercer

Dating: C. Malcolm Watkins, *The Cultural History of Marlborough* (Washington, D.C.: Smithsonian Institution Press, 1968), 14.

Ancestry: James M. Garnett, "James Mercer," *WMQ,* 1st ser., 17 (1908–9): 85–86, 87; George H. S. King, "Notes from the Journal of John Mercer, Esquire, (1704/05–1768) of Marlborough, Stafford County, Virginia," *Virginia Genealogist* 4 (1960): 161–62.

Vital Statistics: King, "Notes from the Journal of John Mercer," 99; Fredericksburg District Court Suit Papers, John Francis Mercer v. John Hedgman, 1787–1798, photocopy, LVA.

Marriage: Garnett, "James Mercer," 85; King, "Notes from the Journal of John Mercer," 100, 104, 109, 155, 162.

Progeny: King, *Register of Overwharton Parish,* 78; Garnett, "James Mercer," 88–90; King, "Notes from the Journal of John Mercer," 100–102, 104–5, 107, 110, 154–58, 160; *Virginia Gazette* (Purdie and Dixon), 26 September 1766.

Education: *Virginia Gazette* (Purdie and Dixon), 26 September 1766.

Sources of Income: Watkins, *Cultural History of Marlborough,* 15–17, 31; Helen Hill Miller, "John Mercer of Marlborough: A Portrait of an Irascible Gentleman," *Virginia Cavalcade* 26 (Autumn 1976): 74–75; Copeland and MacMaster, *Five George Masons,* 62, 69; "Virginia Councils Journals," 14:233; Robert A. Rutland, ed., *The Papers of George Mason, 1725–1792,* 3 vols. (Chapel Hill: University of North Carolina Press, 1970), 1:lxxix; Mulkearn, *George Mercer Papers,* 198; *Virginia Gazette* (Hunter), 5 March 1752, 24 October 1755; Hening, *Statutes at Large,* 4:268, 363; 5:252; 6:19; *Virginia Gazette* (Purdie and Dixon), 18 April 1766 and ibid. (Rind), 30 May 1766.

Inheritance: "Virginia Council Journals," 14:233–34; Mulkearn, *George Mercer Papers,* 204–5.

Public Office: "Virginia Council Journals," *VMHB* 14 (1905–6): 233; Watkins, *Cultural History of Marlborough,* 26; *EJC,* 5:269, 395.

Monticello I, Albemarle County, 1770, Thomas Jefferson

Dating: Boyd et al., *Papers of Thomas Jefferson,* 1:23–25, 34–37.

Ancestry: Thomas Jefferson, *Autobiography* (New York: Capricorn Books, 1959), 19; Lyon G. Tyler, "Jefferson Family," *Tyler's Quarterly Magazine* 6 (1924–25): 199–201, 264–70; 7 (1925–1926): 49–54, 119–24; 8 (1926–27): 39–41.

Vital Statistics: Boyd et al., *Papers of Thomas Jefferson,* 1:409; Tyler, "Jefferson Family," 6:265; Albemarle County Will Book 8, 1824–1826, 248–50, LVA.

Marriage: Boyd et al., *Papers of Thomas Jefferson,* 1:86–87.

Progeny: Tyler, "Jefferson Family," 6:267; Dumas Malone, *Jefferson and His Time,* 6 vols. (Boston: Little, Brown, 1948–81), 1:434.

Education: Jefferson, *Autobiography,* 20–21; Malone, *Jefferson and His Time,* 1:65–74; cf. Douglas L. Wilson, "Thomas Jefferson's Early Notebooks," *WMQ,* 3rd ser., 42 (1985): 435 n. 7.

Sources of Income: Frank L. Dewey, "Thomas Jefferson's Law Practice," *VMHB* 85 (1977): 289–301; Boyd et al., *Papers of Thomas Jefferson,* 1:99, 156–59; Malone, *Jefferson and His Time,* 3:217–20, 300; 4:40; 5:666; 6:3, 81–82; Edwin M. Betts, *Thomas Jefferson's Garden Book, 1766–1824* (Philadelphia: American Philosophical Society, 1944), 42, 61; Edgar Woods, *Albemarle County in Virginia* (Charlottesville: privately printed, 1901), 56–57.

Inheritance: J.E.S. King, comp., *Abstracts of Wills, Inventories and Administration Accounts of Albemarle County, Virginia (1748–1800), Amherst County, Virginia (1761–1800)* (Beverly Hills, Calif.: privately printed, 1940), 8.

Public Office: Boyd et al., *Papers of Thomas Jefferson,* 1:42–43, 246; *EJC,* 6:413; *JHB,* 11:181, 221; 12:3, 113, 143; 13:3, 67, 167.

Mount Airy, Richmond County, 1760, John Tayloe

Dating: Camille Wells and Mark R. Wenger, "Mount Airy, Richmond County," *The Early Architecture of Tidewater Virginia,* ed. Carl Lounsbury (Williamsburg: CWF, 2002), 28–30.

Ancestry: "Virginia Legislative Papers," 17:369; George H. S. King, *The Registers of North Farnham Parish, 1663–1814, and Lunenburg Parish, 1783–1800, Richmond County, Virginia* (n.p., 1966), 182; King, *Marriages of Richmond County,* 205.

Vital Statistics: Lucille M. Watson, *In Memoriam: Benjamin Ogle Tayloe* (Philadelphia: Sherman, 1872), 344, 346; Richmond County Will Book 7, 1767–1787, 354–58, LVA.

Marriage: [Christopher Johnson], "Plater Family," *Maryland Historical Magazine* 2 (1907): 370–71.

Progeny: "Marriage Records from Ralph Wormeley's Bible," 153–54; "John Tayloe II and His Children," *VMHB* 25 (1917): 191.

Education: "Virginia Legislative Papers," 17:372.

Sources of Income: *EJC,* 4:433; Greene, *Diary of Colonel Landon Carter,* 1:543; 2:710, 928, 1049; [Harrison], *Landmarks of Old Prince William,* 427, 435; Account Book of John Tayloe 1749–1774, VHS; Richmond County Will Book 7, 1767–1787, 356–57, LVA; G. MacLaren Brydon, "The Bristol Iron Works in King George County," *VMHB* 42 (1934): 97–102; Walter E. Minchinton, ed., "The Virginia Letters of Isaac Hobhouse, Merchant of Bristol," *VMHB* 66 (1958): 280–82.

Inheritance: Richmond County Will Book 5, 1725–1753, 547–53, LVA.

Public Office: Greene, *Diary of Colonel Landon Carter,* 1:69; Meade, *Old Churches, Ministers and Families,* 2:173, 178–82; *EJC,* 5:104, 394, 6:40; Hening, *Statutes at Large,* 7:427, 431.

Rosewell, Gloucester County, 1726, Mann Page I

Dating: "Carter Papers," *VMHB* 5 (1897–98): 427; 6 (1898–99): 7.

Ancestry: [Page], "Governor Page," 142–43; "Virginia Council Journals," 32:37, 45.

Vital Statistics: "Virginia Council Journals," 32:37, 42–43, 45.

Marriage: Byrd, *Secret Diary,* 555–56; "Marriage Bonds in Lancaster County," 107.

Progeny: "Virginia Council Journals," 32:38, 39, 45; Page, *Genealogy of the Page Family,* 58, 60–61.

Education: Joseph Foster, ed., *Alumni Oxonienses: The Members of the University of Oxford, 1500–1714,* 4 vols. (Oxford: James Parker, 1891), 3:1105; Richard A. Austen-Leigh, *The Eton College Register, 1698–1752* (Eton: Spottiswoode, Ballantyne, 1927), 258.

Sources of Income: Catesby W. Stewart, ed., *Woodford Letter Book, 1723–1737* (Verona, Va.: McClure Printing Co., 1976), 345; Bassett, *Writings of Colonel William Byrd,* 345; *EJC,* 4:237, 285, 310.

Inheritance: Tyler, "Berkeley Manuscripts," 135–40; Betty Leviner, "Rosewell and the Page Family in the Eighteenth Century," 1979, 3, manuscript, VDHR.

Public Office: *EJC,* 3:420; 3:364–65; Hening, *Statutes at Large,* 4:238.

Sabine Hall, Richmond County, 1738, Landon Carter

Dating: Camille Wells, "Dendrochronology for Early Virginia Houses," unpublished report, CWF, 2002.

Ancestry: Jones, *John Carter I,* 1, 19.

Vital Statistics: Jones, *John Carter I,* 92; Richmond County Will Book 7, 1767–1787, 336–44, LVA.

Marriage: Jones, *John Carter I,* 89; Greene, *Diary of Colonel Landon Carter,* 1:5.

Progeny: Jones, *John Carter I,* 92; Greene, *Diary of Colonel Landon Carter,* 1:127 n. 2, 162 n. 26, 291 n. 5, 452 n. 64, 514 n. 99; 2:965.

Education: Harrison, "Will of Charles Carter," 38; Greene, *Diary of Landon Carter,* 1:3–4; Wright, *Letters of Robert Carter,* 25–26, 82–83; *Provisional List,* 11.

Sources of Income: Greene, *Diary of Landon Carter,* 1:127–28, 133, 137–39, 149, 156, 158, 163, 180–83, 208, 276, 325, 327–28, 334, 402, 432, 470, 482, 521, 534, 539, 542; 2:60, 887, 922, 928–31, 935, 949–51, 1134; Richmond County Court Order Book 11, 1739–1746, 17, LVA; *JHB,* 6:281, 296.

Inheritance: "Carter Papers," 5:424–25, 6:10–11, 13–15; Jones, *John Carter I,* 89.

Public Office: Richmond County Court Order Book, 11, 1739–1746, 231, LVA; Greene, *Diary of Colonel Landon Carter,* 1:6, 333; *EJC,* 4:331; 5:394; *JHB,* 8:viii, x; 9:viii; 10:31, 46, 64, 170, 202, 226, 314; 11:4, 80, 136.

Salubria, Culpeper County, 1763, John Thompson

Dating: Culpeper County Deed Book A, 1749–1753, 423–25, LVA; St. Mark's Vestry Book, 382, LVA; Gertrude E. Gray, *Virginia Northern Neck Land Grants,* 2 vols. (Baltimore: Genealogical Publishing, 1988), 2:152.

Ancestry: Meade, *Old Churches, Ministers and Families,* 2:78.

Vital Statistics: Slaughter, *History of St. Mark's Parish,* 39; Culpeper County Will Book B, 1770–1783, 75–78, LVA.

Marriage: Orange County Deed Book 10, 1745–1747, 472–74, LVA; Raleigh T. Green, *Genealogical and Historical Notes on Culpeper County,,* Virginia (Culpeper, Va.: privately printed, 1900), 8; Meade, *Old Churches, Ministers and Families,* 2:79; T. R. Rootes, "The Rootes Family," *VMHB* 4 (1896–97): 208.

Progeny: Culpeper County Will Book B, 1770–1783, 75–78, LVA; Meade, *Old Churches, Ministers and Families,* 2:79.

Education: Bannatyne Club, *A Catalogue of the Graduates in the Faculties of Arts, Divinity, and Law, of the University of Edinburgh, Since Its Foundation* (Edinburgh: Neill and Co., 1858), 196, 202, 204.

Sources of Income: St. Mark's Parish Vestry Book, 45, LVA; Orange County Deed Book 10, 1745–1747, 364–67, 472–74, LVA; Culpeper County Deed Book A, 1749–1753, 400–403, LVA.

Personal Property Valuation: Culpeper County Will Book B, 1770–1783, 83–88, LVA.

Stratford Hall, Westmoreland County, 1738, Thomas Lee

Dating: Herman J. Heikkenen dendrochronology, CWF, 1988.

Militia Officer: Connie H. Wyrick, "Stratford and the Lees," *Journal of the Society of Architectural Historians* 30 (1971): 75.

Ancestry: W. N. Sainsbury, ed., "Virginia in 1673–76," *VMHB* 20 (1912): 243; Montague, "Richard Lee," 8–9, 11, 13.

Vital Statistics: Alexander, *Stratford and the Lees,* 47; Lee, *Lee Chronicle,* 55, 58, 65, 67; Westmoreland County Deed and Will Book 11, 1747–1753, 311–15, LVA.

Marriage: Lee, *Lee of Virginia,* 112.

Progeny: "Descendants of Col. Richard Lee," 62; Lee, *Lee of Virginia*, 125, 165, 167–68, 170, 172–73, 215, 235, 254.

Education: Lee, *Lee of Virginia*, 103; cf. Ludwell L. Montague "Lee at the Spout of the Potomac," *Arlington Historical Magazine*, no. 4 (1970): 28; *Provisional List*, 25.

Sources of Income: Armes, *Stratford Hall*, 26; [Fairfax Harrison], *Virginia Land Grants* (Richmond: Old Dominion Press, 1925; repr., New York: Arno Press, 1979), 99–100; [Harrison], *Landmarks of Old Prince William*, 146–49; Mulkearn, *George Mercer Papers*, 2–3; Lee, *Lee of Virginia*, 111; Hening, *Statutes at Large*, 5:143; *JHB*, 7:20; *Virginia Gazette* (Parks), 28 July 1738.

Inheritance: Lee, *Lee of Virginia*, 80.

Personal Property Valuation: Westmoreland County Record Book 4, 1756–1767, 77a–79, transcription by Connie Wyrick, photocopy courtesy of Jeanne A. Calhoun, Stratford Hall Plantation.

Public Office: Wyrick, "Stratford and the Lees," 75; *EJC*, 3:371, 398; 4:307; 5:300; *JHB*, 5:xi; 6:viii.

Tazewell Hall, Williamsburg, 1758, John Randolph II

Dating: Hening, *Statutes at Large*, 7:598–99; Patricia Samford, Gregory J. Brown, and Ann Morgan Smart, "Archaeological Excavation on the Tazewell Hall Property," report, 1986, CWF, 6.

Ancestry: Cowden, "Randolphs of Turkey Island," 12, 47–91, 506–56.

Vital Statistics: Cowden, "Randolphs of Turkey Island," 506, 669; Memorial of Ariana Randolph, Loyalist Claims, Series I-Evidence, Virginia, 1783–1786, A.O. 12/54, photocopy, CWF.

Marriage: "Diary of John Blair," 150; Cowden, "Randolphs of Turkey Island," 694–95, 753.

Progeny: Cowden, "Randolphs of Turkey Island," 698.

Education: *Provisional List*, 33.

Sources of Income: Boyd et al., *Papers of Thomas Jefferson*, 1:98–99; *JHB*, 8:390; 9:43; Cowden, "Randolphs of Turkey Island," 674–75, 679, 705–7; *EJC*, 6:463.

Inheritance: "Copy of Will of Sir John Randolph," *VMHB* 36 (1928): 378–79.

Public Office: Cowden, "Randolphs of Turkey Island," 677–79; "Justices of the Peace of Colonial Virginia," 72, 88, 117; *JHB*, 8:3, 11:141, 181; 13:67; *Virginia Gazette* (Purdie and Dixon), 11 June 1767.

Wilton, originally in Henrico County (moved to Richmond), 1751, William Randolph III

Dating: An inscription discovered behind paneling of a second-floor southwest chamber reads: "Samson Darril put up this Cornish [cornice] in the year of our Lord 1753." Construction likely started a few years before.

Ancestry: Cowden, "Randolphs of Turkey Island," 12, 47–91, 141–62.

Vital Statistics: A. J. Morrison, "An Account of the Time of the Births of the Children of William and Eliz'a Randolph," *VMHB* 25 (1917): 403; Cowden, "Randolphs of Turkey Island," 172 n. 209; Robert A. Brock, ed., "The Vestry Book of Henrico Parish, Virginia, 1730–1773," in *Annals of Henrico Parish*, ed. J. Staunton Moore (Richmond: Williams Printing Co., 1904), 118–19; *JHB*, 10:7.

Marriage: Cowden, "Randolphs of Turkey Island," 167, 173.

Progeny: Cowden, "Randolphs of Turkey Island," 167; William G. Stanard, "The Randolph Family," *WMQ*, 1st ser., 7 (1898–99): 195–96.

Education: *Provisional List,* 34.

Sources of Income: Cowden, "Randolphs of Turkey Island," 168–69.

Inheritance: "Virginia Council Journals," 33: 397–98.

Public Office: Cowden, "Randolphs of Turkey Island," 171–72; Brock, "Vestry Book of Henrico Parish," 81; *EJC,* 5:254, 391; *JHB,* 7:vii.

Notes

Abbreviations

PUBLISHED DOCUMENTS

EJC   *Executive Journals of the Councils of Colonial Virginia*. Edited by H. R. McIlwaine et al. 6 vols. Richmond: Virginia State Library, 1925–66.

JHB   *Journals of the House of Burgesses*. Edited by H. R. McIlwaine et al. 13 vols. Richmond: Virginia State Library, 1905–15.

JOURNALS

JSAH   *Journal of the Society of Architectural Historians*
VMHB   *Virginia Magazine of History and Biography*
WMQ   *William and Mary Quarterly*

REPOSITORIES

CWF   Colonial Williamsburg Foundation
HABS   Historic American Buildings Survey, Library of Congress
LVA   Library of Virginia
NPS   National Park Service
UVA   University of Virginia Library
VDHR   Virginia Department of Historic Resources
VHS   Virginia Historical Society

Introduction

1. "Hints to Americans Travelling in Europe," enclosure in a letter of Thomas Jefferson to John Rutledge Jr., Paris, 19 June 1788, in Julian P. Boyd et al., *The Papers of Thomas Jefferson,* 33 vols. (Princeton: Princeton University Press, 1950–2007), 13:269.

2. *Virginia Gazette* (Parks), 28 July 1738.

3. John Summerson, *Architecture in Britain, 1530–1830* (1953; New Haven: Yale University Press, 1993), 58–59.

4. E. Mercer, "The Houses of the Gentry," *Past and Present* 5 (May 1954): 11–31.

5. Cary Carson, "The Consumer Revolution in Colonial British America: Why Demand?" in *Of Consuming Interests: The Style of Life in the Eighteenth Century,* ed. Cary Carson, Ronald Hoffman, and Peter J. Albert (Charlottesville: University Press of Virginia, 1994), 626.

6. Bernard Bailyn, "Politics and Social Structure in Virginia," in *Seventeenth-Century America: Essays in Colonial History,* ed. James Morton Smith, 90–115 (Chapel Hill: University of North Carolina Press, 1959); John C. Rainbolt, "The Alteration in the Relationship between Leadership and Constituents in Virginia, 1660 to 1720,"

WMQ, 3rd ser., 27 (1970): 411–34; Grace L. Chickering, "Founders of an Oligarchy: The Virginia Council, 1692–1772," in *Power and Status: Officeholding in Colonial America,* ed. Bruce C. Daniels, 255–74 (Middleton, Conn.: Wesleyan University Press, 1986).

7. Allan Kulikoff, *Tobacco and Slaves: The Development of Southern Cultures in the Chesapeake, 1680–1800* (Chapel Hill: University of North Carolina Press, 1986), 263.

8. Edith D. T. Sale, *Colonial Interiors,* 2nd ser. (New York: W. Helburn, 1930), ii; Edith D. T. Sale, *Manors of Virginia in Colonial Times* (Philadelphia: Lippincott, 1909), 5–6.

9. Agnes Rothery, *New Roads in Old Virginia,* rev. ed. (Boston: Houghton Mifflin, 1929, 1937), 11, 35–36.

10. William Meade, *Old Churches, Ministers and Families,* 2 vols. (Philadelphia: Lippincott, 1857), 1:331–32.

11. Dell Upton, "New Views of the Virginia Landscape," *VMHB* 96 (1988): 403–70; Barbara Burlison Mooney, "'True Worth Is Highly Shown in Liveing Well': Architectural Patronage in Eighteenth-Century Virginia" (Ph.D. diss., University of Illinois, Urbana-Champaign, 1991), 12–43; Camille Wells, "The Multistoried House: Twentieth-Century Encounters with the Domestic Architecture of Colonial Virginia," *VHMB* 106 (1998): 353–418.

12. Mooney, "True Worth Is Highly Shown in Liveing Well," 1:328–38.

Chapter 1. Defining the Prodigy House

1. Robert Beverley, *The History of Virginia in Four Parts,* 2nd ed. (London: F. Fayram and J. Clarke, and T. Bickerton, 1722), 232, 250.

2. Richard and Elizabeth Ambler to Edward and John Ambler at Wakefield, 1 August 1748, quoted in Lucille Griffith, ed., "English Education for Virginia Youth: Some Eighteenth-Century Ambler Family Letters," *VMHB* 69 (1961): 14–15.

3. Edward A. Chappell, "Housing a Nation: The Transformation of Living Standards in Early America," in *Of Consuming Interests: The Style of Life in the Eighteenth Century,* ed. Cary Carson, Ronald Hoffman, and Peter J. Albert, 167–232 (Charlottesville: University Press of Virginia, 1994).

4. *Encyclopedia of Virginia Biography,* ed. Lyon G. Tyler, 5 vols. (New York: Lewis Historical Publishing, 1915), s.v. "Lee, Richard," 1:117; Edmund Jennings Lee, *Lee of Virginia, 1642–1892* (Philadelphia: privately printed, 1895), 60.

5. Cf. James Deetz, *In Small Things Forgotten: The Archaeology of Early American Life* (Garden City, N.Y.: Anchor Books, 1977), 28–43; William M. Kelso, "Big Things Remembered: Anglo-Virginian Houses, Armorial Devices, and the Impact of Common Sense," in *The Art and Mystery of Historical Archaeology: Essays in Honor of James Deetz,* ed. Anne Elizabeth Yentsch and Mary C. Beaudry, 127–45 (Boca Raton: CRC Press, 2000).

6. Clifton Ellis, "Dissenting Faith and Domestic Landscape in Eighteenth-Century Virginia," in *Exploring Everyday Landscapes: Perspectives in Vernacular Architecture 7,* ed. Annmarie Adams and Sally McMurry, 23–40 (Knoxville: University of Tennessee Press, 1997).

7. Dell Upton, "Imagining the Early Virginia Landscape," in *Earth Patterns: Essays in Landscape Archaeology,* ed. William M Kelso and Rachel Most, 71–86 (Charlottesville: University Press of Virginia, 1990); Camille Wells, "The Planter's Pros-

pect: Houses, Outbuildings, and Rural Landscapes in Eighteenth-Century Virginia," *Winterthur Portfolio* 28, no. 1 (1993): 1–31.

8. Cary Carson, Norman F. Barka, William M. Kelso, Gary Wheeler Stone, and Dell Upton, "Impermanent Architecture in the Southern American Colonies," *Winterthur Portfolio* 16, nos. 2–3 (Summer–Autumn 1981): 135–96; Willie Graham, "Matthew Jones House," in *The Early Architecture of Tidewater Virginia,* ed. Carl Lounsbury (Williamsburg: CWF, 2002), 39–40. See also William T. Buchanan Jr. and Edward F. Heite, "The Hallows Site: A Seventeenth-Century Yeoman's Cottage in Virginia," *Historical Archaeology* 5 (1971): 38–48; Edward R. Carr, "Meaning (and) Materiality: Rethinking Contextual Analysis through Cellar-set Houses," *Historical Archaeology* 34, no. 4 (2000): 32–45.

9. Garry Wheeler Stone, "Seventeenth-Century Wall Tile from the St. Mary's City Excavations, 1971–1985," St. Mary's Research Series, no. 3 (St. Mary's County, Md.: Historic St. Mary's City, 1987), 1–8; William M. Kelso, Nicholas M. Luccketti, and Beverly A. Straube, *Jamestown Rediscovery* 5 (Richmond: Association for the Preservation of Virginia Antiquities, 1999), 34–57; Dennis Pogue, "Standard of Living in the Seventeenth-Century Chesapeake: An Archaeological Perspective," in *The American Home: Material Culture, Domestic Space, and Family Life,* ed. Eleanor McD. Thompson, 155–76 (Winterthur, Del.: Winterthur Museum, 1998).

10. William W. Hening, ed., *The Statutes at Large, Being a Collection of All the Laws of Virginia,* 13 vols. (1819–23; repr., Charlottesville: University Press of Virginia for the Jamestown Foundation of the Commonwealth of Virginia, 1969), 3:15.

11. William Fitzhugh I to Nicholas Hayward, 30 January 1686–87, in Richard D. Davis, ed., *William Fitzhugh and His Chesapeake World* (Chapel Hill: University of North Carolina Press, 1963), 202.

12. Fairfax Harrison, "The Will of Charles Carter of Cleve," *VMHB* 31 (1923): 67.

13. E. Estyn Evans, "Folk Housing in the British Isles in Materials Other Than Timber," *Geoscience and Man* 5, ed. Bob F. Perkins (1974): 53–64; R. A. Meeson and C. M. Welch, "Earthfast Posts: The Persistence of Alternative Building Techniques," *Vernacular Architecture* 24 (1993): 1–17; Richard M. Candee, "First-Period Architecture in Maine and New Hampshire: The Evidence of Probate Inventories," in *Early American Probate Inventories,* ed. Peter Benes (Boston: Boston University, 1989), 101; James Deetz, "Plymouth Colony Architecture: Archaeological Evidence from the Seventeenth Century," in *Architecture in Colonial Massachusetts* (Boston: Colonial Society of Massachusetts, 1979), 43–59; Paul R. Huey, "Archaeological Evidence of Dutch Wooden Cellars and Perishable Wooden Structures at Seventeenth and Eighteenth-Century Sites in the Upper Hudson Valley," in *New World Dutch Studies: Dutch Arts and Culture in Colonial America, 1609–1776,* ed. Roderic H. Blackburn, 13–35 (Albany: Albany Institute of History and Art, 1987).

14. Charles E. Peterson, *Colonial St. Louis: Building a Creole Capital* (St. Louis: Missouri Historical Society, 1949), 38.

15. Michael Olmert, "Peering into Rings of Grain," *Colonial Williamsburg* 24, no. 1 (Spring 2002): 74–78; Willie Graham to author, personal communication, 2 November 2005; Herman J. Heikkenen and Mark R. Edwards, "The Key-Year Dendrochronology Technique and Its Application in Dating Historic Structures in Maryland," *APT Bulletin* 15, no. 3 (1983): 2–25.

16. For the sources of information for table 1, see Appendix: Sources for Study Group Data.

17. William M. Kelso, *Kingsmill Plantations, 1619–1800: Archaeology of Country Life in Colonial Virginia* (San Diego: Academic Press, 1984): 104–8; William M. Kelso, *Archaeology at Monticello* (Charlottesville: Thomas Jefferson Memorial Foundation, 1997), 51–74.

18. Daniel D. Reiff, *Small Georgian Houses in England and Virginia: Origins and Development through the 1750s* (London: University of Delaware Press/Associated University Presses, 1986), 326.

19. Mark R. Wenger, "Lynnhaven House," in *The Early Architecture of Tidewater Virginia,* ed. Carl Lounsbury (Williamsburg: Architectural Research Department, CWF, 2002), 41–42.

20. Bernard L. Herman and David G. Orr, "Pear Valley et al.: An Excursion into the Analysis of Southern Vernacular Architecture," *Southern Folklore Quarterly* 39 (1975): 307–27.

21. Joseph Dye Lahendro, Edward Chappell, Willie Graham, and Dell Upton, "Historic Structure Report for Pear Valley, Northampton County, Virginia, 1992," Association for the Preservation of Virginia Antiquities, Richmond, Va. Available at www.apva.org/apva/pear_valley.php.

22. Hening, *Statutes at Large,* 4:39. Other legislation provided different dimensions: *JHB,* 1702–12, 100; Hening, *Statutes at Large,* 4:236.

23. Gregory A. Stiverson, *Poverty in a Land of Plenty: Tenancy in Eighteenth-Century Maryland* (Baltimore and London: Johns Hopkins University Press, 1977), 72–73.

24. Liz Gallow, "Observations from the 1798 Tax Record for Anne Arundel, Baltimore, Prince George, and Somerset counties, Maryland," unpublished report, 2005, CWF.

25. Wells, "Planter's Prospect," 6.

26. Ashli White, "The Character of a Landscape: Domestic Architecture and Community in Late Eighteenth-Century Berkeley Parish, Virginia," *Winterthur Portfolio* 34, nos. 2–3 (1999): 113.

27. Reiff, *Small Georgian Houses,* 52. For Coleshill, see Giles Worsley, *Classical Architecture in Britain: The Heroic Age* (New Haven and London: Yale University Press for the Paul Mellon Centre for Studies in British Art, 1995), 18–19.

28. Nancy Halverson Schless, "Dutch Influence on the Governor's Palace, Williamsburg," *JSAH* 28 (December 1969): 254–70; H. J. Louw, "Anglo-Netherlandish Architectural Interchange, c. 1600–c. 1660," *Architectural History* 24 (1984): 1–23; W. Kuyper, *Dutch Classicist Architecture: A Survey of Dutch Architecture, Gardens, and Anglo-Dutch Architectural Relations from 1625 to 1700* (Delft, Netherlands: Delft University Press, 1980), 115–24.

29. Maurice Howard, "Brick Building in England: The State of Present Research," in *Les chantiers de la Renaissance,* ed. Jean Guillaume (Paris: Picard, 1991), 106; Alec Clifton-Taylor, *The Pattern of English Building,* 4th ed. (London: Faber and Faber, 1987), 220–23; William Byrd II, *The Secret Diary of William Byrd of Westover, 1709–1712,* ed. Louis B. Wright and Marion Tinling (Richmond: Dietz Press, 1941), 17–18.

30. Bill Weldon, "The Brickmaker's Year," *Colonial Williamsburg Historic Trades Annual* 2 (1990): 1–39; Carl R. Lounsbury, *An Illustrated Glossary of Early Southern Architecture and Landscape* (New York and Oxford: Oxford University Press, 1994), 47–50; R. W. Brunskill, *Brick Building in Britain* (London: Victor Gollancz, 1990), 86–110; Andrew Barry, "Brickwork at the Peyton Randolph Complex," *Colonial Williamsburg* 21, no. 6 (December 1999–January 2000): 24–29.

31. Lounsbury, *Illustrated Glossary,* 73–74.

32. "Seventeenth-Century Precedents in Brick Construction in England and Virginia," research report, CWF, n.d., 6; Susan Buck, "Color Washes and Penciling on Bricks and Mortar Joints in the Chesapeake," research report, CWF, 2003.

33. Nicholas M. Luccketti, Edward A. Chappell, and Beverly A. Straube, *Archaeology at Arlington: Excavation at the Ancestral Custis Plantation, Northampton County, Virginia* (Richmond: Virginia Company Foundation and The Association for the Preservation of Virginia Antiquities, 1999), 21, 27; Abbott Lowell Cummings, "The Old Feather Store in Boston," *Old-Time New England* 48, no. 4 (April–June 1958): 89.

34. John Cloake, *Palaces and Parks of Richmond and Kew,* 2 vols. (Chichester, United Kingdom: Phillimore, 1996), 2:58.

35. Anthea Brian, "The Distribution of Brick Bonds in England up to 1800," *Vernacular Architecture* 11 (1980): 3–11.

36. While ornamented by a carved stair, Lynnhaven used false plates, that is, less complicated connections between the plate and principal rafter than traditional mortise-and-tenon joints. Wenger, "Lynnhaven House," 42; Willie Graham, "Preindustrial Framing in the Chesapeake," in *Constructing Image, Identity, Place: Perspectives in Vernacular Architecture 9,* ed. Alison K. Hoagland and Kenneth A. Breisch (Knoxville: University of Tennessee Press, 2003), 179–96.

37. Philip Alexander Bruce, *Economic History of Virginia in the Seventeenth Century,* 2 vols. (New York: Peter Smith, 1935), 1:135–45. See also J. C. Harrington, "Seventeenth Century Brickmaking and Tilemaking at Jamestown, Virginia," *VMHB* 58 (1950): 16–39; Worth Bailey, "Lime Preparation at Jamestown in the Seventeenth Century," *WMQ,* 2nd ser., 18 (1938): 1–12; Terri Keffert, "Yellow 'Dutch' Brick," research report, 2004, CWF.

38. Michael Olmert, "The House That John Page Built," *Colonial Williamsburg* 19, no. 3 (Spring 1997): 34–41; David F. Muraca, "The John Page Site," research report, 2004, CWF.

39. Hugh Jones, *The Present State of Virginia, From Whence Is Inferred a Short View of Maryland and North Carolina* (1724; repr., Chapel Hill: University of North Carolina Press, 1956), 74; Harold Burton Meyers, "Hugh Jones and the Wren Building," *Colonial Williamsburg* 17, no. 2 (Winter 1994–95): 25–31.

40. William Hugh Grove, "Virginia in 1732: The Travel Journal of William Hugh Grove," ed. Gregory A. Stiverson and Patrick H. Butler III, *VMHB* 85 (1977): 22.

41. Ebenezer Hazard, "The Journal of Ebenezer Hazard in Virginia, 1777," ed. Fred Shelley, *VMHB* 62 (1954): 401, 403, 404, 405.

42. Wells, "Planter's Prospect," 9.

43. White, "Character of a Landscape," 134.

44. Gallow, "Observations from the 1798 Tax Record."

45. The first phase of Tuckahoe's construction occurred in 1733 and the second in either 1740 or 1754. Herman J. Heikkenen, "Report on Tuckahoe" (typescript), 2 November 2000, CWF. See also Susan Kern, "The Material World of the Jeffersons at Shadwell, *WMQ,* 3rd. ser., 62, no. 2 (2005): 213–42.

46. Charles Carter to Landon Carter, 31 July 1738, Carter Family Papers, UVA.

47. Robert F. Dalzell Jr. and Lee Baldwin Dalzell, *George Washington's Mount Vernon: At Home in Revolutionary America* (Oxford: Oxford University Press, 1998), 11.

48. Arthur L. Finney, "The Royall House in Medford: A Re-Evaluation of the Structural and Documentary Evidence," in *Architecture in Colonial Massachusetts,* 30.

49. Frederic C. Detwiller, "The Evolution of the Shirley-Eustis House," *Old-Time New England* 70 (1980): 20–21.

50. Andrea Palladio, *The Four Books of Architecture* (London: Isaac Ware, 1738; repr., New York: Dover, 1965), 94.

51. Samuel Sewall, *The Diary of Samuel Sewall,* ed. M. Halsey Thomas, 2 vols. (New York: Farrar, Straus and Giroux, 1973), 2:714; Sara B. Chase, "A Brief Survey of the Architectural History of the Old State House, Boston, Massachusetts," *Old-Time New England* 68 (January–June 1978): 31–49.

52. Nino Strachey, "The Duke and Duchess of Lauderdale," in *Ham House, Surrey* (London: National Trust, 1995), 65–66.

53. W. G. Hoskins, "An Elizabethan Provincial Town: Leicester," in *Studies in Social History: A Tribute to G. M. Trevelyan,* ed. J. H. Plumb (London: Longmans, Green, 1955), 58; Isabel Davies, "Window Glass in Eighteenth-Century Williamsburg," Colonial Williamsburg research report, 1970, CWF; Ivor Noël Hume, "A Window on Williamsburg," *Colonial Williamsburg* 20, no. 1 (Autumn 1997): 32–39.

54. Noël Hume, "Window on Williamsburg," 38; Wenger, "Lynnhaven House," 41; *JHB*, 1727–40, 65. For sash windows, see Cary Carson, "Settlement Patterns and Vernacular Architecture in Seventeenth-Century Tidewater Virginia" (master's thesis, University of Delaware, 1969), 252–55.

55. Edward Chappell, "The Governor's New Paint Job," *Colonial Willimsburg* 16, no. 2 (Winter 1993–94): 68–69; Mary Miley Theobald, "Repainting the Town," *Colonial Williamsburg* 16, no. 4 (Summer 1994): 54.

56. Julian P. Boyd et al., *The Papers of Thomas Jefferson,* 33 vols. (Princeton: Princeton University Press, 1950–2007), 1:61–62; Edwin Morris Betts, ed., *Thomas Jefferson's Garden Book, 1766–1824* (Philadelphia: American Philosophical Society, 1944), 23, 34, 42.

57. Boyd et al., *Papers of Thomas Jefferson,* 1:154–56.

58. Abbott Lowell Cummings, "The Foster-Hutchinson House," *Old-Time New England* 54 (January–March 1964): 59–76; Abbott Lowell Cummings, "The Beginnings of Provincial Renaissance Architecture in Boston, 1690–1725," *JSAH* 42, no. 1 (March 1983): 43–53.

59. A. F. Kelsall, "The London House Plan in the Later Seventeenth Century" *Post-Medieval Archaeology* 8 (1974): 80–91.

60. Deborah Mathias Gough, *Christ Church, Philadelphia: The Nation's Church in a Changing City* (Philadelphia: University of Pennsylvania Press, 1995), 48.

61. Carl Lounsbury, "Anglican Church Design in the Chesapeake: English Inheritances and Regional Interpretations," in *Constructing Image, Identity, Place: Perspectives in Vernacular Architecture 9,* ed. Alison K. Hoagland and Kenneth A. Breisch (Knoxville: University of Tennessee Press, 2003), 22–38; Thomas C. Parramore with Peter C. Stewart and Tommy L. Bogger, *Norfolk: The First Four Centuries* (Charlottesville: University Press of Virginia, 1994), 62–63, 75–77; cf. Bernard L. Herman, *Town House: Architecture and Material Life in the Early American City, 1780–1830* (Chapel Hill: University of North Carolina Press for the Omohundro Institute of Early American History and Culture, 2005), 33–76. For the architectural transformation of New England meetinghouses, see Kevin M. Sweeney, "Meetinghouses, Town Houses, and Churches: Changing Perceptions of Sacred and Secular Space in Southern New England, 1720–1850," *Winterthur Portfolio* 28, no. 1 (Spring 1993): 59–93; Gretchen Buggeln, "New England Orthodoxy and the Language of the Sacred," in *American Sanctuary: Understanding Sacred Spaces,* ed. Louis P. Nelson, 17–36 (Bloomington: Indiana University Press, 2006).

62. Wilton, National Register of Historical Places nomination form, n.d., VDHR.

63. Rudolf Wittkower, *Palladio and English Palladianism* (London: Thames and Hudson, 1974), 168–73.

64. Malcolm Airs, *The Tudor and Jacobean County House: A Building History* (Phoenix Mill, United Kingdom: Sutton, 1995), 25.

65. William M.S. Rasmussen, "Palladio in Tidewater Virginia: Mount Airy and Blandfield," in *Building By the Book* 1, ed. Mario di Valmarana (Charlottesville: University Press of Virginia, 1984), 90; John Summerson, *Architecture in Britain, 1530–1830,* 9th ed. (New Haven: Yale University Press, 1993), 142–56. The term is defined in Ronald L. Hurst "Furniture: From 'Neat and Plain' to Neoclassical," in *George Washington's Mount Vernon,* ed. Wendell Garrett (New York: Monacelli, 1998), 154–55.

66. James Ayres, *Domestic Interiors: The British Tradition 1500–1850* (New Haven: Yale University Press, 2003), 13–39; Anthony Quiney, *The Traditional Buildings of England* (London: Thames and Hudson, 1990), 93, 97; W. G. Hoskins, "The Rebuilding of Rural England," *Past and Present* 4 (November 1953): 45–46; Richard Harris, *Discovering Timber-Framed Buildings,* 3rd rev. ed. (Buckinghamshire, United Kingdom: Shire, 1993), 27–28; R. Machin, "The Great Rebuilding: A Reassessment," *Past and Present* 77 (November 1977): 33–56.

67. Ivor Noël Hume, "Custis Square," *Colonial Williamsburg* 16, no. 4 (Summer 1994): 12–26; Henry K. Sharp, "Bremo Recess and the Eclipse of Jefferson," *Arris* 11 (2000): 28.

68. Dell Upton, "Toward a Performance Theory of Vernacular Architecture: Early Tidewater Virginia As a Case Study," *Folklore Forum* 12, nos. 2–3 (1979): 173–96.

69. Mark R. Wenger, "The Central Passage in Virginia: Evolution of an Eighteenth-Century Living Space," in *Perspectives in Vernacular Architecture 2,* ed. Camille Wells (Columbia: University of Missouri Press, 1986), 138; Dell Upton, "Vernacular Domestic Architecture in Eighteenth-Century Virginia," *Winterthur Portfolio* 17, nos. 2–3 (Summer–Autumn 1982): 107–8.

70. Wenger, "Central Passage," 142–44. By contrast, another school of thought concerning architectural books asserts the primacy of aesthetic over social or functional motivation.

71. Cf. Curtis Perry, "The Politics of Access and Representation of the Sodomite King in Early Modern England," *Renaissance Quarterly* 53, no. 4 (Winter 2000): 1054–83; and Brian Weiser, *Charles II and the Politics of Access* (Woodbridge, United Kingdom, and Rochester, N.Y.: Boydell Press, 2003), 24–53.

72. Richard A. Goldthwaite, "The Florentine Palace As Domestic Architecture," *American Historical Review* 77, no. 4 (October 1972): 977–1012; Richard A. Goldthwaite, *Wealth and the Demand for Art in Italy, 1300–1600* (Baltimore: Johns Hopkins University Press, 1993), 214; Kim S. Sexton, "A History of Renaissance Civic Loggias in Italy from the Loggia dei Lanzi to Sansovino's Loggetta" (Ph.D. diss., Yale University, 1997), 296–336, 343, and passim.

73. E. Mercer, "The Houses of the Gentry," *Past and Present* 5 (May 1954): 14–15.

74. Nicholas Cooper, *Houses of the Gentry, 1480–1680* (New Haven: Yale University Press, 1999), 293; Mark Girouard, *Life in the English Country House* (New Haven: Yale University Press, 1978), 30, 40.

75. Felicity Heal, "The Idea of Hospitality in Early Modern England," *Past and Present* 102 (February 1984): 66–93.

76. Patricia Waddy, *Seventeenth-Century Roman Palaces: Use and the Art of the Plan* (New York: Architectural History Foundation, 1990).

77. Robert Blair St. George, "'Set Thine House in Order': The Domestication of the Yeomanry in Seventeenth-Century New England," in *Common Places: Readings in American Vernacular Architecture,* ed. Dell Upton and John Michael Vlach (Athens: University of Georgia Press, 1986), 354.

78. Wenger, "Lynnhaven House," 42.

79. James C. Scott, *Domination and the Arts of Resistance: Hidden Transcripts* (New Haven: Yale University Press, 1990), 28–35.

80. Robert Neuman, "French Domestic Architecture in the Early 18th Century: The Town Houses of Robert de Cotte," *JSAH* 39, no. 2 (May 1980): 132–33; Mark Girouard, *Life in the French Country House* (New York: Alfred A. Knopf, 2000), 147–61; Monique Eleb-Vidal with Anne Debarre-Blanchard, *Architectures de la vie privée: Maisons et mentalités, XVIIe–XIXe siècles* (Brussells: Archives d'Architecture Moderne, 1989), 235–39; Sherry McKay, "The 'Salon de la Princess': Rococo Design, Ornamented Bodies and the Public Sphere," *RACAR* 21, nos. 1–2 (1994): 71–84.

81. C. Willemijn Fock, "The Décor of Domestic Entertaining at the Time of the Dutch Republic," *Nederlands Kunsthistorisch Jaarboek* 51 (2000): 102–35.

82. Mark R. Wenger, "The Dining Room in Early Virginia," in *Perspectives in Vernacular Architecture 3,* ed. Thomas Carter and Bernard L. Herman (Columbia: University of Missouri Press, 1989), 149–59.

83. Luccketti, Chappell, and Straube, *Archaeology at Arlington,* 10; John H. Sprinkle Jr., "The Wealth of a Rebellion That Was: The Material Culture and Domestic Space of Bacon's Rebellion in Virginia, 1677," in *The American Home: Material Culture, Domestic Space and Family Life,* ed. Eleanor McD. Thompson (Winterthur, Del.: Winterthur Museum, 1988), 241–42; James P. P. Horn, "'The Bare Necessities:' Standards of Living in England and the Chesapeake, 1650–1700," *Historical Archaeology* 22 (1988): 85.

84. Cf. Wenger, "Central Passage," 137–49.

85. Girouard, *Life in the English Country House,* 14–60.

86. Summerson, *Architecture in Britain,* 152; John Harris, *The Palladians* (London: Trefoil Books, 1981), 83; Maurice Howard, "The Ideal House and Healthy Life: The Origins of Architectural Theory in England," in *Les traités d'architecture de la Renaissance,* ed. Jean Guillaume (Paris: Picard, 1988), 425–26.

87. Edward A. Chappell, "Arlington as Architecture," in Luccketti, Chappell, and Straube, *Archaeology at Arlington,* 25.

88. Wenger, "Central Passage," 139.

89. Grove, "Virginia in 1732," 28.

90. Herman and Orr, "Pear Valley," 311 and passim.

91. For the English origins of the centralized passageway, see Reiff, *Small Georgian Houses,* 139–41; and Kelsall, "London House Plan," 80–91.

92. Edward Chappell, "Dendrochronology in Context: Williamsburg's Everard House," *Colonial Williamsburg* 24, no. 1 (Spring 2002): 78–79; Margaret Pritchard and Willie Graham, "Rethinking the Brush-Everard and George Wythe Houses," *Colonial Williamsburg* 18, no. 2 (Winter 1995–96): 25–31.

93. Richard M. Candee, *Building Portsmouth: The Neighborhoods and Architecture of New Hampshire's Oldest City* (Portsmouth: Portsmouth Advocates, 1992), 40–44; Walter Kendall Watkins, "The Hancock House and Its Builder," *Old-Time New England* 18, no. 1 (1926): 2–17; Margaret Henderson Floyd, "Measured Drawings of

the Hancock House by John Hubbard Sturgis: A Legacy to the Colonial Revival," in *Architecture in Colonial Massachusetts,* 87–111. For James, see Sally Jeffrey, "John James: An Early Disciple of Inigo Jones," in *The Georgian Villa,* ed. Dana Arnold, 32–47 (Phoenix Mill, United Kingdom: Sutton, 1996); Eileen Harris, *British Architectural Books and Writers, 1556–1785* (Cambridge: Cambridge University Press, 1990), 242–45.

94. Alice T. Friedman, "Architecture, Authority, and the Female Gaze: Planning and Representation in the Early Modern Country House," *Assemblage* 18 (August 1992): 40–61.

95. John Harris, "Disneyland in Greenwich: The Restoration of the Queen's House, *Apollo* 132, no. 344 (September 1990): 256–57.

96. Rasmussen, "Palladio in Tidewater Virginia," 75–109.

97. Edward Chappell, "The Restoration of Blandfield," *Colonial Williamsburg* 22, no. 3 (Autumn 2000): 45.

98. Mark R. Wenger, "Thomas Jefferson and the Vernacular Tradition" (paper delivered at the University of Virginia Architectural Conference, Charlottesville, 1993).

99. John K. Nelson, *A Blessed Company: Parishes, Parsons, and Parishioners in Anglican Virginia, 1690–1776* (Chapel Hill: University of North Carolina Press, 2001), 51.

100. Jones, *Present State of Virginia,* 74.

101. Grove, "Virginia in 1732," 22, 24.

102. Ibid., 26.

103. Graham, "Matthew Jones House," 39–40.

104. White, "Character of a Landscape," 113, 135. White found that hardly any of these outbuildings served as discrete slave quarters.

105. Reed Benhamou, "Parallel Walls, Parallel Worlds: The Places of Masters and Servants in the *Maisons de Plaisance* of Jacques-François Blondel," *Journal of Design History* 7, no. 1 (1994): 1–11.

106. Cooper, *Houses of the Gentry,* 55, 307–8.

107. Palladio, *Four Books of Architecture,* 47–50.

108. For Pennsylvania Statehouse attribution see Charles E. Peterson, "Early Architects of Independence Hall," *JSAH* 11, no. 3 (October 1952): 23.

109. Dell Upton, *Holy Things and Profane: Anglican Parish Churches in Colonial Virginia,* (New York: Architectural History Foundation, 1986), 208.

Chapter 2. "Blind Stupid Fortune"

1. Philip Vickers Fithian, *Journal and Letters of Philip Vickers Fithian: A Plantation Tutor of the Old Dominion, 1773–1774,* ed. Hunter D. Farish (Charlottesville: University Press of Virginia, 1957), 161.

2. Bernard Bailyn, "Politics and Social Structure in Virginia," in *Seventeenth-Century America: Essays in Colonial History,* ed. James Morton Smith (Chapel Hill: University of North Carolina Press for the Institute of Early American History and Culture, 1959), 90–115; John C. Rainbolt, *From Prescription to Persuasion: Manipulation of Eighteenth-Century Economy* (Port Washington, N.Y.: Kennikat Press, 1974), 11, 22–23, 35, 144–45; Carole Shammas, "English-Born and Creole Elites in Turn-of-the-Century Virginia," in *The Chesapeake in the Seventeenth Century: Essays on Anglo-American Society,* ed. Thad W. Tate and David L. Ammerman (Chapel Hill: University of North Carolina Press, 1979), 274–96.

3. Thad W. Tate, "The Seventeenth-Century Chesapeake and Its Modern Historians," in *The Chesapeake in the Seventeenth Century: Essays on Anglo-American Society,* ed. Thad W. Tate and David L. Ammerman (Chapel Hill: University of North Carolina Press, 1979), 10, 15, 47, 49; Rainbolt, *From Prescription to Persuasion,* 11.

4. Bailyn, "Politics and Social Structure in Virginia," 98.

5. Some of these families, however, may have held shares in the Virginia Company. See, for example, the list of names in "Shareholders in London Company," *VMHB* 4 (1896–97): 299–310.

6. Thomas J. Wertenbaker, *The Planters of Colonial Virginia* (Princeton: Princeton University Press, 1922), 124–48; Russell R. Menard, "The Tobacco Industry in the Chesapeake Colonies, 1617–1730: An Interpretation," *Research in Economic History* 5 (1980): 113–14; Rainbolt, *From Prescription to Persuasion,* 56; Gloria L. Main, *Tobacco Colony: Life in Early Maryland, 1650–1720* (Princeton: Princeton University Press, 1982), 6; Anita H. Rutman, "Still Planting the Seeds of Hope: The Recent Literature of the Early Chesapeake Region," *VMHB* 85 (1987): 5, 9–11.

7. John Oldmixon, *The British Empire in America* (London, 1708).

8. "Heraldry in Colonial Virginia," *Chesopiean: A Journal of North American Archaeology* 11 (October 1973): 112–14; William M. Kelso, *Kingsmill Plantations, 1619–1800: Archaeology of Country Life in Colonial Virginia* (San Diego: Academic Press, 1984), 188–90; Worthington C. Ford, ed., "Some Letters of William Beverley," *WMQ,* 1st ser., 3 (1894–95): 234n; William M. Kelso, "Big Things Remembered: Anglo-Virginia Houses, Armorial Devices, and the Impact of Common Sense," in *The Art and Mystery of Historical Archaeology: Essays in Honor of James Deetz,* ed. Ann Elizabeth Yentsch and Mary C. Beaudry (Boca Raton, Fla.: CRC Press, 1992), 136–40.

9. Diary of Robert Carter I, quoted in Mary A. Stephenson, *Carter's Grove Plantation: A History* (Williamsburg: Colonial Williamsburg, 1964), 237.

10. Robert Carter to Landon Carter, 27 December 1765, Carter Family Papers, microfilm, UVA; Carol Edith Curtis, "The Library of Landon Carter of Sabine Hall, 1710–1778" (master's thesis, University of Virginia, 1981), 40, 42.

11. Fairfax County Will Book D, 1776–1783, 368–82, photocopy of transcription of inventory, courtesy of Julia Claypool, curator of the Carlyle House, Alexandria.

12. George Washington to Mrs. Ruthy Jones, 25 September 1783, in John C. Fitzpatrick, ed., *The Writings of George Washington,* 39 vols. (Washington, D.C.: U.S. Government Printing Office, 1931–44), 27:166–67; 32:25–31; Thomas Jefferson, *Autobiography* (New York: Capricorn Books, 1959), 19.

13. C. Ray Keim, "Primogeniture and Entail in Colonial Virginia," *WMQ,* 3rd ser., 25 (1968): 545–86; Carole Shammas, "English Inheritance Law and Its Transfer to the Colonies," *American Journal of Legal History* 31 (1987): 145–63.

14. James W. Deen Jr., "Patterns of Testation: Four Tidewater Counties in Colonial Virginia," *American Journal of Legal History* 16 (1972): 154–76.

15. Darrett B. Rutman and Anita H. Rutman, *A Place in Time: Middlesex County, Virginia, 1650–1750* (New York: Norton, 1984), 114.

16. Main, *Tobacco Colony,* 271; Deen, "Patterns of Testation," 167; Alice Hanson Jones, *Wealth of a Nation to Be: The American Colonies on the Eve of the Revolution* (New York: Columbia University Press, 1980), 172, 198, 223.

17. Jack P. Greene, ed., *The Diary of Colonel Landon Carter of Sabine Hall, 1752–1779,* 2 vols. (Charlottesville: University Press of Virginia for the Virginia Historical Society, 1965), 1:468, 487.

18. Julian P. Boyd et al., eds., *The Papers of Thomas Jefferson*, 33 vols. (Princeton: Princeton University Press, 1950–2007), 15:393.

19. James M. Gallman, "Mortality among White Males: Colonial North Carolina," *Social Science History* 4 (1980): 300, 303; Daniel S. Levy, "The Life Expectancies of Colonial Maryland Legislators," *Historical Methods* 20 (Winter 1987): 18.

20. T. H. Hollingsworth, "A Demographic Study of the British Ducal Families," in *Population in History: Essays in Historical Demography*, ed. D. V. Glass and D.E.C. Eversley (Chicago: Aldine, 1965), 361.

21. Darrett B. Rutman and Anita H. Rutman, "'Now-Wives and Sons-in-Law': Parental Death in a Seventeenth-Century Virginia County," in *The Chesapeake in the Seventeenth Century: Essays on Anglo-American Society*, ed. Thad W. Tate and David L. Ammerman (Chapel Hill: University of North Carolina Press, 1979), 158 n. 12.

22. George Reese, ed., *The Official Papers of Francis Fauquier, Lieutenant Governor of Virginia, 1758–1768*, 3 vols. (Charlottesville: University Press of Virginia, 1980), 2:1015.

23. Main, *Tobacco Colony*, 14.

24. Hollingsworth, "Demographic Study of the British Ducal Families," 365.

25. Gallman, "Mortality among White Males," 613; Daniel Blake Smith, "Mortality and Family in the Colonial Chesapeake," *Journal of Interdisciplinary History* 8 (1977–78): 423.

26. Allan Kulikoff, *Tobacco and Slaves: The Development of Southern Culture in the Chesapeake, 1680–1800* (Chapel Hill: University of North Carolina Press, 1986), 59–60.

27. Diary of Robert Carter I, 3 June 1725, quoted in Stephenson, *Carter's Grove Plantation*, 234.

28. Fairfax Harrison, "The Will of Charles Carter of Cleve," *VMHB* 31 (1923): 54.

29. Edmund Jennings Lee, *Lee of Virginia, 1642–1892* (Philadelphia: privately printed, 1895), 123.

30. William G. Stanard, "The Corbin Family," *VMHB* 29 (1921): 525.

31. George Mason to John Mason, 22 May 1792, in Kate Mason Rowland, *The Life of George Mason, 1725–1792*, 2 vols. (New York: Putnam's, 1892), 2:357–58.

32. Jo Zuppan, ed., "Father to Son: Letters from John Custis IV to Daniel Parke Custis," *VMHB* 98 (1990): 88 n. 24.

33. This represents a rise from 45 percent in the mid-seventeenth century. Kenneth A. Lockridge, *Literacy in Colonial New England: An Enquiry into the Social Context of Literacy in the Early Modern West* (New York: Norton, 1974), 73–74, 77.

34. Lockridge, *Literacy in Colonial New England*, 82; Richard R. Beeman, *The Evolution of the Southern Backcountry: A Case Study of Lunenburg County, Virginia, 1746–1832* (Philadelphia: University of Pennsylvania Press, 1984), 206.

35. This represents a rise from 20 percent in the mid-seventeenth century. Lockridge, *Literacy in Colonial New England*, 92, 97.

36. As Lorena M. Walsh noted, skills other than literacy were fundamental to economic survival. Walsh, "'Till Death Us Do Part': Marriage and Family in Seventeenth-Century Maryland," in *The Chesapeake in the Seventeenth Century: Essays on Anglo-American Society*, ed. Thad W. Tate and David L. Ammerman (Chapel Hill: University of North Carolina for the Institute of Early American History and Culture, 1979), 150.

37. Kulikoff, *Tobacco and Slaves*, 196–97, 198 n. 63. Kulikoff's figure is based upon inventories from Prince George's County, Maryland. Gloria Main found that up to

1720, only about 5 percent of the population owned other types of books. Main, *To-bacco Colony,* 244. Kulikoff, however, states that later in the eighteenth century the number increased to 16 percent. Kulikoff, *Tobacco and Slaves,* 199 n. 66. A survey of Lancaster County inventories recorded between 1731 and 1740, though, revealed that 75 percent of testators owned at least one book. Carter L. Hudgins, "Patrician Culture, Public Ritual and Political Authority in Virginia, 1680–1740" (Ph.D. diss., College of William and Mary, 1984), 227.

38. A. G. Roeber, "'The Scrutiny of the Ill-Natured Ignorant Vulgar': Lawyers and Print Culture in Virginia, 1716 to 1774," *VMHB* 91 (1983): 394–99, 410 n. 57.

39. Jack P. Greene, "Society, Ideology, and Politics: An Analysis of the Political Culture of Mid-Eighteenth-Century Virginia," in *Society, Freedom, and Conscience: The American Revolution in Virginia, Massachusetts, and New York,* ed. Richard M. Jellison (New York: Norton, 1976), 15–22.

40. Edgar W. Knight, ed., *A Documentary History of Education in the South before 1860,* 5 vols. (Chapel Hill: University of North Carolina Press, 1949), 1:654, 657–59.

41. Quoted in Elizabeth Donnan, "Eighteenth-Century English Merchants: Micajah Perry," *Journal of Economic and Business History* 4 (1931): 93.

42. "Diary of William Beverley of 'Blandfield' during a Visit to England, 1750," *VMHB* 36 (1928): 27.

43. Fithian, *Journal,* 6–7.

44. Educational data for the College of William and Mary are tentative at best. Evidence for matriculation at English and Scottish colleges and the London Inns of Court is somewhat more reliable. "Notes Relating to Some of the Students Who Attended the College of William and Mary, 1753–1770," *WMQ,* 2nd ser., 1 (1921): 27; Earl G. Swem, "The Lee Free School and the College of William and Mary," *WMQ,* 3rd ser., 16 (1959): 207 n. 1; *A Provisional List of Alumni, Grammar School Students, Members of the Faculty, and Members of the Board of Visitors of the College of William and Mary in Virginia, from 1693 to 1888* (Richmond: Division of Purchase and Printing, 1941).

45. Knight, *Documentary History of Education,* 1:511; "Notes Relating to Some of the Students Who Attended the College of William and Mary," 28.

46. Fithian, *Journal,* 65.

47. Jones, *Wealth of a Nation to Be,* 357, table A.1.

48. Hudgins, "Patrician Culture, Public Ritual," 217, table VI-6.

49. *Provisional List of Alumni,* 5–48.

50. Willard Connely, "Colonial Americans in Oxford and Cambridge," *American Oxonian* 29 (1942): 74, 76–77; J. G. de Roulhac Hamilton, "Southern Members of the Inns of Court," *North Carolina Historical Review* 10 (1933): 278–79, 281; Edward A. Jones, *American Members of the Inns of Court* (London: Saint Catherine Press, 1934), xii–xiv.

51. Charles E. Mallet, *A History of the University of Oxford,* 3 vols. (London: Methuen, 1927), 3:65 n. 2, 68 n. 1, 70; V.H.H. Green, *A History of Oxford University* (London: Batsford, 1974), 118–19.

52. G. E. Mingay, *English Landed Society in the Eighteenth Century* (London: Routledge and Kegan Paul, 1963), 135.

53. William L. Sachse, *The Colonial American in Britain* (Madison: University of Wisconsin Press, 1956), 52–53, 58, 67; Knight, *Documentary History of Education,* 1:564–65.

54. Louis B. Wright, ed., *Letters of Robert Carter, 1720–1727, The Commercial Interests of a Virginia Gentleman* (San Marino, Calif.: Huntington Library, 1940), 26.

55. Richard and Elizabeth Ambler to Edward and John Ambler at Wakefield, 1 August 1748, quoted in Lucille Griffith, ed., "English Education for Virginia Youth: Some Eighteenth-Century Ambler Family Letters," *VMHB* 69 (1961): 14–15.

56. Richard Ambler to Edward and John Ambler at Wakefield, 20 May 1749, quoted in Griffith, "English Education for Virginia Youth," 16.

57. Nathaniel Burwell to James Burwell, 13 June 1718, quoted in Louis B. Wright, *The First Gentlemen of Virginia: Intellectual Qualities of the Early Colonial Ruling Class* (San Marino, Calif.: Huntington Library, 1940), 114.

58. John Smith to Edward Ambler at Wakefield, 2 June 1751, quoted in Griffith, "English Education for Virginia Youth," 19.

59. Lee, *Lee of Virginia,* 103.

60. See, for example, letter of John Mercer, 26 September 1766, *Virginia Gazette* (Purdie and Dixon), 26 September 1766.

61. The estimates here are comprised of land inherited directly from a father, grandfather, or upon becoming principal heir after the death of a sibling. There is much room for error in the estimates provided.

62. Wertenbaker, *Planters of Colonial Virginia,* 54, 183–247.

63. Michael B. Katz, "Occupational Classification in History," *Journal of Interdisciplinary History* 3 (1972–73): 63–88.

64. T. H. Breen, *Tobacco Culture: The Mentality of the Great Tidewater Planters on the Eve of Revolution* (Princeton: Princeton University Press, 1985).

65. Benedict Leonard Calvert to Charles Lord Baltimore, 26 October 1726, quoted in John R. Commons et al., eds., *A Documentary History of American Industrial Society,* 10 vols. (New York: Russell and Russell, 1958), 1:282–83.

66. Peter V. Bergstrom, *Markets and Merchants: Economic Diversification in Colonial Virginia, 1700–1775* (New York: Garland, 1985); John J. McCusker and Russell R. Menard, *The Economy of British America, 1607–1789* (Chapel Hill: University of North Carolina Press, 1985): 125–31.

67. Rainbolt, *From Prescription to Persuasion,* 86; cf. Carole Shammas, "How Self-Sufficient Was Early America?" *Journal of Interdisciplinary History* 13 (1982–83): 247–72.

68. John Custis to Peter Collinson, 1736, quoted in Earl G. Swem, "Brothers of the Spade: Correspondence of Peter Collinson, of London, and of John Custis, of Williamsburg, Virginia, 1734–1746," *Proceedings of the American Antiquarian Society,* n.s., 58, pt. 1 (1948): 50.

69. William W. Hening, ed., *The Statutes at Large, Being a Collection of All the Laws of Virginia,* 13 vols. (Richmond, 1819–23; repr., Charlottesville: University Press of Virginia for the Jamestown Foundation of the Commonwealth of Virginia, 1969), 1:420, 9:239; Richard B. Davis, ed., *William Fitzhugh and His Chesapeake World* (Chapel Hill: University of North Carolina Press, 1963), 163; *JHB,* 12:17.

70. McCusker and Menard, *Economy of British America,* 130.

71. Harry J. Carman, ed., *American Husbandry* (1775; repr., Port Washington, N.Y.: Kennikat Press, 1939), 163, 177.

72. Landon Carter, "Observations concerning the Fly-weevil that destroys the Wheat, with some useful discoveries and calculations, concerning the propagation and progress of the pernicious insect, and the methods to be used to prevent the de-

struction of the grain by it," *Transactions of the American Philosophical Society,* 2nd ed., 1 (1789): 274.

73. Richard Corbin Tobacco Book, microfilm, CWF. Some of the tobacco Corbin sold was produced by his neighbors. The price of tobacco in 1760 is taken from U.S. Bureau of the Census, *Historical Statistics of the United States, Colonial Times to 1970,* 2 vols. (Washington, D.C.: U.S. Department of Commerce, 1975), 2:1198, ser. Z, 578–82.

74. John S. Bassett, "The Relation between the Virginia Planter and the London Merchant," *Annual Report of the American Historical Association* (1901): 564–69.

75. Aubrey C. Land, "Economic Behavior in a Planting Society: The Eighteenth-Century Chesapeake," *Journal of Southern History* 33 (1967): 473 n. 11.

76. John Smith to Edward Ambler, 2 June 1751, quoted in Griffith, "English Education for Virginia Youth," 20.

77. Thomas Jefferson to James Monroe, 22 February 1826, quoted in Paul L. Ford, ed., *The Writings of Thomas Jefferson,* 10 vols. (New York: Putnam's, 1892–99), 10:379.

78. Aubrey C. Land, "Economic Base and Social Structure: The Northern Chesapeake in the Eighteenth Century," *Journal of Economic History* 25 (1965): 649; Bergstrom, *Markets and Merchants,* 162–206.

79. Sarah Taliaferro Brooke owned what was called a furnace, although the word could also mean a brick kiln.

80. Land, "Economic Base and Social Structure," 648–49; Land, "Economic Behavior in a Planting Society," 480–82.

81. John Smith to Edward Ambler, 2 June 1751, quoted in Griffith, "English Education for Virginia Youth," 20.

82. A. G. Roeber, *Faithful Magistrates and Republican Lawyers: Creators of Virginia Legal Culture, 1680–1810* (Chapel Hill: University of North Carolina Press, 1981), 130 n. 29. See also Land, "Economic Base and Social Structure," 651–52.

83. Roeber, "Scrutiny of the Ill-Natured Ignorant," 407–8.

84. John K. Nelson, *A Blessed Company: Parishes, Parsons, and Parishioners in Anglican Virginia, 1690–1776* (Chapel Hill: University of North Carolina Press, 2001), 51–56.

85. Harold B. Gill Jr. and George M. Curtis III, "Virginia's Colonial Probate Policies and the Preconditions for Economic History," *VMHB* 87 (1979): 68–73; Fairfax County Will Book B-1, 1752–1767, 206–7, LVA.

86. Culpeper County Will Book B, 1770–1783, 75–78, LVA; Aubrey C. Land, "The Tobacco Staple and the Planter's Problems: Technology, Labor, and Crops," *Agricultural History* 43 (1969): 78–79.

87. Jones, *Wealth of a Nation to Be,* 357, table A.1.

88. Kulikoff, *Tobacco and Slaves,* 137, table 11; 154, table 16.

89. Jones, *Wealth of a Nation to Be,* 114, table 4.9; 119, table 4.14.

90. Richard S. Dunn, "Servants and Slaves: The Recruitment and Employment of Labor," in *Colonial British America: Essays in the New History of the Early Modern Era,* ed. Jack P. Greene and J. R. Pole (Baltimore: Johns Hopkins University Press, 1984), 177, table 6.3.

91. U.S. Bureau of the Census, *Historical Statistics of the United States,* 2:1174, ser. Z, 165–68; Jones, *Wealth of a Nation to Be,* 114, table 4.9.

92. Jackson T. Main, "The One Hundred," *WMQ,* 3rd ser., 11 (1954): 355; Jackson T. Main, "Sections and Politics in Virginia, 1781–1787," *WMQ,* 3rd ser., 12 (1955): 100;

Lewis C. Gray, *History of Agriculture in the Southern United States to 1860,* 2 vols. (New York: Peter Smith, 1941), 1:405.

93. Kulikoff, *Tobacco and Slaves,* 135, table 10; 156, table 17.

94. Cf. Bailyn, "Politics and Social Structure in Virginia," 100.

95. Cf. Land, "Economic Base and Social Structure," 646–47.

96. Allan Kulikoff, "The Economic Growth of the Eighteenth-Century Chesapeake Colonies," *Journal of Economic History* 39 (1979): 288; Rhys Isaac, *The Transformation of Virginia, 1740–1790* (Chapel Hill: University of North Carolina Press for the Institute of Early American History and Culture, 1982), 21.

97. Jackson T. Main, *The Upper House in Revolutionary America, 1763–1788* (Madison: University of Wisconsin Press, 1967), 256 n. 145; Greene, *Diary of Colonel Landon Carter,* 1:548. By "family," Carter is referring to his entire household, not just his immediate blood relations.

98. Mingay, *English Landed Society,* 19–22.

99. Estimates based on Kulikoff, *Tobacco and Slaves,* 133, fig. 17; and U.S. Bureau of the Census, *Historical Statistics of the United States,* 2:1174, ser. Z, 165–68.

100. Richard Pares, "Merchants and Planters," *Economic History Review,* supplement no. 4 (1960): 25; Richard B. Sheridan, "Planter and Historian: The Career of William Beckford of Jamaica and England, 1744–1799," *Jamaican Historical Review* 4 (1964): 38–39.

101. Rutman, "Still Planting the Seeds of Hope," 22–23; Jacob M. Price, "The Last Phase of the Virginia-London Consignment Trade: James Buchanan & Co., 1758–1768," *WMQ,* 3rd ser., 43 (1986): 70 n. 24.

102. Jacob M. Price, "One Family's Empire: The Russell-Lee-Clerk Connection in Maryland, Britain, and India, 1707–1857," *Maryland Historical Magazine* 72 (1977): 166–67.

103. Carman, *American Husbandry,* 174.

104. William Eddis, *Letters from America . . . 1769, to 1777,* quoted in John Clive and Bernard Bailyn, "England's Cultural Provinces: Scotland and America," *WMQ,* 3rd ser., 11 (1954): 209.

Chapter 3. "Reason Reascends Her Throne"

1. "Randolph Tucker Letters," *VMHB* 42 (January 1934): 49–50.

2. Mrs. Jane Pratt Taylor to William Byrd II, 8 June 1741[?], in Marion Tinling, ed., *The Correspondence of the Three William Byrds of Westover, Virginia, 1684–1776,* 2 vols. (Charlottesville: University Press of Virginia for the Virginia Historical Society, 1977), 2:590.

3. Lawrence Stone, *The Family, Sex and Marriage in England, 1550–1800* (1977; repr., New York: Harper and Row, 1979), 149–80; Lawrence Stone, "The Rise of the Nuclear Family in Early Modern England: The Patriarchal Stage," in *The Family in History,* ed. Charles E. Rosenberg (Philadelphia: University of Pennsylvania Press, 1975), 13–57; cf. Alan Macfarlane, book review, *History and Theory* 18, no. 1 (1979): 103–26; and Eileen Spring, "Law and the Theory of the Affective Family," *Albion* 16, no. 1 (Spring 1984): 1–20.

4. Anthony Giddens, *The Transformation of Intimacy: Sexuality, Love and Eroticism in Modern Societies* (Stanford: Stanford University Press, 1992), 37–48; cf. Stone, *Family, Sex and Marriage,* 183–84.

5. Edwin Morris Betts, ed., *Thomas Jefferson's Garden Book, 1766–1824* (Philadelphia: American Philosophical Society, 1944), 16, 17, 33.

6. Thomas Jefferson to George Washington, 21 December 1788, quoted in Sarah N. Randolph, *The Domestic Life of Thomas Jefferson* (1871; repr., Charlottesville: Thomas Jefferson Memorial Foundation), 158.

7. *JHB*, 1727–40, 398–400, 407, 419, 421, 424–25; ibid., 1752–58, 131.

8. Ibid., 1727–40, 398.

9. Ibid., 1727–40, 399; Mary Miley Theobald, "The Widows of Williamsburg," *Colonial Williamsburg* 15, no. 3 (Spring 1993): 57–63.

10. Will of Mrs. Sarah Brooke, dated 19 August 1763, proved in court on 21 May 1764, Essex County Will Book 12, 1762–1775, 113–14, LVA.

11. Alice T. Friedman, "Architecture, Authority and the Female Gaze: Planning and Representation in the Early Modern Country House," *Assemblage* 18 (1992): 40–61; John G. Dunbar, "The Building-Activities of the Duke and Duchess of Lauderdale, 1670–82," *Archaeological Journal* 132 (1975): 202–30; Elizabeth V. Chew, "'Repaired by me to my exceeding great Cost and Charges': Anne Clifford and the Uses of Architecture," in *Architecture and the Politics of Gender in Early Modern Europe,* ed. Helen Hills (Aldershot: Ashgate, 2003), 99–114.

12. Tinling, *Correspondence of the Three William Byrds,* 2:752.

13. Lund Washington to George Washington, 15 October 1775, in *The Papers of George Washington, Revolutionary War Series,* ed. Philander D. Chase, 14 vols. (Charlottesville: University Press of Virginia, 1987), 2:174.

14. Lund Washington to George Washington, 24 November 1775, in *Papers of George Washington, Revolutionary War Series,* 2:421–22.

15. Philip Vickers Fithian, *Journal and Letters of Philip Vickers Fithian: A Plantation Tutor of the Old Dominion, 1773–1774,* ed. Hunter D. Farish (Charlottesville: University Press of Virginia, 1957), 80–81.

16. Marylynn Salmon, "The Legal Status of Women in Early America: A Reappraisal," *Law and History Review* 1 (1983): 129–51; Joan R. Gunderson and Gwen Victor Gampel, "Married Women's Legal Status in Eighteenth-Century New York and Virginia," *WMQ,* 3rd ser., 39 (1982): 114–34; Linda L. Sturtz, *Within Her Power: Propertied Women in Colonial Virginia* (London: Routledge, 2002), 43–70; cf. Janelle Greenberg, "The Legal Status of the English Woman in Early Eighteenth-Century Common Law and Equity," *Studies in Eighteenth-Century Culture 4,* ed. Harold E. Paglain (Madison: University of Wisconsin Press, 1975), 171–81.

17. William Blackstone, *Commentaries on the Laws of England,* 4 vols. (1765–69; repr., Chicago: University of Chicago Press, 1979), 1:430.

18. C. Ray Keim, "Primogeniture and Entail in Colonial Virginia," *WMQ,* 3rd ser., 25 (1968): 548–49.

19. H. J. Habbakkuk, "Marriage Settlements in the Eighteenth Century," in *Transactions of the Royal Historical Society,* 4th ser., 32 (London: Royal Historical Society, 1950), 15–30; Keim, "Primogeniture and Entail in Colonial Virginia," 545–86; James W. Deen, "Patterns of Testation: Four Tidewater Counties in Colonial Virginia," *American Journal of Legal History* 16 (1972): 154–76; Carole Shammas, "English Inheritance Law and Its Transfer to the Colonies," *American Journal of Legal History* 31 (1987): 145–63; Jean Butenhoff Lee, "Land and Labor: Parental Bequest Practices in Charles County, Maryland, 1732–1783," in *Colonial Chesapeake Society,* ed. Lois Green Carr, Philip D. Morgan, and Jean B. Russo (Chapel Hill: University of North Carolina Press, 1988), 306–41.

20. Lee, "Land and Labor," 323–29.

21. Jack P. Greene, ed., *The Diary of Colonel Landon Carter of Sabine Hall, 1752–1779,* 2 vols. (Charlottesville: University Press of Virginia for the Virginia Historical Society, 1965), 2:830; Rhys Isaac, *Landon Carter's Uneasy Kingdom: Revolution and Rebellion on a Virginia Plantation* (Oxford: Oxford University Press, 2004), 37–54.

22. Linda E. Speth, "More Than Her 'Thirds': Wives and Widows in Colonial Virginia," *Women and History* 4 (Winter 1982): 5–41; Marylynn Salmon, *Women and the Law of Property in Early America* (Chapel Hill: University of North Carolina Press, 1986), 141–84.

23. William W. Hening, ed., *The Statutes at Large, Being a Collection of All the Laws of Virginia,* 13 vols. (1819–23; repr., Charlottesville: University Press of Virginia for the Jamestown Foundation of the Commonwealth of Virginia,, 1969), 2:212, 3:371–76.

24. Theodore John Rivers, "Widows' Rights in Anglo-Saxon Law," in *Women and the Law: The Social Historical Perspective,* ed. D. Kelly Weisberg, 2 vols. (Cambridge, Mass.: Schenkman, 1982), 2:37, 42 n. 15.

25. Tinling, *Correspondence of the Three William Byrds,* 2:598.

26. J. A. Leo Lemay, ed., *Robert Bolling Woos Anne Miller: Love and Courtship in Colonial Virginia* (Charlottesville: University Press of Virginia, 1990), 51–76; Daniel Blake Smith, *Inside the Great House: Planter Family Life in Eighteenth-Century Chesapeake Society* (Ithaca: Cornell University Press, 1980), 126–40.

27. Jan Lewis, "Domestic Tranquility and the Management of Emotion among the Gentry of Pre-Revolutionary Virginia," *WMQ,* 3rd ser., 39, no. 1 (January 1982): 136–40.

28. Salmon, *Women and the Law of Property,* 81–119; Pre-nuptial agreement between Mary Mann Page and John Page, 1705, reprinted in Claude O. Lanciano, *Rosewell, Garland of Virginia* (Gloucester, Va.: Gloucester County Historical Committee, 1978), 28–29.

29. Albert Alan Rogers, "Family Life in Eighteenth Century Virginia" (Ph.D. diss., University of Virginia, 1939), 122–23.

30. William Byrd II to "Vigilante" [John Smith], 18 February 1718, in Tinling, *Correspondence of the Three William Byrds,* 2:311–12.

31. Maria Taylor Byrd to Daniel Parke Custis, 20 November 1742, Chicago Historical Society.

32. William Byrd II to Daniel Parke Custis, 23 September 1742, in Tinling, *Correspondence of the Three William Byrds,* 2:595.

33. Hening, *Statutes at Large,* 5:408–10; Marylynn Salmon, "Women and Property in South Carolina: The Evidence from Marriage Settlements, 1730–1830," *WMQ,* 3rd ser., 39 (October 1982): 655–85.

34. *JHB,* 1727–40, 398.

35. "Grymes of Brandon," *VMHB* 27 (1919): 408.

36. "Notes from the Records of Richmond County," *VMHB* 29 (1921): 361–62.

37. George H. S. King, "Will of the Honorable Peter Randolph, of Chatsworth, Henrico County," *Virginia Genealogist* 2 (1958): 4.

38. Those wives whose dowries are unknown: the three wives of John Banister III (Battersea); the three wives of William Fairfax (Belvoir); the second wife of John Carlyle (Carlyle House); the two wives of Richard Henry Lee (Chantilly); the third wife of Charles Carter (Cleve); the first wife of Robert Carter I (Corotoman); the wife of Lewis Burwell III (Kingsmill); the second wife of John Mercer (Marlborough); and

the third wife of Landon Carter (Sabine Hall). The second wife of Robert Carter I (Corotoman) was Elizabeth Landon, the widow of Richard Willis, whose personal estate was worth as much as £4,710. The value of her "widow's thirds" may have amounted to £1,570, but how much of this property was in cash, as opposed to furniture and implements, has not been determined. Sarah Taliaferro Brooke (Brooke's Bank) had a life interest in her deceased husband's estate, including his £466 2s. 6d. in personal property and at least 3,375 acres of land. The value of his personal and real property at the time of marriage, however, cannot be determined.

39. This figure is based on eleven years of marriage to his first wife, who received a £250 sterling per annum annuity from the estate of her first husband, Alexander Spotswood. She also accrued an unknown amount of rent from property in England.

40. Alice Hanson Jones, *Wealth of a Nation to Be: The American Colonies on the Eve of the Revolution* (New York: Columbia University Press, 1980), 357, table A.1. William Fitzhugh's father-in-law left his daughter £350 current money, which, at the time his will was proved, October 1768, equaled about £280 sterling. John J. McCusker, *Money and Exchange in Europe and America, 1600–1775: A Handbook* (Chapel Hill: University of North Carolina Press, 1978), 211, table 3.10.

41. Alexander Spotswood (Germanna) and secondly John Thompson (Salubria) received the profits, presumably from rents, on the English land of Anne Butler Brayne.

42. Annie Laurie Wright Smith, *The Quit Rents of Virginia* (Richmond: Expert Letter Writing Co., 1957).

43. "Carter Papers," *VMHB* 5 (1897–98): 418.

44. Dell Upton, *Holy Things and Profane: Anglican Parish Churches in Colonial Virginia* (New York: Architectural History Foundation, 1986), 15.

45. C. G. Chamberlayne, ed., *The Vestry Book of Stratton Major Parish, King and Queen County, Virginia, 1729–1783* (Richmond: Division of Purchase and Printing, 1931), 131–33.

46. Pohick Church Vestry, *Minutes of the Vestry: Truro Parish, Virginia, 1732–1785* (Lorton, Va.: Pohick Church Vestry, 1974), 113–15, 132–35.

47. Jo Zuppan, ed., "Father to Son: Letters from John Custis IV to Daniel Parke Custis," *VMHB* 98 (1990): 84 n. 6.

48. C. G. Chamberlayne, ed., *The Vestry Book of St. Paul's Parish, Hanover , Virginia, 1706–1786* (Richmond: Division of Purchase and Printing of the Library Board, 1940), 157–58, 163.

49. Tinling, *Correspondence of the Three William Byrds*, 2:600.

50. McCusker, *Money and Exchange*, 205–13; Ed Crews, "How Much Is That in Today's Money?" *Colonial Williamsburg* 23, no. 2 (Summer 2002): 20–25.

51. Smith, *Inside the Great House*, 140–50.

52. "Kennon Letters," *VMHB* 31 (1923): 299.

53. *Virginia Gazette*, 27 October 1738; 12 November 1736. The word "tit" can mean either a loose woman or a young girl. *Oxford English Dictionary*, s.v. "tit."

54. Salmon, *Women and the Law of Property*, 88.

55. G. E. Mingay, *English Landed Society in the Eighteenth Century* (London: Kegan Paul, 1963), 35; Betsy C. Corner, *William Shippen, Jr.: Pioneer in American Medical Education* (Philadelphia: American Philosophical Society, 1951), 39 n. 22.

56. Horace Walpole, *Anecdotes of Painting in England,* 3 vols. (London: Henry G. Bohn, 1862), 3:725; Arthur S. Weisinger and W. B. Coley, *Hogarth on High Life: The*

Marriage á la Mode *Series from Georg Christoph Lichtenberg's Commentaries* (Middleton, Conn.: Wesleyan University Press, 1970), 20–22, 28, 131–32.

57. "Conversation Piece—Family Group around Man Sitting at Writing Table," File G 57-196, Department of Collections, CWF.

58. Edmund Jennings Lee, *Lee of Virginia, 1642–1892* (Philadelphia: privately printed, 1895), 113; Cazenove G. Lee Jr., *Lee Chronicle: Studies of the Early Generations of the Lees of Virginia,* ed. Dorothy Mills Parker (New York: New York University Press, 1957), 64; Ludwell L. Montague, "Thomas Lee at the Spout of the Potomac," *Arlington Historical Magazine,* no. 4 (1970): 31; Ethel Armes, *Stratford Hall: The Great House of the Lees* (Richmond: Garret and Massie, 1936), 39–40.

59. Quoted in Paul Buchanan, *Stratford Hall and Other Architectural Studies* (Stratford, Va.: Robert E. Lee Memorial Association, 1998), 59.

60. "Ludwell Family," *WMQ,* 1st ser., 19 (1910–11): 213; Virginia B. Price, "Constructing to Command: Rivalries between Green Spring and the Governor's Palace, 1677–1722," *VHMB* 113, no. 1 (2005): 7–9.

61. "Will of Richard Taliaferro," *WMQ,* 1st ser., 12 (1903–4): 124.

62. Richmond County Will Book 7, 1767–1787, 356, LVA.

63. Camille Wells, "Dower Play/Power Play: Menokin and the Ordeal of Elite House Building in Colonial Virginia," in *Constructing Image, Identity, and Place: Perspectives in Vernacular Architecture 9,* ed. Alison K. Hoagland and Kenneth A. Breisch, 2–21 (Knoxville: University of Tennessee Press, 2003).

64. Quoted in Abbott Lowell Cummings, "The Old Feather Store in Boston," *Old-Time New England* 48, no. 4 (April–June, 1958): 88.

65. "Carter Papers," *VMHB* 5 (1897–98): 427–28.

66. "Virginia Council Journals," *VMHB* 32 (1924): 39.

67. William Byrd, *The London Diary, 1717–1721 and Other Writings,* ed. Louis B. Wright and Marion Tinling (New York: Oxford University Press, 1958), 524–25.

68. Diary of Robert Carter I, microfilm, UVA.

69. Will of Benjamin Harrison IV in "Harrison of James River," *VMHB* 32 (1924): 98–99.

70. "Carter Papers," *VMHB* 5 (1897–98): 418.

71. Tinling, *Correspondence of the Three William Byrds,* 2:600.

72. Fairfax Harrison, "The Will of Charles Carter of Cleve," *VMHB* 31 (1923): 50.

73. Will of John Tayloe, 3 January 1744 and 31 January 1744, Richmond County Will Book 5, 1725–1753, LVA; M. Bridget Maley, "'A Very Genteel Manner': Virginia Architecture and the Tayloe Family" (master's thesis, University of Virginia, 1993), 126–30.

74. Will of Mann Page II, dated 7 November 1780, proved in court 19 April 1781, Spotsylvania Will Book E, 1772–1798, 387–90, LVA.

75. Sturtz uses the term "ghost family" to refer to this acknowledgment of the original nuclear family on the part of later family configurations. *Within Her Power,* 19–41.

76. Amerigo Salvetti to the Grand Duke of Tuscany, 31 July 1626; reprinted in "The Manuscripts of Henry Duncan Skrine, Esquire, of Claverton Manor, Somerset," *Great Britain Historical Manuscripts Commission,* Eleventh Report, Appendix, pt. 1 (London: Her Majesty's Stationery Office by Eyre and Spottiswoode, 1887), 81–82.

77. Mr. Garrard to the Lord Deputy, 11 January 1635, reprinted in William Knowler, ed., *The Earl of Strafforde's Letters and Dispatches,* 2 vols. (London: William Bow-

yer, 1739), 1:359. See also Lawrence Stone, *Crisis of the Aristocracy, 1558–1641* (Oxford: Clarendon Press, 1965), 176, 552, 618–19, 717; and Howard Colvin's 1954 article, "The South Front of Wilton House," reprinted in *Essays in English Architectural History* (New Haven: Yale University Press, 1999), 136–57.

78. Elizabeth Cust, "James Stuart, Duke of Lenox and Richmond, of Cobham Hall," *Archaeologia Cantiana* 12 (1878): 72–73; Reverend Mr. Garrard to the Lord Deputy, 15 March 1635, reprinted in Knowler, *The Earl of Strafforde's Letters,* 1:524.

79. Glenys Popper and John Reeves, "The South Front of Wilton House," *Burlington Magazine* 124, no. 951 (1982): 358–61.

80. Memorial of Ariana Randolph, Loyalist Claims, Series I-Evidence, Virginia, 1783–1786, A.O. 12/54, photocopy, CWF.

81. Louise Pecquet du Bellet, *Some Prominent Virginia Families,* 4 vols. (1907; repr., Baltimore: Genealogical Publishing, 1976), 1:63–65; Ann L. Miller, *Antebellum Orange* (Orange, Va.: Orange County Historical Society, 1988), 59–60.

82. Elizabeth Barbour Ambler to John Jaquelin Ambler and Laura B. Ambler, 12 April 1859, in Elizabeth Barbour Ambler Collection, UVA.

83. Jacqueline Eales, *Women in Early Modern England, 1500–1700* (London: UCL Press, 1998), 52.

Chapter 4. "Each Rascal Will Be a Director"

1. William Fitzhugh I to Nicholas Hayward, 30 January 1687, and Fitzhugh to Doctor Ralph Smith, 22 April 1686, in Richard B. Davis, ed., *William Fitzhugh and His Chesapeake World* (Chapel Hill: University of North Carolina Press for the Virginia Historical Society, 1963), 202–3, 175.

2. William Fitzhugh I to John Cooper, 7 June 1681, ibid., 90.

3. Thomas Jefferson, query XV, "Colleges, Buildings and Roads," in *Notes on the State of Virginia,* in *The Portable Thomas Jefferson,* ed. Merrill D. Peterson (New York: Penguin, 1979), 203.

4. William W. Hening, ed., *The Statutes at Large, Being a Collection of All the Laws of Virginia,* 13 vols. (Richmond, 1819–23; repr., Charlottesville: University Press of Virginia for the Jamestown Foundation of the Commonwealth of Virginia, 1969), 1:193.

5. Henry Hartwell, James Blair, and Edward Chilton, *The Present State of Virginia,* ed. Hunter Dickinson Farish (Williamsburg: Colonial Williamsburg, 1940), 9.

6. Camille Wells, "Dower Play/Power Play: Menokin and the Ordeal of Elite House Building in Colonial Virginia," in *Constructing Image, Identity, and Place: Perspectives in Vernacular Architecture 9,* ed. Alison K. Hoagland and Kenneth A. Breish (Knoxville: University of Tennessee Press, 2003), 2–21.

7. Carl R. Lounsbury, *An Illustrated Glossary of Early Southern Architecture and Landscape* (Oxford: Oxford University Press, 1994), 385.

8. John Summerson, *Georgian London,* 3rd ed. (Cambridge: MIT Press, 1978), 69–73; Howard Colvin, "Architect and Client in Georgian England," in *Essays in English Architectural History* (New Haven: Yale University Press, 1999), 268–75.

9. Marcus Whiffen, *The Public Buildings of Williamsburg* (Williamsburg: Colonial Williamsburg, 1958), 21–22.

10. Edward M. Riley, "The Colonial Courthouses of York County, Virginia," *WMQ,* 2nd ser., 22 (1942): 400–401; Whiffen, *Public Buildings of Williamsburg,* 41; *Encyclopedia of Virginia Biography,* ed. Lyon G. Tyler, 5 vols. (New York: Lewis His-

torical Publishing Co., 1915), 1:205; William G. Stanard and Mary N. Stanard, *The Colonial Virginia Register* (Albany, 1902; repr., Baltimore: Genealogical Publishing Co., 1965), 26, 89, 93, 95–97; Carter L. Hudgins, "Patrician Culture, Public Ritual and Political Authority in Virginia, 1680–1740" (Ph.D. diss., College of William and Mary, 1984), 104–6.

11. "Diary of John Blair," *WMQ,* 1st. ser., 7 (1898–99): 151.

12. Ralph E. Fall, ed., *The Diary of Robert Rose* (Verona, Va.: McClure Press, 1977), 39, 52, 73. The record of Charles Carter's payment to Walker is found in a nineteenth-century transcript of a receipt discovered by Carl Lounsbury in Box 8, Minor Collection-Carter Family, James Monroe Law Office Museum, Fredericksburg, Va.

13. Robert Carter I to Edward Turner, 27 May 1721, quoted in Lewis B. Wright, ed., *Letters of Robert Carter, 1720–1727, The Commercial Interests of a Virginia Gentleman* (San Marino, Calif.: Huntington Library, 1940), 97.

14. Robert Carter I to Micajah and Richard Perry, quoted in Wright, *Letters of Robert Carter,* 22–23.

15. Letter of Robert Carter, 15 July 1727, quoted in Betty C. Leviner, "The Pages and Rosewell," *Journal of Early Southern Decorative Arts* 13 (1987): 45–46 n. 24; Summerson, *Georgian London,* 76.

16. For Carter's legal problems with his builders, see Richmond County Court Order Book 10, 1732–1739, 147, LVA; Richmond County Criminal Trials, 1710–1754, 53–54, LVA; Richmond County Records: Account Book 1, 1724–1783, 68, LVA; Mary A. Stephenson, *Carter's Grove Plantation: A History* (Williamsburg: Colonial Williamsburg for Seatlantic Fund, 1964), 233.

17. Richmond County Court Order Book 10, 1732–1739, 646, LVA; Richmond County Court Order Book 11, 1739–1746, 119, LVA.

18. Jack P. Greene, ed., *The Diary of Colonel Landon Carter of Sabine Hall, 1752–1779,* 2 vols. (Charlottesville: University Press of Virginia for the Virginia Historical Society, 1965), 1:328.

19. Charles Carter to Landon Carter, 31 July 1738, Carter Family Papers, microfilm, UVA.

20. C. Malcolm Watkins, *The Cultural History of Marlborough: An Archaeological and Historical Investigation of the Port Town for Stafford County and the Plantation of John Mercer, Including Data Supplied by Frank M. Setzler and Oscar M. Darter,* Smithsonian Institution Press Bulletin No. 253 (Washington, D.C.: Smithsonian Institution Press, 1968), 35–39; Eileen Harris, *British Architectural Books and Writers, 1556–1785* (Cambridge: Cambridge University Press, 1990), 23–63.

21. *Virginia Gazette* (Hunter), 7 February 1751, 29 August 1751; Pat Gibbs, ed., "Carter Burwell Account Book, 1738–1756," n.d., 22, 46, 48, 51, 53–56. 58–68, 79, CWF.

22. Richard Corbin to John Robinson, 20 August 1758, Richard Corbin Letterbook, microfilm, CWF.

23. Mary Kate Black, "My Dear Brother: John Carlyle of Alexandria as Revealed in Letters to George Carlyle," *Northern Virginia Heritage* 6 (October 1984): 6, 20 n. 29.

24. James D. Munson, *Colo. John Carlyle, Gent., A True and Just Account of the Man and His House* (Alexandria: Northern Virginia Regional Park Authority, 1986), 42.

25. James C. Ballagh, *The Letters of Richard Henry Lee,* 2 vols. (New York: Macmillan, 1911–14), 1:24–25; J. Kent McGaughy, *Richard Henry Lee of Virginia: A Portrait of an American Revolutionary* (Lanham, Md.: Rowman and Littlefield, 2004), 87–88.

26. Ballagh, *Letters of Richard Henry Lee,* 1:66, 76–77.

27. Richard Henry Lee Account Book, 1776–1794, microfilm, Huntington Library, San Marino, Calif.

28. Ballagh, *Letters of Richard Henry Lee,* 1:49, 53, 65–66; Paul C. Nagel, *The Lees of Virginia: Seven Generations of an American Family* (New York: Oxford University Press, 1990), 89.

29. *American National Biography,* ed. John A. Garraty and Mark C. Carnes (New York: Oxford Univeristy Press, 1999), s.v. "Buckland, William."

30. "Chronology of George Mason's Land, Business and Trade Affairs," 1990, typescript, Gunston Hall Library.

31. Robert A. Rutland, ed., *The Papers of George Mason, 1725–1792,* 3 vols. (Chapel Hill: University of North Carolina Press, 1970), 1:56–57; *Minutes of the Vestry: Truro Parish Virginia, 1732–1785* (Lorton, Va.: Pohick Church Vestry), 115.

32. "The Recollections of John Mason," unabridged transcript by Terry Dunn, Gunston Hall Library, Lorton, Virginia, 48. The author wishes to thank Susan Borchardt for making this transcript available.

33. George Mason to John Mason, 22 May 1792, in Kate Mason Rowland, *The Life of George Mason, 1725–1792,* 2 vols. (New York: Putnam's, 1892), 2:357–58.

34. Edwin M. Betts, ed., *Thomas Jefferson's Garden Book* (Princeton: Princeton University Press for the American Philosophical Society, 1953), 17, 18, 23, 29, 42, 57, 69, 80, 102; Jack McLaughlin, *Jefferson and Monticello: The Biography of a Builder* (New York: Henry Holt, 1988), 67, 166–67.

35. Calvin B. Coulter Jr., "The Import Trade of Colonial Virginia," *WMQ,* 3rd ser., 2 (1945): 312; William M. S. Rasmussen, "Palladio in Tidewater Virginia: Mount Airy and Blandfield," in *Building by the Book 1,* ed. Mario di Valmarana (Charlottesville: University Press of Virginia 1984), 88; Julian P. Boyd et al., eds., *The Papers of Thomas Jefferson,* 33 vols. (Princeton: Princeton University Press, 1950–2007), 1:71–72.

36. Hugh Jones, *The Present State of Virginia, From Whence Is Inferred a Short View of Maryland and North Carolina,* ed. Richard L. Morton (Chapel Hill: University of North Carolina Press for the Virginia Historical Society, 1956), 76.

37. Inventory of the Estate of Robert Carter, November 1733, VHS.

38. Fairfax Harrison, "The Will of Charles Carter of Cleve," *VMHB* 31 (1923): 66–67.

39. Richard Corbin to John Robinson, 20 August 1758, Richard Corbin Letterbook, microfilm, CWF.

40. William G. Stanard, "The Corbin Family," *VMHB* 30 (1922): 82.

41. Colonel John Tayloe to Landon Carter, 16 October 1762, Sabine Hall Collection, UVA.

42. Greene, *Diary of Colonel Landon Carter,* 1:253, 259, 295.

43. Quoted in John R. Commons et al., eds., *A Documentary History of American Industrial Society,* 10 vols. (New York: Russell and Russell, 1958), 2:82–83.

44. *Virginia Gazette* (Rind), 5 October 1769.

45. Greene, *Diary of Colonel Landon Carter,* 1:568.

46. Letter of Peter Fontaine, 30 March 1757, quoted in Commons et al., *Documentary History of American Industrial Society,* 2:29–30; E. H. Phelps Brown and Sheila V. Hopkins, "Seven Centuries of Building Wages," *Economica,* n.s., 22 (1955): 205; Edward M. Riley, ed., *The Journal of John Harrower: An Indentured Servant in the Colony of Virginia, 1773–1776* (Williamsburg: distributed by Holt, Rinehart and Winston, 1963), 109.

47. Dell Upton, *Holy Things and Profane: Anglican Parish Churches in Colonial Virginia* (New York: Architectural History Foundation, 1986), 11–34; Carl R. Lounsbury, *The Courthouses of Early Virginia: An Architectural History* (Charlottesville: University of Virginia Press, 2005), 168–215.

48. When a new parish was created, however, the first vestrymen were elected by the freeholders. Thereafter, only members of the vestries elected new vestrymen, unless the General Assembly ordered a new election.

49. Carl R. Lounsbury, "The Plague of Building: Construction Practices on the Frontier, 1650–1730," in *Architects and Builders in North Carolina: A History of The Practice of Building* (Chapel Hill: University of North Carolina Press, 1990), 436 n. 60.

50. St. Mark's Parish Vestry Book, 15, 18, 34, 50 51, 52, 60, 61, 68, 70–71, 80, 83, 92, LVA.

51. Ibid., 50, 59, 61, 64 67, 71, 85, 88, 89, 92, 101, 102, 360, 371, 384, 394, 396, 405, 408, 411, LVA.

52. *Virginia Gazette* (Rind), 5 September 1771.

53. Ibid., 14 July 1768.

54. Bristol Parish Vestry Book, 173, 184, 187, 188, 201, 205–6, LVA.

55. *JHB,* 7:203; Hening, *Statutes at Large,* 7:151; Upton, *Holy Things and Profane,* 17; Watkins, *Cultural History of Marlborough,* 35, 37.

56. *EJC,* 4:238.

57. R. A. Brock, ed., "The Vestry Book of Henrico Parish, Virginia, 1730–1773," in *Annals of Henrico Parish,* ed. J. Staunton Moore (Richmond: Williams Printing Co., 1904), 82, 84, 93, 95, 98, 110.

58. *JHB,* 7:129; "Diary of John Blair," 4; Upton, *Holy Things and Profane,* 82, fig. 81; Hening, *Statutes at Large,* 6:197–98, 528.

59. Lancaster County Court Order Book 4, 1696–1702, 53–54, LVA.

60. Lancaster County Court Order Book 4, 1696–1702, 1009, LVA; cf. Robert Tittler, *Architecture and Power: The Town Hall and the English Urban Community c. 1500–1640* (Oxford: Oxford University Press, 1991), 106–22.

61. Cary Carson, Norman F. Barka, William M. Kelso, Garry Wheeler Stone, and Dell Upton, "Impermanent Architecture in the Southern American Colonies," *Winterthur Portfolio* 16 (Summer–Autumn 1981): 195–96.

62. *LJC,* 1:355.

63. "Carter Papers," *VMHB* 6 (1898–99): 3; Diary of Robert Carter I, microfilm, UVA; "Carter Papers," 6:3; Upton, *Holy Things and Profane,* 15, 44.

64. Richmond County Court Order Book 12, 1746–1752, 144, LVA.

65. Carl R. Lounsbury, "'An Elegant and Commodious Building': William Buckland and the Design of the Prince William County Courthouse," *JSAH* 46 (1987): 233–37.

66. Richmond County Court Order Book 12, 1746–1752, 207, LVA.

67. Greene, *Diary of Colonel Landon Carter,* 1:457.

68. Andrea Palladio, *The Four Books of Architecture* (London: Isaac Ware, 1738; repr., New York: Dover, 1965), 75 and plate 18.

69. Fairfax County Court Order Book, 1749–1754, 49, 180–81, 196, 373, LVA; *EJC,* 5:379, 387; Munson, *Colo. John Carlyle,* 33, 37–38, 42–43, 85; Fairfax County Minute Book, 1756–1763, pt. 1, 42, 205, LVA.

70. *Virginia Gazette,* 10 January 1751; Robert M. Moxham, *Early Colonial Churches of Northern Virginia* (North Springfield, Va.: Colonial Press, 1974), 15–16.

71. Philip Slaughter, *History of Truro Parish in Virginia,* ed. Edward L. Goodwin (Philadelphia: Jacobs, 1907), 45; Munson, *Colo. John Carlyle,* 109–11; Upton, *Holy Things and Profane,* 130, fig. 153.

72. Munson, *Colo. John Carlyle,* 150 n. 28, 151 n. 14.

73. C. G. Chamberlayne, ed., *The Vestry Book of Stratton Major Parish, King and Queen County, Virginia, 1729–1783* (Richmond: Division of Purchase and Printing, 1931), 63, 67, 74, 89, 107–8, 130–31, 135, 142, 150, 159, 173, 175, 196, 200, 205.

74. Pohick Church Vestry, *Minutes of the Vestry: Truro Parish,* 69, 78–80, 82; Slaughter, *History of Truro Parish,* 34; Luke Beckerdite, "William Buckland and William Bernard Sears: The Designer and the Carver," *Journal of Early Southern Decorative Arts* 8 (1982): 14–16.

75. Pohick Church Vestry, *Minutes of the Vestry: Truro Parish,* 114, 115–17, 121–22, 129. The will of Daniel French was dated 20 May 1771 and proved 6 May 1772. J.E.S. King, comp., *Abstracts of Wills and Inventories, Fairfax County, Virginia, 1742–1801* (Baltimore: Southern Book Co., 1959; repr., Baltimore: Genealogical Publishing Co., 1983), 18.

76. Pohick Church Vestry, *Minutes of the Vestry: Truro Parish,* 132–35, 142. Mason also worked on a church enclosure, vestry house, and new glebe for Truro Parish.

77. William M. S. Rasmussen, "Designers, Builders, and Architectural Traditions in Colonial Virginia," *VMHB* 90 (1982): 201.

78. *Virginia Gazette* (Purdie and Dixon), 26 September 1766.

79. James L. Axtell, ed., *The Educational Writings of John Locke,* (Cambridge: Cambridge University Press, 1968), 314–16.

80. Mary Hollingsworth, "The Architect in Fifteenth-Century Florence," *Art History* 7, no. 4 (1984): 385–410; H. J. Habakkuk, "Daniel Finch, 2nd Earl of Nottingham: His House and Estate," in *Studies in Social History: A Tribute to G. M. Trevelyan,* ed. J.H. Plumb (London: Longmans, Green, 1955).

Chapter 5. Learning to Become "Good Mechanics in Building"

1. Martha Jaquelin to "Dear Boys," 28 April 1748, Elizabeth Barbour Ambler Collection, UVA.

2. Robert Beverley to unknown correspondent, 1776, Robert Beverley Letterbook, quoted in James B. Slaughter, *Settlers, Southerners, Americans: The History of Essex County, Virginia, 1608–1984* (Tappahannock, Va.: Essex County Board of Supervisors, 1985), 31.

3. Richard Ambler to Edward and John Ambler, 20 May 1749, quoted in Lucille Griffith, ed., "English Education for Virginia Youth: Some Eighteenth-Century Ambler Family Letters," *VMHB* 69 (1961): 15; Richard and Elizabeth Ambler to Edward and John Ambler at Wakefield, 1 August 1748, in the Elizabeth Barbour Ambler Collection, UVA; George K. Smart, "Private Libraries in Colonial Virginia," *American Literature* 10 (1938–39): 24–52.

4. Daniel McDonald, ed., *Joseph Addison and Richard Steele: Selected Essays from "The Tatler," "The Spectator" and "The Guardian"* (Indianapolis and New York: Bobbs-Merrill, 1973), 183; William Byrd, "A Progress to the Mines," in John Spencer Bassett, ed., *The Writings of Colonel William Byrd of Westover in Virginia Esqr.* (1901; repr., New York: Burt Franklin, 1970), 356, 360–61.

5. McDonald, *Joseph Addison and Richard Steele,* 183; Marion Tinling, ed., *The*

Correspondence of the Three William Byrds of Westover, Virginia, 1684–1776, 2 vols. (Charlottesville: University Press of Virginia for the Virginia Historical Society, 1977), 2:453; John Ashton, *The Fleet: Its River, Prison, and Marriages* (1888; repr., Detroit: Singing Tree Press, 1968), 255–91; Richard B. Davis, "William Byrd II: Taste and Tolerance," in *Literature and Society in Early Virginia* (Baton Rouge: Louisiana State University Press, 1973), 97–132.

6. Francis Bacon, *The Essayes, or Counsels, Civill and Morall,* ed. Michael Kiernan (Oxford: Clarendon Press, 1985), 135.

7. William Bottorff and Roy Flannagan, eds., "The Diary of Frances Baylor Hill of Hillsborough, King and Queen County Virginia (1797)," *Early American Literature* 2, no. 3 (1967), 12–13.

8. Jeanne A. Calhoun, "A Virginia Gentleman of the Eve of the Revolution: Philip Ludwell Lee of Stratford," research report, Robert E. Lee Memorial Association, 1996; Robert Manson Myers, "The Old Dominion Looks to London," *VMHB* 54, no. 3 (July 1946): 197.

9. Bassett, *Writings of Colonel William Byrd,* xliii–xliv; Tinling, *Correspondence of the Three William Byrds,* 1:195.

10. J. A. Bennett, "Architecture and Mathematical Practice in England, 1550–1650," in *English Architecture, Public and Private: Essays for Kerry Downes,* ed. John Bold and Edward Chaney (London: Hambledon Press, 1993), 23–29.

11. Edgar W. Knight, ed., *A Documentary History of Education in the South Before 1860,* 5 vols. (Chapel Hill: University of North Carolina Press, 1949), 1:564–65.

12. James L. Axtell, ed., *The Educational Writings of John Locke* (Cambridge: Cambridge University Press, 1968), 264–65; Baldesar Castiglione, *The Book of the Courtier* (1528), trans. Leonard Eckstein Opdycke (New York: Scribner's, 1903), 65; Philip Vickers Fithian, *Journal and Letters of Philip Vickers Fithian: A Plantation Tutor of the Old Dominion, 1773–1774,* ed. Hunter D. Farish (Charlottesville: University Press of Virginia, 1957), 222.

13. William Byrd, *The London Diary, 1717–1721, and Other Writings,* ed. Louis B. Wright and Marion Tinling (Oxford: Oxford University Press, 1958), 49, 89; Tinling, *Correspondence of the Three William Byrds,* 195.

14. Ann Bermingham, "'An Exquisite Practice': The Institution of Drawing as a Polite Art in Britain," in *Towards a Modern Art World,* ed. Brian Allen (New Haven: Yale University Press, 1995), 47–66.

15. Maya Hambly, *Drawing Instruments, 1580–1980* (London: Sotheby's Publications, 1988), 23–28, 37–51; "New Items in the John D. Rockefeller, Jr. Library's Special Collection," *Colonial Williamsburg Interpreter* 26, no. 1 (Spring 2005): 21.

16. Fithian, *Journal,* 135, 146, 148; Bottorff and Flannagan, "Diary of Frances Baylor Hill," 22 and passim; "Francis Nicholson in Perspective," *Virginia Historical Society Occasional Bulletin* 16 (April 1969): 6–8.

17. Fithian, *Journal,* 148; William Howard Adams, ed., *The Eye of Thomas Jefferson* (Charlottesville: University Press of Virginia, 1981), figs. 400, 464; Christina K. Hough, "New Discoveries on the Architectural Drawings of Thomas Jefferson," *Magazine of Albemarle County History* 50 (1992): 31–36; Douglas L. Wilson, "Dating Jefferson's Early Architectural Drawings," *VMHB* 101, no. 1 (1993): 53–76. For the use of the pencil in architectural design, see Hambly, *Drawing Instruments,* 65–66.

18. Ronald Bailey, "A Surveyor for the King," *Colonial Williamsburg* 23, no. 2 (Summer 2001): 26–31.

19. For Washington's drawings, see Charles Brownell, Calder Loth, William M.

S. Rasmussen, and Richard Guy Wilson, *The Making of Virginia Architecture* (Richmond: Virginia Museum of Fine Arts, 1992), 204–7. For the Ayrault plan, see Antoinette F. Downing and Vincent J. Scully Jr., *The Architectural Heritage of Newport, Rhode Island, 1640–1915,* 2nd ed. (New York: Clarkson N. Potter, 1967), plate 71.

20. W.A.R. Goodwin, *Historical Sketch of Bruton Church, Williamsburg, Virginia* (Petersburg: Franklin Press, 1903), 33.

21. C. G. Chamberlayne, ed., *The Vestry Book of Stratton Major Parish, King and Queen County, Virginia, 1729–1793* (Richmond: Division of Purchase and Printing, 1931), 130–33.

22. *Virginia Gazette* (Purdie and Dixon), 23 March 1769.

23. St. Mark's Parish Vestry Book, 405, 408–10, LVA.

24. Jo Zuppan, ed., "Father to Son: Letters from John Custis IV to Daniel Parke Custis," *VMHB* 98 (1990): 88.

25. "Diary of John Blair," *WMQ,* 1st ser., 7 (January 1898–99): 133–53; 8 (1899–1900): 1–17.

26. Variation in the precision of contractual language is explored in Catherine W. Bishir, "Good and Sufficient Language for Building," in *Perspectives in Vernacular Architecture 4,* ed. Thomas Carter and Bernard L. Herman (Columbia: University of Missouri Press, 1991), 44–52.

27. "Memorandum of an Agreement made between John Johnson and Col. James Patton, 1755," quoted in John R. Commons et al., eds., *A Documentary History of American Industrial Society,* 10 vols. (New York: Russell and Russell, 1958), 2:275.

28. Carl R. Lounsbury, *The Courthouses of Early Virginia: An Architectural History* (Charlottesville: University of Virginia Press, 2005), 180–87; William M. S. Rasmussen, "Architectural Drawings and Design in the Virginia Colony," in Brownell et al., *Making of Virginia Architecture,* 133–44.

29. Lois Mulkearn, ed., *George Mercer Papers Relating to the Ohio Company of Virginia* (Pittsburgh: University of Pittsburgh Press, 1954), 194–95.

30. T. H. Breen, *Tobacco Culture: The Mentality of the Great Planters on the Eve of the Revolution* (Princeton: Princeton University Press, 1985), 40–83.

31. *JHB,* 5:39.

32. Lounsbury, *Courthouses of Early Virginia,* 168–80, 198; Hugh Jones, *The Present State of Virginia, From Whence Is Inferred a Short View of Maryland and North Carolina,* ed. Richard L. Morton (Chapel Hill: University of North Carolina Press for the Virginia Historical Society, 1956), 76.

33. William L. Sachse, *The Colonial American in Britain* (Madison: University of Wisconsin Press, 1956), 36; John Harris, "English Country House Guides, 1740–1840," in *Concerning Architecture,* ed. John Summerson (London: Allen Lane, 1968), 61; Esther Moir, *The Discovery of Britain: The English Tourists, 1540–1840* (London: Routledge and Kegan Paul, 1964), 58–76.

34. John Banister III (Battersea); William Fairfax (Belvoir); Robert Beverley (Blandfield); John Carlyle (Carlyle House); Richard Henry Lee (Chantilly); Charles Carter (Cleve); Robert Carter I (Corotoman); Alexander Spotswood (Germanna); John Mercer (Marlborough); Mann Page I (Rosewell); Landon Carter (Sabine Hall); John Thompson (Salubria); Thomas Lee (Stratford Hall); and John Randolph II (Tazewell Hall).

35. Many scholars have cited travel as an important factor in high-style design. See Hugh Morrison, *Early American Architecture from the First Settlements to the National Period* (Oxford: Oxford University Press, 1952; repr., New York: Dover, 1987),

290; Carter L. Hudgins, "Patrician Culture, Public Ritual and Political Authority in Virginia, 1680–1740" (Ph.D. diss., College of William and Mary, 1984), 164–65; Camille Wells, "Interior Designs: Room Furnishings and Historical Interpretations at Colonial Williamsburg," *Southern Quarterly* 31, no. 3 (Spring 1993): 105.

36. Bacon, *Essayes,* 56–63.

37. Axtell, *Educational Writings of John Locke,* 321.

38. David Fordyce, *Dialogues Concerning Education* (1745 and 1768), quoted in George C. Brauer Jr., *The Education of a Gentleman: Theories of Gentlemanly Education in England, 1660–1775* (New York: Bookman, 1959), 162; Moir, *Discovery of Britain,* 91–107.

39. George B. Parks, "John Evelyn and the Art of Travel," *Huntington Library Quarterly* 10 (1946–47): 251–76.

40. Richard Ambler to Edward and John Ambler at Wakefield, 20 May 1749; Richard Ambler to Edward Ambler, 31 October 1751, quoted in Griffith, "English Education for Virginia Youth," 16, 22.

41. Betsy C. Corner, *William Shippen, Jr., Pioneer in American Medical Education* (Philadelphia: American Philosophical Society, 1951), 17, 18, 20, 29, 32.

42. Moir, *Discovery of Britain,* 77–90.

43. Brauer, *Education of a Gentleman,* 160–61.

44. G. E. Mingay, *English Landed Society in the Eighteenth Century* (London: Routledge and Kegan Paul, 1963), 138, 141.

45. Quoted in Sachse, *Colonial American in Britain,* 221 n. 34.

46. "Diary of William Beverley of "Blandfield' during a Visit to England, 1750," *VMHB* 36 (1928): 162, 163, 166–69.

47. John Harris, *William Talman, Maverick Architect* (London: George Allen and Unwin, 1982); Marcus Whiffen, *Thomas Archer: Architect of the English Baroque* (Los Angeles: Hennessey and Ingalls, 1973).

48. Thomas T. Waterman, "'Rosewell,' Gloucester County, Virginia," *Architectural Forum* 52 (January 1930): 17–30; Morrison, *Early American Architecture,* 336; Marcus Whiffen, "Some Virginia House Plans Reconsidered," *JSAH* 16 (May 1957): 17–19; Betty C. Leviner, "The Pages and Rosewell," *Journal of Early Southern Decorative Arts* 13 (1987): 27–40.

49. James D. Munson, *Colo. John Carlyle, Gent., A True and Just Account of the Man and His House* (Alexandria: Northern Virginia Regional Park Authority, 1986), 120–21.

50. Alan Simpson, "Robert Carter's Schooldays," *VMHB* 94 (1986): 161; Peter Guillery, *The Small House in Eighteenth-Century London* (New Haven: Yale University Press, 2004), 161–69.

51. Carter L. Hudgins, "Robert 'King' Carter and the Landscape of Tidewater Virginia in the Eighteenth Century," in *Earth Patterns: Essays in Landscape Archaeology,* ed. William M. Kelso and Rachel Most (Charlottesville: University Press of Virginia, 1990), 63; William M. Kelso, "Big Things Remembered: Anglo-Virginian Houses, Armorial Devices, and the Impact of Common Sense," in *The Art and Mystery of Historical Archaeology: Essays in Honor of James Deetz,* ed. Ann Elizabeth Yentsch and Mary C. Beaudry (Boca Raton, Fla.: CRC Press, 1992), 134–35; Harris, *William Talman,* plate 13.

52. Daniel D. Reiff, *Small Georgian Houses in England and Virginia* (Cranbury, N.J.: Associated University Presses, 1986).

53. S. Fiske Kimball, *Domestic Architecture of the American Colonies and Early*

Republic (New York: Scribner's, 1922), 56; John Harris, "The Pattern Book Phenomenon," in *Building by the Book 2,* ed. Mario di Valmarana (Charlottesville: University Press of Virginia,1986), 101–15.

54. Roger G. Kennedy, *Architecture, Men, Women and Money in America, 1600–1860* (New York: Random House, 1985), 118.

55. Morrison, *Early American Architecture,* 290–91; Marcus Whiffen, *The Eighteenth-Century Houses of Williamsburg,* 2nd rev. ed. (Williamsburg: CWF, 1987), 64; Dell Upton, "Pattern Books and Professionalism: Aspects of the Transformation of American Domestic Architecture, 1800–1860," *Winterthur Portfolio* 19 (1984): 109; Martin Eli Weil, "Interior Details in Eighteenth-Century Architectural Books," *APT Bulletin* 10, no. 4 (1978): 47–66.

56. Quoted in Calhoun, "Virginia Gentleman," 3; *Dictionary of Virginia Biography,* ed. John T. Kneebone et al., 3 vols. (Richmond: LVA, 1998–2006), s.v. "John Ariss."

57. John M. Jennings, *The Library of the College of William and Mary in Virginia, 1693–1793* (Charlottesville: University Press of Virginia for the Earl Gregg Swem Library of the College of William and Mary in Virginia, 1968), 48.

58. Marcus Whiffen, *The Public Buildings of Williamsburg* (Williamsburg: Colonial Williamsburg, 1958), 95; John W. Reps, *Tidewater Towns: City Planning in Colonial Virginia and Maryland* (Williamsburg: CWF, 1972), 126.

59. C. Malcolm Watkins, *The Cultural History of Marlborough,* Smithsonian Institution Press Bulletin No. 253 (Washington, D.C.: Smithsonian Institution, 1968), 37–39.

60. Carol Edith Curtis, "The Library of Landon Carter of Sabine Hall, 1710–1778" (master's thesis, University of Virginia, 1981), 92.

61. Richmond County Court Order Book 12 (1746–1752), 207, LVA.

62. Jack P. Greene, ed., *The Diary of Colonel Landon Carter of Sabine Hall, 1752–1779,* 2 vols. (Charlottesville: University Press of Virginia for the Virginia Historical Society, 1965), 1:457.

63. William M. S. Rasmussen, "Sabine Hall, A Classical Villa in Virginia" (Ph.D. diss., University of Delaware, 1980), 23–24; Andrea Palladio, *The Four Books of Architecture* (London: Isaac Ware, 1738; repr., New York: Dover, 1965), 63–64.

64. S. Fiske Kimball, *Thomas Jefferson, Architect, Original Designs in the Coolidge Collection of the Massachusetts Historical Society* (1916; repr., New York: Da Capo Press, 1968), 90–101; William B. O'Neal, *Jefferson's Fine Arts Library, His Selections for the University of Virginia Together with His Own Architectural Books* (Charlottesville: University Press of Virginia, 1976); E. Millicent Sowerby, *Catalogue of the Library of Thomas Jefferson,* 5 vols. (Washington, D.C.: Library of Congress, 1952–59).

65. Marquis de Chastellux, *Travels in North America in the Years 1780, 1781 and 1782,* trans. Howard C. Rice Jr., 2 vols. (Chapel Hill: University of North Carolina Press, 1963), 2:391.

66. Hudgins, "Patrician Culture, Public Ritual," 252; Eileen Harris, *British Architectural Books and Writers, 1556–1785* (Cambridge: Cambridge University Press, 1990), 401.

67. Mary A. Stephenson, *Carter's Grove Plantation: A History* (Williamsburg: Colonial Williamsburg for Seatlantic Fund, 1964), 249–50; Harris, *British Architectural Books,* 331–33.

68. Louis B. Wright, "The 'Gentleman's Library' in Early Virginia: The Literary Interests of the First Carters," *Huntington Library Quarterly* 1 (1937): 42, 59; Douglas

Chambers, "The Legacy of Evelyn's *Sylva* in the Eighteenth Century," *Eighteenth-Century Life* 12 (1988): 29.

69. Quoted in Rasmussen, "Sabine Hall," 183 n. 29.

70. Leviner, "Pages and Rosewell," 50 n. 92; *Dictionary of National Biography,* ed. Leslie Stephen and Sidney Lee, 22 vols. (London: Smith, Elder, 1908–9), s.v. "Evelyn, John," "Markham, Gervase"; William H. Adams, *The French Garden, 1500–1800* (New York: George Braziller, 1979), 37.

71. Joseph Moxon, *Mechanick Exercises: or the Doctrine of Handy-Works* (London, 1703; repr., Morristown, N.J.: Astragal Press, 1989), 253; Rosamond R. Beirne and John H. Scarff, *William Buckland, 1731–1774: Architect of Virginia and Maryland* (Baltimore: Maryland Historical Society, 1958), 142–43.

72. Mark R. Wenger, "Westover: William Byrd's Mansion Reconsidered" (master's thesis, University of Virginia, 1981), 94–95, 132; Whiffen, *Eighteenth-Century Houses of Williamsburg,* 62–63.

73. Morrison, *Early American Architecture,* 336. Primatt's H-shaped plan is illustrated in Kimball, *Domestic Architecture of the American Colonies,* 54, fig. 30.

74. Calder Loth, "Palladio in Southside Virginia: Brandon and Battersea," in *Building by the Book* 1, ed. Mario di Valmarana (Charlottesville: University Press of Virginia, 1984), 25–46.

75. S. Fiske Kimball, "Gunston Hall," *JSAH* 13 (1954): 4, 7; Gunston Hall, 1982, HABS, 7. For Buckland's inventory, including the books he owned at his death, see Beirne and Scarff, *William Buckland,* 149–50.

76. Beirne and Scarff, *William Buckland,* 142–43; Fithian, *Journal,* 6–7, 200.

77. Thomas Jefferson to James Oldham, 24 December 1804, Thomas Jefferson Papers Series 1, General Correspondence, 1651–1827, Library of Congress.

78. Douglas E. Ross, "The Birds Are Coming Home to Roost: Re-evaluating the Architectural History of Turkey Island Plantation," *Archeological Society of Virginia Quarterly Bulletin* 58, no. 1 (March 2003): 6–7, 9.

79. Smart, "Private Libraries in Colonial Virginia," 24–52; Helen Park, *A List of Architectural Books Available in America Before the Revolution,* (Los Angeles: Hennessey and Ingalls, 1973).

80. [John Page], "Governor Page," *Virginia Historical Register* 3 (1850): 146–47.

81. Thomas Jefferson, *The Autobiography of Thomas Jefferson* (New York: Capricorn, 1959), 20–21; Harold Burton Meyers, "Enlightened Governor Fauquier," *Colonial Williamsburg* 16, no. 2 (Winter 1993–94): 28–35; Herbert L. Ganter, "William Small, Jefferson's Beloved Teacher," *WMQ,* 3rd ser., 4, no. 4 (October 1947): 505–11.

82. Edmund Jenings to John Tayloe II, 9 June 1754, Letterbook of Edmund Jenings, VHS, transcribed and quoted in Rasmussen, "Palladio in Tidewater Virginia," 77–78.

83. Quoted in Rasmussen, "Palladio in Tidewater Virginia," 90–91.

84. Quoted in ibid., 91.

85. Greene, *Diary of Colonel Landon Carter,* 1:362.

86. Carl R. Lounsbury, "'An Elegant and Commodious Building': William Buckland and the Design of the Prince William County Courthouse," *JSAH* 46 (1987): 228–40.

87. Luke Beckerdite, "William Buckland and William Bernard Sears: The Designer and the Carver," *Journal of Southern Decorative Arts* 8 (1982): 6–41; M. Bridget Maley, "'A Very Genteel Manner': Virginia Architecture and the Tayloe Family" (master's thesis, University of Virginia, 1993).

88. Peter Collinson to John Bartram, 17 February 1737, quoted in "Letters of John Clayton, John Bartram, Peter Collinson, William Byrd, Isham Randolph," *WMQ*, 2nd ser., 6 (1926): 304.

Chapter 6. Epistemologies of Female Space

A substantial portion of this chapter was presented in a paper entitled "Spike Marks and Props: The Theatrics of Architectural Gentility" on 8 October 2005 at the Creating an American Style, Art and Architecture, 1600–1900 Symposium at the University of Virginia, Charlottesville, Virginia.

1. William Byrd II to Charles Boyle, in Marion Tinling, ed., *The Correspondence of the Three William Byrds of Westover, Virginia, 1684–1776,* 2 vols. (Charlottesville: University Press of Virginia for the Virginia Historical Society, 1977), 1:355; Kenneth A. Lockridge, *On the Sources of Patriarchal Rage: The Commonplace Books of William Byrd and Thomas Jefferson and the Gendering of Power in the Eighteenth Century* (New York: New York University Press, 1992), 38–39.

2. Rhys Isaac, *The Transformation of Virginia, 1740–1790* (Chapel Hill: University of North Carolina Press, 1982).

3. Henri Lefebvre and Donald Nicholson-Smith, *The Production of Space* (Oxford: Basil Blackwell, 1991), 68–168; Donna Birdwell-Pheasant and Denise Lawrence-Zúñiga, "Introduction: Houses and Families in Europe," in *House Life: Space, Place and Family in Europe,* ed. Donna Birdwell-Pheasant and Denise Lawrence-Zúñiga (Oxford: Berg, 1999), 1–35.

4. Jane Duran, *Toward a Feminist Epistemology* (Savage, Md.: Rowman and Littlefield, 1991), 147–48, 185–200; *The Stanford Encyclopedia of Philosophy* (Stanford, Calif.: Metaphysics Research Lab, Center for the Study of Language and Information, Stanford University, 2007), s.v. "Feminist Epistemology and Philosophy of Science." http://plato.stanford.edu/entries/feminism-epistemology/.

5. Mark P. Leoni and Paul A. Schackel, "Plane and Solid Geometry in Colonial Gardens in Annapolis, Maryland," in *Earth Patterns: Essays in Landscape Archaeology,* ed. William M. Kelso and Rachel Most (Charlottesville: University Press of Virginia, 1990), 153.

6. Kathleen M. Brown, *Good Wives, Nasty Wenches, and Anxious Patriarchs: Gender, Race and Power in Colonial Virginia* (Chapel Hill: University of North Carolina Press, 1996), 283, 298–99.

7. Lisa Nevett, "Separation or Seclusion? Towards an Archaeological Approach to Investigating Women in the Greek Household in the Fifth to Third Centuries, BC," in *Architecture and Order: Approaches to Social Space,* ed. Michael Parker Pearson and Colin Richards (London: Routledge, 1994), 98–112; Alexander P. Kazhdan, "Women at Home," and Robert F. Taft, "Women at Church in Byzantium: Where, When—and Why?" in *Dumbarton Oaks Papers* 52 (1998), 1–17 and 27–87, respectively.

8. Ed Lilley, "The Name of the Boudoir," *JSAH* 53, no. 2 (1994): 193–98; Jill H. Casid, "Commerce in the Boudoir," in *Women, Art and the Politics of Identity in Eighteenth-Century Europe,* ed. Melissa Hyde and Jennifer Milam (Aldershot, United Kingdom: Ashgate, 2003), 91–114.

9. Jessica Kross, "Mansions, Men, Women, and the Creation of Multiple Publics in Eighteenth-Century British America," *Journal of Social History* 33, no. 2 (1999): 385–408.

10. Mark R. Wenger, "The Dining Room in Early Virginia," in *Perspectives in Vernacular Architecture 3,* ed. Thomas Carter and Bernard L. Herman (University of Missouri Press, 1989), 149–59; Dell Upton, "Vernacular Domestic Architecture in Eighteenth-Century Virginia," *Winterthur Portfolio* 17, nos. 2–3 (1982): 95–119.

11. Erasmus Jones, *The Man of Manners or Plebian Polished* (1737; repr., Sandy Hook, Conn.: Hendrickson Group, 1993), 8.

12. Philip Vickers Fithian, *Journal and Letters of Philip Vickers Fithian, 1773–1774: A Plantation Tutor of the Old Dominion* (Charlottesville: University Press of Virginia, 1957), 42.

13. Mark R. Wenger, "Gender and the Eighteenth-Century Meal," in *A Taste of the Past: Early Foodways of the Albemarle Region, 1585–1830,* ed. Barbara E. Taylor (Elizabeth City, N.C.: Museum of the Albemarle, 1991), 32.

14. See, for example, Elizabeth V. Chew, "'Repaired by me to my exceeding great Cost and Charges:' Anne Clifford and the Uses of Architecture," in *Gender and the Architecture of Politics in Early Modern Europe,* ed. Helen Hills (Aldershot, United Kingdom: Ashgate Press, 2003), 104–5.

15. Robert Neuman, "French Domestic Architecture in the Early Eighteenth Century: The Town House of Robert de Cotte," *JSAH* 39, no. 2 (May 1980): 130; Monique Eleb-Vidal and Anne Debarre-Blachard, *Architectures de la vie privée: Maisons et mentalités, XVIIe–XIXe siècles* (Brussels: Archives de l'Architecture Modern, 1989), 234–39.

16. Marion Nelson Winship, "Safety and Danger in a Puritan Home: Life in the Hull-Sewall House, 1676–1717," in *The American Home: Material Culture, Domestic Space, and Family Life,* ed. Eleanor McD. Thompson (Winterthur, Del.: Henry Francis du Pont Winterthur Museum, 1998), 257–71.

17. William Byrd II, *The Secret Diary of William Byrd of Westover, 1709–1712,* ed. Louis B. Wright and Marion Tinling (Richmond: Dietz Press, 1941), 20, 27, 210–11, 228–29, 242, 272, 275, 293.

18. Mrs. Maria Taylor Byrd to William Byrd III, 15 August 1760, in Tinling, *Correspondence of the Three William Byrds,* 2:701.

19. John C. Fitzpatrick, ed., *The Last Will and Testament of George Washington and His Schedule of Property to which is appended the Last Will and Testament of Martha Washington* (Mount Vernon, Va.: Mount Vernon Ladies' Association of the Union, 1939), 58; Fithian, *Journal,* 80, 127, 141, 152; Andrew Levy, *The First Emancipator: The Forgotten Story of Robert Carter, the Founding Father Who Freed His Slaves* (New York: Random House, 2005), 111.

20. Edward T. Hall, "A System for the Notation of Proxemic Behavior," *American Anthropologist* 65, no. 5 (October 1963): 1003–26; Edward T. Hall, *The Hidden Dimension* (Garden City, N.Y.: Doubleday, 1966), 85–105.

21. Fithian, *Journal,* 39; Carol Duncan, "Happy Mothers and Other New Ideas in Eighteenth-Century French Art," *Art Bulletin* 55 (December 1973): 570–83.

22. "The Recollections of John Mason," unabridged transcript by Terry Dunn, Gunston Hall Library, Lorton, Va., 12, 33–34, 39, 41. Room use is analyzed at length at: http://gustonhall.org/architecture/roomuse/public.html. For the Virginia study, see Jan Kirsten Gilliam and Betty Crowe Leviner, *Furnishing Williamsburg's Historic Buildings* (Williamsburg: CWF, 1991), 48–55.

23. Essex County Will Book 12, 1762–1775, 113–14, LVA; cf. K. L. Sandall, "The Unit System in Essex," *Archaeological Journal* 132 (1975): 195–201.

24. Robert F. Dalzell Jr. and Lee Badwin Dalzell, *George Washington's Mount Vernon: At Home in Revolutionary America* (Oxford: Oxford University Press, 1998), 16, 55, 69, 91.

25. Charles C. Wall et al., *Mount Vernon: A Handbook* (Mount Vernon: Mount Vernon Ladies' Association, 1985), 77.

26. Ibid., 71–74.

27. Ron Hurst, "Just Arrived," *Colonial Williamsburg* 27, no. 5 (2005): 10; Fitzpatrick, *Last Will and Testament,* 58.

28. Melissa Hyde, "The Makeup of the Marquise: Boucher's Portrait of Pompadour at the Toilette," *Art Bulletin* 82, no. 3 (September 2000): 453.

29. Cary Carson, "The Consumer Revolution in Colonial British America: Why Demand," in *Of Consuming Interests: The Style of Life in the Eighteenth Century,* ed. Cary Carson, Ronald Hoffman, and Peter J. Albert (Charlottesville: University Press of Virginia, 1994), 566.

30. Benno M. Forman, "Furniture for Dressing in Early America, 1650–1730: Forms, Nomenclature, and Use," *Winterthur Portfolio* 22, nos. 2–3 (Summer 1987): 149–64; Fithian, *Journal,* 128; Byrd, *Secret Diary,* 296.

31. Ronald L. Hurst and Jonathan Prown, *Southern Furniture, 1680–1830: The Colonial Williamsburg Collection* (Williamsburg: CWF, 1997), 280; Carson, "Consumer Revolution," 575, 579–80. For wig practices, see Karin Calvert, "The Fiction of Fashion in Eighteenth-Century America," in *Of Consuming Interests: The Style of Life in the Eighteenth Century,* ed. Cary Carson, Ronald Hoffman, and Peter J. Albert (Charlottesville: University Press of Virginia, 1994), 263–70.

32. Mimi Hellman, "Furniture, Sociability, and the Work of Leisure in Eighteenth-Century France," *Eighteenth-Century Studies* 32, no. 4 (1999): 415–45.

33. Byrd, *Secret Diary,* 324.

34. Alice T. Friedman, "Architecture, Authority, and the Female Gaze: Planning and Representation in the Early Modern Country House," *Assemblage* 18 (1992): 40–61; Mark Girouard, *Life in the English Country House* (New Haven: Yale University Press, 1978), 230; J. T. Smith, "The Evolution of the English Peasant House to the Late Seventeenth Century: The Evidence of Buildings," *Journal of the British Archaeological Association,* 3rd ser., 33 (1970): 137–38; Bruce Boucher, *Andrea Palladio: The Architect in His Time* (New York: Abbeville, 1998), 87, 90; Andrea Palladio, *The Four Books of Architecture* (London: Isaac Ware, 1738; repr., New York: Dover, 1965), 39.

35. Upton, "Vernacular Domestic Architecture," 95–119.

36. W. G. Hoskins, "An Elizabeth Provincial Town: Leicester," in *Studies in Social History: A Tribute to G. M. Trevelyan,* ed. J. H. Plumb (London: Longmans, Green, 1955), 57; Bernard L. Herman, *Town House: Architecture and Material Life in the Early American City, 1780–1830* (Chapel Hill: University of North Carolina Press, 2005), 40–42.

37. Byrd, *Secret Diary,* 43, 387, 576.

38. Ibid., 206; Fithian, *Journal,* 90.

39. Richard Beale Davis, *A Colonial Southern Bookshelf: Reading in the Eighteenth Century* (Athens: University of Georgia Press, 1979), 113–15; Ned C. Landsman, *From Colonials to Provincials: American Thought and Culture, 1680–1760* (Ithaca: Cornell University Press, 1997), 38–42; Richard Beale Davis, "Literary Tastes in Virginia before Poe," *WMQ,* 2nd ser., 19 (1939): 55–68; Robert Manson Myers, "The Old Dominion Looks to London: A Study of English Literary Influences upon the *Virginia Gazette* (1736–1766)," *VMHB* 54, no. 3 (1946): 187–217.

40. Fithian, *Journal*, 20, 37.

41. Davis, *Colonial Southern Bookshelf*, 119–24.

42. Robert Dodsley (attributed), *The Economy of Human Life* (Leominster, Mass.: Charles Prentiss, 1797), 48; William Bottorff and Roy Flannagan, eds., "The Diary of Frances Baylor Hill of 'Hillsborough,' King and Queen County, Virginia, 1797," *Early American Literature* 2, no. 3 (1967): 14, 45–48; Fanny Burney, *Evelina*, ed. Kristina Straub (Boston: Bedford Books, 1997), 82, 103, 113, 135; Catherine Kerrison, "The Novel As Teacher: Learning to Be Female in the Early American South," *Journal of Southern History* 69, no. 3 (2003): 513–48.

43. Timothy Clayton, *The English Print, 1688–1802* (New Haven: Yale University Press, 1997), 122.

44. *An Inventory of the Contents of the Governor's Palace Taken after the Death of Lord Botetourt* (Williamsburg: CWF, 1981), 18; Fithian, *Journal*, 83.

45. Richmond County Wills and Inventory Book (1725–53), transcription in M. Bridget Maley, "'A Very Genteel Manner': Virginia Architecture and the Tayloe Family" (master's thesis, University of Virginia, 1993), 123.

46. Byrd, *Secret Diary*, 324.

47. The social function of portraiture is addressed in Margaretta M. Lovell, "Painters and Their Customers: Aspects of Art and Money in Eighteenth-Century America," in *Of Consuming Interests: The Style of Life in the Eighteenth Century*, ed. Cary Carson, Ronald Hoffman, and Peter J. Albert (Charlottesville: University Press of Virginia, 1994), 300.

48. Fithian, *Journal*, 95; Joan Dolmetsch, "Prints in Colonial America: Supply and Demand in the Mid-Eighteenth Century," in *Prints in and of America to 1850*, ed. John D. Morse (Charlottesville: University Press of Virginia, 1970), 53–74.

49. Ivor Noël Hume, "Custis Square," *Colonial Williamsburg* 16, no. 4 (Summer 1994): 15.

50. Clayton, *English Print*, 130–46.

51. Graham Hood, "The Role of the British Eighteenth-Century Print at Williamsburg: Introductory Remarks," in *Eighteenth-Century Prints in Colonial America*, ed. Joan D. Dolmetsch (Williamsburg: CWF, 1979), 1–10.

52. See *Spectator*, no. 41 (17 April 1711), in the *Spectator*, ed. Donald F. Bond, 5 vols. (Oxford: Oxford University Press, 1965), 1:173–77.

53. Roy Moxham, *Tea: Addiction, Exploitation and Empire* (London: Constable, 2003), 16–19; Denys Forrest, *Tea for the British: The Social and Economic History of a Famous Trade* (London: Chatto and Windus, 1973), 21–31.

54. Julie B. Curtis, "Chinese Export Porcelain in Eighteenth-Century Tidewater Virginia," *Studies in Eighteenth-Century Culture* 17 (1987): 121.

55. Ann Smart Martin, "Commercial Space as Consumption Arena: Retail Stores in Early Virginia," in *Perspectives in Vernacular Architecture 7*, ed. Sally McMurry and AnnMarie Adams (Knoxville: University of Tennessee Press, 2000), 202.

56. Rodris Roth, "Tea Drinking in Eighteenth-Century America: Its Etiquette and Equipage," in *Material Life in America, 1600–1860*, ed. Robert Blair St. George (Boston: Northeastern University Press, 1988), 439–62; Beth Kowaleski-Wallace, "Women, China, and Consumer Culture in Eighteenth-Century England," *Eighteenth-Century Studies* 29 (1995–96): 152–67.

57. Barbara Carson, *Ambitious Appetites: Dining, Behavior, and Patterns of Consumption in Federal Washington* (Washington, D.C.: American Institute of Architects, 1990), 27–29; Carson, "Consumer Revolution," 504–5, 546.

58. Joan Sayers Brown, "Silver Associated with George Mason IV at Gunston Hall," *Antiques* 118, no. 2 (August 1980): 285–89.

59. Sarah Richards, *Eighteenth-Century Ceramics: Products for a Civilised Society* (Manchester: Manchester University Press, 1999), 99–104, 131–42.

60. *Spectator,* 3:367.

61. Carl Van Doren, ed., *The Letters of Benjamin Franklin and Jane Mecom* (Princeton: Princeton University Press, 1950), 35.

62. Mary Beth Norton, *Liberty's Daughters: The Revolutionary Experience of American Women, 1750–1800* (Boston: Little, Brown, 1980), 157, 159; *Virginia Gazette* (Purdie and Dixon), 6 November 1774.

63. Forrest, *Tea for the British,* 52; Brown, *Good Wives,* 283–87.

64. David S. Shields, *Civil Tongues and Polite Letters in British America* (Chapel Hill: University of North Carolina Press, 1997), 99–126; Beth Kowaleski-Wallace, "Tea, Gender, and Domesticity in Eighteenth-Century England," *Studies in Eighteenth-Century Culture* 23 (1994): 131–45; Elizabeth Kowaleski-Wallace, *Consuming Subjects: Women, Shopping, and Business in the Eighteenth Century* (New York: Columbia University Press, 1997), 32–36.

65. Hurst and Prown, *Southern Furniture,* 300. Average dimensions are: 28 inches high, 31½ inches wide, and 21 inches deep. Wallace B. Gusler, "The Tea Tables of Eastern Virginia," *Antiques* 135 (May 1989): 1238–57.

66. Linda Baumgarten, John Watson, and Florine Carr, *Costume Close-Up: Clothing Construction and Pattern, 1750–1790* (Williamsburg: CWF, 2000), 29–30; Linda Baumgarten, *What Clothes Reveal: The Language of Clothing in Colonial and Federal America* (Williamsburg: CWF, 2002), 64.

67. The author wishes to thank Brenda Rosseau, costume curator at Colonial Williamsburg, who on 5 May 2005 patiently measured the dimensions of a mid-1770s reconstructed gown that would have been appropriate for tea.

68. Fithian, *Journal,* 124–25.

69. Linda Baumgarten, *Eighteenth-Century Clothing at Williamsburg* (Williamsburg: CWF, 1986), 18, 20.

70. Hurst and Prown, *Southern Furniture,* 313. Averages are based on examples in Gusler, "Tea Tables of Eastern Virginia," 1245–57. For a more detailed description of the origins and evolution of tea tables of various design, see Ann Smart Martin, "Tea Tables Overturned: Rituals of Power and Place in Colonial America," in *Furnishing the Eighteenth Century: What Furniture Can Tell Us about the European and American Past,* ed. Dena Goodman and Kathryn Norberg (New York and London: Routledge, Taylor and Francis Group, 2007), 169–81.

71. Stephenson B. Andrews, ed., *Bacon's Castle* (Richmond: APVA, 1984), 17.

72. Christopher Rowell, "Tour of the House," in *Ham House, Surry* (London: National Trust, 1995), 35–37.

73. Byrd, *Secret Diary,* 246.

74. Ibid., 15, 74.

75. Fithian, *Journal,* 61, 74, 80, 92, 110, 117.

76. Ibid., 48.

77. Gilliam and Leviner, *Furnishing Williamsburg's Historic Buildings,* 74; Katherine E. Harbury, *Colonial Virginia's Cooking Dynasty* (Columbia: University of South Carolina Press, 2004), 42; Jane Carson, "Plantation Housekeeping in Colonial Virginia," research report, 1974, CWF, 4–12.

78. Carson, "Consumer Revolution," 506.

79. Gregory A. Stiverson and Patrick H. Butler III, eds., "Virginia in 1732: The Travel Journal of William Hugh Grove," *VMHB* 85 (1977): 29.

80. Sidney Wilfred Mintz, *Tasting Food, Tasting Freedom: Excursions into Eating, Culture, and the Past* (Boston: Beacon Press, 1996), 46–47; Anne Elizabeth Yentsch, *A Chesapeake Family and Their Slaves: A Study in Historical Archaeology* (Cambridge: Cambridge University Press, 1994), 149–56, 160–61; Karen Hess, *The Carolina Rice Kitchen: The African Connection* (Columbia: University of South Carolina Press, 1992), 5; Carson, *Ambitious Appetites,* 111–16; J. Jean Hecht, "Continental and Colonial Servants in Eighteenth-Century England," *Smith College Studies in History* 40 (1954): 1–6; Harbury, *Colonial Virginia's Cooking Dynasty,* 58–59.

81. Fithian, *Journal,* 32.

82. Samuel Pepys quoted in Lorna Weatherell, *Consumer Behavior and Material Culture in Britain 1660–1760,* 2nd ed. (London: Routledge, 1996), 139.

83. Bottorff and Flannagan, "Diary of Frances Baylor Hill," 50.

84. Mrs. Maria Taylor Byrd to William Byrd III, 6 November 1757, in Tinling, *Correspondence of the Three William Byrds,* 2:632.

85. Catherine Clinton, *The Plantation Mistress: Woman's World in the Old South* (New York: Pantheon Books, 1982), 26–28.

86. Mary Randolph, *The Virginia House Wife* (1824; repr., Baltimore: Plaskitt and Cugle, 1828), ix–xii.

87. Web site for African American experience at Stratford: http://www.stratfordhall .org/africa.html; Hannah Glasse, *The Art of Cookery* (1747; Alexandria, Va.: Cottom and Steward, 1805), n.p.; Isaac Jefferson, "Memoirs of a Monticello Slave," in *Jefferson and Monticello,* ed. James A. Bear (Charlottesville: University Press of Virginia, 1967), 3.

88. Jeanne A. Calhoun, "The African American Experience at Stratford: 1782," Robert E. Lee Memorial Association, 2002.

89. Philip D. Morgan, *Slave Counterpoint: Black Culture in the Eighteenth-Century Chesapeake and Low Country* (Chapel Hill: University of North Carolina Press for the Omohundro Institute of Early American Culture, 1998), 244; Carson, *Ambitious Appetites,* 94; Washington inventory from Gunston Hall probate inventory database.

90. Lucia C. Stanton, *Free Some Day: The African-American Families of Monticello* (Charlottesville: Thomas Jefferson Foundation, 2000), 125–31; Lucia C. Stanton, *Slavery at Monticello* (Charlottesville: Thomas Jefferson Foundation, 2002), 31, 35–36.

91. Hannah to Thomas Jefferson, 15 November 1818, Massachusetts Historical Society. The author is indebted to Barbara J. Heath, archaeologist at Poplar Forest, for kindly providing a transcription of Hannah's letter. For slave literacy, see also Barbara J. Heath, *Hidden Lives: The Archaeology of Slave Life at Thomas Jefferson's Poplar Forest* (Charlottesville: University Press of Virginia, 1999), 55.

92. Andrew Nunn McKnight, "Lydia Broadnax, Slave and Free Woman of Color," *Southern Studies* 5, nos. 1–2 (1994): 18, 23, 26.

93. Carole Shammas, "Black Women's Work and the Evolution of Plantation Society in Virginia," *Labor History* 26, no. 1 (1985): 5–28.

94. "Carter Papers," *VMHB* 6 (1899): 367–68; Allan Kulikoff, *Tobacco and Slaves: The Development of Southern Cultures in the Chesapeake, 1680–1800* (Chapel Hill: University of North Carolina Press, 1986), 276.

95. Oliver Millar, *Sir Peter Lely, 1618–80* (London: National Portrait Gallery, 1978), 47–48; Paul H. D. Kaplan, "Titian's 'Laura Dianti' and the Origins of the Motif of the Black Page in Portraiture," *Antichità Viva* 21, no 1 (1982): 11–18; 21, no. 4 (July–August 1982): 10–18; Hecht, "Continental and Colonial Servants," 33, 36.

96. Marley R. Brown III and Joanne Bowen, "An Archaeological Perspective on the Material Life of Williamsburg's Artisan Community," in *Common People and Their Material World: Free Men and Women in the Chesapeake, 1700–1830,* ed. David Harvey and Gregory Brown (Williamsburg: CWF, 1995), 55–59.

97. Fithian, *Journal,* 38, 199.

98. Durand de Dauphiné, *A Huguenot Exile in Virginia,* trans. Gilbert Chinard (New York: Press of the Pioneers, 1934), 119–20.

99. Nicholas Cooper, *Houses of the Gentry: 1480–1680* (New Haven: Yale University Press, 1999), 307–8.

100. Thomas Tileston Waterman and John Barrows, *Domestic Colonial Architecture of Tidewater Virginia* (1932; repr., New York: Dover, 1969), 104–5.

101. The walking distance was estimated by Steven Bashore. Steven Bashore, Stratford Hall Plantation, personal communication, 18 June 2004; Stratford Hall site plan, sheet no. 27, 1969, HABS.

102. Bottorff and Flannagan, "Diary of Frances Baylor Hill," 51.

103. Fithian, *Journal,* 81.

104. Mary Miley Theobald, "Repainting the Town," *Colonial Williamsburg* 16, no. 4 (Summer 1994): 53.

105. Norton, *Liberty's Daughters,* 28.

106. Fithian, *Journal,* 67.

107. John Harrower, *The Journal of John Harrower: An Indentured Servant in the Colony of Virginia, 1773–1776,* ed. Edward M. Riley (Williamsburg: distributed by Holt, Rinehart and Winston, 1963), xviii, 42, 155.

108. Peter Martin, *Pleasure Gardens of Virginia: From Jamestown to Jefferson* (Princeton: Princeton University Press, 1991), 100–133.

109. Harrower, *Journal,* 46; Fithian, *Journal,* 74–75, 123, 125, 145, 150, 178, 189, 193.

110. Fithian, *Journal,* 32, 44, 45, 63.

111. Carmen A. Weber et al., "Mount Claire," in *Earth Patterns: Essays in Landscape Archaeology,* ed. William M. Kelso and Rachel Most (Charlottesville: University Press of Virginia, 1999), 137, 144–45. For John Randolph's interest and work in gardening, see Marley R. Brown and Patricia M. Samford, "Recent Evidence of Eighteenth-Century Gardening in Williamsburg, Virginia," in *Earth Patterns: Essays in Landscape Archaeology,* ed. William M. Kelso and Rachel Most (Charlottesville: University Press of Virginia, 1999), 104, 117–18.

112. Barbara A. Hanawalt, "Medieval English Women in Rural and Urban Domestic Space," *Dumbarton Oaks Papers* 52 (1998): 19–26.

113. Shields, *Civil Tongues,* 109–11; Byrd, *Secret Diary,* 9, 22.

114. Bottorff and Flannagan, "Diary of Frances Baylor Hill," 31–33.

Chapter 7. Political Power and the Limits of Genteel Architecture

1. For political offices, see Appendix, Sources of Study Group Data.

2. Dell Upton, *Holy Things and Profane: Anglican Parish Churches in Colonial Virginia* (New York: Architectural History Foundation, 1986), 6–7.

3. Don Higginbotham, "Military Leadership in the American Revolution," in

Leadership in the American Revolution, Library of Congress Symposium on the American Revolution (Washington, D.C.: Library of Congress, 1974), 96.

4. Col. John Thornton to Governor Dinwiddie, 29 October 1757, quoted in Merrow E. Sorley, comp., *Lewis of Warner Hall: The History of a Family* (Columbia, Mo.: E. W. Stephens, 1937), 137.

5. Charles Campbell, ed., *The Bland Papers: Being a Selection from the Manuscripts of Colonel Theodorick Bland, Jr. of Prince George County, Virginia,* 2 vols. (Petersburg: Edmund and Julian C. Ruffin, 1840), 2:62–63.

6. For a more detailed explanation of the duties and authority of the vestry, see John K. Nelson, *A Blessed Company: Parishes, Parsons, and Parishioners in Anglican Virginia, 1690–1776* (Chapel Hill: University of North Carolina Press, 2001), 13–84.

7. The scope of the vestry's powers is examined in greater detail in Upton, *Holy Things and Profane,* 6–10.

8. The role of the vestry is discussed in William H. Seiler, "The Anglican Church: A Basic Institution of Local Government in Colonial Virginia," in *Town and County: Essays on the Structure of Local Government in the American Colonies,* ed. Bruce C. Daniels (Middletown, Conn.: Wesleyan University Press, 1978), 134–59.

9. A. G. Roeber, *Faithful Magistrates and Republican Lawyers: Creators of Virginia Legal Culture, 1680–1810* (Chapel Hill: University of North Carolina Press, 1981), 41–46; Robert Wheeler, "The County Court in Colonial Virginia," in *Town and County: Essays on the Structure of Local Government in the American Colonies,* ed. Bruce C. Daniels (Middletown, Conn.: Wesleyan University Press, 1978), 111–33; Carl R. Lounsbury, *The Courthouses of Early Virginia: An Architectural History* (Charlottesville: University of Virginia Press, 2005), 16–28.

10. John G. Kolp, "The Dynamics of Electoral Competition in Pre-Revolutionary Virginia," *WMQ,* 3rd ser., 49 (1992): 652–74.

11. Roeber, *Faithful Magistrates,* 42; William G. Stanard and Mary N. Stanard, *The Colonial Virginia Register* (Albany, 1902; repr., Baltimore: Genealogical Publishing Co., 1965), 9.

12. John C. Rainbolt, "The Alteration in the Relationship between Leadership and Constituents in Virginia, 1660–1720," *WMQ,* 3rd ser., 27 (1970): 411–34; Carter L. Hudgins, "Patrician Culture, Public Ritual, and Political Authority in Virginia, 1680–1740" (Ph.D. diss., College of William and Mary, 1984), 101–2, 115–18, 130–31.

13. Jack P. Greene, ed., *The Diary of Colonel Landon Carter of Sabine Hall, 1752–1779,* 2 vols. (Charlottesville: University Press of Virginia for the Virginia Historical Society, 1965), 2:1008.

14. Campbell, *Bland Papers,* 1:27.

15. William Fairfax (Belvoir); John Carlyle (Carlyle House); and John Mercer (Marlborough).

16. The father of John Banister III (Battersea) was not elected to the House of Burgesses, but served as customs collector of the Upper James River Naval District.

17. William Fairfax (Belvoir) was an immigrant, but his record of office holding undoubtedly was affected by the stature of his uncle Thomas, Lord Fairfax, the proprietor of the Northern Neck. The father of Richard Corbin (Laneville) was not a councilor, but both Corbin's father-in-law and brother-in-law did serve on the Council.

18. Carter Burwell (Carter's Grove); William Fitzhugh (Chatham); Robert Carter I (Corotoman); George Mason IV (Gunston Hall); Thomas Jefferson (Monticello I); John Tayloe II (Mount Airy); Mann Page I (Rosewell); Thomas Lee (Stratford Hall); and John Randolph II (Tazewell Hall).

19. John Banister III (Battersea); Benjamin Harrison IV (Berkeley); Robert Beverley (Blandfield); Richard Henry Lee (Chantilly); Charles Carter (Cleve); Lewis Burwell III (Kingsmill); Mann Page II (Mannsfield); Landon Carter (Sabine Hall); and William Randolph III (Wilton).

20. William Byrd II, *The Secret Diary of William Byrd of Westover, 1709–1712,* ed. Louis B. Wright and Marion Tinling (Richmond: Dietz Press, 1941), 159.

21. John Banister III (Battersea); John Carlyle (Carlyle House); Richard Henry Lee (Chantilly); William Fitzhugh (Chatham); George Mason IV (Gunston Hall); Mann Page II (Mannsfield); John Mercer (Marlborough); Thomas Jefferson (Monticello I); John Tayloe II (Mount Airy); and Landon Carter (Sabine Hall).

22. Robert Beverley (Blandfield); Richard Corbin (Laneville); and John Randolph II (Tazewell Hall). The division made here between Patriots and Loyalists is of course oversimplified. Men expressed various degrees of political passion in regard to the issue of separation from Great Britain. Nevertheless, they have been judged by their actions, not whether they acted out of expedience or conviction.

23. The apolitical character of high-style architecture may not hold true for other colonies. See Kevin M. Sweeney, "Mansion People: Kinship, Class, and Architecture in Western Massachusetts in the Mid-Eighteenth Century," *Winterthur Portfolio* 19 (Winter 1984): 250–52.

24. Patricia Waddy, *Seventeenth-Century Roman Palaces: Use and the Art of the Plan,* (New York: Architectural History Foundation, 1990), 3–13.

25. Upton, *Holy Things and Profane,* 206–9.

26. John S. Bassett, ed., *The Writings of Colonel William Byrd of Westover in Virginia Esqr.* (1901; repr., New York: Burt Franklin, 1970), 356.

27. Eugene D. Genovese, *Roll, Jordan, Roll: The World the Slaves Made* (New York; Vintage Books, 1976), 587–637; Shane White and Graham White, *Stylin': African American Expressive Culture from Its Beginnings to the Zoot Suit* (Ithaca: Cornell University Press, 1998), 5–62; William D. Piersen, "A Resistance Too Civilized to Notice," in *Signifyin(g), Sanctifin' & Slam Dunking: A Reader in African American Expressive Culture,* ed. Gena Dagel Caponi (Amherst: University of Massachusetts, 1999), 348–70.

28. Byrd, *Secret Diary*, 15, 46, 112–13, 197–202, 254, 257.

29. Philip Vickers Fithian, *Journal and Letters of Philip Vickers Fithian: A Plantation Tutor of the Old Dominion, 1773–1774,* ed. Hunter D. Farish (Charlottesville: University Press of Virginia, 1957), 161.

30. Byrd, *Secret Diary,* 436.

31. Marion Tinling, ed., *The Correspondence of the Three William Byrds of Westover, Virginia, 1684–1776,* 2 vols. (Charlottesville: University Press of Virginia for the Virginia Historical Society, 1977), 2:464–65.

32. *Calendar of Virginia State Papers and Other Manuscripts, 1652–1781, Preserved in the Capitol at Richmond,* 11 vols. (Richmond: R. F. Walker, Superintendent of Public Printing, 1875–93), 1:173.

33. Stephen Saunders Webb, *The Governor's-General* (Chapel Hill: University of North Carolina Press, 1979), 512–13.

34. Jack P. Greene, "The Opposition to Lieutenant Governor Alexander Spotswood, 1718," *VMHB* 70 (1962): 36; Roeber, *Faithful Magistrates,* 64–71; Robert P. Thomson, "The Merchant in Virginia, 1700–1775" (Ph.D. diss., University of Wisconsin, 1955), 98–101, 108.

35. James D. Kornwolf, *"So Good a Design": The Colonial Campus of the College of William and Mary: Its History, Background, and Legacy* (Williamsburg: College of William and Mary, 1989), 44; Hugh Jones, *The Present State of Virginia, From Whence Is Inferred a Short View of Maryland and North Carolina,* ed. Richard L. Morton (Chapel Hill: University of North Carolina Press for the Virginia Historical Society, 1956), 26; Harold Burton Meyers, "Hugh Jones and the Wren Building," *Colonial Williamsburg* 17, no. 2 (Winter 1994–95): 25–31.

36. Carl Lounsbury, "Bruton Parish Church," in *The Early Architecture of Tidewater Virginia,* ed. Carl Lounsbury (Williamsburg: CWF, 2002), 5–6.

37. W. A. R. Goodwin, *Historical Sketch of Bruton Church, Williamsburg, Virginia* (Petersburg: Franklin Press, 1903), 33.

38. *JHB,* 5:38–39.

39. *Calendar of Virginia State Papers,* 1:174–75; Goodwin, *Historical Sketch of Bruton Church,* 35.

40. *JHB,* 6:19.

41. [Robert Beverley], *The History of Virginia in Four Parts,* 2nd ed. (London: Printed for B. and S. Tooke, 1722), 250.

42. Harold B. Gill Jr., "Building the Capitoll [*sic*]," *Colonial Williamsburg* 20, no. 4 (Summer 1998): 52–56.

43. Peter Martin, *The Pleasure Gardens of Virginia: From Jamestown to Jefferson* (Princeton: Princeton University Press, 1991), 42–53.

44. Byrd, *Secret Diary,* 429, 440, 444; Geoffrey Parnell, "The King's Guard Chamber," *Apollo* 140 (August 1994): 60–64.

45. Martin, *Pleasure Gardens of Virginia,* 37–39.

46. *JHB,* 5:203, 205.

47. Ibid., 5:206.

48. Ibid., 5:284; 6:39.

49. Ibid., 5:290, 296–97.

50. John Fontaine, "Journal of John Fontaine," in *Memoirs of a Huguenot Family,* trans. Ann Maury (New York: Putnam, 1872), 245–310; Ian Marshall, "Landscape Aesthetics and Literary History: The Knights of the Golden Horseshoe in Journal, Poem, and Story," *Mississippi Quarterly* 44 (1990–91): 71.

51. William Byrd, *The London Diary, 1717–1721, and Other Writings,* ed. Louis B. Wright and Marion Tinling (New York: Oxford University Press, 1958), 475, 479.

52. *Dictionary of American Biography,* 21 vols. (New York: Charles Scribner's Sons, 1928–37), s.v. "Jones, Hugh"; Robert A. Brock, *Official Letters of Alexander Spotswood, Lieutenant-Governor of the Colony of Virginia, 1710–1722,* 2 vols. (Richmond: Virginia Historical Society, 1882), 2:253; *JHB,* 5:175, 221, 251; Kornwolf, *"So Good a Design,"* 70 n. 28; Lyon G. Tyler, "Education in Colonial Virginia," *WMQ,* 1st ser., 6 (1897–98): 85.

53. *Calendar of Virginia State Papers,* 1:198; *EJC,* 3:540; Louis Des Cognets Jr., comp., *English Duplicates of Lost Virginia Records* (Princeton: privately printed, 1958), 114.

54. William S. Perry, ed., *Historical Collections Relating to the American Colonial Church,* 5 vols. (Hartford, Conn.: Church Press Co., 1870–78; repr., New York: AMS Press, 1969), 1:249; Byrd, *London Diary,* 479–80, 511.

55. Louis B. Wright, ed., *Letters of Robert Carter, 1720–1727, The Commercial Interests of a Virginia Gentleman* (San Marino, Calif.: Huntington Library, 1940), 89–91; Byrd, *London Diary,* 509.

56. Brock, *Official Letters of Alexander Spotswood,* 2:351.

57. Jones, *Present State of Virginia,* 91.

58. Enchanted Castle Projected Plan, 1984, VDHR; Kerri Saige Barile, "Archaeology, Architecture, and Alexander Spotswood: Redefining the Georgian Worldview at the Enchanted Castle, Germanna, Orange County Virginia" (Ph.D. diss., University of Texas, Austin, 2004), 252–63.

59. Carter L. Hudgins to author, 31 January 1991; Keith Egloff, "Spotswood's Enchanted Castle, 44OR3, Orange County,"1977, 1, 5, VDHR; Douglas W. Sanford, "The Enchanted Castle in Context: Archaeological Research at Germanna, Orange County, Virginia," *Quarterly Bulletin of the Archaeological Society of Virginia* 44 (1989): 102.

60. William W. Hening, ed., *The Statutes at Large, Being a Collection of All the Laws of Virginia,* 13 vols. (1819–23; repr., Charlottesville: University Press of Virginia for the Jamestown Foundation of the Commonwealth of Virginia, 1969), 4:77–79.

61. Bassett, *Writings of Colonel William Byrd,* 356.

62. *Virginia Gazette* (Parks), 29 October 1736.

63. Douglas Sanford, "The Gardens at Germanna, Virginia," in *Earth Patterns: Essays in Landscape Archaeology,* ed. William M. Kelso and Rachel Most (Charlottesville: University Press of Virginia, 1999): 53–56.

64. Spotswood Inventory, Orange County Will Book 1, 181–85, transcription in Barile, "Archaeology, Architecture, and Alexander Spotswood," 307–15.

65. "William and Mary College: Recently Discovered Documents," *WMQ,* 2nd ser., 10 (1930): 246–50.

66. W. W. Scott, *A History of Orange County, Virginia,* (Richmond: Everett Waddey Co., 1907), 80–83; Lester J. Cappon, *Iron Works at Tuball: Terms and Conditions for Their Lease as Stated by Alexander Spotswood on the Twentieth Day of July 1739* (Charlottesville: University of Virginia, 1945), 12.

67. Hening, *Statutes at Large,* 4:364–65; E. Lee Shepard, "'The Ease and Convenience of the People': Courthouse Location in Spotsylvania County, 1720–1740," *VMHB* 87 (1979): 83–84.

68. Merrill D. Peterson, ed., *The Portable Thomas Jefferson* (New York: Penguin, 1979), 203.

69. Fred Shelley, ed., "The Journal of Ebenezer Hazard in Virginia, 1777," *VMHB* 62 (1954): 407

70. "Williamsburg's Second Capitol," *Colonial Williamsburg* 10, no. 1 (Autumn 1987): 12.

71. Giles Worsley, *Classical Architecture in Britain: The Heroic Age* (New Haven: Yale University Press, 1995), 1–43.

72. See, for example, book 4, chapter 4, in Andrea Palladio, *The Four Books of Architecture* (London: Isaac Ware, 1738; repr., New York: Dover, 1965), 83.

73. Advertisement reprinted in Peterson, *Portable Thomas Jefferson,* 25. Douglas L. Wilson, "The Evolution of Jefferson's *Notes of the State of Virginia,*" *VMHB* 112, no. 2 (2004): 99–133.

74. Peterson, *Portable Thomas Jefferson,* 103.

75. John W. Reps, *The Making of Urban America: A History of City Planning in the United States* (Princeton: Princeton University Press, 1965), 314–21; John W. Reps, "Thomas Jefferson's Checkerboard Towns," *JSAH* 20, no. 3 (October 1961): 108–14.

76. Robert M. Owens, "William Harrison's Indiana: Paternalism and Patriotism on the Frontier, 1795–1812" (Ph.D. diss., University of Illinois, Urbana-Champaign,

2003), 199–212; John D. Barnhart, "Southern Contributions to the Social Order of the Old Northwest," *North Carolina Historical Review* 17 (1940): 247.

77. Harold R. Shurtleff, *The Log Cabin Myth* (1939; repr., Gloucester, Mass.: Peter Smith, 1967), 186–208.

Conclusion

1. William Bainter O'Neal, *Jefferson's Fine Arts Library: His Selections for the University of Virginia Together with His Own Architectural Books* (Charlottesville: University Press of Virginia, 1976), 22–24.

2. Leon Battista Alberti, *The Ten Books of Architecture, The 1755 Leoni Edition* (New York: Dover, 1986), 113.

Index

Beckford, Peter, 115, 270

bedchambers, 229, 230–32, 234, 236–38,
240–41, 247, 249

Beecher, Catherine, 259

Belvoir (Fairfax County), 15*t*, 66, 203,
294–95; plan of, *67*

Bennett, J. A., 189

Berkeley, Sally, 131

Berkeley (Charles City County), 15*t*, 87,
87; brickwork at, 26; commemorative stone at, *140;* data sources about,
295–96; dressing tables at, 240; ownership of, 129, 137–38; plan of, *65*, 89; size
of, 105; style of, 55

Bermingham, Ann, 190

Bess of Hardwick, 67, 119, 240

Beverley, Robert (1673–1722), 9–10, 78,
274

Beverley, Robert (patron of Blandfield),
48, 50, 55, 68, 165, 186, 220–21; ancestry
of, 83*t*, 84; business interests of, 109;
data sources about, 296; education of,
97, 99*t*, 202; income sources of, 106*t*;
inheritance of, 86*t*, 103, 104*t*; involve-
ment in building process by, 35, 74;
marriage of, 91*t*, 92; political ideology
of, 268, 346n22; political offices held
by, 261, 263*t*, 346n19; progeny of, 93*t*;
property valuation of, 113*t*; travels of,
334n34; vital statistics of, 88*t*. *See also*
Blandfield

Beverley, William, 11, 84, 97, 202–3, 206,
207

birth order of patrons, 85

Bishir, Catherine W., 194

Blackhouse, John, 165

Blackstone, William, 121

Blair, James, 273

Blair, John, 95, 153, 157, 194

Blanchard, Joshua, 66

Bland, Richard, 152, 171, 179

Bland, Theodorick, Sr., 265

Blandfield (Essex County), 15*t*, *36, 221;*
brickwork at, 48, *50;* data sources about,
296; fenestration at, 35; outbuildings of,
74; plan of, 68, *69;* size of, 103; style of,
55, 213; wallpaper at, 220–21

Blenheim Palace (Oxfordshire, England),
198

Blickling Hall (Norfolk, England), 51, *54*

Blondel, Jacques-François, 73

Bollett, A., *The Old Virginia Capitol, 281*

Bolling, Robert, 122–23

Book of Architecture, A (Gibbs), 40, *44,*
208–9, 213, *214*

Book of the Courtier, The (Castiglione), 190

Booth, Richard B., 189, 191

Boston City Hall, crown glass windows
in, 36–37

Botetourt, Baron de, 242

Boucher, François, 243

Boudet, Dominic W., portraits by, *163, 233*

boudoir, 228, 230, 231

Bourdieu, Pierre, 278

Bowles, Carrington, 191; *Charles Concluding a Treaty of Marriage . . . , 123*

Boyd, Benjamin, 165–66

Boyle, Charles (4th Earl of Orrery), 225

brackets, scrolled, 43

Brafferton building (Williamsburg), 19,
21, 55, 66; plan of, *65*

Brayne, Anne Butler. *See* Thompson, Anne
Butler Brayne Spotswood

breastfeeding practices, 234

Breen, T. H., 196

Bremo Recess (Fluvanna County), 58

Brent, James, 162, 222

Brent, John, 164

Brewer, John, 165

breweries, 110, 196

bricklayers, 23, 26, 149, 154, 165, 167, 291

brick makers and brick making, 21–23,
165, 291

brick vernacular buildings, 13–16

brickwork: bonding types, 23–26; brick
types, 23; glazed (vitrified), 23, 26, *28,*
50; molded, 48, *53,* 58; mortar, 164;
rubbed and gauged, 50, *53;* as status
symbol, 21; for water tables and stringcourses, 48, 50

Bridges, Charles, portraits by/attributed
to, *101, 135, 195, 272*

bridges, 174, *175, 176*

British Architect, The (Swan), 215

broad sheet glass, 36

Bromley, William, 156, 181

Brooke, Sarah Taliaferro, 26, 50, 261,
263*t*, 268, 322n79; ancestry of, 83*t*; data
sources about, 296; education of, 99*t*;
house built by, 119, 234, 236; income
sources of, 106*t*; inheritance of, 86*t*,
104*t*, 326n38; marriage of, 91*t*; progeny

Harrison, Benjamin, V, 38

Harrison, Carter Henry, 129, 138

Harrison, Peter, 45

Harrison, William Henry, 271, 283–84, *284*, 286, 288. *See also* William Henry Harrison House

Harrower, John, 167, 254, 256

Hayward, Nicholas, 149

Hazard, Ebenezer, 30, 280

Hellman, Mimi, 240

Hemings, James, 251

Hendryx, Mrs., drawing by, *287*

Henry VIII, king of England, 2

heraldic devices, 84

Herbert, Philip (Earl of Pembroke), 144

Hesselius, John, portraits by, *150, 160, 168*

Hill, Frances Baylor, 187, 191, 242, 249–50, 253, 258

Hillsborough (King and Queen County), 30, *31*, 191, 249–50, 253

Hinch, Gregory, 154, 156

Historic St. Mary's City, Maryland, 12; hole-set dwelling reconstruction at, *13*

History of Virginia in Four Parts, The (Beverley), 9–10, 274

Hogarth, William, 131–32, 243; illustrations by, *132, 243*

hole-set buildings, 12–13, *13*, 15, 29, 173

Holmes, Lucy, 254

Hoppus, Edward, 157, 209

hôtels particulier, 73, 230

housekeepers, 254

Hudson, Thomas, 79, 219; portrait by, *80*

indentured servants: as mine workers, 269, 276, 279; resistance of, 269–70; as skilled laborers, 149, 154, 156, 157, 159–60, 162, 165, 168, 170, 211–12, 217, 222, 257

inheritance of patrons, 85–87, 90, 103–5, 267; dowries and, 118–19, 121–22, 124–25, 291

Inns of Court, London, 98, 320n44

insecurity of patrons, 6, 10, 84, 100, 102, 114, 115–16, 270–71, 292

intercolumniation, 280, 282

inventories, 112–14, 227–28, 240, 247, 249, 278

Isaac, Rhys, 114

Isaac Royale House (Medford, Massachusetts), 32, *33*

Italian Renaissance architecture and plans, 2, 11, 59, 66, 67, 183–84

Ivory, Thomas, remodeling by, *54*

jack arches, 50

Jacob Faulcon House (Surry County), 14, *14*, 232, 234; bedchamber of, *235*

James, John, 66

James City County courthouse, 23, 192

James I, king of England, 2

Jamestown townhouses, brickwork for, 23, 26

Jaquelin, Martha, 183, *184,* 185, 191

Jefferson, Isaac, 251

Jefferson, Thomas, *281;* ancestry of, 82, 83*t,* 84; architecture's value viewed by, 1, 271; books owned by, 210–11, 217–18; business interests of, 110, 114; colonial architecture viewed by, 150, 201, 280; data sources about, 304; debts of, 6; drawings by, 191–92, *193;* education of, 99*t;* erroneous attributions to, 71; European travels of, 198; William Henry Harrison influenced by, 283, *284;* income sources of, 106*t;* inheritance of, 86*t,* 104*t,* 105; life expectancy of, 89; marriage of, 89, 91*t,* 129; at Monticello, 33, 38, 89, 164–65, 180, 222; political ideology of, 268, 346n21; political offices held by, 263*t,* 345n18; as president, 112; progeny of, 93*t;* pursuit of knowledge by, 219–20, 291; sheep owned by, 109; slaves owned by, 13, 118–19, 251; tobacco grown by, 109; vital statistics of, 88*t;* writings of, 81, 225, 282–83. *See also* Monticello I; *Notes on the State of Virginia*

Jefferson, Ursula, 251

Jenings, Edmund, 220

John Brush House (Williamsburg), 66

John Custis House (Williamsburg), 56, 58

John Foster House (Boston, Massachusetts), 39, *40*

Johnson, Randolph, 165

joiners, 4, 66, 157, 161, 170, 208, 216–18, 291

jointure, 124, 128, 144

Jones, Alice Hanson, 112

Jones, Hugh, 29, 72, 165, 198, 201, 273, 276–77

Jones, Inigo, 37, 68, 144, 282

justices of the peace, 169, 176, 197, 261, 264, 267

Pembroke, Earl of. *See* Herbert, Philip

Pennsylvania Statehouse (Philadelphia, Pennsylvania), 74; plan of, *75*

Pepys, Elizabeth, 249

Pepys, Samuel, 249

Perrault, Claude, 210

Perry, Micajah, 97

Peter Jefferson/Joshua Fry Map, 119

Philosophical Transactions (Royal Society), 271

Piganiol de la Force, Jean-Aimar, 209

pilasters, 19, *24,* 39, *40,* 43, 48, 184, *185*

plan, 58–59, 192–93, 212, 227, 269. *See also specific plan types*

plantation management as source of architectural knowledge, 195–98

political ideology and architecture, 268

political offices: architectural patrons and, 261–67, 283–84, 286, 288, 292; public building projects and, 169–79, 192, 194, 197–98, 273–76; selection process for, 170; wealth and, 10, 111–12. *See also* burgesses; councilors; justices of the peace; lieutenant governors; militia officers; offices of power and profit; vestrymen

politics of access, 59–62, 240–41, 269

Pond, William, 165

poorhouses, 168

porticoes, 39, 40, 156, 220; double, 43, 280, 282

Port Royal, South Carolina, 30

post-in-ground. *See* hole-set buildings

power: androcentric perspective on, 225, 227; architectural expressions of, 260, 268–71, 273–80, 282–84, 286, 288; resistance to, 166–67, 279, 286, 288, 292; of slave cooks, 251. *See also* political offices

Practical Essay on Cement . . . , A (Loriot), 209

Pratt, Roger, 19, 68

prenuptial agreements, 123, 131, 134

Present State of Virginia, The (Jones), 165, 277

Price, Joseph, 165

Primatt, Stephen, 212

primogeniture, 85, 121, 236

Prince's Lodgings (Newcastle, England), 37, 282

prints, imported, 242–44

prisons, 9, 169, 172–73, 187, 273

privacy issues, 11, 241

prodigy houses: building costs of, 130, 149, 266, 292; building process of, 153–54, 156–62, 164–65, 291; daily life in, 58; in Indiana Territory, 283–84, 286; power and, 260, 277–79, 289; problems in building of, 149–53; role of design in, 9–14, 289; room function specialization in, 11, 61, 240–41, 269; scale and relative size of, 15–16, 18–19, 29; significance of, 1–2; study group of, 15*t,* 81; term used in England, 2–3; term used in Virginia, 3; vernacular houses contrasted with, 6; women's influence on, 119–20, 291–92; women's legal position in, 120–35, 137–38, 140, 143–47, 234, 236. *See also specific buildings and patrons by name*

progeny of patrons. *See* children of patrons

property valuation, 112–14, 167; British standards compared with, 114–16, 131

proxemics, 234

Pyle, Howard, *Old State House, Williamsburg, 46*

quadrant hyphens, 74–75

quarrels, 36, 37, 38

Queen's House (Greenwich, England), 68

Quintine, Jean de la, 209

quoins, 47, 51, *52,* 178

Randolph, Anne, 117, 121

Randolph, Ariana Jennings, 145–46

Randolph, Beverley, 131

Randolph, John, II, 145–46, 204, 257; ancestry of, 83*t;* data sources about, 307; education of, 99*t;* income sources of, 107*t;* inheritance of, 86*t,* 103, 104*t;* marriage of, 91*t,* 92, 128; political ideology of, 268, 346n22; political offices held by, 112, 261, 263*t,* 264, 266–67, 345n18; progeny of, 93*t;* travels of, 334n34; vital statistics of, 88*t. See also* Tazewell Hall

Randolph, Mary, 250, 254

Randolph, Peter, 128

Randolph, Ryland, 218; plan of house of, *219*

Randolph, Susannah, 119

Randolph, William, III, 15–16, 18, 21, *22, 50–51;* ancestry of, 83*t;* business interests of, 109; data sources about, 307–8; education of, 99*t;* European travels of, 198; income sources of, 107*t;* inheritance of, 86*t,*

Spotswood, Alexander (*continued*)
  management skills of, 197; political offices held by, 112, 261, 263*t*, 266; progeny
  of, 93*t*; property valuation of, 113*t*; travels of, 201–2, 334n34; visit to Westover
  by, 270; vital statistics of, 88*t*; widow of,
  111, 128, 326n39. *See also* Germanna

Spotswood, Anne Butler Brayne. *See*
  Thompson, Anne Butler Brayne
  Spotswood

stairways, 63, *64*, 66–67, 68, *210*, 234, 236,
  283

Stanbury, Susanna Walker, 134–35

Stanbury, Thomas, 134–35

Stanstead (King George County), 138, 156,
  197

status of patrons, 3; architecture and,
  94–95, 206; domestic slaves and, 252;
  knowledge acquisition and, 222, 290;
  material culture and, 10, 78, 79; political offices and, 262; politics of access
  and, 59–62

Stephen Van Rensselaer II Mansion (Albany, New York), 68

Stone, Lawrence, 117

stonework, 30, 32, 51, 55, 156, 159–60, 165,
  166, 203–4; imitation, 32–34

Stowe, Harriet Beecher, 259

Stratford Hall (Westmoreland County),
  15*t*, *136*; brickwork at, 26, *28*; chimneys of, 58; data sources about, 306–7;
  doorway of, 48, *49*; dressing tables
  from, 240; Great Hall of, 45, *47*, 184,
  185; kitchen of, 253, *254*; Hannah Lee's
  influence on, 134; outbuildings of, 76,
  77; plan of, *16*, 89, 212; size of, 19, 103;
  slave cooks at, 251; slavery and, 2; transport landing at, 196; William Walker as
  undertaker for, 153

Stratton Major Parish church (King and
  Queen County), 130, 192

stringcourses, *28*, 47, 48, 50, 283

stucco, 120

studies or libraries, 229, 231, 234, 236–37

Summerson, John, 2–3, 55

Surflet, Richard, 211

surveying, 192

Swan, Abraham, 215, 216, 217

Swan Tavern, Yorktown, 192

Sylva, or a Discourse of Forest Trees, 211

symmetry, 35, 62–63, 184

Taliaferro, Peter, 194

Taliaferro, Richard, 134, 162

Talman, William, 203; drawing attributed
  to, *207*

Tasker, Benjamin, 257

Tatler, The, 186

Tayloe, John, I, 242

Tayloe, John, II, 68, 212–13, 269; ancestry
  of, 82, 83*t*; business interests of, 110; data
  sources about, 305; education of, 99*t*;
  estate of, 112, 134; income sources of,
  107*t*; inheritance of, 86*t*, 104*t*; involve-
  ment in building process by, 32, 74, 220;
  marriage of, 91*t*, 92; political ideology
  of, 346n21; political offices held by, 174,
  263*t*, 345n18; progeny of, 93*t*; slaves
  owned by, 166; vital statistics of, 88*t*. *See
  also* Mount Airy

Tayloe, Rebecca, 134

Tazewell Hall (Williamsburg), 15*t*, 145–46,
  264, 266; conjectural elevation, *146*; data
  sources about, 307; plan of, *70*, 71; style
  of, 204, 213

tea drinking and tea tables, 244–48, *245,
  246,* 342n70

Thomas Stanbury House (Boston, Massachusetts), 25, *25*, 134–35

Thompson, Anne Butler Brayne Spotswood,
  33, 128, 129, *129,* 241, 326n39, 326n41

Thompson, John, 33, 48, 263*t*, 268; ancestry
  of, 83*t*; as clergyman, 111, 261; data
  sources about, 306; education of, 99*t*; as
  immigrant, 82; income sources of, 105,
  107*t*, 326n41; inheritance of, 86*t*, 104*t*;
  marriages of, 91*t*, 92, 111, 128; progeny of,
  93*t*; property valuation of, 112–13, 113*t*,
  115, 167; travels of, 334n34; as undertaker, 171; vital statistics of, 88*t*. *See also*
  Salubria

Thomson, James, 256

Thoroughgood House (Princess Anne
  County), 14, 26

Thorpe Hall (Cambridgeshire, England), 62

Thorsby, Ralph, 202

tobacco warehouses, 110, 119, 169, 172, 174,
  176, 196

Todd, Martha, 119

Tower of London (London, England), 275

travel as source of architectural knowledge,
  173, 198–204, 206–7

Treatise on Perspective (Ditton), 191

women in building process, 118–19, 291
Wormeley, Ralph, 131, 211
Wren, Christopher, 46, 188–89, 201, 273;
   drawing attributed to, *207*
Wren, James, 176, 178

Wyatt, Benjamin, 192
Wythe, Elizabeth Taliaferro, 134
Wythe, George, 134, 220, 252

Yorktown, Virginia, 29–30, 72–73